Globalization, Marginalization and Development

Over the past two decades, 'globalization' has become a universally recognized and talked about phenomenon. In economic terms, globalization implies the accelerated integration of world markets, not only with respect to international trade, but also the world's financial markets. In principle, globalization should offer poorer countries an opportunity to grow faster and catch up with more affluent countries. However, more often than not, it has led to the marginalization of low-income countries.

This excellent new book contains contributions from a number of leading experts and is the result of the UNU/WIDER project on globalization and low-income countries. The discussion focuses in on how to harness globalization for the benefit of present day marginalized countries and enhance their meaningful participation in the globalization process.

Vital reading for students and academics interested in the field of development economics, this collection will also prove an invaluable tool for policy-makers.

S. Mansoob Murshed is at The Institute of Social Studies, The Hague, in The Netherlands.

Routledge Studies in Development Economics

1 **Economic Development in the Middle East**
Rodney Wilson

2 **Monetary and Financial Policies in Developing Countries**
Growth and stabilization
Akhtar Hossain and Anis Chowdhury

3 **New Directions in Development Economics**
Growth, environmental concerns and government in the 1990s
Edited by Mats Lundahl and Benno J. Ndulu

4 **Financial Liberalization and Investment**
Kanhaya L. Gupta and Robert Lensink

5 **Liberalization in the Developing World**
Institutional and economic changes in Latin America, Africa and Asia
Edited by Alex E. Fernández Jilberto and André Mommen

6 **Financial Development and Economic Growth**
Theory and experiences from developing countries
Edited by Niels Hermes and Robert Lensink

7 **The South African Economy**
Macroeconomic prospects for the medium term
Finn Tarp and Peter Brixen

8 **Public Sector Pay and Adjustment**
Lessons from five countries
Edited by Christopher Colclough

9 **Europe and Economic Reform in Africa**
Structural adjustment and economic diplomacy
Obed O. Mailafia

10 **Post-Apartheid Southern Africa**
Economic challenges and policies for the future
Edited by Lennart Petersson

11 **Financial Integration and Development**
Liberalization and reform in sub-Saharan Africa
Ernest Aryeetey and Machiko Nissanke

12 **Regionalization and Globalization in the Modern World Economy**
Perspectives on the Third World and transitional economies
Edited by Alex F. Fernández Jilberto and André Mommen

13 **The African Economy**
Policy, institutions and the future
Steve Kayizzi-Mugerwa

14 **Recovery from Armed Conflict in Developing Countries**
Edited by Geoff Harris

15 **Small Enterprises and Economic Development**
The dynamics of micro and small enterprises
Carl Liedholm and Donald C. Mead

16 **The World Bank**
New agendas in a changing world
Michelle Miller-Adams

17 **Development Policy in the Twenty-First Century**
Beyond the post-Washington consensus
Edited by Ben Fine, Costas Lapavitsas and Jonathan Pincus

18 **State-Owned Enterprises in the Middle East and North Africa**
Privatization, performance and reform
Edited by Merih Celasum

19 **Finance and Competitiveness in Developing Countries**
Edited by José María Fanelli and Rohinton Medhora

20 **Contemporary Issues in Development Economics**
Edited by B.N. Ghosh

21 **Mexico Beyond NAFTA**
Edited by Martín Puchet Anyul and Lionello F. Punzo

22 **Economies in Transition**
A guide to China, Cuba, Mongolia, North Korea and Vietnam at the turn of the twenty-first century
Ian Jeffries

23 **Population, Economic Growth and Agriculture in Less Developed Countries**
Nadia Cuffaro

24 **From Crisis to Growth in Africa?**
Edited by Mats Lundal

25 **The Macroeconomics of Monetary Union**
An analysis of the CFA franc zone
David Fielding

26 **Endogenous Development**
Networking, innovation, institutions and cities
Antonio Vasquez-Barquero

27 **Labour Relations in Development**
Edited by Alex E. Fernández Jilberto and Marieke Riethof

28 **Globalization, Marginalization and Development**
Edited by S. Mansoob Murshed

Globalization, Marginalization and Development

Edited by S. Mansoob Murshed

London and New York

First published 2002
by Routledge
11 New Fetter Lane, London EC4P 4EE

Simultaneously published in the USA and Canada
by Routledge
29 West 35th Street, New York, NY 10001

Routledge is an imprint of the Taylor & Francis Group

Typeset in 10/12 Times New Roman by
Newgen Imaging Systems (P) Ltd, Chennai, India
Printed and bound in Great Britain by
Antony Rowe Ltd, Chippenham, Wiltshire

British Library Cataloguing in Publication Data
A catalogue record for this book is available from the British Library

Library of Congress Cataloging in Publication Data
A catalog record for this book has been requested

ISBN 0-415-28850-9

Contents

Figures

Tables

Research

United Nations University World Institute for Development Economics Research (UNU/WIDER) was established by the United Nations University as its first research and training centre and started work in Helsinki, Finland, in 1985. The purpose of the Institute is to undertake applied research and policy analysis on structural changes affecting the developing and transitional economies, to provide a forum for the advocacy of policies leading to robust, equitable and environmentally sustainable growth, and to promote capacity strengthening and training in the field of economic and social policy-making. Its work is carried out by staff researchers and visiting scholars in Helsinki and through networks of collaborating scholars and institutions around the world.

Contributors

Manuel R. Agosin, Director, Center on International Economics and Development, Universidad de Chile, Chile.

David E. Bloom, Professor of Economics and Demography, School of Public Health, Harvard University, USA.

Patrick Bond, Graduate School of Public and Development Management, University of the Witwatersrand, Johannesburg, South Africa.

Deborah Bräutigam, International Development Program, School of International Service, American University, Washington DC, USA.

Linda Cotton, Overseas Development Council, Washington DC, USA.

Nick J. Freeman, Institute of Southeast Asian Studies (ISEAS), Singapore.

Kiichiro Fukasaku, Head of Division, Economic Analysis and Development Policy Dialogue, OECD Development Centre, Paris.

Rukmani Gounder, Department of Applied and International Economics, Massey University, New Zealand.

Rolf J. Langhammer, Kiel Institute of World Economics, Germany.

Matthias Lücke, IMF, USA.

Jörg Mayer, UNCTAD, Division on Globalization and Development Strategies, Switzerland.

Guy Mhone, Graduate School of Public and Development Management, University of Witwatersrand, Johannesburg, South Africa.

S. Mansoob Murshed, ISS, The Netherlands and UNU/WIDER, Helsinki, Finland.

Waseem Noor, Strategic Decisions Group, New York, USA.

Vijaya Ramachandran, Overseas Development Council, Washington DC, USA.

Robert Read, Department of Economics, University of Lancaster, UK.

Matthew J. Slaughter, Department of Economics, Dartmouth College and NBER, USA.

Djono Subagjo, UNU/INTECH, The Netherlands.

P.K.M. Tharakan, University of Antwerp-UFSIA, Belgium.

Michael Woolcock, Development Research Group, The World Bank, Washington DC, USA.

Vilaphonh Xayavong, Massey University, New Zealand.

Foreword

The last two decades have been described as the era of globalization. In economic terms, this implies the accelerated integration of world markets, not only with respect to international trade, but also in the world's financial markets. In principle, this should offer poorer countries an opportunity to grow faster and catch up with more affluent countries. But more often than not, globalization has led to the marginalization of poor low-income countries. This means that their participation in the increased trade that globalization brings is limited, and in many instances is declining in relative terms. Their access to private international financial markets is practically non-existent, and their share of inflows of real inward investment is in many cases declining. Globalization attenuates the policy autonomy of the nation state, thereby offering fewer options for development strategies. Many low-income countries – especially in Africa, but also in Latin America – have had long periods of negative economic growth and declining human development indicators during the era of globalization. Their social sector expenditure has had to be reined in as a result of structural adjustment policies, and many are burdened by unsustainable international debt. Moreover, the rules of the game governing the international trading and financial systems leave many poor countries more vulnerable and disadvantaged in gaining access to western markets than at any time in the past.

This volume is the result of the UNU/WIDER project on Globalization and the Obstacles to the Successful Integration of Small Vulnerable Economies. It focuses on the challenges that globalization creates for poorer developing countries that fall within the UN least developed country grouping, and the World Bank's low-income definition. The purpose is to examine how globalization can be harnessed for the benefit of marginalized countries, and to identify policies that can enhance the meaningful participation of developing countries in the globalization process.

Anthony Shorrocks
Director, WIDER

Acknowledgements

UNU/WIDER gratefully acknowledges the financial support of the Finnish Ministry for Foreign Affairs.

There are a great many intellectual debts that I owe in the production of this volume. Among colleagues at UNU/WIDER I would like to thank Richard Auty, Tony Addison, Giovanni Andrea Cornia, Steve Kayizzi-Mugerwa and Cecilia Ugaz. Among others, who do not appear in the volume as authors, mention must be made of Dorothy Rosenberg, Colin Kirkpatrick, Charles Oman and Carl Greenidge. Taina Iduozee from WIDER's library provided excellent bibliographical assistance. Janis Vehmaan-Kreula, the project secretary performed her tasks superbly, and her help in organizing the project, the two project conferences and a host of other matters was invaluable and will always be remembered. I must also thank the enabling work atmosphere that WIDER produces. Lastly, I would like to thank my partner Mary Conaghan for her patience and support during this project.

1 Perspectives on two phases of globalization

S. Mansoob Murshed

The term globalization is used rather ambiguously. It is used in the positive sense to point at the increased international integration of trade, investment and finance; it is also employed in the normative sense to denote a reaction to increased integration, and the policies that follow from there (Nayyar 1997). Globalization and openness are not new phenomena. The period before the First World War offers parallels to the present day in terms of a highly integrated world economy measured by a high degree of international trade, foreign direct investment (FDI), as well as financial flows (portfolio investment and direct lending to banks and governments). During the inter-war period this highly globalized economy became inward looking and the process of globalization was reversed. Since about 1960 the barriers to globalization have once again been dismantled. This was often a slow process, and many developing countries chose not to participate, at least initially. International trade was the first to be liberalized. FDI followed suit, and finally it was the turn of financial flows. Milanovic (1999) argues that the present phase of globalization began at a date well after 1960, as at that time at least a quarter of the world's population lived under socialist systems. Globalization, therefore, requires the capitalist economic system to be almost ubiquitously present. A convenient date to mark the commencement of the present era of globalization could be circa 1980, following China's adoption of open-door policies.

This volume focuses on globalization and the challenges it creates for developing countries that mainly fall within the UN least developed country (LDC) grouping, and the World Bank low-income definition. It may not be controversial to state that the forces of globalization disadvantage and marginalize most poor countries. We could, however, argue that this is true of globalization processes, both in its current form, and in its earlier late-nineteenth century incarnation. Nineteenth century globalization can be said to have produced the marginalized third world, just as our present experience of globalization further cements, and adds to, these global inequalities.

The first section presents the picture of the marginalization of most low-income countries in the contemporary era of globalization. The second section contains a sketch of the previous historical episode of globalization, comparing and contrasting it with our modern experience. The third section is concerned with problems arising out of present day globalization, and outlines the issues considered in this volume.

Globalization and marginalization

Globalization implies the accelerated integration of the world economy, not just at the regional level. In principle, this should offer poorer countries an opportunity to grow faster and catch up with more affluent countries. But another process could also be in operation. Globalization may serve to cement the polarization between rich and poor. This polarization has been described by Quah (1996) as the 'persistence and stratification' of the differences between rich and poor. Over time, such as with our present spate of globalization, a bi-modal distribution of world incomes emerges; one for affluent nations, the other for low-income countries. Nations are driven to join one or another of these groups.

Globalization can, therefore, produce winners and losers. At present, as in the past, it appears to benefit countries of the North disproportionately more than in the South. Some eleven developing countries account for 66 per cent of total developing country exports, as well as receiving the lion's share of FDI inflows (Nayyar 1997). China, Mexico and Brazil account for 50 per cent of all developing country FDI inflows. Thus, even within the South the gains from globalization have been highly skewed. Dollar and Kraay (2001) identify a group of successful globalizing developing countries. They are defined to be in the top third of trade to GDP increases since 1980 for all non-OECD countries. In other words, these countries were the most successful in trade expansion. Accompanying this has been an increase in their growth rates, which normally results in poverty reduction. The countries concerned include East Asian nations plus China, Brazil and Mexico. They, therefore, account for over half of the developing world's population. This picture of success is highly aggregative, for example, in the case of the two most populous 'successful' globalizers, China and India, aggregate figures mask huge regional variation in income, and the majority of the world's poor continue to remain in those countries. Moreover, there is evidence that the world's income distribution has worsened in the era of globalization (Milanovic 2002).

Notwithstanding the successful globalizers, the majority of the world's citizenry, and entire nations in the developing world remain extremely vulnerable to domestic and external shocks, and seem unable to cash in on the increased internationalization of the world economy. They are, in many senses of the term, *marginalized* from the world economic system. The new rules of the game and the international economic environment prevalent since about 1980, following accelerated globalization, also leaves them *vulnerable* in novel ways. For a nation, failure to achieve acceptable rates of economic growth is linked to its inability to benefit from a globalizing world economy. As is indicated in Table 1.1, the set of economies defined by the UN as the LDC group experienced poor growth rates during both the 1980s and 1990s. Their growth rates were below the developing country average. A more telling picture emerges when we examine real per capita income levels. For the least developed economies they had remained stagnant between 1980 and 1996. As indicated, countries in East Asia and the Pacific have been the most successful in the past two decades. Sub-Saharan Africa (SSA) has been lagging behind most, with unimpressive growth rates and a substantial decline in real per capita income.

Table 1.1 GDP growth rates and per capita income levels in selected regions and countries

Area/country	*1980–90 (% annual average GNP growth)*	*1990–6 (% annual average GNP growth)*	*1980 per capita income level in 1996 US$*	*1996 per capita income level in 1996 US$*
All developing countries	3.1	2.9	985	1,350
UN least developed countries	2.6	2.2	227	228
East Asia and the Pacific	7.7	10.2		1,190
South Asia	5.7	5.6		380
Latin America and Caribbean	1.8	3.2	2,334	3,710
Sub-Saharan Africa	1.7	2.0	594	490

Sources: UNCTAD (1998), World Bank (1998), and IMF (1997).

Unlike Latin America, this region does not appear to have bounced back from the lost decade of the 1980s. The average figures for the geographical regions cited in Table 1.1 often disguise considerable variations in individual country performance within any geographical grouping.

Low *et al.* (1998) show that the world trade share of many developing economies has fallen. SSA's share of world exports declined from 3.1 per cent during the 1950s to 1.2 per cent by 1990. The corresponding decline for Latin America was from 5.6 per cent to 4.9 per cent. On the other hand, between 1985 and 1996, Asia's share of world trade rose by 25 per cent. Low-income countries account for only 2.5 per cent of world merchandise exports, and 1.4 per cent of FDI inflows. The corresponding figures for all developing countries are 19.7 and 21.6 per cent, respectively. Developing country FDI flows are mainly confined to China and middle-income countries. This is *prima facie* evidence that many developing countries, mainly, but not exclusively in Africa, are truly marginalized from the globalization of recent times.

The combined effects of globalization and structural adjustment in the last two decades has contributed towards making the income distribution more skewed, even in countries where per capita incomes have risen (Cornia 1999). As will be seen below, the last quarter century has driven the widest ever wedge in human history between average incomes in rich and poor nations. Globalization, however, does offer the hope of emulating other successful developing nations, in East Asia, say.

I have stated that we are currently experiencing the second historical phase of economic globalization, and I turn to the earlier episode of globalization, during the period 1870–1914, in the next section.

Globalization in historical perspective

It is said that the past informs the present. This section is not meant to be an exhaustive summary of the differences between present and past globalization, but will be concerned with the salient differences between the two episodes. The period between 1870–1914 was an era of unprecedented international economic integration in terms of trade, FDI and other types of investment as well as capital flows. Let us take the example of merchandise trade. Figures cited in Krugman (1995) indicate, for example, that the share of trade in the UK's GDP was 27.7 per cent in 1913, declining to 13.1 per cent in 1950 and recovering to 21.1 per cent in 1987. The same figures, for a more inwardly oriented economy, the USA, are 3.9 per cent, 2.9 per cent and 7.4 per cent, respectively. In the case of Germany they are, 19.9 per cent, 9.8 per cent and 23.3 per cent. Thus the world economy, in terms of the value of trade, has recovered to its pre-First World War golden age, after an inward looking half century, particularly during the inter-war period.

It is useful to summarize the more obvious differences in our present experience of globalization when compared to the previous episode, a century earlier. The first is to do with the nature of trade. There is an increased amount of intra-industry trade, compared to the inter-industry trade of the last century (or even half a century ago). Within the category of intra-industry trade, there is also a great deal of intra-firm trade. This is what is described by Krugman (1995), as the vertical disintegration of production or 'slicing up the value chain', and 'fragmentation' in Arndt and Kierzkowski (2001). Essentially, this refers to the process by which different components of a particular product can be produced in several parts of the world. The second difference stems from the fact that present day FDI is more concentrated: Nayyar (1997) points out that developing countries account for only 22 per cent of the stock of FDI in 1992, compared to 45 per cent in 1914. Third, at present, large proportions of international financial flows occur within the North. Fourth, unlike in the previous century, international labour mobility is extremely restricted, and confined only to the highly skilled, see Baldwin and Martin (1999), on this. Last, the political environment is quite different. Around 1900 colonialization, gunboat-diplomacy and direct interventions in developing countries were rife; these were the means utilized to impose the will of the hegemonic powers. This is less common nowadays. We live in a world where most countries in the developing world are 'sovereign' nation states, and at least superficially democratic. The policy sovereignty, however, of the nation state, and developing countries in particular, is severely limited by globalization. Most decisions regarding the governance of the global system are taken in the small fora of the powerful, such as the G-7. The undemocratic rules that follow are mainly enforced through a nexus of multilateral agreements (such as the World Trade Organization or WTO agreements) and multilateral organizations (such as the IMF and the World Bank).

Williamson (1999) states that nineteenth century globalization was triggered-off not just by policy driven trade and capital flow liberalization, but also by falling transport costs and mass migration from Europe to the 'new' world. To this list, we can add the process of integrating many third world countries, several of which were colonies, to the global trade nexus as suppliers of primary products. One could argue that declining transport costs, induced by technological innovation, was akin to a 'natural' reduction in trade barriers. It must be remembered that international trade was less free of taxes (or artificial trade barriers) in the last century when compared to the present. Granted, the UK and Denmark pursued free trade. But the USA, Germany, France and Russia had considerable import tariffs in place. This was in the interests of their landed classes and other producers. Britain had free trade, because it suited her; it maintained real wages as food prices declined without raising nominal wages: a positive terms-of-trade effect on 'aggregate supply'. Today's liberalization is, by contrast, much more about reductions in artificial or policy-induced trade barriers, and less to do with movements of people.

To give ourselves a lesson in economic history: up to the mid-nineteenth century there was a divergence in real earnings between the 'new' world and Europe – Australia and USA enjoyed the higher wages. Globalization in the nineteenth century, which is said to have occurred post-1870, implied the *convergence* of real wages (and wage–land rental ratios) in the 'Atlantic' economies, as described in Williamson (1999). Irish wages grew and moved towards British levels as the result of mass emigration. Furthermore, there was also an intra-European convergence – Ireland and Scandinavia doing the main catching up. Nordic countries moved from the periphery to the centre during the pre-1914 globalization, with Sweden and Denmark doing best. Austria did well, but Italy performed poorly, the Iberian Peninsula fared worse, as did much of South Eastern Europe. The same Atlantic economies, with new European and East Asian countries added, continue to be successful in present day globalization.

A question mark remains over why much of the third world was, and still remains, excluded, in terms of economic convergence, from both episodes of globalization. In fact, it can be argued that the previous phase of globalization *created* the third world and marginalization (Davis 2001), whereas the present system of globalization *perpetuates* the third world. This can be seen from examining the gap in average or per capita incomes between the richest and poorest countries in the world. UNDP (1999) reproduces figures to show that this gap was only 3 : 1 during the dawn of the industrial revolution in 1820, rising to 11 : 1 by the end of the first episode of globalization in 1913. Then, it grew to 35 : 1 in 1950, rising slightly to 44 : 1 by 1973. More recently, after the commencement of the present round of globalization, this figure has acquired a staggering magnitude of 72 : 1. This is the most conclusive evidence of the process of marginalization of developing countries during the two great phases of globalization. The great first wave of globalization produced a sizeable North–South income gap for the first time. This gap has been widened during the more recent globalization experience.

Baldwin and Martin (1999) allude to the important, but often ignored historical fact that the industrialization of the North, preceding nineteenth century globalization, was at the expense of the South. Bairoch (1982) presents evidence that China and India were just as industrialized in the eighteenth century as the parts of Europe (such as England) who had developed manufacturing. Market penetration by Britain following colonialization caused the manufacturing sectors in these countries of the South to practically vanish. Figures to be found in

Davis (2001: table 9.3) show that Europe's and the UK's share of world manufacturing output rose from 23.1 per cent and 1.9 per cent, respectively, in 1750 to 63 per cent and 18.5 per cent by 1900. The corresponding figures for China and India, the two most successful globalizers of the post-1980 period according to Dollar and Kraay (2001) make interesting reading. They fell from 32.8 per cent of world manufacturing output in 1750 to 6.2 per cent in 1900 for China, and from 24.5 per cent in 1750 to 1.7 per cent in 1900 for India. Baldwin and Martin (1999), however, argue that in the present globalized context knowledge or 'ideas' spillovers are less costly than a century ago. This has enabled a small part of the South to industrialize, whereas the manufacturing share of employment has dwindled in the North. It offers a window of opportunity to poorer countries given the current pattern of consumption where product and brand innovation plays a leading part. But the barriers to entry to such a process of industrialization are still very formidable.

The creation of the proto-third world during the turn of the nineteenth century has been analysed in Davis (2001). There are five points to consider here. The first is the integration of the peasant producer in China, India and elsewhere into global primary product markets. In many parts of the third world there was a switch from food production for domestic consumption to cash or food crops for export. In other parts of the world, in Africa and Latin America minerals production commenced or was expanded. This shift in production patterns was, more often than not, induced by 'subsistence adversity': the combination of debt, tax burdens, famine, drought, the loss of common resources and the disappearance of traditional safety nets. Not only did this switch in production patterns reduce food security during the two international tropical famine episodes of 1876–9 and 1896–1902, but, ironically, was associated with the great slump in the global terms of trade of commodity prices during the great depression of 1873–96. The shift towards commodity exports formed the basis of the present-day staple trap, described by Auty (1997). Other parallels exist today in the form of a host of 'open' policies pursued in developing countries in the hope of gaining from globalization. Despite these measures, most low-income developing countries are marginalized from world trade. Their participation in world trade a century ago was, perhaps greater, even if it was only primary goods exports.

The second is the burden of taxation and debt. In India, which was under British rule, the burden of taxation was succinctly summarized by the great nationalist economist Dadabhai Naoroji in 1876 (see Naoroji 1901; also Dutt 1902, 1904). He put the average tax burden in India at twice that of contemporary England, although average income there was fifteen times greater at that point in time. Moreover, during the great famine of 1876–9 an extra salt tax was levied to finance a war in Afghanistan. This was criticized by the Victorian philanthropist Florence Nightingale and the politician William Gladstone (Davis 2001). At this time of fiscal exigency, import duties on manufactured cotton goods from England were lowered at the behest of British interests (the Lancashire textile industry), so other taxes had to be levied. By contrast, there is ample evidence to suggest that under the Mughal pre-British rulers in India the burden of taxation was lower. In China too there is evidence pointing to a low agrarian tax burden in the eighteenth century. But the combination of drought, increased military expenditure induced by wars, bureaucratic mismanagement, fiscal measures enforced by colonial powers, and reparation payments all conspired to raise the burden of taxation on the Chinese peasantry during the late-nineteenth century. Other examples of crippling agrarian taxation include late-nineteenth century Algeria. Similarly, a number of independent nations were also saddled with large international debt-servicing burdens such as in Morocco in the late 1870s during a period of drought-induced famine. The tax burden of a century ago bears huge similarities to present day international debt servicing burdens of the highly indebted developing countries.

Third, the burden of taxation was not counterbalanced by expenditure on infrastructure or human development. This specially applies to irrigation works in India and China, but also to public health and education. Rather, as Davis (2001) and others point out, taxes in India were used to finance imperial wars. Among them were numerous campaigns in Afghanistan, the siege of Beijing (1860), the Ethiopian war (1868), the suppression of the revolt in Egypt (1882) and the conquest of the Sudan (1896–8). Military and police expenditure was never lower than 34 per cent of central government expenditure in British India (Davis 2001: Chapter 9). In the developing world of today social sector expenditure is also low, not just because of venal governments, but also because of fiscal restraint (implying expenditure reduction) under the aegis of structural adjustment programmes.

Fourth, the operation of the international payments and currency systems under the gold standard militated against developing countries. Much has been written on this. Naoroji (1901) analysed the famous colonial drain of resources from India to Britain. The combined effect of the hefty home charge levied on Indian taxpayers by the India Office in London, and the lodgement of other financial surpluses in London meant that Britain enjoyed a surplus in her total financial transactions with India. Similarly, she had a surplus in financial dealings with China. India's role as a major market for British manufactures is well known (Davis 2001 and references therein), but, crucially, trade with India allowed the continuation of free trade in Britain, and the ability of British FDI to be diversified and untied to British exports (Cain and Hopkins 1993). During the late-nineteenth century industrial depression in the UK, caused by a decline in competitiveness of her manufacturing sector relative to new rivals, she nevertheless imported heavily from, and had trade deficits with the USA, Germany, Scandinavian countries, Australia and other white dominions. This fostered the latter group's industrialization and growth behind tariff walls in many cases. Moreover, since India was on the silver standard and Britain operated under the gold standard the monetary terms of trade continually depreciated for India. The home charges were paid in gold, and as silver depreciated in value, British export prices to India appreciated, while her imports from India declined in value. At present, most developing countries receive few private financial flows; Those who do, suffer from banking and currency crises, as well as being subject to financial contagion.

Fifth, there are the attitudes to free market forces that can explain the marginalization of much of the third world from globalization both at present and in the past. A good example to consider would be attitudes to famines that raged through much of the tropical world in Africa, Latin America and Asia (especially China and India) in the last quarter of the nineteenth century, extensively documented in Davis (2001). In Africa, drought-induced famine aided colonial expansion by assisting military victories over debilitated native powers, such as the defeat of the Zulus in South Africa and the Mahdists in the Sudan. It also aided the nascent mining sector by providing it with labour displaced from traditional herding activities. In India, famines coincided with periods of massive grain exports. There was a marked reluctance, in virtually all of the famine episodes in India and elsewhere, to interfere with global grain markets for the sake of famine relief. Thus, the obdurate refusal to interfere with the workings of the market during complex humanitarian disasters is not new. For example, the Economist magazine in July 1874, asserted that it was not the duty of government to keep Indians alive during famine (cited in Davis 2001: 37). This in spite of a contemporary scientific paper (Walford 1878), which states that there had been 120 serious famines in British India from 1757 to 1877, compared to seventeen episodes in two millennia prior to British rule. At the time, a Malthusian view of the lower classes was in vogue, which viewed starvation or famine to be the product of fecundity and indolence. Compare that to the present group of thinkers who ascribe all the woes of low-income countries to bad policies of domestic origin. Another present day parallel is the refusal, until recently, of the international trading system (WTO rule-based trade) to allow the production of cheaper generic drugs protected by patent laws in response to the AIDS pandemic. Going back to nineteenth century famines, attitudes of colonial rulers to famine relief were less than lukewarm Davis (2001). There was the infamous Temple wage (after Sir Richard Temple, Lieutenant Governor of Bengal and in charge of Famine Relief in the Deccan) during the Indian famine of 1876–9, which provided famine relief of a pound of rice a day in return for hard labour. Thus the relief was means tested, and bears a striking resemblance to the World Bank's international poverty standard of a dollar a day (which in many instances fetches little more than a pound of rice). In contrast the Mughal rulers in India, and earlier Chinese emperors, had extensive systems of famine relief, which were provided without any economic *quid pro quo*. Above all, they did not hesitate to interfere in grain markets to manipulate prices, and granted tax relief to hard pressed farmers.

Both historical episodes of globalization have produced a backlash, involving both intellectual opposition as well as direct action. Williamson (1999) has pointed out that during 1870–1914, income inequality rose in the USA as landowners gained from trade and mass migration, whereas the opposite effect took place in Europe. In the USA, around 1914 there was a pronounced resentment of the forces of globalization, particularly mass migration. Thus immigration restrictions crept into the 'new' world even before 1917. In Europe protectionism took the form of trade restrictions. France, for example, restricted trade in grain, raising the real wages of agricultural workers. There are similar processes in train in present day globalization, which has also produced substantial inequality inside richer OECD countries. The main disadvantaged group are unskilled workers. Any backlash to globalization from this group is likely to be much more muted at present. Unskilled workers in the North receive social security benefits. Trade restrictions do exist, but are subtle and selective, non-tariff barriers and agricultural subsidies, directed mainly against third-world interests.

The intellectual critics of globalization came from the radical-left, then and now. The alternative ideology a century ago was socialism; no such substitute exists today, unless it is radical Islam evidenced in a few Muslim states such as Iran (Milanovic 1999). Crucially, the marginalization of the third world during nineteenth century globalization produced nationalism and rebellion. Examples of the former include the founding of the Indian National Congress, which later led the vanguard of the independence movement, as well as home-grown critics of immiserization such as the economists Dutt (1902, 1904) and Naoroji (1901).

The Boxer revolt in China is a good example of an armed rebellion against the effects of globalization. Direct action against globalization can be seen at present in the form of violent protests at the Seattle WTO meeting in 1999, the wrecking of the Davos summit in 2001 and the disruptions during the G-8 meeting in Genoa in 2001. Even the tragic destruction of the World Trade Centre on 11 September 2001 may have, in part, contained an anti-globalization message.

Critics of nineteenth century policies included disenchanted officials such as Allan Octavian Hume, formerly of the Indian Civil Service, just as today's globalization policies attract rebukes from the likes of Joseph Stiglitz, formerly of the World Bank. The eponymous development non-governmental organizations (NGOs) of today had their counterparts in Victorian philanthropists (Florence Nightingale), journalist-politicians (William Digby), and above all in the Socialist International, and other socialist parties.

In our own millennium globalization looks set fair to extend itself further. We must, therefore, turn our minds to harnessing it for the benefit of present day marginalized countries. Consequently, I return to contemporary issues in the next section.

Globalization at present

Macroeconomic issues

Scant attention is paid in the literature to North–South interaction in the context of globalization. The North–South terms of trade have interested development economists ever since the Prebisch–Singer hypothesis about declining primary goods prices relative to manufactures (see Singer 1950). Nowadays, countries in the South are increasingly exporting manufactured goods. There is also concern about the informalization of employment and a shift in income shares from labour to capital (Standing 1999). Bloom and Murshed (Chapter 3) present an analytical North–South growth model where the informal sector in the South also produces an exportable. This good may also be an illegal narcotic substance, representing a global public 'bad'. The stylized facts for many developing countries suggest that the informal sector is large and may even be growing. In some countries, the contribution of narcotic substances to overall national income is substantial (estimated at 20 per cent of GNP in Bolivia, for example). Bloom and Murshed (Chapter 3) find that an expansion in the informal or illegal sector in the South, when captured mainly by 'entrepreneurs' or crime-bosses, can have major immiserizing consequences for that region in terms of its capital stock and terms of trade.

In general, increased globalization attenuates the ability of national governments to pursue independent macroeconomic policy. Macroeconomic stabilization is important even if nations decide to avoid full participation in the globalized system. Sound anti-inflationary monetary policies, a movement towards fiscal balance and a stable exchange rate system are the corner stones of good macroeconomic management. If a developing economy is not well managed in these areas, it will have no recourse but to seek assistance from the IFIs, who will in turn demand macroeconomic reforms via structural adjustment. In their influential paper, Sachs and Warner (1995) stress the growth promoting aspects of openness. Openness implies less protectionism and the absence of a bias against a more outward-looking economic development. On the face of it, a less than open policy regime will not be able to seize the opportunities presented by increased globalization. Rodriguez and Rodrik (1999), however, argue that indicators of trade restrictions may be highly correlated to other factors that retard economic growth. Similarly, countries that grow faster might do so for reasons other than mere openness.

Mhone and Bond (Chapter 16) are critical of structural adjustment and the associated policies of openness in Zimbabwe. They cite widespread failure during this era ranging from falling incomes to the stagnation of child mortality indicators. Notwithstanding the negative supply shocks suffered by Zimbabwe, they point to balance of payment crises, financial fragility, rising debt and falling government revenues, which they show are linked to policies carried out at the behest of the Fund and the Bank. As an alternative, they endorse the strategies suggested by the UNDP Human Development Report. These include more inward-looking policies, capital controls and trade restrictions, as well as a more people-centric development approach.

Crippling international debt, and debt servicing burdens are certainly a major constraint on growth-promoting investment in human capital. Based on Mayer's (Chapter 5) statistical analysis indebtedness and balance of payments constraints retard investment in both human and physical capital. Agosin (Chapter 15) has emphasized the need for more expenditure on health and human capital; the paucity of government revenues is a major cause for the lack of investment in this area in Honduras and Nicaragua. Macroeconomic reforms are also necessary in poorer countries in East Asia (Laos and Vietnam) if robust FDI inflows are to resume (Freeman, Chapter 7). This is also true of the Pacific Island nations of Fiji and the Solomon Islands (Gounder and Xayavong, Chapter 14) in their attempts to attract more FDI.

Financial sector regulation

The private international financial system, to which small nations are increasingly hostage, is extremely volatile. Herding behaviour, financial contagion and volatile behaviour characterize world capital markets. This implies that nations should proceed with caution before liberalizing the financial sector. The presence of a fragile banking sector makes the defence of the currency under speculative attack even more difficult. More often than not, twin (banking and currency) crises appear, and cumulative losses to GDP in any year can be substantial. There is sometimes a high degree of correlation between indicators of banking and currency crises (Kaminsky 1998).

A related issue concerns the prudential regulation of domestic financial markets, an area that has received a great deal of attention in a globalized context following the Asian crisis of 1997. The importance of a well-regulated financial system to the success of any economy, but especially one that is outward-oriented, cannot be overemphasized, as it lowers financial sector fragility. This is because of the disproportionate externality that malfunctions in the financial sector have on the real side of the economy (Greenwald and Stiglitz 1993). As far as commercial banks are concerned, there are important issues in their regulation related to the principal-agent literature, as analysed in Chapter 2 by Murshed and Subagjo. There is considerable moral hazard on the part of bank managers as they perform multiple tasks, and are often accountable to multiple principals (the common agency problem). The chapter also discusses the relative merits of various types of regulatory instruments ranging from direct controls to incentive-based regulation for low-income countries.

Technological progress, FDI and product diversification

In order to fully benefit from greater economic integration low-income countries need to diversify and upgrade their export base. This requires enhancing production techniques and increasing the skill base of the labour force, with a view to moving up the product cycle into technologically more sophisticated goods and services. This can be achieved both by the increased import of relatively more sophisticated machinery and capital equipment, and/or via FDI inflows.

The statistical analysis in Mayer (Chapter 5) on technology imports by low-income countries suggests that the technological integration of these countries as a group has increased, but relatively few countries account for most of this change. These include relatively large and small countries, and economies with a large minerals sector. An interesting development is the growth in technology imports from technologically more advanced developing countries. Even if it still remains small compared to such imports from developed countries, it has substantially risen over the past two decades. The sectoral composition of technology imports suggests that it has been strongest for mineral-based activities, and low-skilled labour-intensive activities. Mayer (Chapter 5) also finds that labour productivity increases in low-income countries are confined to a few cases, India and Pakistan prominent amongst them. This suggests among other things a greater need for investment in education and training, a finding also stressed by Agosin (Chapter 15) in his case study of Honduras and Nicaragua, as well as Gounder and Xayavong (Chapter 14) for Fiji and the Solomon Islands.

Cotton and Ramachandaran (Chapter 6) find that in three African economies: Zimbabwe, Ghana and Kenya, the gross value added by firms is higher where the majority ownership of the firm is foreign, when compared to indigenously owned firms in the same category. Skills and technological know-how are key factors in explaining this difference. They also analyse prospects for Asian FDI in Africa, which appear to be growing. Infrastructural development is key to attracting FDI. Power shortage in Ghana, following a drought, is a case in point. One encouraging sign is that a large single project can provide the springboard for attracting more FDI (Mozal in Mozambique, for example). Also, cross-border projects to attract FDI, such as the Maputo corridor, are likelier to provide greater dividends.

Freeman (Chapter 7) describes the increase in export-oriented FDI to Vietnam (in garments, for example) and Laos (electricity for Thailand). Both nations witnessed a decline in FDI inflows following the Asian crisis of 1997. There has to be a stronger pre-commitment to broader reform and institutional overhaul before growth in FDI flows resumes. Piecemeal tinkering, and the odd tax incentive is unlikely to be a workable strategy for other low-income countries when it comes to attracting FDI. In Central America, Honduras and Nicaragua have set up export promotion zones (EPZs) to foster inward investment with major tax holidays. Yet, as Agosin (Chapter 15) describes, economic activities in these EPZs bring about negligible backward linkages to the rest of the economy. Honduras with a more clearly defined property rights regime has been more successful than Nicaragua in attracting export-oriented FDI. Also, unlike in Costa Rica (electronics), some of the FDI is in more footloose areas such as textiles. The market signals of policy changes are weak; supply-side responses inappropriate because of the lack of investment in human capital. These experiences provide important lessons for all developing countries. In Fiji and the Solomon Islands, poorly defined, and badly enforced, property rights are a major hindrance to investment (Gounder and Xayavong, Chapter 14). These problems are exacerbated by political upheavals, such as coups in Fiji, where earlier agreements are reneged upon.

Does smallness cause economic vulnerability or is it institutions of governance?

Are small economies more vulnerable to external economic forces in an era of globalization? Conventionally, smallness refers to the nation state's inability to affect world prices and interest rates, making all areas except the USA, Japan and the European Union small. Other measures of smallness could pertain to demographic or geographic size, as discussed in Read (Chapter 12). But such smallness need not be associated with economic weakness. A small population does not imply small economic size. For example, in spite of being forty times larger than Singapore (3 million) in terms of its population, Bangladesh (122 million) has a smaller absolute economic size in terms of GNP. Also, as Read (Chapter 12), as well as Bräutigam and Woolcock (Chapter 13) indicate, there is no tendency for small countries (defined in different ways) to have lower growth rates, and few of them are low-income countries. Countries such as Fiji and the Solomon Islands, however, have performed poorly in recent years (Gounder and Xayavong, Chapter 14). The Solomon Islands are particularly aid-dependent. Small states are also able to free ride the international system in several areas such as defence expenditure (Read, Chapter 12). But they are less wary of globalization and openness compared to more populous states such as Vietnam (Freeman, Chapter 7).

Then we come to the question of economic vulnerability. All economies are susceptible to demand and supply shocks, as well as the vagaries of the rapidly shifting pattern of competitive advantage. It has been argued that small nations experience greater income and growth fluctuations (Bräutigam and Woolcock, Chapter 13). Therefore vulnerability can be related to a weak and undiversified production/export structure, which is prone to shocks and fluctuations in earnings, and not size *per se* (Read, Chapter 12). Some authors, such as Auty (1997), have defined this as the 'staple' trap.

Another notion of vulnerability is linked to good governance and well-functioning institutions. According to Hall and Jones (1999) these institutions prevent the diversion of the output of an economy into wasteful activities. The importance of state capacity and the institutions of conflict management are tested for a cross section of countries in Bräutigam and Woolcock (Chapter 13). In their analysis, they find that the contribution of various socio-economic variables, capturing state capacity and conflict management, works in the same direction for all states, large or small. But given greater growth volatility in small states, the role of good institutions may be even more important there than in large states. Mayer (Chapter 5) finds that the adoption of newer technology is also correlated to low political risk. So better institutions and superior state capacities are important factors in promoting the adoption of better production techniques. Even nations such as Laos and Vietnam, in a relatively successful region of the world, may find it difficult to encourage a new upsurge of FDI inflows, following the slump of 1997, if they do not improve institutional capacity (Freeman, Chapter 7). Pacific Island nations such as Fiji and the Solomon Islands desperately need private inflows to supplement official assistance, which may be less forthcoming in the future (Gounder and Xayavong, Chapter 14). But apart from institutional weaknesses, these countries suffer from low absorptive capacities, due to the shortage of skilled manpower, exacerbated by emigration in Fiji in response to racial discrimination. In analysing the experience of Honduras and Nicaragua with globalization, Agosin (Chapter 15) emphasizes the growth-retarding role of poor governance. There may be a greater tendency towards rent-seeking behaviour and collusive activity in small states (Read, Chapter 12), but this does not necessarily result in greater corruption (Bräutigam and Woolcock, Chapter 13).

Read (Chapter 12) analyses the various 'vulnerability' indices that exist to explain the losses due to greater fluctuations in smaller nations. These indices are susceptible to the usual problems associated with weighting; even with endogenous weighting techniques difficulties arise due to the paucity of data for small countries.

It is important to emphasize the newer vulnerabilities for all low-income countries engendered by the rapid pace of globalization during the past two decades. There are the cumulatively debilitating effects of the oil shocks of the 1970s and the debt crisis of the 1980s, which have left many economies in a weak position. Public finances are susceptible to the vicissitudes of export earnings. The imposition of structural adjustment as well as multilateral donor conditionality has resulted in much less room for manoeuvre in the macroeconomic sphere. As Mhone and Bond (Chapter 16) argue, structural adjustment in Zimbabwe produced de-industrialization, and coupled with droughts led to a major decline in government revenues and rising government debt. See Cornia (2001) on the idea of social funds managing vulnerability arising from income variations.

Why has Africa benefited least from globalization?

There is a literature stressing pure geographical position as a *fixed* factor governing long-term economic development. It is concerned mainly with the recent poor economic performance in SSA. The central thesis of Bloom and Sachs (1998), as well as Gallup *et al.* (1998), is that there are two factors, impacting like fixed costs that disadvantage Africa. These are (1) tropical location and (2) demographic burden. The tropics, especially tropical Africa, is said to have lower agricultural productivity compared to the mid-latitudes, where most of humanity resides. A lot of SSA is extremely vulnerable to drought, has the highest variance around annual average rainfall, and a lot of coastal East Africa is hot and arid. More to the point, transportation is most difficult in Africa; only 19 per cent of Africa's population live within 100 kilometres of the coast. Also, there is said to be a special disease burden in tropical Africa, involving infectious and parasitic diseases, such as malaria. It is also suggested that the poor geographical and demographic endowments in Africa can in turn cause policy failure and hinder good governance. Other commentators place greater emphasis on policy failure rather than locational factors in explaining Africa's poor performance.

Bräutigam and Woolcock (Chapter 13) discuss one of the two successful countries in SSA, Mauritius. In contrast with war-torn Sierra Leone, government interventions have been judicious, and expenditure in the social sector quite substantial. Mhone and Bond (Chapter 16) analyse the experience of Africa's other success story, Botswana. Despite its huge success in the regional context, they express a degree of scepticism about Botswana, pointing out to the continued undiversified nature of the economy, the relative failure to attract FDI and rising unemployment/underemployment. Zimbabwe, by contrast, is an unequivocal failure. Badly designed liberalization of trade and finance during the period of structural adjustment in the 1990s is to blame according to Mhone and Bond (Chapter 16). These led to the demise of industries set up during an earlier era of sanctions-induced import substitution policies. That may be no bad thing, but the economy has failed to diversify successfully into new areas.

Geography need not be destiny, despite Easterly and Levine's (1998) stress on contagion effects from bad neighbours in Africa. Let us not forget that a generation ago it was Asia that was considered to be the laggard in terms of economic development (Myrdal 1968). The pursuit of good policies in a well-functioning institutional context is of paramount importance.

The world trading system and vulnerable economies

Developments in the arrangements for conducting multilateral trade and technology transfer have left nations in the South more vulnerable than in the past. At a more fundamental level, authors such as Bhagwati (1994) have indicated that there is a growing concern in the North (particularly, the US) for fair as opposed to free trade. This particularly depends very much on the USA's perception of fairness and what is in her interests. It also leads, as Nayyar (1996) points out, to an increasing asymmetry in the application of the principle of free trade when it comes to the rules governing North–South trade, see also Murshed (1992).

There is the issue of membership of the WTO (Langhammer and Lücke, Chapter 10). Of the thirty-two countries that had applied for WTO membership as of November 1999, five are both LDCs and low-income economies. The question then arises, will WTO membership enable these countries to participate meaningfully in the globalized system? The benefits, aside from the value of entering into orderly arrangements, may be elusive. Langhammer and Lücke (Chapter 10) argue that an additional benefit of WTO membership to low-income countries might come from giving a strong signal about the country's willingness to participate in rules-based international trade, and serve to attract FDI. At the operational level, many small developing countries are experiencing difficulties in meeting some of their complex WTO trade obligations. These problems include procedural notification obligations as well as implementing agreements. Skill shortages and lack of permanent missions have been cited as reasons for non-compliance with WTO treaties. Fukasaku (Chapter 11) analyses the special and differential (S&D) treatment clauses still remaining within the WTO system. These are meant to allow developing countries preferential access to OECD markets without their having to return the favour. He argues that these clauses are artefacts of a bygone era, and that they were always ineffective because of derogations excluding developing country exports that pose a threat to OECD country import-competing goods, as in agriculture and textiles. In many cases favourable market access, such as to ACP countries by the European Union, is being diluted. It would be better not to ask for the extension of S&D treatment for LDCs, and concentrate on the real job of providing LDCs better market access in the OECD.

Tharakan (Chapter 9) examines the most frequently used form of contingent protection allowable under WTO rules, the anti-dumping (AD) mechanism. Market shares of low-income economies, and vulnerable lower middle income countries are sometimes cumulated with those of co-respondents like the USA, Russia and Brazil in AD actions. This is inherently unfair, as it drags in exporters from poorer countries struggling to export and with a small market share. There is also an alarming trend whereby larger and more successful developing nations are increasingly instituting AD actions against smaller more vulnerable developing countries. Tharakan proposes alternatives to the AD mechanism based on existing safeguard systems that take a broader view of public interest, by extending this to consumer welfare in importing countries.

The general shift of competitive advantage in labour-intensive manufacturing production from North to the South has attracted a good deal of attention from commentators in developed countries. Indeed, much of the South's exports to the North are already heavily subject to protectionist measures (Page 1994). Such protectionist calls, and the managed trade measures already in place, constitute a very grave threat to the meaningful participation of developing countries in the international system. In developed countries like the USA and the UK there has been an increase in wage dispersion (Slaughter, Chapter 8). In other words, the earnings differential between the skilled and unskilled has widened. This may be due to increased imports of manufactured goods from developing countries, but given the low value of North–South trade compared to intra-North trade, it is more likely due to technical progress favouring more skilled workers in the North. Slaughter (Chapter 8) examines whether protectionist tendencies, in terms of both policy preferences and policy actions in the USA seem to be an obstacle to the integration into the world economy of small, vulnerable developing countries. He makes three related points. First, current trade barriers in the North appear to cost the South billions of dollars annually. Second, although some WTO-governed trade barriers in the North are declining, it appears that there is an increasing US resistance to further globalization via trade, investment and immigration liberalization. Third, he presents evidence on the forces driving this rising resistance to further liberalization, in terms of unskilled worker preferences in the USA.

Then, there is the question of incorporating environmental and labour standards into the international trade policy regulatory framework, specifically the demand that they should be enshrined within WTO rules, giving members the right to use retaliatory trade policy if imports do not conform to these standards. In other words, poor countries interested in exporting to the North would have to implement these standards or face trade sanctions. There is the danger, however, that protectionist interests could manipulate altruistic motivation regarding environmental and specially labour standards. The prominent trade theorist T.N. Srinivasan has said: 'The real danger of using trade sanctions as an instrument for promoting basic rights is that the trade-standards link could become hijacked by protectionist interests attempting to preserve activities rendered uncompetitive by cheaper imports', World Bank (1995: 79). Noor (Chapter 4) considers an analytical North–South model where the imposition of a labour standard by the North in the presence of a distortionary minimum wage in the North raises employment in its import-competing sector. The key insight in his model is that if industrial countries are explicitly constrained by WTO rules regarding the imposition of an import tariff to gain advantage in trade, they will resort to second-best policy options – demanding labour standard policies for their trading partners. The successful implementation of a labour standard in developing countries acts as a substitute for higher tariffs in the industrial countries on goods imported from the South, and partially alleviates the distortion caused by the industrial bloc's own labour standard.

Even when there is universal acceptance of standards regarding the rights of workers, the method of implementation is open to question. They need not be enforced via second-best trade sanctions under the aegis of WTO rules, but their adoption could be made a condition of aid, and by strengthening existing ILO conventions regarding workers' rights. In any case, as incomes rise and poverty diminishes, labour standards tend to emerge and child labour diminishes. Another method for introducing labour standards is through consumer-group pressure in the North. Freeman (1998) argues that the consumer in the North who has altruism built into his/her utility function, and is prepared to pay for more humane conditions for workers as well as the abolition of child labour, can do so via purchasing goods appropriately labelled, such as with 'rugmark'.

Low-income economies have become caught up in the wave of accelerated globalization sweeping through the world in the last two decades. Besides being intrinsically vulnerable, they face new constraints in the processes of trade, technology transfer, investment and international finance. Economic policy-making powers of the nation state are considerably less in the present globalized context; this at least places greater restraints on the world's more non-altruistic governments. But societies and states do retain some residual room for manoeuvre over the pace at which they embrace the full implications of globalization. Thus, choices should be wisely exercised, and capacities built up before rushing into the globalized world. Besides humanitarian reasons, there are compelling security considerations as to why the affluent world should be concerned with the development of the really disadvantaged and marginalized countries of the world. Otherwise the dangers of wars and localized conflicts loom large, which in the end affect everyone. There is also the dreaded prospect of a vast swathe of mass migration from the immiserized and marginalized parts of the world into richer countries to consider.

References

Arndt, S. and Kierzkowski, H. (eds) (2001) *Fragmentation – New Production Patterns in the World Economy*, Oxford: Oxford University Press.

Auty, R.M. (1997) 'Natural Resources, the State and Development Strategy', *Journal of International Development*, 9, 651–63.

Bairoch, P. (1982) 'International Industrialisation Levels from 1750 to 1980', *Journal of European Economic History*, 2, 268–333.

Baldwin, R. and Martin, P. (1999) 'Two Waves of Globalisation: Superficial Similarities, Fundamental Differences', in H. Siebert (ed.), *Globalisation and Labour*, Tübingen: JCB Mohr.

Bhagwati, J. (1994) 'Free Trade: Old and New Challenges', *Economic Journal*, 104, 231–46.

Bloom, D.E. and Sachs, J.D. (1998) 'Geography, Demography and Economic Growth in Africa', *Brookings Papers on Economic Activity*, 2, 207–95.

Cain, P.J. and Hopkins, A.G. (1993) *British Imperialism: Innovation and Expansion, 1688–1914*, London: Longmans.

Cornia, G.A. (1999) 'Liberalization, Globalization and Income Distribution', WIDER Working Paper 157, Helsinki: UNU/WIDER.

Cornia, G.A. (2001) 'Social Funds in Stabilization and Adjustment Programmes: A Critique', *Development and Change*, 32, 1–32.

Davis, M. (2001) *Late Victorian Holocausts: El Niño Famines and the Making of the Third World*, London: Verso.

Dollar, D. and Kraay, A. (2001) 'Trade, Growth and Poverty', Presented at the UNU/WIDER Conference on Growth and Poverty, Helsinki, 25–6 May 2001, available at www.wider.unu.edu.

Dutt, R.C. (1902, 1904) *Economic History of British India*, 2 volumes, London: Kegan, Paul.

Easterly, W. and Levine, R. (1998) 'Troubles with the Neighbours: Africa's Problem, Africa's Opportunity', *Journal of African Economies*, 7, 120–42.

Freeman, R.B. (1998) 'What Role for Labor Standards in the Global Economy?' Harvard University (processed).

Gallup, J.L., Sachs, J.D., and Mellinger, A.D. (1998) 'Geography and Economic Development', National Bureau of Economic Research (NBER) Working Paper 6849.

Greenwald, B. and Stiglitz, J.E. (1993) 'Financial Market Imperfections and Business Cycles', *Quarterly Journal of Economics*, 108, 77–114.

Hall, R.E. and Jones, C.I. (1999) 'Why Do Some Countries Produce So Much More Output Per Worker Than Others?', *Quarterly Journal of Economics*, 114(1), 83–116.

IMF (International Monetary Fund) (1997) *International Financial Statistics Yearbook*, Washington, DC: IMF.

Kaminsky, G.L. (1998) 'Currency and Banking Crises: The Early Warnings of Distress', International Finance Discussion Paper No. 629, Washington, DC: Board of Governors of the Federal Reserve System.

Krugman, P. (1995) 'Growing World Trade: Causes and Consequences', *Brookings Papers on Economic Activity*, 25, 327–77.

Low, P., Olarreaga, M., and Suarez, J. (1998) 'Does Globalization Cause a Higher Concentration of International Trade and Investment Flows?', ERAD Working Paper 98-8, Geneva: WTO.

Milanovic, B. (1999) 'On the Threshold of the Third Globalization: Some Historical Angles', unpublished manuscript.

Milanovic, B. (2002) 'True World Income Distribution, 1988 and 1993. First Calculations Based on Household Surveys Alone', *Economic Journal*, 112 (January).

Murshed, S.M. (1992) *Economic Aspects of North–South Interaction: Analytical Macroeconomic Issues*, London: Academic Press.

Myrdal, K.G. (1968) *Asian Drama: An Inquiry into the Poverty of Nations*, London: Allen Lane.

Naoroji, D. (1901) *Poverty and Un-British Rule in India*, London: Swan Sonnenschein.

Nayyar, D. (1996) 'Free Trade: Why, When and for Whom?', *Banca Nazionale del Lavoro Quarterly Review*, 198, 333–50.

Nayyar, D. (1997) 'Globalization: The Game, the Players and the Rules', in S.D. Gupta (ed.), *The Political Economy of Globalization*, London: Kluwer Academic Publishers.

Page, S. (1994) *How Developing Countries Trade: The Institutional Constraints*, London: Routledge.

Quah, D. (1996) 'Twin Peaks: Growth and Convergence in Models of Distribution Dynamics', *Economic Journal*, 106, 1045–55.

Rodriguez, F. and Rodrik, D. (1999) 'Trade Policy and Economic Growth: A Skeptic's Guide to the Cross-National Evidence', NBER Working Paper 7081, Cambridge, MA: National Bureau of Economic Research.

Sachs, J. and Warner, A. (1995) 'Economic Reforms and the Process of Global Integration', *Brookings Papers on Economic Activity*, 1, 1–118.

Singer, H.W. (1950) 'The Distribution of Gains Between Borrowing and Investing Countries', *American Economic Review*, 40, 473–85.

Standing, G. (1999) *Global Labour Flexibility. Seeking Distributive Justice*, Basingstoke: Macmillan.

UNCTAD (1998) *Least Developed Countries Report*, Geneva: United Nations Conference on Trade and Development.

UNDP (1999) *Human Development Report 1999*, New York: United Nations Development Programme.

Walford, C. (1878) 'The Famines of the World: Past and Present', *Journal of the Statistical Society*, 41, 434–42.

Williamson, J.G. (1999) 'Globalization, Labor Markets and Convergence in the Past', in P. Aghion and J.G. Williamson (eds), *Growth, Inequality, and Globalization*, Cambridge: Cambridge University Press.

World Bank (1995) *World Development Report*, Washington, DC: World Bank.

World Bank (1998) *World Development Indicators*, Washington, DC: World Bank.

2 Financial sector regulation in a globalized context

S. Mansoob Murshed and Djono Subagjo

In his presidential address to the American Economics Association, Milton Friedman gave us the authoritative version of the *monetarist* creed:

> … monetary policy can prevent money itself from being a major source of economic disturbance … A second thing monetary policy can do is to provide a stable background for the economy.
>
> Milton Friedman (1968: 12–13)

This statement has become the cornerstone of macroeconomic policy advice dispensed to all developing and transitional economies. It also constitutes the *raison d'être* for the primacy of inflation control, as well as the stabilization and structural adjustment programmes of the 1980s, and the associated liberalization of financial markets. But as we all know, with hindsight, this view (generally described as the Washington consensus) ignored the need for prudential regulation of the financial sector as a prerequisite for sound monetary policy. The converse is equally true: stable monetary policies are needed if an efficient financial sector is to flourish. Simple (or simple-minded) capital account liberalization, as part of a strategy of integration into the global economy, has become discredited in the wake of the Asian crisis of 1997 (see Rodrik 1998). In addition, it is recognized that monetary policy reform geared to controlling inflation will not benefit the economy fully unless and until the private financial sector is well functioning. Also in the presence of many other distortions in the economy, financial liberalization may be undesirable, due to second-best considerations. The over-arching problem lies in the weak nature of institutions and the type of strategic interaction between the state and various groups in developing countries (LDCs).

This chapter aims to make a policy-oriented contribution to the literature on prudential bank regulation for LDCs. It does three things: first, it argues that there is a need to place banking sector regulation high on the policy agenda. Second, it provides some theoretical insights, emphasizing the difficulties of the regulation process. Finally, it critically analyses policy advice in a taxonomic style with regard to prudential regulation, paying close attention to the capabilities of low-income and small LDCs. The first section examines the need to pay attention to banking regulation, the second section is devoted to the theoretical and policy analysis on bank regulation, and, finally, the third section concludes with policy recommendations.

Motivation for more robust banking sector policy

In the 1990s, foreign portfolio investment and short-term bank lending to the financial-services sector experienced more dramatic growth than trade and direct investment flows (Crafts 2000; Bordo *et al.* 1998). Financial integration, however, is largely confined to a small group of emerging economies in the context of the developing world. The globalization of capital markets carries its own price. National governments have become more vulnerable to changes in circumstances often unrelated to the stance of domestic economic fundamentals, due to the sudden reversal of capital flows and shifts in investor sentiment.

After the recent crises in Mexico, East Asia and Russia, the reality of excessive volatility in international capital markets or contagion is becoming more widely accepted, although the reasons for vulnerability of countries to contagion are still not clearly understood (Dornbusch *et al.* 2000). Kaminsky and Reinhart (1996) show that currency and banking crises have generally increased since the 1980s following a wave of financial liberalization allowing more banks to operate. Table 2.1 summarizes a part of their survey findings combined with data on gross fiscal costs of selected crises from different sources. The gross costs include outpayment of guaranteed liabilities, liquidity support, recapitalization and acquisition of non-performing loans. The net costs will only be known after incorporating proceeds from recoveries and reprivatization.

Table 2.1 also indicates that financial crises are more costly for developing countries. Honohan (1996) establishes the vulnerability of small countries with his finding that economic size appears to be a more robust explanatory variable compared to a set of macroeconomic indicators in regressions on crisis resolution cost. The very disproportional resolution cost as a share of GDP combined with the harmful impact of disorderly financial liberalization casts doubts on whether financial integration is viable or sensible for developing countries (Rodrik 1998).

In addition to the contagion factor, reduced profitability as a result of tougher competition in a more deregulated market is an important explanation for the higher number of banking crises. However, as argued by Kaufmann and Mehrez (2000), the increased likelihood of banking crises in the periods after liberalization is not an excuse for countries not to liberalize their financial sector. They show that banking crises are not more likely in *any* liberalized financial system, as pointed out by Demirgüç-Kunt and Detragiache (1998a), but in countries where banks have little time to gather information, update their knowledge and make adjustments during periods of transition to a more deregulated system. The lesson is that in countries with poor transparency financial liberalization should be carried out cautiously.

Despite the debate on whether or not liberalized and financially integrated countries are more vulnerable to contagion and boom–bust cycles in banking, hardly any researcher is found to challenge the urgency of supervision, regulation,

Table 2.1 Financial liberalization, banking crises, currency crises and the gross fiscal costs

Country	*Dates of financial liberalization (FL)*[a]	*Number of banking and currency crises since FL*[b]	*Total number of crises during survey period (1970–97)*[b]	*Gross costs as % of GDP (selected banking crises)*
Argentina	1977	8	10	55.3 (1980–2)[c]
Indonesia	1983–8	4	6	42 (1998–9)[d]
Chile	1974–6	5	8	41.2 (1981–2)[c]
Israel			5	30 (1977–83)[c]
Thailand	1989–90	1	6	26 (1997–9)[d]
Côte d'Ivoire				25 (1988–91)[c]
Malaysia	1978–85	2	3	11 (1998–9)[d]
Senegal				17 (1988–91)[c]
Spain	1974	6	6	16.8 (1977–85)[c]
Bulgaria				14 (1990s)[c]
Mexico	1974 and 1991	4 and 2	4 and 2	13.5 (1995)[c]
South Korea				10 (1997–9)[d]
Hungary				10 (1991–3)[c]
Finland	1982–91	4	5	7.5 (1991–4)[e]
Sweden	1980–90	4	5	5.2 (1991–3)[e]
Sri Lanka				5 (1989–93)[c]
Norway	1980–90	4	5	3 (1988–92)[e]
United States				3.2 (1984–91)[e]
Australia				1.6 (1989–91)[c]
Colombia	1980	3	3	
Denmark	early 1980s	2	5	
Bolivia	1985	2	4	
Brazil	1975	7	7	
Peru	1991	0	3	
Philippines	1980–4	5	6	
Uruguay	1975–9	2	4	
Turkey	1980 and 1987 (Dec. 1983–June 1987 controls reimposed)	3	4	
Venezuela	1981 and 1989 (1984–Jan. 1989 controls reimposed)	5	6	

Sources

a Kaminsky and Reinhart (1996).

b Counted from Kaminsky and Reinhart (1996) with the addition of one count for Indonesia, Thailand, Malaysia, South Korea and the Philippines due to the recent Asian crisis.

c Caprio and Klingebiel (1996a).

d Merrill Lynch (1999).

e Edey and Hviding (1995).

contract enforcement, rule of law and transparency for a strong banking sector, *both* in liberalized and unliberalized financial systems. In fact, studies on the causes of Mexican and Asian crises have shown a shift in conventional wisdom from emphasizing macroimbalances to weaknesses in the financial sector. Recent years have seen a stream of studies looking for determinants of banking crises (for example, Demirgüç-Kunt and Detragiache 1998b; Kaufmann and Mehrez 2000; and Hardy and Pazarbaşioğlu 1999). We find, however, that relative significance of determinants of banking crises shown in existing literature, be they macroeconomic, financial or institutional, are quite sensitive to different crisis definitions, sample selection and model specification (Frydl 1999). Murshed and Subagjo (2000) test empirically for the probability of banking crises utilizing logit estimates. The main finding is that a floating exchange regime does not significantly lower the probability of a banking crisis; in fact countries with a managed float are more prone to such crises. Under managed floating banks lack incentives to hedge their foreign currency exposure because governments are believed to have an interest in smoothing the fluctuation of exchange rates. The other noteworthy finding is that the inclusion of corruption indices (from Transparency International) does not statistically significantly contribute to banking crises.

Prudential financial regulation

We now turn to issues regarding the prudential regulation of the banking sector by a regulatory agency in LDCs. We focus on the banking sector because the *sine qua non* for a robust financial sector is a strong banking system.

One of the main results of the empirical analysis in Murshed and Subagjo (2000) is that bank regulators should be particularly alert about the rapid growth of credit and tightened liquidity in the banking sector. This is consistent with the Honohan and Stiglitz (1999) statement that over-optimism and deliberate gambling together with self-dealing or looting are three endemic components present in every banking crisis. Similarly, Caprio and Klingebiel (1996b) show that poor supervision and regulation is the most prevalent feature for a sample of twenty-nine bank insolvencies in twenty-one developing countries. Notwithstanding this, low-income developing countries face particular impediments, mainly in terms of social capability, human resources and general infrastructure, in establishing prudential banking standards as outlined in the Basle Core Principles (Basle Committee 1997).

This section attempts to fill in the gap between the need for prudential standards and the limitations of many LDCs. The next subsection reviews the hurdles in the path of strengthening the domestic financial system and applying prudential standards. We also discuss a series of controversies concerning the selection of regulatory measures, followed by a search for a prudential, but also viable, set of banking regulations that suit general developing countries conditions. A simple framework that reduces misalignment between the policy makers' goals of a sound banking sector and banks' pursuit of profitability by rewarding prudent risk taking while punishing misconduct and incompetence is required.

Obstacles to building a robust financial sector

Before selecting an appropriate set of policy options, it is imperative to document a number of stylized obstacles and limitations that are often more serious in LDCs. The first major obstacle is related to difficulties in devising efficient regulation because regulators themselves have multiple tasks and multiple principals. While it is also relevant for industrial countries, the problem is exacerbated in developing countries due to weaker institutions. Other remaining constraints to a more robust financial sector stem from a lack of regulatory infrastructure, the smallness of the banking sector and reputational inadequacies.

Who guards the guardians?

The regulators of a banking system themselves require regulation. They may be acting as principals as regulators of the private sector, but in turn they are appointed by governments to whom they must answer. In that sense they are agents, as well. What happens if they have several masters or principals and perform several tasks? Examples of several masters include such instances as answering not only to the government but other powerful special interest groups. Tirole (1994) cites the example of the legislature and the executive in the US system. In developing countries, and elsewhere, one can think of other interest groups and lobbies. When we come to the agent (regulator in this case) she or he may have multiple tasks: prudentially manage the financial sector, but also promote economic growth and take into account the interests of powerful stakeholder groups. In general, as demonstrated by Holmström and Milgrom (1991), this will yield low-powered incentives to perform any task. The essence of any principal–agent relationship is unverifiable effort exerted by the agent in carrying out the task for the principal. There is, however, a verifiable output. One cannot usually prove effort levels undertaken by those who act on our behalf, but the outcome or output is fully verifiable.

Following the set-up in Dixit (1999) we specify a multiple principal, multi-task framework. Let the two tasks to be done be denoted by x_1 and x_2 corresponding to commissions made by Principal 1 and 2, respectively. Each job entails symmetric costly effort levels, e. We abstract from uncertain variations in the agent's efforts (the influence of luck). Principal 1 derives a benefit $= B$ for task 1 but none from job 2, and the same in reverse applies to Principal 2. Both principals will need to satisfy the participation constraint of the agent. The first principal's profit function takes the following form:

$$P_1 = Bx_1 - w\left[x_1 + ex_1^2 + ex_2^2 + 2kx_1x_2\right] \tag{1}$$

The terms inside the square brackets indicate the costs of exerting effort by the agent, which the principal must meet in order to satisfy the agent's participation constraint. Observe the jointness of effort, because the agent must simultaneously carry out both tasks x_1 and x_2. The payment made to the agent is indicated by w, and the payment schedule is linear. The last term refers to how carrying out one task affects effort levels in the other. If k is positive then the two tasks are substitutes: more effort in one direction implies less effort elsewhere. If k is negative the two jobs are complements.

The second principal's profit function by symmetry is

$$P_2 = Bx_2 - w\left[x_2 + ex_1^2 + ex_2^2 + 2kx_1x_2\right] \tag{2}$$

Maximization of (1) with respect to x_1 will lead to

$$\frac{\partial P_1}{\partial x_1} = B - w - 2wx(e+k) = 0 \tag{3}$$

where $x_1 = x_2 = x$ by symmetry. An identical expression can also be obtained for Principal 2. Rearrangement in terms of w yields the following payment schedule:

$$w = \frac{B}{1 + 2x(e+k)} \tag{4}$$

Note the following:

a Incentive payments to the agent are less high-powered if the two tasks conducted by the agent are substitutes, as efforts in one direction detract from the other function. This is not the case if the jobs are complements.

b Incentive payments related to effort and output to the agent increase, if the principals act together in a cooperative or collusive manner. Thus, incentives to the agent to exert optimal effort become stronger. This can be demonstrated by summing equations (1) and (2) and then jointly maximizing for x. In the resultant expression for w in equation (4), the term 2 will vanish. The most frequently cited reason for the failure of cooperation is that people suspect one another, and are unsure of how the benefits of acting jointly will eventually be divided up between the different parties. In other words, there is coordination failure. Clearly, this problem is more acute the larger the number of potential principals.

c Equation (4) states that incentive payments to a multi-task agent decline as the number of principals, stakeholders or masters increases, as the magnitude of the term 2 in the denominator of equation (4) rises with the number of principals.

In summary, the presence of multiple tasks and multiple principals increases the difficulties associated with efficient regulation. A political system has many stakeholders, often deliberately so constructed, so as to minimize the chances of a corrupt dictator emerging. The downside is a weaker set of incentives for regulators, which in turn adversely affects their efficiency. Other problems associated with multiple principals (the common agency problem) in the context of adverse selection are discussed in Murshed and Sen (1995).

A related problem is that of regulatory capture. This occurs when regulators are bribed or controlled by groups they are meant to supervise. The existence of powerful vested interests, and strong informal social networks often results in regulatory capture. Vested interests and informal networks are, however, notoriously resistant to reform. Thus, it is important for the policy maker to attempt to work with the existing institutional structure rather than suggest piece-meal reform, see Rodrik (2000). In the context of monetary policy and financial regulation, Romer and Romer (1996) call for a two-tiered regulatory structure: a board of trustees and a separate body of policy makers, each with different tenures in office. The idea is to limit the influence of any government of the day by appointing trustees on non-renewable long-term contracts, with more short-term periods of office for regulators.

Other obstacles

Banking regulators in developing countries are believed to face more serious obstacles and limitations in promoting banking stability, which are related to their low bureaucratic capability. Four stylized obstacles can be stated:

1 LDCs have more serious information, contracting and monitoring problems. Information problems refer to the difficulty of determining product, project and borrower quality; contracting problems are related to the difficulties of detecting fraud and of attaching collateral; while by monitoring problems, we mean the difficulty of verifying the compliance of covenants.
2 The provision of required public infrastructure and services for a sound financial system is subject to constraints related to a lack of economies of scale.
3 The profitability of the banking sector tends to be squeezed by high overall unit costs of operation due to smallness and technological backwardness. There is a limited choice of financial assets, thereby making risk pooling less effective.
4 Most LDCs suffer from the so-called Peso Problem. This arises because risk-neutral investors require an extra premium owing to their perception that the government benefits from inflation tax by depreciating its currency (Hausmann *et al.* 1999).

Given the above, the question now is which set of prudential standards LDCs should adopt. There is a large menu of policy tools for a sound bank regulation. The cornerstone of the BIS regulation (1988) is the 8 per cent capital adequacy ratio (CAR). This may be adequate for international banks, but for banks in smaller LDCs, this standard regulatory capital ratio should be complemented with other robust policy tools.

An appropriate regulatory framework

Recommendations from various bank regulation studies differ as to what should be controlled: whether it concerns banks' output, input or process. Restraints on input mainly relate to incentives: capital adequacy, liability composition and proper tests for bank managers. Those on output fit and pertain to direct controls. They include administrative ceilings on a number of identified high-risk assets, total asset growth, lending rate ceilings and other permissible activities. For simplicity, the term restraint on processes can be replaced with *supervision*. It refers to regulators' involvement in overseeing and influencing banks' risks policy framework, internal reporting standards and procedures concerning market and credit risk management.

Restraint on output are generally considered to be the least effective, but they do have the lowest verification costs. At the other end of the spectrum, prudential restraint on processes potentially produces the least crisis-prone financial sector (Honohan and Stiglitz 1999). But because of complexity and costs, they are also the most expensive and difficult to implement in developing countries where rent-seeking activities are ubiquitous.

With regard to whether regulators target restraint on banks' input or output, Honohan and Stiglitz (1999) argue for more direct regulatory restraints on output. Others put more weight on more indirect measures based on incentives (e.g. Galloway *et al.* 1997; Caprio and Summers 1995).

A simplistic conclusion from various empirical findings would be to limit credit expansion and maintain ample liquidity in the banking sector. But, while these measures may prevent countries from experiencing crises, they are usually at the expense of financial sector performance that is important for stimulating general economic activity. In addition, restraints on output tend to lose effectiveness as a result of financial innovation, and if underlying incentives driving bankers' actions are not taken into account. Measures by the Indonesian government to curb foreign exchange syndicated loans issued by banks are a notable example. As the government had not worked on the underlying incentives by preserving a crawling peg exchange rate regime, thus allowing foreign investors to exploit interest rate differentials with guaranteed predictability of exchange rate depreciation, banks' external borrowing was not held back. In fact, financial innovation and advancing technology facilitated the continuing build up of foreign debt through issuance of short-term promissory notes and commercial paper that were not entirely covered by rules and constraints.

As the alternative to the direct approach, the incentive-based regulatory framework is also subject to question. Proponents of more direct restraints point out that two banks having the same capital adequacy ratio and employing a similar risk management procedure, may have thoroughly different risk profiles if the interests of bank owners and managers diverge. To clarify this, assume that, according to a new regulation, bank owners have to inject more equity into the banking sector. The higher CAR will theoretically motivate bank owners to act prudently. However, as a result, bank managers may be enticed to gamble in riskier asset allocation if the higher CAR puts them under pressure to perform.[1] They could also make changes in the loan composition that maintains the agreed capital ratio constant but actually increases the risk profile by lending more than warranted to government bodies, and by expanding short-term loans to financial institutions, which under the present Basle CAR framework have a lower risk weighting (capital arbitrage). There could also be incentives towards the manipulation of interest income recognition. Imposing more direct restraint on output, in the form of administrative ceilings on asset composition or total loan growth, could restrain such unwanted responses of agents. Hence, the critics of incentive-based bank regulation highlight the ineffectiveness of fine tuning incentives in situations where bankers respond differently from what has been assumed in the underlying model. In the worst case scenarios, Honohan and Stiglitz (1999) argue that incentive-based measures can lead to perverse outcomes.

However, in the case of small LDCs, the differences in policy recommendations between proponents of direct (restraint on output) and indirect measures turn out not to be so striking. Both views take into account the limitations of developing countries in adopting best practise in bank regulation and supervision.

With regard to the problems associated with the use of the minimum CAR, we find that in the developing country context with little fragmentation of shareholding and absence of stock listing, bank owners (principals) are usually involved in important decision making (see Claessens *et al.* (2000) on East Asia). The agency problem where bank managers' (agent's) interests are not aligned with their principals', therefore, becomes less pertinent in this setting.

Further, Honohan and Stiglitz (1999) persuasively demonstrate that information and monitoring problems in correctly pricing deposit insurance premia can lead to perverse outcomes when bankers exploit their ability to manipulate the loan book. However, it is questionable if the schedule of deposit insurance premia will play such a substantive role for banks in developing countries where the institution of deposit insurance is itself absent (explicitly or implicitly). In fact, most LDCs included in Demirgüç-Kunt and Huizinga (1999) have no deposit insurance premium schedule (Colombia being a notable exception).

Hence, for less developed countries, focusing on aligning bank owners' and agents' incentives with prudent risk taking will potentially render a more feasible set of robust bank regulatory standards. Inefficient regulation due to the presence of multiple tasks and multiple principals can be alleviated, as the interests of regulators and the financial sector in favour of financial stability become closer.

Another reason for stressing incentive-compatible mechanisms is that supervision cannot be the main line of defence against bank failures, even in developed countries (Caprio and Summers 1995). The supervisory agency could be starved of resources and suffer from an inferior remuneration package. Training and education of quality bank supervisors takes many years.[2] Furthermore, even in developed countries, supervisors face political and other pressures, and are frequently inclined to be silent about chronic banking problems until net worth becomes negative. Ironically, depositors and bank analysts in sophisticated financial systems are found to fail to anticipate the downgrading of banks to problem status (Simons and Cross 1991).

The first evident option to induce bankers to exercise safe and sound banking is a higher CAR. Besides providing a financial cushion against unforeseen losses, a bank with a substantial capital base is less prone to gambling and looting

(Akerlof and Romer 1993). In a case of too few net assets and in the presence of a government safety net, a bank tends to take more risks to enable it to attract deposits more aggressively.

The absence of supporting conditions can, however, undermine the effectiveness of the higher CAR. First, deficiencies in accounting and reporting standards could compromise the integrity of capital when a bank faced with non-performing loans refuses to recognize falling interest income and make the necessary provisioning (Brownbridge and Kirkpatrick 1998). Second, as noted above, a bank can change the composition of its risk assets to meet a higher CAR while actually increasing the riskiness of its loan book. The new capital adequacy framework that is now being proposed by the Bank for International Settlement (Basle Committee 1999) will in principle reduce the possibility of capital arbitrage and the first-order differences between regulatory and economic capital requirement (see Berger *et al.* 1995). The new required regulatory capital should be set using models involving various relevant portfolio characteristics that drive credit risk. These comprise individual asset risk, portfolio size, and behaviour of defaulted assets and the correlation of individual loan credit losses. It should be pointed out that important barriers to adoption still remain under discussion, especially concerning technical and empirical uncertainty about the dimensions of credit risks (see Carey 2000). Third, the effectiveness of the higher CAR could be eroded by high intra-group lending, especially when protecting the funds put in the bank is less attractive for bank owners than exploiting the bank as a financing vehicle for their more profitable non-bank business interests. The latter problem can be specifically solved by making the banking sector more profitable and by imposing restraints on the percentage of capital invested in own group companies, a form of restraint on output.

In addition to the increasing minimum CAR, the banking sector can be strengthened with a rise in liability limits on bankers. Saunders and Wilson (1995) draw lessons from the success of Scottish banking adopting contingent liability provision in the nineteenth century, which was a period of relatively frequent banking failures in England and the USA. The system created a powerful incentive to bank owners to stay prudent because their liability extended to both personal and inheritable wealth. Unlike the case of higher CARs above, it does not require an accompanying restriction on intra-group lending. A drawback of imposing this measure is disintermediation in financial services. Moreover, the penalty for risk taking becomes so high that necessary investment in growth inducing, but risky, activities like infrastructure and technological development may not be undertaken.

While raising capital ratios and liability limits might be suggested to small countries with insufficient supervisory skills, the two policy tools could induce either banking disintermediation in the case where both measures are imposed, or gambling if only the minimum capital ratios apply. To guarantee profitability, limiting entry could be a solution. The downside of this alternative is that the financial sector will not benefit from static and dynamic efficiency in the form of lower interest and service charges and technical progress. The presence of foreign banks may mitigate the welfare losses and lack of innovation characterizing a monopolistic banking market. In some African countries, ex-colonial banks are well established. Claessens *et al.* (1998) provide empirical evidence that foreign bank entry improves the functioning of domestic financial sector, with positive welfare implications for banking customers, despite the reduced franchise value of bank licences.

Another possible drawback of entry barriers is that banks become excessively profitable, which in turn gives rise to non-bank financial institutions. Rent-seeking activities will emerge (Honohan and Stiglitz 1999) when bank licences are so valuable. But small banks operating in small markets are unlikely to be excessively profitable. Entry barriers have the advantage that they are compatible with the limited oversight abilities of most banking authorities in small countries. The Indonesian pre-crisis experience was probably the best example of an excessively liberal competition policy, where the number of banks mushroomed following the 1988 banking deregulation. This situation was sustainable, and poor supervision remained unpunished, only as long as investment was buoyant. It was a matter of time before a banking crisis forced rationalization in the business.

Entry policies determining the degree and ease of entry are not independent of the two incentive-based measures discussed above. If the capital requirement is high, and owners as well as managers face increased liability in case of failures, only those who know how to bank will venture into the financial sector. One may argue that this is not enough if incentives to gambling and looting are high in the presence of implicit deposit insurance. An additional restraint on banks' input should be requiring potential owners and bank managers to pass 'fit and proper' tests. While the latter will also engender rent-seeking opportunities in countries with low transparency, the fit and proper test requirement can be applied when the instruments are ready.

An important issue relevant to entry policy, which proponents of more direct restraint on output point out, is the extent of permissible operations and limits on products. Again, there is a need for balancing, on the one hand, sufficient profit opportunities for banks, and, on the other hand, guarding against excessive risk taking. Recalling the limited supervisory capacity of small countries, extensive and complicated rules should be avoided. In an extensive survey of more than sixty countries, Barth *et al.* (2000) find that restrictions with respect to what a bank is permitted to do are not beneficial for the performance and stability of the banking sector. Restrictions placed on securities and bank ownership of non-financial firms are especially harmful to financial stability; see also Kono and Schuknecht (1998) who come to a similar conclusion.

Nonetheless, in developing countries, where economic structure is less diversified, restrictions on exposure concentration in certain commodities and real estate are to be encouraged. Although banks, acting under a robust incentive-compatible regulatory regime will voluntarily avoid risk concentration, government intervention to limit systemic crises is necessary. Due to bounded rationality, banks may be compelled to follow herd behavioural patterns during booms, as bankers believe that when bank failures occur across the board the government will refrain from applying the increased liability rule.

Several other incentive-based bank regulations may be inappropriate for LDCs because of an unfavourable cost–benefit balance as well as the unfeasibility of implementation. One is a curb on deposit rates allowing banks to earn high interest margins. A major flaw of this option is that the typical low-income country has low saving rates. Low or negative real deposit rates are not conducive to financial sector deepening. Another is the proposal for risk-calibrated deposit premia (e.g. Bhattacharya *et al.* 1998). The implementation of this regulation assumes, however, that regulators are able to price the risk of the loan book fairly and accurately. A third is, increasing the monitoring efforts of depositors through a co-insurance rule, where depositors face a deductible in their insured funds, for example, 25 per cent of their deposit. The advantage of this instrument is that it reduces moral hazard associated with deposit insurance. Unfortunately, the ability of depositors to influence bank behaviour is seriously contestable even in developed countries. Finally, the idea that the banking sector in LDCs form long-term mutual ties with each other, resulting in self-policing arrangements (Bossone and Promisel 1998) may not always be realistic.

Table 2.2 Incentive compatible policy instruments under stylized LDCs circumstances

	Information, contracting and monitoring problem	*Poor endowment of infrastructure for adequate supervision*	*Smallness of banking sector*	*Credibility and reputation problem of government agencies in regulatory enforcement*
Minimum capital requirement[a]	***	*****	***	****
Contingent liability limit	*****	*****	*****	*
Entry barriers with openness to foreign bank	**	*****	****	***
Fit and proper test of bankers	*	*	***	*
Curb on deposit rate	**	****	*	****
Risk calibrated deposit premia	*	*	*	*
Self-policing arrangements	*	***	****	***
Co-insurance	*	****	****	*
Restrictions on bankable activities	***	***	*	*

Note

a Assuming that the formula of capital ratio follows the existing BIS capital adequacy framework, the friendliness of policy instruments is ranked from * (least suitable) to ***** (most suitable) under the four stylized impediments to building a strong financial sector in small countries.

Conclusions and policy implications

It has been argued that LDCs need a regulatory framework that rewards prudent risk taking more handsomely, but punishes misconduct more harshly. Regulation and restrictions on banking activities will be counterproductive if they erode franchise value while banks have a lot at stake due to higher capital ratio and increased liability limits. It has also been argued that the portfolio of this incentive-compatible bank regulation should be 'LDCs friendly'. The various policy options discussed, and their degree of friendliness in terms of the four stylized obstacles to building a strong financial sector are summarized in Table 2.2.

Promoting the *right* incentive-compatible policy regime does not mean that policy makers neglect strengthening the credibility and capacity of supervisory cadres, auditing and reporting standards and other public infrastructure necessary for a healthy and profitable banking sector. The building of institutional capacities together with the elimination of corruption cannot be overemphasized, because they are the backdrop to efficient regulation, and to alleviating the obstacles to building a robust financial sector.

Notes

1 Gorton and Rosen (1995) also show how in well-capitalized banks, managers take excessive risks in order to convince shareholders that they are good managers. When disappointing results emerge, 'bad managers' can easily hide behind bad luck arguments.

2 For a similar reason, some argue that it is ironic that after the recent Asian crises the IMF rescue package includes conditionality for comprehensive structural changes including reforms in banking supervision, business–government relationships, bankruptcy laws, etc. (Feldstein 1998). It is better to strive for more compatibility between market-oriented reforms and pre-existing institutional capabilities in order to have higher probability of success (Rodrik 2000).

References

Akerlof, G. and Romer, P. (1993) 'Looting: The Economic Underworld of Bankruptcy for Profit', *Brookings Papers on Economic Activity*, 2, 1–73.

Barth, J.R., Caprio, G. Jr., and Levine, R. (2000) 'Banking Systems around the Globe: Do Regulation and Ownership Affect Performance and Stability?', Policy Research Working Paper, Washington, DC: World Bank, February.

Basle Committee on Banking Supervision (1997) 'Core Principles for Effective Banking Supervision (Basle Core Principles)', Basle, Switzerland: Bank for International Settlements, April.

Basle Committee on Banking Supervision (1999) 'A New Capital Adequacy Framework', Basle, Switzerland: Bank for International Settlements, June.

Berger, A., Richard, N., Herring, J., and Szego, Giorgio P. (1995) 'The Role of Capital in Financial Institutions', *Journal of Banking and Finance*, 19, 393–430.

Bhattacharya, S., Boot, A., and Thakor, A. (1998) 'The Economics of Bank Regulation', *Journal of Money, Credit and Banking*, 30, 745–70.

BIS (1988) 'International Convergence of Capital Measurement and Capital Standards', Basle, Switzerland: Bank for International Settlements, July.

Bordo, M.D., Eichengreen, B., and Kim, J. (1998) 'Was There Really an Earlier Period of Financial Integration Comparable to Today?', NBER Working Paper No. 6738, September, Cambridge, MA: National Bureau of Economic Research.

Bossone, B. and Promisel, L. (1998) 'The Role of Self-Regulation in Developing Economies', Washington, DC: World Bank.

Brownbridge, M. and Kirkpatrick, C. (1998) 'Financial Sector Regulation: The Lessons of the Asian Crisis', Manchester: Institute for Development Policy and Management, University of Manchester.

Caprio, G. Jr. and Klingebiel, D. (1996a) 'Bank Insolvencies: Cross–Country Experience', World Bank Policy Research Working Paper No. 1620, Washington, DC: World Bank.

Caprio, G. Jr. and Klingebiel, D. (1996b) 'Bank Insolvency: Bad Luck, Bad Policy, or Bad Banking?', *Proceedings of the Annual World Bank Conference on Development Economics*, Washington, DC: World Bank.

Caprio, G. Jr. and Summers, L.H. (1995) 'Financial Reform: Beyond Laissez Faire', available at www.worldbank.org/finance/cdrom/library/docs/caprio2/capr201a.htm.

Carey, M. (2000) 'Dimensions of Credit Risk and their Relationship to Economic Capital Requirements', NBER Working Paper No. 7629, Cambridge, MA: National Bureau of Economic Research.

Claessens, S., Demirgüç-Kunt, A., and Huizinga, H. (1998) 'How Does Foreign Entry Affect the Domestic Banking Market?', World Bank Working Paper No. 1918, Washington, DC: World Bank.

Claessens, S., Djankov, S., and Long, L.H.P. (2000) 'The Separation of Ownership and Control in East Asian Corporations', *Journal of Financial Economics*, 58, 81–112.

Crafts, N. (2000) 'Globalization and Growth in the Twentieth Century', IMF WP/00/44, Washington, DC: IMF.

Demirgüç-Kunt, A. and Detragiache, E. (1998a) 'Financial Liberalization and Financial Fragility', Research Working Paper No. 1917, Washington, DC: World Bank.

Demirgüç-Kunt, A. and Detragiache, E. (1998b) 'The Determinants of Banking Crises in Developing and Developed Countries', *IMF Staff Papers*, 45, 81–109.

Demirgüç-Kunt, A. and Huizinga, H. (1999) 'Market Discipline and Financial Safety Net Design', World Bank Working Paper, June, Washington, DC: World Bank.

Dixit, A.K. (1999) 'Some Lessons from Transaction-Cost Politics for Less-Developed Countries', unpublished manuscript, Princeton University.

Dornbusch, R., Park, Y.C., and Claessens, S. (2000) 'Contagion: Understanding How it Spreads', *World Bank Research Observer*, 15, 177–97.

Edey, M. and Hviding, K. (1995) 'An Assessment of Financial Reform in OECD Countries', Economic Department Working Paper No. 154, Paris: OECD.

Feldstein, M. (1998) 'Refocusing the IMF', *Foreign Affairs*, March/April.

Friedman, M. (1968) 'The Role of Monetary Policy', *American Economic Review*, 68, 1–17.

Frydl, E.J. (1999) 'The Length and Cost of Banking Crises', IMF Working Paper, WP/99/30, March, Washington, DC: IMF.

Galloway, T.M., Lee, W.B., and Roden, D.M. (1997) 'Banks' Changing Incentives and Opportunities for Risk Taking', *Journal of Banking and Finance*, 21, 509–27.

Gorton, G. and Rosen, R. (1995) 'Corporate Control, Portfolio Choice, and the Decline of Banking', *Journal of Finance*, 50, 1377–420.

Hardy, D.C. and Pazarbaşioğlu, C. (1999) 'Leading Indicators of Banking Crises: Was Asia Different?', *IMF Staff Papers*, 46, 241–58.

Hausmann, R., Gavin, M., Pages-Serra, C., and Stein, E. (1999) 'Financial Turmoil and the Choice of Exchange Rate Regime', WP-400, Washington, DC: Inter-American Development Bank.

Holmström, B. and Milgrom, P. (1991) 'Multi-task Principal Agent Analysis', *Journal of Law, Economics and Organization*, 7, 24–51.

Honohan, P. and Stiglitz, J.E. (1999) 'Robust Financial Restraint', Policy Research Working Paper, Washington, DC: World Bank.

Honohan, P. (1996) 'Financial System Failures in Developing Countries: Diagnosis and Prediction', Washington, DC: IMF (mimeo).

Kaminsky, G. and Reinhart, C. (1996) 'The Twin Crises: Causes of Banking and Balance-of-Payments Problems', Discussion Paper No. 544, Washington, DC: Board of Governors of the Federal Reserve System.

Kaufmann, D. and Mehrez, G. (2000) 'Transparency, Liberalization and Banking Crises', Policy Research Working Paper No. 2286, Washington, DC: World Bank.

Kono, M. and Schuknecht, L. (1998) 'Financial Services Trade, Capital Flows, and Financial Stability', Staff Working Paper *ERAD*, Geneva: WTO.

Merrill Lynch (1999) 'Asia-Pacific Banks: Progress and Issues in Bank Restructuring', Global Fundamental Equity Research Department, February.

Murshed, S.M. and Sen, S. (1995) 'Aid Conditionality and Military Expenditure Reduction in Developing Countries: Models of Asymmetric Information', *Economic Journal*, 105, 498–509.

Murshed, S.M. and Subagjo, D. (2000) 'Prudential Regulation of Banks in Less Developed Economies', WIDER Working Paper No. 199, Helsinki: UNU/WIDER.

Rodrik, D. (1998) 'Who Needs Capital-Account Convertibility?', in S. Fischer *et al.* (eds), *Should the IMF Pursue Capital-Account Convertibility?* Essays in International Finance No. 207, International Finance Section, Department of Economics, Princeton University.

Rodrik, D. (2000) 'Governing the Global Economy: Does One Architectural Style Fit All?', Brookings Trade Policy Forum, Washington DC, forthcoming.

Romer, C.D. and Romer, D.H. (1996) 'Institutions for Monetary Stability', NBER Working Paper No. 5557, Cambridge, MA: National Bureau of Economic Research.

Saunders, A. and Wilson, B. (1995) 'Contingent Liability in Banking: Useful Policy for Developing Countries?', World Bank Working Paper No. 1538, Washington, DC: World Bank.

Simons, K. and Cross, S. (1991) 'Do Capital Markets Predict Problems in Large Commercial Banks?', *New England Economic Review*, May/June, 51–6.

Tirole, J. (1994) 'The Internal Organization of Government', *Oxford Economic Papers*, 46, 1–29.

3 Globalization, informalization, criminalization and North–South interaction

David E. Bloom and S. Mansoob Murshed

This chapter examines the effects of an increase in criminal and informal activities following globalization on growth in a North–South model. By globalization we mean an increased world demand for various goods, including products and services which are illegal or produced in the informal sector in the South. We analyse the effects of these shocks on growth and capital stocks in a North–South macroeconomic model, along the lines of Findlay (1980). We begin by outlining some stylized facts in the first section on globalization, informalization and increasing criminal activity. This is followed, in the second section, by a sketch of different approaches to understanding criminal, informal and shadowy activities and a discussion of the North–South model employed in the chapter. The third section analyses the North–South growth model, where the North is represented by a one-sector neoclassical growth model, and the South has surplus labour. An innovation of our model is that the institutionally given fixed real wage in the South is determined in the informal sector. We examine an increase in illicit/informal sector activity in the South, and increased migration from South to the North. Finally, the fourth section concludes with some policy implications.

Stylized facts on globalization, informalization and criminality

Globalization involves the accelerated international exchange of goods/services, capital, labour and ideas or knowledge. It arises from the lowering of barriers to exchange combined with technological developments. The reductions of the impediments to international exchange are a result of deliberate policies pursued in the last quarter of the twentieth century. Accompanying this has been a shift in power, and even income shares, from labour to capital (Standing 1999). Globalization may also create longer lasting 'bads', such as environmental degradation or decreased national security. Increased crime and/or shadowy activities are among the most frequently cited of these bads. Just as globalization creates new opportunities and incentives for legitimate behaviour, it also alters the framework within which criminal actions are taken: crime may increase or decrease; new forms of criminal organization may develop, as well as new initiatives to combat crime.

Accompanying globalization has been an increase in informal sector economic activity. According to the ILO (1999) the majority of new jobs created in Africa and Latin America were in the informal sector. The same report goes on to state that in countries like Bolivia, Bangladesh, Colombia, Côte d'Ivoire, Gambia, Tanzania and Uganda the informal sector accounts for more than 50 per cent of total employment. See also Levenson and Maloney (1998) on patterns of informal sector employment. According to the Global Labour Institute (2000) the informal sector accounts for 80 per cent of all employment in low-income countries, and 40 per cent in middle-income countries. Table 3.1 summarizes this data, for the three major developing regions of the world, and underscores the importance of the magnitude of informal employment.

Whereas most criminal activities are part of the informal sector, not all informal activity is criminal. The informal sector is, therefore, larger than the criminalized sector. We will employ the term informal/criminal/shadowy to cover a wide spectrum of activities in the informal sector, including legal, semi-legal, evasive, underground and illegal but acceptable actions, as well as 'morally' indefensible activities. This is because the analysis that follows in the North–South model in the third section is macroeconomic, encompassing both informal and criminal.

Crime is a complex phenomenon. Not every illegal activity diminishes total output or is growth retarding. Certain illegalities, such as the evasion of draconian and excessive regulation, might even benefit the economy. Parallel, but illegal, organizations may compete with the state and bring about a Pareto superior allocation of public goods such as security and property rights (see Grossman 1995). An excellent survey of issues surrounding corruption and the underground economy can be found in Tanzi (2000). Globalization has an impact on crimes committed across borders (transnational crime), but it also has an indirect impact on national crime through changes in the global economy. More narrowly, a global economic shock – or the pain of adjusting to greater openness to global economic forces – may also have an impact on national crime rates. Some crimes increase with globalization, but others may become less common. For example, smuggling of goods was rife because of prohibitive tariff or quota restrictions. As barriers to trade are dismantled, so are the incentives to smuggle.

A distinctive feature of organized, transnational crime is how closely it mirrors the legitimate transnational and international system. This type of crime can be

Table 3.1 Size of the informal sector (%)

Informal sector, share of	*Latin America/Caribbean*	*Africa*	*Asia*
Total employment excluding agriculture	15	18	15–30
Total employment including agriculture	45	75	75–85
Non-agricultural employment	57	78	45–85
Urban employment	40	61	40–60
Poor employment	50	n/a	n/a
New jobs	84	93	n/a

Source: Global Labour Institute (2000).

classified according to three categories: illegal global trade, defined as activities that shadow and compete with legitimate trade; illegal politics, defined as activities that shadow and compete with legitimate politics; and corruption linked to the global system.

Illegal global trade includes illicit drug trafficking; import/export of stolen goods; illicit traffic in arms; trafficking in people or body parts; and theft of art and cultural objects. Some of these activities are now huge industries. Half the global trade in light weapons is thought to be illicit (*Arms Trade News* 1997). Smuggling people is thought to be worth US$9 billion per year (Savona 1998), while the world drug industry is now thought to be worth US$500 billion (UNDCP 1994). In certain countries the illicit drugs sector can account for a large fraction of national income, for example, the coca-cocaine industry in Bolivia may account for 20 per cent of GNP (UNRISD 1995). Illegal global politics include terrorism; aircraft hijacking; environmental crime; and human rights abuses. Other examples involve the link between corruption and globalization. These include the proceeds from looting national natural resource revenues by politicians and others, such as in Russia and Nigeria, that are laundered through the international banking system. Other types of technology-based global crime include the theft of intellectual property; computer crime; insurance fraud; fraudulent bankruptcy; fraudulent appropriation of funds; and infiltrations of legal businesses.

Most importantly, many of the civil wars in today's world are, at least partially, motivated by banditry and the criminal desire to control natural resource rents. For example, the conflict over diamonds associated with the civil wars in the Democratic Republic of Congo and Sierra Leone. Similarly, narcotics play a major part in sustaining the civil war in Colombia. See Addison *et al.* (2000) for a theoretical model of conflict driven by greed, but where injustice too plays a leading role. Crime, conflict and the forces of globalization are inextricably intertwined. To revert back to the example of conflict over diamonds in Africa: these diamonds have to be shipped to OECD markets, and the proceeds of the sales need to be laundered through offshore financial centres. Similarly, the arms required by the protagonists in these civil wars have to be procured via a complex chain of intermediaries. The point is that the financing of international conflict and crime is part of the process of economic globalization, involving a vast set of actors and institutions, across different countries and continents.

Modelling crime and informal activity

The schema (Figure 3.1) attempts to characterize non-altruistic human economic interaction, motivated by the discussion in Garfinkel and Skaperdas (2000). The main distinction is between contract-based and conflictual interaction. Of course, not all contracts are explicitly written or legally enforceable; some are based on social and ethical conventions. Similarly, the judicial system and other social organizations are also utilized for conflict resolution and dispute settlement. Activities involving conflict can be divided into violent and non-violent actions, with shadowy activities positioned uncomfortably in between.

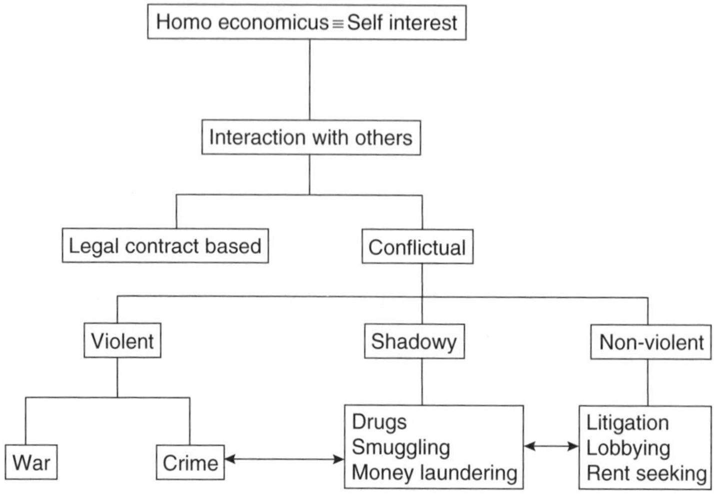

Figure 3.1 Economic interaction between humans.

This chapter is not about the choice-theoretic basis for crime or the technology of violence. Excellent models exist to explain these: Hirshleifer (1995) and Skaperdas (1992) are among many. We are concerned with increased informalization and crime in the context of globalization, as well as consequences for growth in a global North–South paradigm.

The model we outline is based on the seminal work of Findlay (1980), as well as the Burgstaller and Saavedra-Rivano (1984) extension of the Findlay model allowing for capital mobility between the North and the South. The essence of both these models lies in the asymmetry of North–South interaction, with the former wielding the greater economic power. Basically, the growth rate of the South, equal to its terms-of-trade adjusted profit rate has to conform to the growth rate of the North, defined as the growth in its effective labour force. This does not imply convergence to the higher income of the North, as long as there is surplus labour in the South.

The economy of the North corresponds to a Solow (1956) one-sector growth model, with full employment, and factor rewards are determined by marginal product. Saving is out of total income. The South, unlike the North, is meant to have surplus labour with an institutionally determined real wage rate. The innovation in our model is that the 'institution' determining this is the informal or shadowy sector. Our justification for making this assertion is based on Lewis's notion of surplus labour force (1954). There the exogenous wage rate is meant to reflect the fixed average product of labour in subsistence agriculture. We substitute the informal or shadowy economy for subsistence agriculture. An expansion in illicit activity due to 'globalization' will, therefore, impact on the South's, otherwise fixed, wage–rental ratio.

Our model is macroeconomic as it involves a sectoral delineation involving the North producing a single composite good; the South produces two types of goods: one in the formal sector, and the other in the informal sector (which could be illegal). The production of the informal sector or illicit commodity in the South does not directly detract from the capital stock, as it only utilizes surplus labour abundantly available in the hinterland. The effect on equilibrium capital stock, however, occurs via changes in the wage–rental ratio. This in turn will affect steady-state growth rates in the two regions. Also there is a role for capital flows (akin to foreign direct investment) from North to South. The model in the chapter will be concerned with steady-state effects on capital stocks, and not with short-run considerations.

A North–South model

We begin with the structure of production in the North. The production function there is

$$q_{NP} = f_{NP}(k_{NP}) \qquad f'_{NP} > 0 \tag{1}$$

where q_{NP} represents per capita output of the northern product (NP) as a function of the capital–labour ratio (k_{NP}) in the North. Both per capita output and the capital–labour ratio are in terms of the fully employed labour force in the North, L_N. Profit maximization gives the equilibrium wage and profit rates. The northern profit rate, r_N, is equal to the marginal product of capital. The real wage rate, in terms of the North's good, is a residual, given by the Euler equation.

A similar process drives production decisions in the South, except that in the South the real wage rate, w_S is taken as given in the formal sector. Let us denote formal sector per capita output in the South as $q_{SP} = f_{SP}\,(k_{SP})$. Profit maximization will give us a unique capital–labour ratio (k_{SP}) and real rental rate (r_S) in southern formal sector production given the fixity of the wage and rental rate in that sector. The real rental rate on capital in the South's production may be written as

$$r_S = r^*_S = f'_{SP}\,(k^*_{SP}) \tag{2}$$

The rate of profit, however, varies with the terms of trade, P_S (the North's price is set at unity). Thus, the rate of profit in the South is the real rental rate on capital times the terms of trade.

We turn now to the production of the informal sector good which is produced exclusively in the South, for final use in the North. In our simple formulation this activity utilizes labour, but not capital, serving to highlight its cottage industry nature. We can specify a simple mark-up pricing rule, consistent with constant returns for the production of this good, C, whose price is given by P_C in the South's currency:

$$\begin{aligned} P_C &= (1+x)aw_S \\ D_C &= f(P_C, Y_{NC}, \theta) \end{aligned} \tag{3}$$

where the parameter $a = L_C/C$ stands for the labour input–output coefficient in this area, and x is a profit mark-up coefficient. It (x) can also be viewed as the coercive rent extracted by informal sector entrepreneurs, warlords or organizers of crime. Note that in (3) the shares of x and wages in total output are not determined by marginal productivity but by coercive and/or exogenous political factors. This particular formulation has its origins in the work of Kalecki (1971), who argued that x reflected the monopoly power of firms. This allows us to visualize x also as the power of warlords, gang leaders, informal sector entrepreneurs and other forces of coercion including rogue governments. Note that the formulation in (3) does allow us to say something about distributional issues. The second line in (3) specifies the demand for the shadowy good as a function of prices, income in the North and a positive demand shift parameter, θ.

Our characterization above of the production differences could also be generalized for a single country. The North would be the modern sector, the South's formal sector production the semi-modern sector, and the criminal and informal activities the production activity of the ghetto (whether in Bangkok, Lagos, St Petersburg, Los Angeles or Bogota) or the rural hinterland (Afghanistan or Colombia). The underprivileged have two choices: stay in the ghetto or rural backwater or work in smokestack industries or services that use capital. The really modern sector would be associated with advanced technology, 'competitive' in the economic sense, and where factors are paid their just deserts or marginal product.

Events in the informal or shadowy economy will alter the institutionally given real wage rate in the South. Consider a rise in P_C due to globalization (an increase in demand, θ). Totally, differentiating (3), holding a constant,

$$dP_C = (1 + x)a \, dw_S + aw_S \, dx \tag{4}$$

For a given technology (fixed a), the rise in shadowy activities, reflected by an increase in P_C, can either lead to: (i) no changes in the shares of labour or x, (ii) a rise in the share of x or (iii) increases in the share of wages in the production of C. We rule out the first possibility. A rise in x relative to w_S will cause the profit rate to rise in the South; whereas an increase in wages will have the opposite effect. This occurs because a change in the wage rate automatically alters the rate of return on the other factor, capital, used in formal sector production, even though capital is not employed in the informal/shadow economy. Either way, an increase in the demand for informal sector goods will impact on the given wage–rental ratio in the other sector in the South. This in turn will have implications for the steady-state growth rates of the two regions. In what follows, we will claim that a rise in the rent associated with the informal sector is mainly expropriated by warlords or informal sector entrepreneurs leading to a fall in the wage rate and a rise in the profit rate.

Moving on to the outline of income, and capital mobility we have to bear in mind that international capital mobility requires us to distinguish between domestic product and national income. Capital owned in the North could be employed in the production in the South, for example. Per capita national income in the North is

$$Y_{\mathrm{N}} = f_{\mathrm{NP}}(\cdot) + r_{\mathrm{N}}(k_{\mathrm{N}} - k_{\mathrm{NP}}) \tag{5}$$

where k_{N} is nationally owned capital and k_{NP} is capital employed in northern production. The second term indicates the profit earned by northern capital that is repatriated from the South. Per capita consumption (Y_{NC}) is

$$Y_{\mathrm{NC}} = (1 - s_{\mathrm{N}})Y_{\mathrm{N}} \tag{6}$$

where s_{N} is the constant savings propensity in the North. We can also postulate that a constant fraction of consumption will fall on the South's informal or illicit good.

In the South, total income per employed worker (L_{S}) is

$$Y_{\mathrm{S}} = w_{\mathrm{S}} + \left(r_{\mathrm{S}}^{*}k_{\mathrm{S}}/\lambda\right) + xw_{\mathrm{S}} \tag{7}$$

where $\lambda = L_{\mathrm{S}}/L_{\mathrm{N}}$, $k_{\mathrm{S}} = K_{\mathrm{S}}/L_{\mathrm{N}}$ in terms of labour units in the North. Note that part of the South's income will be used to finance debt servicing or profit repatriation against northern ownership of part of the productive capital stock in the South. Consumption per worker in the South is given by

$$Y_{\mathrm{SC}} = w_{\mathrm{S}} + (1 - s_{\mathrm{S}})\left[\left(r_{\mathrm{S}}^{*}k_{\mathrm{S}}/\lambda\right) + xw_{\mathrm{S}}\right] \tag{8}$$

where s_{S} is the savings propensity in the South. Note that workers do not save in the South, following Findlay (1980).

We now turn to the question of capital mobility. It is postulated that international capital mobility serves to equate profit rates across regions. Thus,

$$r_{\mathrm{N}} = P_{\mathrm{S}}r_{\mathrm{S}}^{*} \tag{9}$$

or

$$f'_{\mathrm{NP}}(k_{\mathrm{NP}}) = P_{\mathrm{S}}r_{\mathrm{S}}^{*} \tag{10}$$

Assuming that the excess demand functions are Walrasian stable, and that the Marshall–Lerner conditions hold such that North–South trade is balanced, the following reduced form function relates the terms of trade to the regional capital–labour ratios (see Burgstaller and Saavedra-Rivano 1984 for details):

$$P_{\mathrm{S}} = P_{\mathrm{S}}(k_{\mathrm{N}}(r_{\mathrm{N}}), k_{\mathrm{S}}(r_{\mathrm{S}})), \qquad k_{\mathrm{N1}}, k_{\mathrm{S1}} > 0 \tag{11}$$

Both partial derivatives with respect to P_{S} and k_{N}, k_{S} will be negative. In other words, a rise in the capital stock owned by either region will cause the equilibrium terms of trade of the South to decline. This is because of the combination of (i) full employment in the North, (ii) an institutionally determined real wage in the

South, and (iii) perfect capital mobility, equations (9) and (10). The fixed wage in the South gives a unique r_S^*; given that perfect capital mobility equalizes profit rates, we have a unique k_{NP} (capital–labour ratio in the production of the northern good). As there is full employment in the North any rise in national capital stocks irrespective of the region in which it occurs leads to the relocation of capital towards production in the South. This leads to an excess supply of output in the South, and its terms of trade decline.

It is assumed that initially the rate of profit is greater in the South than in the North. Once international capital mobility is introduced, and profit rates across the regions are equalized, certain disadvantageous characteristics emerge for the South in the steady-state equilibrium. Due to the fact that production in the South is more profitable, the world capital stock is redistributed so that more output is produced in the South and less in the North. The capital stock owned by the North is greater than under autarky in international capital flows. Hence the North's per capita income is greater than if there were no capital flows, and the North–South income differential is widened. This is all the more the case because part of the South's domestic product has to be devoted to profit repatriation.

We have already noted that the North follows a pattern resembling a Solow neoclassical growth model. There is an exogenously given growth rate of the effective labour force, denoted by n. Given that a constant fraction (s_N) of total income (Y_N) is saved in the North, the evolution of its capital stock is given by

$$\dot{k}_N = s_N Y_N - n k_N \tag{12}$$

In the steady state, the growth of k_N is zero. Note that the rate of growth in the North, following the Solow model, is given by the exogenous growth rate of the effective labour force, n.

In the South saving is out of profits alone. Thus the evolution of the South's indigenously owned capital stock is its savings rate times the rate of profit. This is also the growth rate (g_S) in that region. Hence,

$$g_S = s_S P_S r_S^* \tag{13}$$

The job of the terms of trade, given free trade, is to equate the growth rates of the two regions, in the steady-state equilibrium. This happens when n (growth in the North) is equated to the left-hand side of (13) for the South:

$$P_S^* = \frac{n}{s_S r_S^*} \tag{14}$$

Equation (14) conveys the central message of the model: the South's growth rate, given by profitability in that region, must equal the North's growth rate. To reiterate, this does not mean per capita income or even conditional convergence between North and South. See Bloom and Murshed (2001) for the steady-state dynamics, solution technique and other properties of the model.

Figure 3.2 describes the evolution of the capital stocks in the two regions in k_N and k_S space. The growth of the two nationally owned capital stocks, hence, the

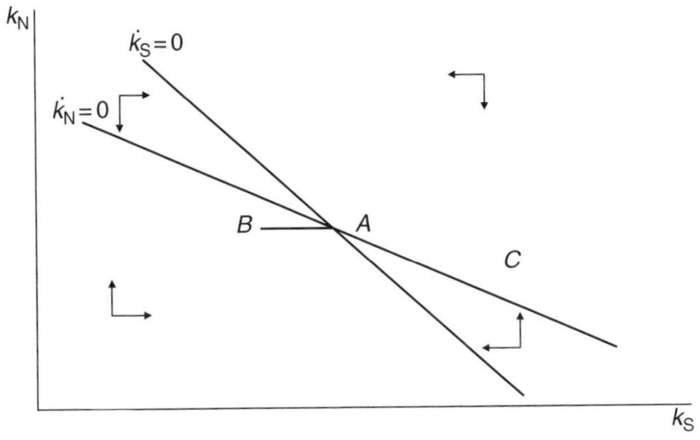

Figure 3.2 Capital stocks in the North and South.

growth rates of the North and the South, are constant along the k_N and k_S schedules. An increase in the equilibrium capital stock in one region leads to a decline in the other region's capital stock.

We are concerned with the steady-state effects on the capital stocks of the two regions of two parameter changes. (See Bloom and Murshed (2001) for details of mathematical derivations.) The first parameter change is associated with increased demand for the informal or shadowy economy good in the North; the second to do with possibly increased migration from South to North. Legal migration is much less than what it was in the nineteenth century, and we make no effort to model the hazards and uncertainties of illegal migration to today's affluent countries.

The first type of change occurs via an alteration in the South's wage–rental ratio (exogenous datum for the legitimate economy). A rise in r_S^*, the profit rate in the South, occurs if the increased revenues from rising informal sector activity go relatively more to x (drug barons and so on), rather than to wages. The equilibrium capital stock in the North will remain unaltered. In the South, however, the nationally owned capital stock engaged in formal sector production declines. These results are shown at point B in Figure 3.2. Upon impact, there is a rise in the South's terms of trade due to increased demand for its products. In the long run, however, P_S has to fall; see equation (11). Since the role of the terms of trade is to equate growth rates of the two regions, and since no crucial parameter has changed in the North, there is an inverse relation between the terms of trade and the rental rate on capital in the South. As P_S falls, so does overall profitability $r_S^*P_S$, and k_S declines. Recall that the informal or grey activity does not utilize capital. Formal sector output declines in the South, as does employment in that sector. Eventually, foreign direct investment or capital flows to the South will also decline, as P_S falls (equation 9). Note that the total effect on national income is less clear-cut. The shadowy or informal economy expands, but the formal sector contracts. Per-worker consumption from (8) will decline, as the share of the majority (labour) in national income falls. Employment falls in the formal sector but could rise in the informal/shadowy economy. There is an unambiguous loss to the South associated with the expansion in the informal sector in terms of its capital stock, terms of trade, and the real compensation of workers, the group that includes the poorest of the poor.

The second change results in an increase in the North's effective labour force, n. The North's equilibrium capital stock declines, and the South's is likely to increase as illustrated by point C in Figure 3.2. So, legitimate economic activity rises in the South, and its terms of trade improve, by equation (14). This is all beneficial for the South, but part of its capital stock will be owned by the North via increased capital flows from North to South, and part of this increased output will take the form of profit repatriation. Emigration from the South to the North encourages foreign direct investment in the opposite direction. In the North, however the equilibrium wage rate declines, due to the presence of full employment. But national income may not decline.

Conclusions and policy implications

Crime is one of the most obvious public bads that can arise from the powerful economic and social trend termed globalization. Crime, shadowy or informal sector activity in the South is modelled here as being produced by labour only, with a rent extracted by an 'entrepreneur' or Mafia boss. In our model, the institutionally given wage–rental ratio in the South is determined in its informal/shadowy economy. Let us say that an expansion in these activities in the South due to globalization lowers the wage–rental ratio, as is empirically plausible, with the entrepreneurs expropriating most of the gains. Then, there is a very serious loss for the South via falling terms of trade, capital stock, lower foreign direct investment and employment in the regular activity. There could also be an increase in poverty as workers are worse off in the South. These results have a number of policy implications.

1 Reducing the power of gang leaders and other coercive forces raises the institutional real wage rate in the South. This generates a real virtuous cycle for the South as its terms of trade and capital stock increase. Also the well being of all workers, including those in the informal sector improves.
2 If the North does attempt to stem the flow of certain 'bads' such as narcotics from the South, demand side restrictions within the North would be better than lowering supply in the South. The latter type of policy may simply strengthen the hands of warlords and drug barons; see Murshed (2001).
3 Increased migration from South to the North raises the equilibrium capital stock and the South's terms of trade. There is also more investment from the North to the South. It increases the well being of the South. National income in the North may rise. Workers in the North receive lower wages in the presence of full employment in flexible labour markets. However, in the presence of social protection, where displaced workers in the North receive compensation

as they do in practice, South–North migration may even enhance world welfare.

Acknowledgements

The authors are grateful to Ajay Mahal, Jaypee Sevilla, Ragnar Torvik and River Path Associates for their input.

References

Addison, T., Le Billon, P., and Murshed, S.M. (2000) 'On the Economic Motivation for Conflict in Africa', paper presented at the Annual World Bank Conference on Development Economics, Paris, June.

Arms Trade News (1997) 'Conventional Arms Transfer Project', November, available at www.clw.org/cat/atn1197.html#WeaponsProfile.

Bloom, D.E. and Murshed, S.M. (2001) 'Globalization, Global Public "Bads", Rising Criminal Activity and Growth', WIDER Discussion Paper 2001/50, Helsinki: UNU/WIDER, available at www.wider.unu.edu.

Burgstaller, A. and Saavedra-Rivano, N. (1984) 'Capital Mobility and Growth in a North-South Model', *Journal of Development Economics*, 15, 213–37.

Findlay, R. (1980) 'The Terms of Trade and Equilibrium Growth in the World Economy', *American Economic Review*, 70, 291–99.

Garfinkel, M. and Skaperdas, S. (2000) 'Contract or War? On the Consequences of a Broader View of Self-Interest in Economics', Irvine: University of California (mimeo).

Global Labour Institute (2000) 'Notes on Trade Unions and the Informal Sector', available at www.global-labour.org.

Grossman, H.I. (1995) 'Rival Kleptocrats: The Mafia versus the State', in Gianluca Fiorentini and Sam Peltzman (eds), *The Economics of Organized Crime*, Cambridge: Cambridge University Press.

Hirshleifer, J. (1995) 'Anarchy and its Breakdown', *Journal of Political Economy*, 103(1), 26–52.

ILO (International Labour Office) (1999) 'Trade Unions and the Informal Sector: Towards a Comprehensive Strategy', Geneva: ILO.

Kalecki, M. (1971). 'Class Struggle and the Distribution of Income', *Kyklos*, 24, 1–9.

Levenson, A.R. and Maloney, W.F. (1998) 'The Informal Sector, Firm Dynamics and Institutional Participation', available at www.worldbank.org.

Lewis, W.A. (1954) 'Economic Development with Unlimited Supplies of Labour', *Manchester School*, 22, 139–91.

Murshed, S.M. (2001) 'Quantitative Restrictions on the Flow of Narcotics: Supply and Demand Restraints in a North–South Macro-Model', WIDER Discussion Paper 2001/60, Helsinki: UNU/WIDER, available at www.wider.unu.edu.

Savona, E.U. (1998) 'The Organizational Framework of European Crime in the Globalization Process', Transcrime Working Paper No. 20, February. Research Group on Transnational Crime, University of Trento.

Skaperdas, S. (1992) 'Cooperation, Conflict and Power in the Absence of Property Rights', *American Economic Review*, 82, 720–39.

Solow, R. (1956) 'A Contribution to the Theory of Economic Growth', *Quarterly Journal of Economics*, 70, 65–94.

Standing, G. (1999) *Global Labour Flexibility. Seeking Distributive Justice*, Basingstoke: Macmillan.

Tanzi, V. (2000) *Policies, Institutions and the Dark Side of Economics*, Cheltenham: Edward Elgar.

UNDCP (1994) 'Drugs and Development', Discussion Paper prepared for the World Summit on Social Development, June.

UNRISD (United Nations Research Institute for Social Development) (1995) 'States of Disarray: The Social Effects of Globalization', Geneva: UNRISD.

4 Labour standards in exports and developing countries

Waseem Noor

> The failure of any nation to adopt humane conditions of labour is an obstacle in the way of other nations which desire to improve the conditions in their own countries.
>
> Preamble to the International Labour Organization Constitution

Background to the debate on labour standards

The debate surrounding the issue of including certain types of labour standards, collectively referred to as a 'social clause', into multilateral free-trade negotiations has recently attracted much public attention. Labour standards can be defined loosely as any rule or regulation adopted by a government that affects some aspect of the labour market. These policies cover a wide range of social and political issues, such as maternity leave, unemployment insurance, time lost from work, minimum working age requirements, safe working conditions, and collective bargaining. As of 1994, 168 countries, including close to 98 per cent of the world's population, were members of the International Labour Organization (ILO), which is responsible for formulating and implementing these standards, or conventions, worldwide. Member countries of the ILO are free to choose whether or not to ratify a convention. However, once they ratify the convention, they are required to apply the convention in industrial legislation and 'to submit to supervision by the appropriate ILO bodies' (ILO 1994). Supervision is carried out to ensure that the obligations assumed are continually fulfilled. In 1994, the number of ILO conventions stood at 174, with the average member country having ratified thirty-four standards, applied mostly through industrial legislation. More than 120 countries have signed conventions dealing with basic labour rights, such as freedom from forced labour, freedom to organize and bargain collectively, and equal remuneration for equal work.

The international social clause would potentially ban the use of child labour, require basic safety conditions in work environments, and perhaps require a minimum level of compensation to workers. The impetus for adopting such a clause has come mostly from the US and the European Union, which argue that the delinquency of some developing countries in adopting these standards has given poorer countries an unfair advantage in the production of goods. To compete with this inflow of goods produced under unjust conditions, the US and the European Community maintain that they are forced to participate in a 'race to the bottom' where countries with the lowest labour standards win the prize in international trade.

Insistence by the US and France on including labour standards formally on the agenda of the World Trade Organization (WTO) almost held up the signing of the Uruguay Round of the General Agreement on Tariffs and Trade in April 1994. In addition, due to deliberations in the US Congress about the inclusion of labour and environmental standards in trade agreements, Chile's inclusion in the North American Free Trade Agreement was delayed indefinitely in December 1995. More recently in 1999, labour standards was one of the issues brought forward during the WTO meetings in Seattle.

US claims of poor labour conditions are exemplified in a range of circumstances varying from the extremely low wages of workers in Shenzen, China, to the use of children in carpet and textile production in Pakistan, and to the employment of slave labour in Peru. In November 1995, the US Department of Labor published a 210-page report called *By the Sweat and Toil of Children*, which cited the practice of child labour from the tobacco plantations of Brazil to the coffee fields in Guatemala and Honduras (US Department of Labor 1995).

To counter these arguments, developing countries argue that adoption of some of the labour standards would impose an undue burden on their countries. As the Human Resources Minister of Malaysia has pointed out, 'We certainly would not agree to reflect those [labour] standards rigidly in our legislations as this will stifle economic growth, resulting in the eventual displacement of workers' (*New Straits Times* 1995: 15). In addition, many of the countries potentially affected by such a social clause contend that the humanitarian claims are simply a guise for protectionist policies. India's former Prime Minister P.V.N. Rao stated, 'Such causes [labour standards] could become an alibi for raising protectionist trade barriers' (*Economist* 1994: 13).

Many international organizations dealing with trade issues have sided with developing countries. One of the conclusions of the World Bank's World Development Report (1995) is that the costs of trying to link national labour standards to international trade relations will almost certainly outweigh any benefits'. The WTO's former Director General, Renato Ruggiero, concurred with this viewpoint, stating 'Using trade restrictions to enforce labour standards would not only be susceptible to protectionist abuse but could, by reducing their economic growth, also reduce the ability of low income countries to afford better labour standards' (*BNA Management Briefing* 1995: 12). The ILO even recognizes a serious disadvantage in using negative economic incentives in encouraging labour standards in countries. The ILO argues that, in cases such as child labour, the policy may have the 'effect of driving child labour underground, further into the shadows and into even more unregulated sectors' (*National Journal* 1995: 24).

In contrast, labour unions in industrial countries have advocated the inclusion of a social clause linked to international trade negotiations. For example, in the

US after the release of the World Bank's Report (1995), the American Federation of Labor and Congress of Industrial Organizations criticized the Bank's recommendation of divorcing trade from labour market issues. On the issues of Mexico and Chile's inclusion into the North American Free Trade Agreement treaty, the American Federation of Labor and Congress of Industrial Organizations and the Canadian Labor Conference have been extremely vocal in endorsing the inclusion of various labour market regulations into the trade treaty.

The economics literature also varies widely in its opinions on the issue of incorporating a social clause into trade negotiations. Bhagwati (1995, 1996) has argued against a social clause on the grounds that proposals for such clauses are usually asymmetrically stacked against developing countries, thereby betraying a protectionist intent or design. More efficient ways of achieving better standards are desirable and should be used. Casella (1996) argues that many standards, like child labour standards, are similar to public goods, because the benefits spill over to the entire community. Therefore, differences in standards among countries reflect diverse preferences and incomes. Zhang (1994) echoes this result by showing that increased income through free trade naturally brings about higher standards in developing countries. By contrast, Rodrik (1996) proposes the creation of a global 'social-safeguards clause', which would provide adherence to a 'widely held ethical standard or social preference'. In a similar vein, Fields (1995) calls for a distinction between labour rights, which should be required internationally because they are basic human rights, and labour standards, which should not be subject to harmonization. Freeman (1994) argues that inter-country equity can be improved by providing information to consumers about labour conditions in various countries. Informed consumers will adjust their demands in accordance with their taste for labour market conditions in other countries. This 'labelling' alternative, which was also suggested for environmental concerns, has received serious consideration in the US Congress, where in November 1995 Senator Tom Harkin introduced a bill to carry out such measures.

An important question raised by these debates is whether implementation of standards can have strategic benefits for industrial countries. At first, answers to this question seem to exist. One possible reason that industrial countries call for labour standards abroad is that these countries wish to artificially protect their competitiveness in labour-intensive goods that are domestically produced, such as textiles. Perhaps the less straightforward question is why, in a climate of trade negotiations, would industrial countries choose to impose industrial labour standards, which prima facie incur industrial costs by creating distortions in the labour market. Could the adoption of an industrial labour standard improve welfare for an industrial country through the policy's effect on the international trade market? In addition, once such a policy is instituted, what possible gains are there in encouraging the establishment of standards abroad?

This chapter analyses these questions and presents mechanisms through which protectionist goals may lead an industrial country to maintain a labour standard domestically, as well as advocate adoption of these standards among its trading partners. For purposes of exposition, labour standards in industrial countries are modelled as minimum wage policies, while labour standards for developing countries are represented as reductions in labour supply, for example, policies abolishing child labour, banning forced prison labour, and so forth. Brecher (1974a,b) first analysed the effects of a minimum wage policy on international trade, and showed that the unilateral tariff policy of a country may be different with a minimum wage policy. This chapter builds on Brecher's analysis by looking at what happens when the trading partner reacts to the industrial country's labour standard. Thus the analysis allows for strategic interaction between countries.

The rest of the chapter is organized as follows: The second section outlines the basic model, the third section analyses the issue with a labour standard in the industrial country only, in the fourth section both the industrial and developing country have a labour standard, and finally the fifth section concludes.

The basic framework

The tariff-war model

We use a standard two-country trade model with two countries, Industrial and Developing, which have similar production and consumption structures. An asterisk (*) indicates the developing country's variables. Both countries produce two goods, cloth and computers, and the two industries use capital and labour. Factors of production are perfectly mobile between sectors within a country, but not between countries, and both economies are perfectly competitive with constant returns to scale in production. The two goods move freely between the two countries, and each country has the ability to place an *ad valorem* import tax. Both countries share identical production technologies, and the industrial country is relatively capital abundant and thus imports the labour-intensive good, cloth. The developing country is relatively labour abundant and imports the relatively capital-intensive good, computers. The countries' *ad valorem* tariffs on their importable good are represented by τ and τ^*.

Johnson (1953–4), updated by Mayer (1981) and Dixit (1987), showed that both countries' welfare (V, V^*) can be solved simply in terms of the tariff levels, $V(\tau, \tau^*)$ and $V^*(\tau, \tau^*)$. Industrial will set τ to optimize its welfare, given any level of Developing's tariff. A derivation of the optimal tariff-reaction function, $R(\tau, \tau^*)$, for a Cobb–Douglas production and preferences is presented in Noor (2000). The key relationship is that the optimal tariff is inversely related to the other country's tariffs. Deriving a similar tariff-reaction curve for the developing country $R^*(\tau, \tau^*)$, we can combine the two tariff-reaction curves, Figure 4.1, to find the Cournot equilibrium of the tariff game at (τ_n, τ_n^*). The term Cournot equilibrium (and not Bertrand equilibrium) is used to describe the outcome of a Cournot–Nash non-cooperative game in tariffs on two non-homogenous goods. At the equilibrium, both countries reach a 'prisoner's dilemma' equilibrium. Each country, by individually attempting to improve its own terms of trade, has succeeded in making world welfare worse. Another possible tariff equilibrium is a Stackelberg outcome, see Noor (2000).

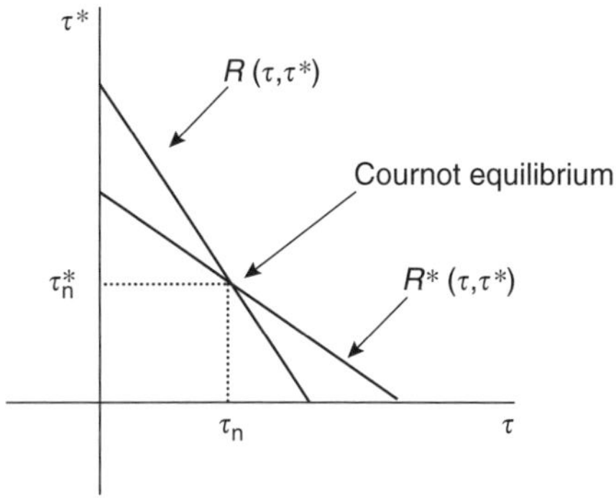

Figure 4.1 Cournot tariff-war equilibrium.

The minimum wage model

Labour standards in the industrial country are modelled by a minimum wage policy. The standard not only represents minimum wage policies *per se*, but can be interpreted as any labour market regulation that causes price rigidities in the industrial labour market, such as restrictions on hiring and firing, wage indexing, and so forth. We assume throughout that the minimum wage policy holds in both sectors of the economy and fixes the real marginal product of labour above the rate that would prevail without the policy.

As Brecher (1974a,b) shows, a minimum wage in the industrial country raises the relative price of cloth and fixes the other prices in the economy, because firms must earn zero profits under perfect competition. Production of cloth declines due to the higher cost of labour. If product prices were any lower than the price implicitly set by the minimum wage, then production of both goods in the economy would not be possible. All the firms would switch to production of computers. In the international market, the minimum wage flattens Industrial's import demand curve at a price determined by the level of the wage.

Figure 4.2 reveals that the minimum wage raises the international price from p to p'. This increase in the world price translates into a deterioration of Industrial's terms of trade and an increase in the total quantity traded. As the minimum wage rises, the relative price in the world market increases, and the amount imported from the developing country increases.

The labour standard in the industrial country essentially acts as an import subsidy policy, increasing imports while deteriorating Industrial's terms of trade. In terms of welfare, the minimum wage policy only hurts the industrial country because it creates unemployment while simultaneously worsening the country's trade position. From a protectionist point of view, such a standard, by itself, would be completely undesirable because it decreases production of the import-competing good (cloth).

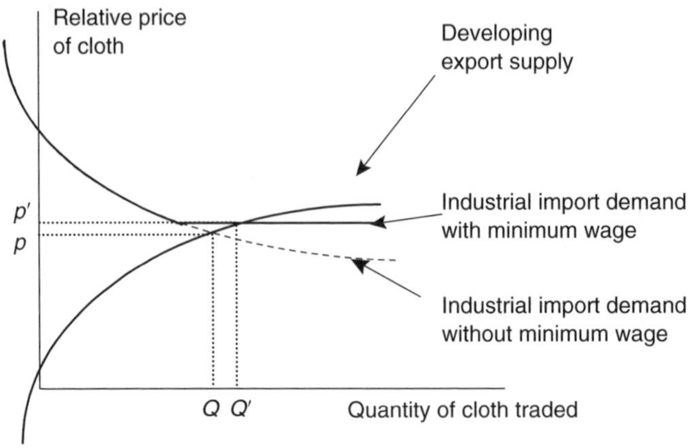

Figure 4.2 Effect of a minimum wage on trade.

Trade with a labour standard in the Industrial country

Effect of a minimum wage on Industrial's tariff-reaction function

We begin the analysis by assuming that two countries are initially in the trading scenario described in the previous section. Because both countries have the ability to set tariffs, they will set tariffs in their own interests so that they are at the Johnson/Nash equilibrium. From this initial tariff-war equilibrium where no internal distortions exist, such as labour standards, we assume the industrial country implements a minimum wage.

We assume that Industrial can set its minimum wage at any level between the wage that prevails under free trade (w_F), where both countries tariffs are set at zero, and the wage that prevails in Industrial under autarky (w_A). Compared to autarky, the introduction of trade will lead to a decrease in the price of cloth and a simultaneous decrease in the industrial country's wage. Thus, the autarky wage will be higher than the wage prevailing under free trade, $w_F < w_A$. These boundaries are chosen for the minimum wage because, if it were set below w_F, the wage would not be binding under free trade, while a wage set higher than w_A would induce the country to cut off trade completely. The minimum wage is set in terms of the numeraire good, which in this case is the Industrial price of the capital-intensive (exported) good in the industrial country. The minimum wage causes a shift in Industrial's tariff-reaction function (Figure 4.3) such that in the presence of an effective minimum wage level for certain ranges of τ^*, τ is higher. If the minimum wage is set at the level w_F, the tariff-reaction function is the same as in Figure 4.1, because with any positive tariff the policy will no longer be binding. With a minimum wage higher than this level the optimal Industrial tariff will be higher.

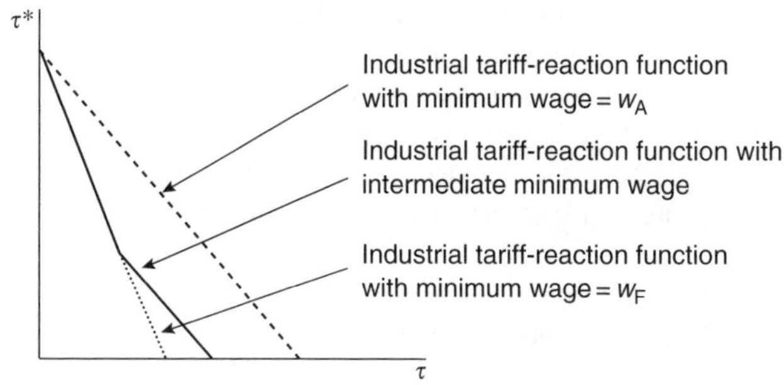

Figure 4.3 Effect of a minimum wage on Industrial's tariff-reaction function.

The entire tariff-reaction schedule does not necessarily change if the developing country tariff is high enough, Industrial's minimum wage will no longer be binding. An import tariff in the developing country decreases its own import demand for computers, while placing upward pressure on the world price of cloth. This pressure will eventually lead to enough of an increase in the industrial country's labour demand to bring Industrial out of the minimum wage regime. In this case, the optimal tariff for the industrial country is the same as it was before the labour standard. A higher and higher minimum wage, however, shifts out a larger part of the industrial country's tariff-reaction function, up to the point where the minimum wage is set at w_A and the entire tariff-reaction function has been shifted out.

The most important characteristic of Industrial's new tariff-reaction function is that every tariff bundle on the curve describes a situation of full employment in the economy. The section where the tariff-reaction curve 'breaks away' from the old curve describes points of full employment, with the minimum wage regime barely holding, while the section where the tariff-reaction curve is the same as the old curve describes points of full employment where the minimum wage regime is not binding. Thus, all tariff combinations to the north-west of the curve must be points of full employment as well, while combinations south-east of the curve describe situations when labour is not fully employed.

Effect of a minimum wage on Developing's tariff-reaction function

To describe the new tariff equilibrium, we also need to understand how the labour standard will impact on the tariff-reaction curve of the trading partner, the developing country. In the end, an effective minimum wage will cause the developing country's optimal tariff to decline. To begin the analysis, we initially assume that Industrial's tariff is set to zero ($\tau = 0$) and then later drop this restriction.

At this point, the developing country has two options: (a) accept the minimum wage and set its own tariffs to zero ($\tau^* = 0$), thus losing any tariff revenues, or (b) place an import tariff on computers that will put upward pressure on labour demand in Industrial. If Developing's tariff is set high enough, global labour demand will be enough to bring Industrial out of the minimum wage regime. By successfully carrying out the second option, the developing country can regain its tariff revenues, but at the cost of tariff distortions.

Which option is chosen depends on the level of the minimum wage set in the industrial country. We can determine the chosen option by comparing Developing's welfare with and without a tariff under different levels of the minimum wage and by assuming that Industrial's tariffs are initially zero.

- If the industrial country's minimum wage is set at w_F, Developing's welfare is maximized by placing the optimal tariff that would have been set without the minimum wage (τ^*_{opt}). At this level of the developing country tariff, the relative price of cloth has been bid up, and the minimum wage is no longer binding.
- With higher and higher levels of the Industrial minimum wage, the terms of trade keep improving for the developing country. Finally, at some intermediate level of the minimum wage, w_I ($w_F \leq w_I \leq w_A$), the benefits from the industrial country labour standard are so high that it is optimal for the developing country to set its tariffs to zero. At this point, the developing country's welfare is higher with a zero tariff.
- If the minimum wage was to be set at w_A, the world prices are fixed on the world market, and the developing country realizes a large gain in its terms of trade. In this case, Developing definitely finds it optimal to set its own tariff at zero.

We then redraw the developing country tariff-reaction function (Figure 4.4), assuming a minimum wage in Industrial such that $\overline{w} \in (w_I, w_A)$. Initially, the optimal Developing tariff will be zero if the Industrial tariff is equal to zero. Eventually, though, once the Industrial tariff is large enough, the developing country will find it optimal to jump back to its old tariff-reaction function.

The downward sloping line indicates the original tariff-reaction function. At the discontinuity, points a and b provide the developing country the same level of

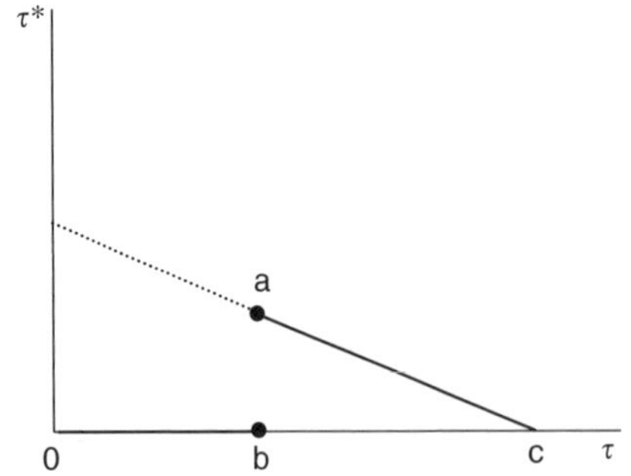

Figure 4.4 The developing country's tariff-reaction function.

utility, for example, the country is indifferent between two very different states of the world. At point b, the minimum wage is binding, and the developing country tariff is set to zero. At point a, Developing has a positive tariff and has managed to raise relative world prices of cloth so much that the minimum wage is no longer binding in the industrial country.

The shape of the developing reaction curve is then determined. It must have this breakpoint, but where the break occurs depends on the level of the minimum wage. If the minimum wage is set equal to w_I, the smallest level of the minimum wage for which Developing's curve is discontinuous, the break will occur at the origin. As the minimum wage increases towards w_A, the flat portion becomes bigger and bigger, and the break occurs closer and closer to point c. If the minimum wage is less than w_I, the tariff-reaction function will not change, because any tariff combination on the tariff-reaction function is sufficient to raise Industrial labour demand and to make the minimum wage non-binding.

The discontinuity in Developing's tariff-reaction function is a direct result of the elbow or 'kink' in Industrial's import demand function (see Noor 2000). This kink occurs due to the assumptions that Industrial and Developing's goods are perfect substitutes for each other and that firms have zero profits because of perfect competition.

New tariff equilibrium

Having derived the shapes of the reaction functions with a minimum wage, we now determine the new tariff equilibrium. Because the reaction functions change under different levels of the minimum wage, we concentrate on the circumstances where the minimum wage is set between the level w_I and w_A. We focus the investigation for this range of the minimum wage, because, as discussed above, when the wage is set below the level w_I, the tariff-reaction functions do not change. Only one of three possible equilibria can occur (Figure 4.5).

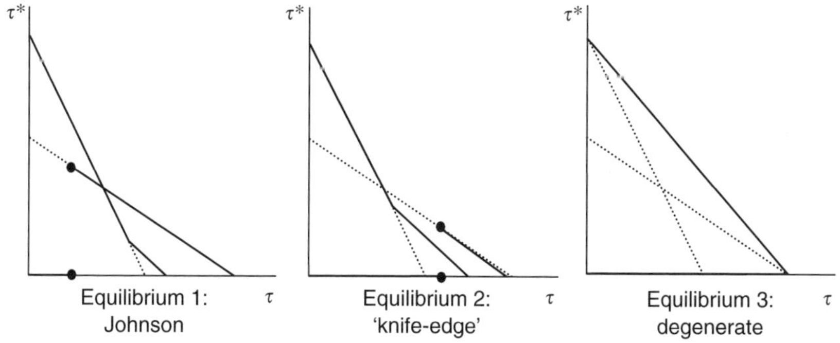

Figure 4.5 Possible tariff equilibria.

In Figure 4.5, the old tariff-reaction functions, the ones that would occur in the absence of the minimum wage policy, are also drawn with a dotted line. Equilibrium 1 describes a situation where the tariff reactions do not alter very much because the minimum wage is not set very high above w_I. Thus, for certain values of the minimum wage, we should always get back the old Johnson equilibrium. We call Equilibrium 3 the degenerate equilibrium. This equilibrium occurs only if the minimum wage is set at the level w_A, at the wage that prevails under autarky. In this case, the optimal Developing tariff is always zero, and the Industrial tariff is set so high that all trade is cut off. We are most interested in Equilibrium 2 because it is the one where the Industrial reaction function intersects the Developing reaction function through the discontinuity. The equilibrium, in this case, is a 'knife-edge' solution, which is known more formally in the literature as a mixed-strategy Nash solution. From Figure 4.6, we can see that the developing country, if Industrial places the tariff τ_e, can choose between two radically different tariff options, τ_h^* and τ_0^*. As both options give equivalent levels of welfare, Developing is indifferent between them.

The industrial country, by contrast, reacts in the following way. If Industrial knows Developing will set its tariff at τ_h^*, Industrial's optimal tariff would be τ_e'. However, if Developing were to play τ_0^*, Industrial would set its tariff at τ_e''. In this sense, no single 'best reaction' to the tariff exists. In order for Industrial to choose τ_e, Developing must play a combination of the two tariffs, for example, play either tariff with a positive probability. Although all three of the equilibria listed above are possible, from simulations, we found that the 'knife-edge' equilibria is the one that is most prevalent over a wide range of minimum wage values above w_I.

One interpretation for the seemingly random nature of Developing's actions in the knife-edge equilibria comes from Harsanyi (1973). Developing's tariff policy is a manifestation of the idea that the industrial country has incomplete information about the variables that affect Developing's decision making. In this case, uncertainty can arise for a number of reasons. For example, Industrial may be

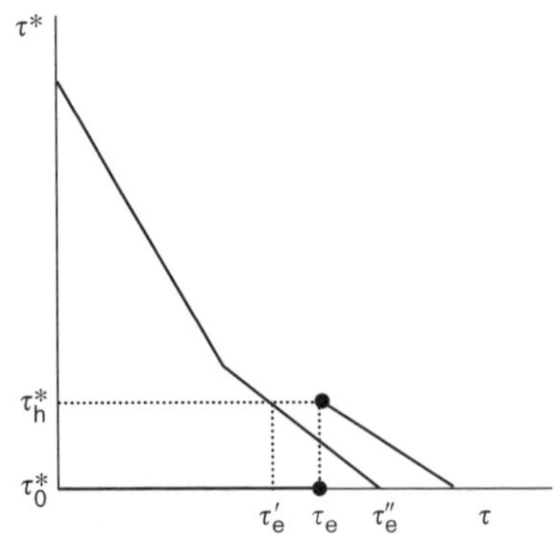

Figure 4.6 Knife-edge tariff equilibrium.

unsure exactly how much weight the other country places on the welfare of their workers, what the current political situation is in the developing country, or even how Developing makes its decisions on tariff policy.

Welfare in the knife-edge equilibrium

When investigating the welfare implications of the different equilibria, welfare for the two countries in Equilibrium 1, where we get back the old Johnson tariff-war solution, is the same as if the minimum wage policy were never established. Although the minimum wage changes the tariff-reaction functions of both countries to a certain extent, the relevant parts of the tariff-reaction curves are not affected, so the original equilibrium is not altered.

Similarly, welfare in Equilibrium 3, where the minimum wage in the industrial country is set at the wage level prevailing in autarky, is the same as welfare for both countries in autarky. At this level of the minimum wage, the industrial country places a tariff that completely halts all trade in the world market. Therefore, prices in the Industrial economy and the Developing economy due to the tariff are now at the same level as they were in autarky for both countries.

Welfare for Equilibrium 2, the knife-edge case, is a bit harder to calculate. In this case, the developing country will randomize between two different tariff levels, τ_{h}^{*} and τ_{0}^{*}, given a fixed level of the Industrial tariff, τ_{e}. Because Developing's utility for both tariff options is exactly the same, any mixture of the tariffs will also give the same level of welfare. Equilibrium occurs, though, when the randomization Developing chooses makes τ_{e} the solution to the industrial country's maximization of expected utility. A small increase in the minimum wage from the Johnson equilibrium may improve welfare for the industrial country (see Noor 2000). In simulations with Cobb–Douglas demand and production, the change in expected welfare always comes out as positive. The welfare improvement derives from the fact that the minimum wage moves the industrial country closer to the Stackelberg point on Developing's reaction function. Even though the increase in the minimum wage causes additional employment distortions industrially, for small increases it primarily acts as a commitment device to achieve the Stackelberg equilibrium, which forces an increase in the Industrial tariff, and a subsequent decline in Developing's tariff.

Dropping the assumption that Industrial and Developing are relatively similar in size does not alter the outcome of the tariff game. The surprising result of the model is that the minimum wage, a purely distortionary policy, may actually serve to improve Industrial's welfare in the face of a tariff-war situation. By implementing legislation in the Industrial factor arena, the industrial country is able to determine the outcome in the international policy arena as well. Thus, the institution of the standard for humanitarian purposes can actually serve to improve the country's welfare along tariff lines. The minimum wage policy is able to increase the wage of workers, raise import tariffs, increase production in the import-competing sector, maintain full employment, reduce the tariffs of the developing country, and improve Industrial's welfare.

Trade with a labour standard in both countries

Until now we have examined the situation where the industrial country imposes the labour standard while the trading partner does not. Many times in the current political climate, industrial countries have insisted through the WTO that a core set of labour standards be implemented abroad as well. This section models a possible reason why the industrial country would encourage such a policy.

We imagine a situation where the countries have already engaged in a tariff war and the industrial country has implemented a welfare-optimizing minimum wage policy. We now introduce to this framework an institution like the WTO, which has the goal of reducing tariffs or at least constraining them to the levels currently prevalent. The explicit constraint on tariff levels will prevent the industrial country from alleviating the distortion caused by the minimum wage solely through industrial tariff policies. By contrast, a labour standard in the developing country could achieve the same goal as the industrial tariff policy. Thus, as a prerequisite to entering WTO-type tariff negotiations, the industrial country, recognizing that such negotiations will lead to Industrial unemployment, demands international labour standards.

Rather than calling for labour standards abroad, the industrial country's first-best option to alleviate unemployment would be to dismantle the minimum wage policy – the source of the domestic distortion. This could be achieved through a production tax along with a subsidy, as Brecher (1974b) points out. We assume though that, due to internal pressure or because of international regulations on production subsidies, the reversal of such a policy would be impossible. In the absence of a minimum wage at home, a labour standard in the developing country provides no benefit to the industrial country, because the policy would not only reduce world welfare, but would also deteriorate Industrial's terms of trade and its exports (Brown *et al.* 1996).

To avoid degenerate or multiple equilibrium conditions as explained in Noor (2000), we model the implementation of the standard in Developing by assuming that the legislation in effect reduces the labour supply of the country. For example, one of the labour standards currently in discussion is the exploitation of child labour. If a developing country were to impose such a standard, the primary effect would be to reduce the developing country's labour supply. In this case, because quantities are controlled rather than an additional price, a unique solution to the problem can still be found.

Analytically, we introduce the policies of the WTO as a restriction on the maximum tariffs allowable by both countries. The tariff limit is set at the levels currently prevalent in the world economy. From the third section, we have seen that Industrial's tariff will be set at the level τ_e (Figure 4.6), which is determined by the level of the minimum wage. The developing country's tariff, on the other hand, can be at either τ_h^* or τ_0^*. The analysis will focus on the situation where the developing country has set its tariffs at τ_h^*. As we will see, with the WTO restriction, the case where the tariff is set at τ_0^* gives exactly the same conclusions.

With the tariff combination (τ_e, τ_h^*) no unemployment exists in the industrial economy because the tariffs are high enough to pull the economy out of the minimum wage regime. With the WTO constraints, the tariff-reaction functions for the two countries will once again change. In Figure 4.7, the dotted lines indicate the tariff-limit levels. For levels of the developing country's tariff below τ^*_w, the industrial country would like to set a tariff higher than the WTO limit, but is not allowed to do so. Thus, Industrial's reaction for these tariff levels stays constant at τ_e. By contrast, Developing's tariff-reaction function remains unchanged by the restrictions.

With a restriction on the maximum tariff levels allowable, the new tariff equilibrium will occur at a point of unemployment for the industrial country. The intersection of the newly altered tariff-reaction functions occurs when Industrial sets its tariffs at τ_e and Developing drops its tariffs to zero. Because this tariff combination is below Industrial's 'unconstrained' tariff-reaction function, it represents a point of unemployment for the Industrial economy.

A WTO restriction on tariffs would precipitate a change in tariff policies, which in turn results in unemployment for the industrial country. Under this new tariff regime, the minimum wage policy, which before was a source of welfare improvement, now reveals its distortionary characteristics. Because the industrial country by assumption is unable to dismantle the policy, it finds that an alternative method of avoiding the unemployment loss is to require a labour standard in the developing country as well. A reduction in Developing's labour supply will cause a reduction in Developing's exports of the labour-intensive good. At fixed world prices, this reduction in trade leads to an increase in Industrial's production of the import-competing good, as well as an increase in labour demand and thus an improvement in employment and welfare.

The Developing labour standard acts essentially as a second best policy to alleviate the distortion of the minimum wage industrially. Because Industrial no longer has tariffs available as a policy tool for securing welfare improvements in the face of a minimum wage policy, Industrial finds it optimal instead to require a labour standard abroad.

The call for labour standards adoption universally through the WTO, although they may inherently contain a humanitarian motive, could also be seen as a way

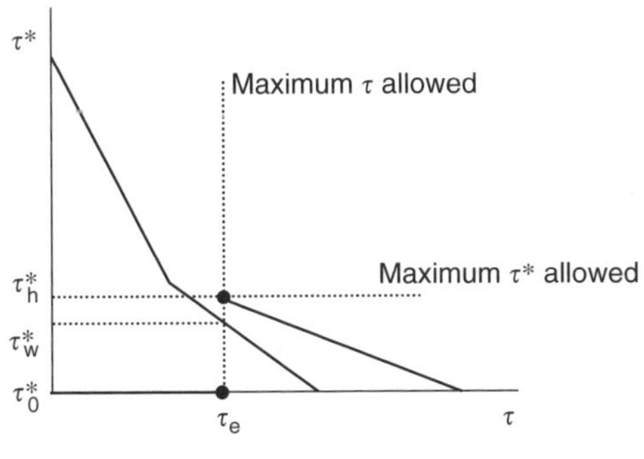

Figure 4.7 Restrictions on tariff setting.

for industrial countries to escape the unemployment that would ensue if tariff restrictions were carried out. The universal call for labour standards adoption, at the level of WTO trade policy making, may simply be a means for ensuring protection of the industrial country's import-competing sector.

Conclusion

This chapter has shown how a country's labour policies can radically change the international tariff equilibrium. By introducing a labour standard, an industrial country can improve welfare through the policy's effect on industrial and developing countries' tariff positions. The standard effectively acts to increase the industrial country's optimal tariff on its labour-intensive imports (cloth) while forcing the trading partner to drop its own tariffs, thereby moving the industrial economy closer to an optimal Stackelberg tariff. The surprising result of the model is that the minimum wage, an otherwise purely distortionary policy, may improve the industrial country's welfare in the face of a tariff-war situation.

Furthermore, labour standards adoption is encouraged in the developing country when multilateral trade agreements limit the use of traditional trade tariffs. By securing a reduction in the labour force of the developing countries, industrial countries can prevent unemployment, and thus welfare losses, in their own countries. Therefore, arguments for global labour standards, while perhaps motivated by a high moral stance, can easily be subverted by more protectionist interests. Labour standards are thus 'second-best' strategic trade policy tools. While the analysis in this chapter is carried out in a two-country, two-good framework with a minimum wage already present in the developed country, the broader message is that the adoption of labour standards for humanitarian reasons should be de-linked from trade policy. Other means, such as consumer pressure via certification procedures like rugmark, should be utilized to encourage their implementation in low-income developing countries.

References

Bhagwati, J. (1995) 'Trade Liberalization and "Fair Trade" Demands: Addressing the Environmental and Labour Standards Issues', *World Economy*, 18(11), 745–60.

Bhagwati, J. (1996) 'The Demand to Reduce Domestic Diversity among Trading Nations', in J. Bhagwati and R.E. Hudec (eds), *Fair Trade and Harmonization: Prerequisites for Free Trade*, Boston, MA: MIT Press.

BNA Management Briefing (1995) 'WTO Makes "Good Beginning" in 1995, Director General Says', 13 December.

Brecher, R.A. (1974a) 'Minimum Wage Rates and the Pure Theory of International Trade', *Quarterly Journal of Economics*, 88(1), 98–116.

Brecher, R.A. (1974b) 'Optimal Commercial Policy for a Minimum-Wage Economy', *Journal of International Economics*, 4, 139–49.

Brown, D., Deardorff, A.V., and Stern, R.M. (1996) 'International Labor Standards and Trade: A Theoretical Analysis', in J. Bhagwati and R.E. Hudec (eds), *Fair Trade and Harmonization: Prerequisites for Free Trade*, Boston, MA: MIT Press.

Casella, A. (1996) 'Free Trade and Evolving Standards', in J. Bhagwati and R.E. Hudec (eds), *Fair Trade and Harmonization: Prerequisites for Free Trade*, Boston, MA: MIT Press.

Dixit, A. (1987) 'Strategic Aspects of Trade Policy', in T.F. Bewley (ed.), *Advances in Economic Theory: Fifth World Congress*, Cambridge: Cambridge University Press.

Economist (1994) 'Free Trade or Foul?', 9 April, 13.

Fields, G.S. (1995) *Trade and Labor Standards: A Review of the Issues*, Paris: OECD.

Freeman, R.B. (1994) 'A Hard-Headed Look at Labour Standards', in W. Sengenberger and D. Campbell (eds), *International Labour Standards and Economic Interdependence*, Geneva: ILO.

Harsanyi, J. (1973) 'Games with Randomly Disturbed Payoffs: A New Rationale for Mixed-Strategy Equilibrium Points', *International Journal of Game Theory*, 2, 1–23.

ILO (International Labour Office) (1994) *Report of the Committee of Experts on the Application of Conventions and Recommendations*, Geneva: ILO.

Johnson, H.G. (1953–4) 'Optimum Tariffs and Retaliation', *Review of Economic Studies*, 21, 142–53.

Mayer, W. (1981) 'Theoretical Consideration on Negotiated Tariff Adjustments', *Oxford Economic Papers*, 33, 135–53.

National Journal (1995) 'A Noble Cause', 11 November.

New Straits Times (1995) 'ILO Standards Not Just Yet', 17 June.

Noor, W. (2000) 'Labour Standards in Exports and Developing Countries', WIDER Working Paper No. 212, Helsinki: UNU/WIDER.

Rodrik, D. (1996) 'Labor Standards in International Trade: Do They Matter and What Do We Do About Them?' in R. Lawrence, D. Rodrik and J. Whalley (eds), *Emerging Agenda for Global Trade: High Stakes for Developing Countries*, Washington, DC: Overseas Development Council.

US Department of Labor (1995) *By the Sweat and Toil of Children*, Vols. I and II, A Report to the Committees on Appropriations United States Congress by the Bureau of International Labor Affairs.

World Bank (1995) *World Development Report 1995: Workers in an Integrating World*, Oxford: Oxford University Press.

Zhang, Z.J. (1994) 'Labor Standards, Trade and Industrial Competitiveness', Discussion Paper No. 356, Research Forum on International Economics, Ann Arbor, MI: Institute of Public Policy Studies, The University of Michigan.

5 Globalization, technology transfer and skill accumulation in low-income countries

Jörg Mayer

Introduction

Both standard neoclassical growth theory and recent endogenous growth theory explain persistent poverty in developing countries as being partly due to differences in technology between rich and poor countries. Neoclassical theory considers technology as both universally available and applicable, and technological differences as gaps in the endowments of objects, such as factories or roads. By contrast, endogenous growth theory considers that gaps in the endowment of ideas and the limited capability of developing countries to absorb new knowledge are the main reasons for poverty. The latter implies that development policy should concentrate on the interaction between technology and skills with a view to facilitating the reduction of the idea gap.

One of the main opportunities which globalization – the integration of national economies – is said to offer to developing countries is that they would have better access to the technical advances in developed countries. Integration would help to reduce the technology gap and to raise the level of total factor productivity and per capita income in developing countries. Coe and Helpman (1995), Keller (1998) and Coe, Helpman and Hoffmaister (1997) – henceforth CHH (1997) – have shown empirically that countries which have imported more from the world's technology leaders have experienced faster growth in total factor productivity.

The role of technology adoption in the process of economic development has been a recurrent theme in the economic literature. It highlights that the cross-country distribution of per capita income will move up over time with no change in its range if the distribution of technology adoption is constant over time, that is, all countries adopt new technology equally. To reduce this range, backward countries will need to upgrade their level of technology faster than the advanced countries. The realization of technological improvements in backward countries is closely interrelated with their educational attainment: their skill supply influences the amount and degree of sophistication of technology which can be adopted and efficiently used, while in turn the amount and sophistication of newly introduced technology impacts on the demand for skills. This means that globalization can ignite a virtuous circle of technological upgrading and skill accumulation in technological latecomers.

The objective of the chapter is to concentrate on trade flows as a vehicle for technology transfer to developing countries and to assess empirically two phenomena: (1) the evolution of machinery and equipment imports and their sectoral bias, and (2) the change in the demand for skilled labour. The second section presents a simple framework regarding the interaction between technology upgrading and skill accumulation. The third section assesses technology imports by low-income countries from both developed countries and developing countries with significant domestic research and development (R&D) spending, where the latter group will be called 'technologically more advanced developing countries'. The fourth section discusses changes in labour productivity and the demand for skilled labour, and the fifth section provides some concluding remarks. Throughout the chapter, specific emphasis will be placed on low-income countries.

Technology and skill accumulation

The shortage of modern technology is widely assumed to hold down the level of per capita income in low-income countries. But there is little empirical evidence on whether the improved access to modern technology which has come about with globalization has helped alleviate this shortage. It is clear that their improved access to modern technology alone does not guarantee that low-income countries will realize productivity increases. They need the human capital required to absorb and efficiently use modern technology. Moreover, economic policies and institutional arrangements impact on the actual amount of modern technology which low-income countries can import.

The combined role of education and technology can be formalized building on a model by Nelson and Phelps (1966). The model shows that the rate at which technological latecomers realize technology improvements made in technologically advanced countries is a positive function of their educational attainment (with $\partial\alpha/\partial h > 0$) and proportional to the gap between the technology level in advanced countries $T(t)$ and their own $A(t)$:

$$\frac{\dot{A}(t)}{A(t)} = \alpha(h)\left[\frac{T(t) - A(t)}{A(t)}\right]$$

Assuming that technology in advanced countries improves exogenously each year by δ per cent:

$$T(t) = T_0\, e^{\delta t}$$

implies that the equilibrium path of potential technological development of a technological latecomer is

$$A(t) = \left[\frac{\alpha(h)}{(\alpha(h) + \delta)}\right] T_0\, e^{\delta t}$$

Accordingly, the potential level of technology which is employed in a technologically backward country depends on its own educational attainment h and the rate of technological progress in the advanced countries which becomes available to the backward countries. Assuming that production is characterized by a low elasticity of substitution between imported technology and domestic skilled labour, there are rapidly decreasing returns to the increase of either (imported technology or domestic skilled labour) in the absence of rising supply of the other.

The introduction of new technology is constrained by barriers to technology adoption. When such constraints are present, the technology inflows which can be realized (δ_F) will be lower than the potential inflows of modern technology (δ).

$$A(t) = \left[\frac{\alpha(h)}{(\alpha(h) + \delta_F)}\right] T_0 \, e^{\delta_F t}$$

Several factors determine the difference between δ and δ_F. Import rules and restrictions will limit technology imports – one effect of trade integration is the decline of such limits. Natural trade barriers such as geographical distance can reduce technology imports. From a micro-economic perspective, high costs of firms to invest in new technology limit its adoption (see Parente and Prescott 1994, for a detailed discussion) including a cumbersome legal and regulatory framework or high real interest rates and an unstable exchange rate, which do not enable potential investors to make long-term plans.

From a macroeconomic perspective, a country's ability to import new technology will be seriously limited if it is subject to a balance-of-payments constraint. Increased trade integration has a composition effect on the country's production structure. As argued above, this composition effect impacts on the direction of change up or down the technology ladder brought about by the sectoral bias of the new technology. On the import side, an inflow of new technology that raises productivity of all sectors equally will not alter comparative advantage in the framework of standard trade theory. But the opposite will be the case if the inflow of technology is sectorally biased, since this will alter comparative advantage.

On the export side, the composition effect works through two channels that can pull in different directions. The first channel concerns the terms of trade: to maximize its export earnings, the country should strive to export those products which are not subject to declining terms of trade. The second channel regards the country's comparative advantage: to maximize its export earnings, the country will need to change its production and export structure towards those sectors in which it has a competitive edge. Concern has often been expressed in this regard as developing countries might experience de-industrialization, and lower growth because their comparative advantage is usually not in manufacturing.

Globalization further complicates the composition effect of trade integration. With an increasing number of countries integrating into the world economy, a specific country's comparative advantage changes over time depending on the evolution of effective global factor endowments in addition to changes in the country's own factor combination. The effective global factor endowment changes according to the additional factor supply from newly integrating countries. It has been argued by Wood (1997), for example, that China's increased trade integration in the early 1980s has significantly increased the effective world supply of labour with basic skills and that this has significantly lowered the comparative advantage which integrating Latin American countries would have had in low-skilled-labour-intensive activities in the absence of China's integration.

This suggests that the interrelationship between technology imports, the sectoral composition of production and skill accumulation depends on two measurable magnitudes: (1) the inflow of modern technology, and (2) the sectoral bias of technology inflows.

Trade integration and technology imports: some evidence

This section examines indirect measures of technological integration by looking at the GDP-ratios of trade, total imports and, most importantly, machinery imports. The group of forty-six low-income countries (see Appendix for the country list) analysed includes all developing countries with a per capita income of under US$800 in 1995 for which data are available.

The analysis of technology imports builds on CHH (1997) who provide evidence which suggests that there is significant technology transfer from the developed to developing countries. They measure the stock of foreign technology which a developing country can access as a weighted average of the domestic R&D capital stocks of its developed-country trading partners, with bilateral machinery and equipment import shares of each developing country with respect to the developed country serving as weights.

The statistical analysis[1] in this chapter diverges from that in CHH (1997) in three main respects. First, the technology imports of low-income countries are not weighted according to the domestic R&D capital stock of the country's trading partners. Coe and Hoffmaister (1999) in fact note that using simple import averages instead of bilateral import weights leads to essentially similar results. In other words, it matters for a developing country how much technology it imports from the developed countries, but it is unimportant whether it imports 50 per cent from the US and 30 per cent from Japan or the other way round.

Second, due to data problems in the calculation of the foreign R&D capital stock, CHH (1997) do not take into account technology imports from other developing countries. However, such imports are likely to be important, especially for the technologically least advanced economies, because technology imports from technologically more advanced developing countries can be considered less sophisticated than those from developed countries as they are likely to be of an older vintage or a lower technological level. Hence, technology imports from those developing countries with – according to CHH (1997) – significant domestic R&D expenditure (see Appendix), will be examined in addition to imports from developed countries.

Third, CHH (1997) follow conventional practice in the analysis of technology imports and limit their analysis to aggregate data on machinery and transport equipment (that is, section 7 of SITC Rev. 2). By contrast, a finer data breakdown appears to be suited better to the purposes of this chapter. First, parts of such imports are better classified as consumption or imports for re-export, rather than capital equipment. Second, whereas general-purpose technology imports can be considered as raising productivity in all sectors equally, sectorally-biased technology imports affect the importing country's comparative advantage. As a result, a change in the structure of production (and exports) is likely to be associated with sectorally-biased technology imports. Third, a finer breakdown of technology imports allows us to assess whether technology transfer in any given sector to low-income countries has been faster from the developed or from the technologically more advanced developing countries.

Figure 5.1 shows that the weighted GDP-ratio of machinery imports for the group of forty-six low-income countries has been higher[2] over the last few years than during the 1970s and 1980s, despite the sharp drop after 1995 to its level during the second half of the 1980s.[3] The figure also shows that technology imports from technologically more advanced developing countries have considerably gained in importance and that they represent between one-fifth and one-fourth of all technology imports by low-income countries.

Figure 5.2 assesses the sectoral bias of technology imports by plotting the ratio of sectorally-specific to general-purpose technology imports. The sectorally-specific technology imports have been classified according to the primary factors which are intensively employed in their use: agricultural land (agricultural machinery and tractors), mineral and fuel resources (metalworking machinery, construction,

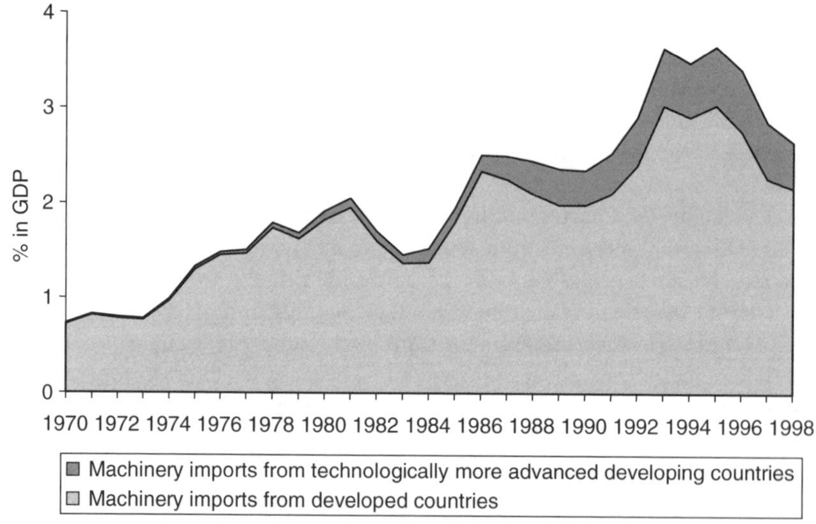

Figure 5.1 GDP-ratio of machinery imports by low-income countries, 1970–98.

Sources: Trade data from COMTRADE and GDP-data from UNCTAD database.

Note: See Appendix for the composition of country and product groups.

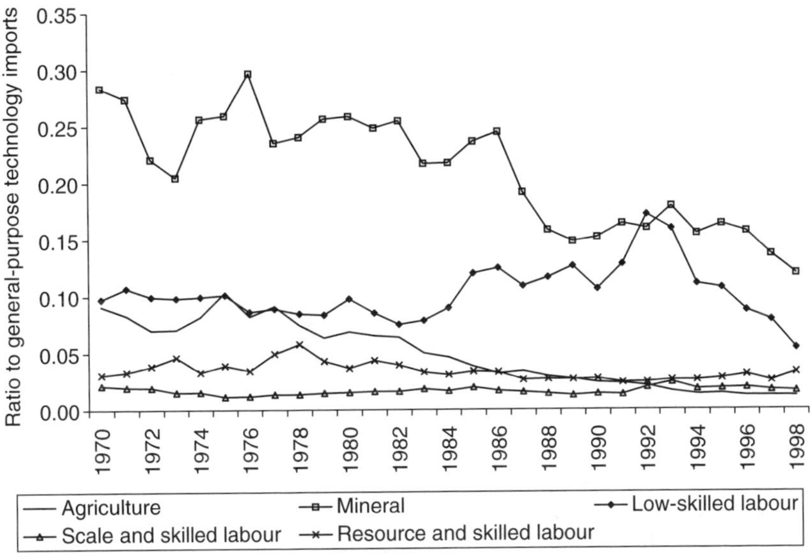

Figure 5.2 Specialized and general-purpose machinery imports by low-income countries, 1970–98.

Source: COMTRADE.

mining and metal crushing machinery), low-skilled labour (textile and leather machinery), agricultural land and skilled labour (food-processing machinery and paper and pulp-mill machinery), and scale and skilled labour (printing and bookbinding machinery).[4]

The figure shows that specialized-technology imports have always been small compared to imports of general-purpose technology, and that this fraction has become even smaller over the past few years. While the combined GDP-ratio of specialized-technology imports from both developed and technologically more advanced developing countries was about half that of general-purpose technology imports, it fell to about one-third during the 1990s. This drop in the combined ratio is due to the drop in technology imports related to activities in the primary sector – both agricultural and, in particular, mineral- and fuel-based.

Whereas the ratio of skill-related technology imports has by and large remained constant, that of labour-related technology imports strongly increased during the second half of the 1980s and the early 1990s, reaching the same level as that of mineral-related technology, before falling in a similar way as technology imports related to the minerals sector. This means that, for low-income countries as a whole, the sectoral bias of technology imports is small, and that this bias has shifted from primary-sector-related to low-skilled-labour-intensive technology.

In addition to their GDP-ratios, the evolution of technology imports can also be assessed by their rate of growth compared to that of total imports. Table 5.1

Table 5.1 Imports by low-income countries, selected categories 1970–98, average growth rates (%)

	1970–9	*1980–9*	*1990–8*
Total imports from world	20.1	3.6	10.4
Imports from developed countries, by category			
Total	21.5	3.0	8.1
Machinery and transport equipment (SITC7)	11.1	1.2	9.5
of which			
Transport equipment	10.7	−3.6	4.6
Technology-including consumption goods	11.1	5.0	0.4
Transistors and semiconductor devices	11.9	28.0	27.2
Machinery	11.4	3.0	11.2
of which			
Agricultural machinery	10.3	−6.9	0.1
Textile and leather machinery	8.8	10.0	1.2
Paper and pulp mill machinery	14.6	−1.9	22.1
Printing and bookbinding machinery	6.0	2.6	15.4
Food-processing machinery	16.8	1.1	9.0
Construction, mining and metal-crushing machinery	14.2	−5.3	6.5
Metalworking machinery	6.4	6.7	11.6
Imports from technologically more advanced developing countries, by category			
Total	30.3	11.1	13.6
Machinery and transport equipment (SITC7)	25.8	11.6	14.0
of which			
Transport equipment	25.9	−0.8	9.4
Technology-including consumption goods	37.9	5.3	9.1
Transistors and semiconductor devices	73.3	42.2	26.2
Machinery	23.1	18.5	14.4
of which			
Agricultural machinery	24.9	3.0	15.0
Textile and leather machinery	18.9	17.5	9.0
Paper and pulp mill machinery	26.9	11.9	15.4
Printing and bookbinding machinery	15.3	22.3	9.9
Food-processing machinery	32.3	2.4	9.2
Construction, mining and metal-crushing machinery	55.3	−1.0	19.5
Metalworking machinery	24.2	12.8	20.4

Sources: 'Total imports from world' from UNCTAD database and all other data from COMTRADE.

shows that the average growth rate of the absolute value of machinery imports by low-income countries from both developed and technologically more advanced developing countries has exceeded that of total imports for all sub-periods since 1970. The growth rate of imports from both developed and advanced developing countries regarding textile and leather machinery, as well as those regarding consumption goods embodying technology, has dropped sharply during the 1990s, while the growth rate of transistor and semiconductor imports has risen strongly. It is also noteworthy that all categories of technology imports from technologically more advanced developing countries have grown faster than total imports in all of the sub-periods, except the 1990s where the growth of several categories is lower than that of total imports.

To understand the reasons for the cross-country discrepancies in the ratio of machinery imports to GDP, it may be helpful to look for correlations across low-income countries between the change in the GDP-ratio of technology imports between the 1970s and the 1990s and variables which come readily to mind as influencing technology imports: low investment, factor combinations and geographical location which are not conducive to industrial development, high tariffs and other impediments to machinery and equipment imports, and a lack of foreign exchange to pay for such imports. From a methodological point of view, a pairwise correlation analysis is preferable to an analysis which combines the variables in multiple regressions because of the endogeneity between technology imports and, for example, educational attainment or investment.

For this purpose, the set of forty-six countries was modified by omitting the two countries for which comprehensive data for the 1970s are not available (Angola and Mozambique), as well as the four countries with a population below one million inhabitants (Comoros, Equatorial Guinea, Guyana and Sao Tomé & Principe) whose very high technology imports ratios are statistical outliers. The first column of Table 5.2 reports the coefficients of correlation (R) across the forty remaining countries between fourteen variables and the absolute discrepancy between the GDP-ratio of machinery imports during 1990–8 and that during 1970–9 (or, as indicated for three variables, the absolute level of the GDP-ratio of machinery imports during 1990–8). A glance down the column reveals that the sign of only one of the correlations (with external debt) is contrary to expectations, indicated by square brackets around the number, and that the correlation with only two other variables (distance to the closest major port, and change in total import charges between the 1980s and 1990s) are weak.

The first four rows of the column (Panel A) shows positive relationships between the size of the change in GDP-ratios of machinery imports and measures of investment and investment climate: the average share of gross domestic investment in GDP in the 1990s, its absolute increase between the 1970s and the 1990s, the December-1995 value of the index of the international country risk guide (ICRG) which reflects the risk perception of international investors, and the average GDP-ratio of inflows of foreign direct investment (FDI) in the 1990s. It is widely accepted that inward foreign direct investment should play a substantial role in the international diffusion of technology. Unsurprisingly, the correlation coefficients in Panel A are the highest of all, even though the correlation between inward FDI and machinery imports is comparatively weak.

The selection of endowment-related and geographical variables in Panel B is based on the assumption that production activities in the manufacturing and minerals sectors require more machinery imports than agricultural production, and

Table 5.2 Factors associated with variation among low-income countries in technology imports

Explanatory variable (number of countries, if <40)	*Means of explanatory variables for countries with*					
	Correlation (R) with absolute discrepancy between machinery imports during 1990–8 and during 1970–9 (1)	*Proportional difference about double or more (good performers)* (2)	*Drop in absolute level by more than 2% points (poor performers)* (3)	*No significant change (average performers)* (4)	*P-value of t-test of difference of means (good vs poor performers)* (5)	*P-value of t-test of difference of means (good vs average performers)* (6)
A. Investment and risk						
Gross domestic investment (% of GDP), 1990–7 (37)	0.58	23.2	11.8	15.9	0.15	0.01
Change in gross dom. investment, 1990s − 70s (32)	0.68	5.6	−9.8	−1.6	0.06	0.02
Risk index 1995 (ICRG): high = good (32)	0.50	61.5	41.3	53.3	0.16	0.02
Inflows of FDI (% of GDP), 1990–8	0.46[a]	1.5	0.2	0.9	0.03	[0.31]
B. Factor endowment and geography						
Square km of land per 100 workers, 1995 (30)	−0.25	2.0	1.6	9.1	[0.76]	0.00
Years of schooling, 1995 (30)	0.43	4.3	3.0	2.6	0.04	0.01
Population, 1995 ('000)	0.29	244,466	6,900	18,011	0.12	0.14

Mineral reserves, 1990: \$mn/100 km^2	0.33	23.9	0.2	2.3	0.05	0.07
Distance to closest major port: km (39)	−0.05	5,246	4,773	5,625	[0.75]	[0.54]
C. Charges on imports of machinery and equipment						
Total import charges, most recent year (17)	−0.44[a]	18.1	n/a	15.2	n/a	[0.59]
Change in total import charges, 1990s–80s (11)	−0.02	−35.7	n/a	−12.0	n/a	[0.29]
D. Balance-of-payments constraint						
External debt, 1990–7: % of GDP	[0.38][a]	64.4	130.5	143	0.43	0.00
Change in capacity to import, 1990s–70s (34)	0.36	3.7	1.3	1.4	0.08	0.09
Change in level of exports, 1990s–70s (34)	0.36	3.8	1.5	1.7	0.07	0.09

Source: See Mayer (2000).

Notes: Square brackets around an *R*-value or *P*-value indicate that the direction of relationship is contary to expectations. 'Good performers' group contains ten countries, 'poor performers' group contains three countries and 'average performers' group contains 27 countries. The superscript 'a' indicates that the *R*-value refers to the relationship between the variable and the level of machinery imports during the 1990s.

that transportation of machinery imports is more expensive for countries which are located further away from major ports. Following Wood and Mayer (2001), we can expect that countries with a comparatively small natural-resource endowment (proxied by a country's total land area per worker) and a comparatively high educational attainment (proxied by the years of schooling per worker) have a comparative advantage in manufacturing (requiring more machinery imports), and that a bigger size (proxied by total population) is associated with more manufacturing activities because of economies of scale and external economies. A comparative advantage in the minerals sector is proxied by the value of known mineral reserves per land area, while the distance to the closest major port is used as a proxy for transportation costs associated with machinery imports. While all of the correlation coefficients for this group of variables have the expected sign, the correlation between the proxy for transportation costs and machinery imports is very low.

A low level of machinery imports can be caused by high tariff or non-tariff barriers to such imports (Panel C). A move towards greater trade openness is likely to be accompanied by tariff reform but this does not necessarily imply a decline in the tariffs on intermediate and capital goods. This may explain the relatively low correlation coefficients in this panel.

The variables in Panel D reflect the capacity of countries to pay for imports. The surprising result in this panel is the positive correlation between the ratio of external debt to GDP and the ratio of machinery imports to GDP. However, this may reflect the fact that a number of countries are unable to meet their external debt-servicing obligations and that they may prefer accumulating arrears which are unlikely ever to be paid, rather than foregoing the potential for future growth by renouncing machinery imports.

The correlation between some of the variables and machinery imports may be concealed by the inclusion of countries whose GDP-ratio of machinery imports during the 1990s was lower than during the 1970s. To investigate this possibility, the forty-country set was divided into three sub-groups: 'poor performers' (Haiti, Somalia and Togo) whose GDP-ratio of machinery imports strongly fell between the 1970s and the 1990s, 'good performers' (Bangladesh, China, Ghana, Honduras, India, Nepal, Nigeria, Sri Lanka, Uganda and Zimbabwe) whose GDP-ratio of machinery imports more than doubled proportionally or strongly rose in absolute terms, and the group of 'average performers' which includes the remaining twenty-six countries. The comparison between 'good' performers on the one side and 'bad' or 'average' performers on the other show essentially the same results. But since it could be argued that civil unrest had a sizeable impact on the results of the 'poor performers', it may be useful to focus on the comparison between the 'good' and the 'average performers', reported in columns 3, 4 and 6 of Table 5.2. All of the associations are in the expected direction and significant, except for the geography variable, the charges on machinery and equipment imports, and inward FDI. Regarding the latter, the weak but still existing correlation is driven by the inclusion of China and Nigeria. This result is likely to be due to the fact that flows of FDI to developing countries have often been concentrated in a few middle-income countries plus China, so that the majority of low-income countries – especially those which do not have a large minerals sector – have to rely on other channels for technology transfer.

The statistical analysis of the evolution of technology imports by low-income countries suggests that the technological integration of these countries as a group has increased, but that comparatively few individual countries account for this phenomenon. The heterogeneity of the countries included in the sample makes it difficult to find meaningful criteria which separate these countries from the others. There is some evidence suggesting that economies with either a very small or a very large size, and economies with a large minerals sector have made most advance in technological integration, but it is clear that there are wide discrepancies even among these countries with regard to the barriers of technology adoption discussed in the previous section. The importance of technology imports from technologically more advanced developing countries remains small compared to such imports from developed countries, but has substantially risen over the past two decades. Whereas general-purpose technology has remained the most important part of technology imports from developed countries, specialized technology imports play a substantial role in technology imports from technologically more advanced developing countries. Whereas the sectoral bias of technology imports has remained small, it has been strongest for mineral-based activities; the importance of specialized technology imports related to agricultural activities has fallen, while that related to low-skilled-labour-intensive activities has substantially increased.

Labour productivity and demand for skilled labour

It is clear that a country's productivity gap is influenced – in addition to technology imports – by a large number of domestic factors including structural characteristics, resource endowments and policies pursued. These factors vary from one country to another, and a full account of such influences requires detailed country analysis that goes beyond the scope of this chapter. But as an approximation, it appears reasonable to assume that the introduction of new technology in low-income countries implies a reallocation of labour from low to high-productivity activities – both within and between industrial sectors – which in general are both more capital and skill-intensive. This means that increased technology imports are likely to be accompanied by an increase in labour productivity – in the growth-accounting framework, increases in labour productivity reflect a rising ratio of capital to labour and overall technical progress – and in the demand for skilled labour (see O'Connor and Lunati 1999).

Labour productivity

Table 5.3 provides a simple assessment of the evolution of labour productivity in the US – the world's technology leader – and various low-income countries for a number of low, medium and high-skill industries. Given the lack of data, the evidence needs to be interpreted cautiously. Nonetheless, the table suggests that

Table 5.3 Labour productivity in selected low-income countries and industrial sectors, 1996 (index numbers 1980 = 1)

	Total manufacturing (ISIC 300)	*Food products (ISIC 311/12)*	*Textiles (ISIC 321)*	*Clothing (ISIC 322)*	*Footwear (ISIC 324)*	*Non-ferrous metals (ISIC 372)*	*Metal products (ISIC 381)*	*Electrical machinery (ISIC 383)*	*Printing and publishing (ISIC 342)*	*Transport equipment (ISIC 384)*
Bangladesh	0.8	1.0	0.6	1.0	1.3	n/a	1.1	0.9	1.1	2.7
Cameroon	0.7	0.6	1.2	1.7	n/a	1.0	1.1	1.3	0.2	0.1
Central African Republic	0.7	n/a	n/a	n/a	n/a	n/a	n/a	n/a	n/a	n/a
China	1.0	1.8	0.5	n/a	n/a	1.0	0.3	2.3	1.1	1.4
Gambia	1.2	n/a	n/a	n/a	n/a	n/a	n/a	n/a	n/a	n/a
Ghana	0.8	1.2	0.7	n/a	n/a	0.5	0.9	1.7	0.6	n/a
India	2.6	5.1	1.9	3.1	1.7	3.2	1.8	2.7	2.6	1.8
Kenya	1.1	1.2	0.6	0.8	1.0	n/a	1.1	3.5	0.6	0.9
Malawi	1.6	1.7	1.7	n/a	n/a	n/a	0.9	n/a	n/a	n/a
Pakistan	1.5	1.0	2.5	1.3	1.58	0.8	1.1	2.3	3.7	1.5
Senegal	1.2	0.9	0.5	1.1	0.6	n/a	2.3	1.3	0.9	2.7
Sri Lanka	1.4	2.6	2.3	1.7	1.8	2.5	1.5	1.0	1.5	1.2
Zambia	0.6	1.1	0.4	0.4	0.2	0.2	0.5	n/a	0.5	0.2
Zimbabwe	1.4	1.6	1.3	0.8	1.0	1.4	1.2	1.6	1.1	1.7
Memo item										
United States	1.4	1.3	1.2	1.3	1.1	0.8	1.1	1.8	1.7	1.4

Sources: UNIDO Industrial Statistics Database and UNCTAD database.

Notes: Labour productivity calculated as real value added (in US dollar) per worker. Nominal value added deflated by the GDP-deflator which was derived implicitly by dividing the GDP series at current prices by constant price GDP series referenced to 1995.
All data for Ghana and Kenya for 1995, for Malawi and Zambia for 1994, for Central African Republic and Gambia for 1993, and for Bangladesh and Pakistan for 1992. Data for Sri Lanka are for 1993 except for non-ferrous metals and metals products for 1992.

only some of the fourteen countries for which data are available have experienced rising labour productivity over the past few years. India appears to be the only one of the fourteen countries which has succeeded in reducing the gap in labour productivity with respect to the US across all industrial sectors. Pakistan, Sri Lanka and Zimbabwe have also been relatively successful in keeping up with productivity increases in the US. It is also noteworthy that India achieved the highest increase in labour productivity in labour-intensive sectors (where India raised its specialized technology imports most) and minerals and metal-related sectors (where India's specialized technology imports have traditionally been highest, see Mayer (2000, table 5)). Whereas the evidence for the other countries is less uniform, the table (in conjunction with table 5 in Mayer 2000) suggests that Sri Lanka also managed to raise labour productivity in those sectors where the country's specialized technology imports were highest. This suggests that those countries with high and/or rising specialized technology imports have indeed succeeded in raising sector-specific labour productivity faster than countries with low and/or falling specialized technology imports. But generally speaking, low-income countries have not been very successful in keeping up with productivity increases in the US.

These results can be taken to suggest that even though low-income countries have increased their technology imports over the past few years, this increase has not been sufficiently high to match technological progress in developed countries. But the results can also be taken to support the hypothesis advanced by Acemoglu and Zilibotti (1999) that productivity differences between developed and developing countries continue to exist even with rapid diffusion of new technology. According to these authors, the reason for this is differences in skill scarcities, that is, developed countries design new technologies for the factor combinations which prevail there, so that developing countries which import such technologies must use unskilled workers in tasks performed by skilled workers in developed countries.

Wage differentials and the demand for labour

In addition to affecting cross-country productivity convergence, changes in the GDP-ratio of technology imports are likely also to impact on the wage differential between skilled and unskilled workers. This differential is likely to widen in the short run and to provide incentives to individuals to enhance their investment in education – Bartel and Lichtenberg (1987), for example, show that the process of adjustment to the implementation of new technology uses educated labour – so that over long periods skill supply and demand are likely to grow apace. To the extent that there is such a short-run impact, relative wages follow a path similar to technology imports, while in the long run this impact is conditioned by changes in the supply of skilled labour. An individual's incentive to forego current income and invest in education depends on the wage differential between better and less educated labour, and on the probability of finding employment that adequately rewards the skills achieved.[5] There is evidence of such a differential in low-income countries and for its tendency to widen as education levels increase: the difference between the wages of workers with secondary and primary education tends to exceed that between workers with primary education and those with no schooling.[6]

Recognizing the importance of relative endowments of skilled and unskilled labour under free trade, production in countries with abundant unskilled labour should concentrate on agricultural and manufactured goods that require unskilled labour. According to a simple variant of the theory, this is likely to lead to an increase in the demand for unskilled labour and hence a reduction in wage inequality. However, even if trade integration causes resources to shift towards unskilled-labour-intensive sectors, the degree of skill intensity will tend to increase within each sector if integration is accompanied by increased general-purpose technology imports. If these technology effects are sufficiently strong, the returns to skilled labour will rise not fall.

Unfortunately, available country-specific evidence on the evolution of wage differentials in developing countries is limited to high and middle-income countries. But it is noteworthy that this evidence points to a rapid improvement of the labour incomes of skilled manpower and the reduction or lack of growth in pay levels for workers not taking part in the modernization of production. Many Latin American countries share this experience as shown, for example, by Robbins and Gindling (1999) for Costa Rica. It can also be argued that in countries with surplus labour, employment of unskilled labour can increase without leading to rising real wages, and since unskilled-labour-intensive activities also employ some skilled labour, this could lead to higher wages for skilled labour.

Table 5.3 suggests that not all low-income countries have achieved rising technology imports and that in some low-income countries there has been no increase in labour productivity. This is likely to imply that in many low-income countries globalization has not been associated with an increased demand for skills.[9] Rather, it appears to have been associated with a decline in an individual's returns to skill. Even though this could be welcomed in countries with high initial income inequality, it can also be interpreted as a reduction in the incentive to invest in education. To the extent that lower investment in education today implies reduced future *per capita* income levels and slower long-run growth, governments would need to make special efforts to raise technology imports and simultaneously bolster individual educational incentives.

Concluding remarks

An important determinant of the benefits which low-income countries can reap from globalization is whether they can ignite a simultaneous increase of technology imports and the skill level of the domestic labour force. This implies a need for government policy to sustain incentives for human capital formation and for a reduction in the cost of technology adoption. The coordination of such efforts is crucial because investment in human capital alone will lead to diminishing returns in skill accumulation, while increased technology transfer alone is unlikely to be enduring and might have negative developmental effects from rising income inequality.

This is also one of the lessons from the East Asian development experience where rapid industrialization and skill accumulation were achieved by expansion of the education system in conjunction with a step-by-step upgrading of the skill intensity of economic activities. Doing so not only reduced the technology gap with advanced countries and raised the demand for educated labour, but also provided the training and experience needed to realize the economic potential of educated workers. The difference is that in low-income countries this upward spiral does not necessarily need to occur in skill-intensive manufacturing activities but – depending on the specific sectors in which a country has a competitive edge – might need to be based in primary sectors, unskilled-labour-intensive manufacturing, or services where this diversity reflects the heterogeneity within the group of low-income countries. To the extent that these efforts imply increased budgetary spending, low-income countries are at a disadvantage because the problem of mobilizing additional government revenue is likely to be most acute in the poorest countries, and especially difficult without external sources of finance.

Acknowledgements

The author is grateful to Mark Knell, S. Mansoob Murshed, Robert Read, Matthew J. Slaughter and Adrian J.B. Wood for helpful comments and suggestions on an earlier draft. The opinions expressed in this paper are those of the author and do not necessarily reflect the views of UNCTAD.

Notes

1 The analysis is based on mirror trade data, that is, exports from country A to country B are used to measure imports by country B from country A.

2 A rise in the GDP-import ratio can be caused by purely accounting reasons because of real currency depreciation. However, Table 5.1 shows that machinery imports have grown faster than total imports so that the increase shown in Figure 5.1 is not just a statistical artefact.

3 This drop reflects a general slowdown of world trade caused initially by a sharp deceleration of import growth in developed economies and then by the turmoil following the outbreak of the East Asian crisis.

4 The classification is partly based on OECD (1992: 152). As with any classification, it includes some arbitrariness.

5 A vast empirical literature suggests that education is indeed a major determinant of an individual's earnings, that returns to education respond to this supply, and that educational choice is in large part an investment decision. But to the extent that parents finance their children's education, family income and wealth has an additional impact on the valuation of education, as well as on the interaction between demography and education.

6 This evidence goes against the conventional wisdom that rates of return on education are highest for primary education, followed by secondary and tertiary education, as argued in many papers by Psacharopoulos (e.g. Psacharopoulos 1994). But Bennell (1996, 1998) argues that this pattern does not prevail in sub-Saharan Africa and South Asia (i.e. the geographic location of most low-income countries) because of lacking wage employment opportunities (see also World Bank 1995: 39).

7 Berman and Machin (2000) also find that there has been no increase in the demand for skilled labour in low-income countries (their group of low-income countries includes

only seven countries in spite of a much broader definition of 'low income' than the one used in this chapter).

References

Acemoglu, D. and Zilibotti, F. (1999) 'Productivity Differences', NBER Working Paper No. 6879, January. Cambridge, MA: National Bureau of Economic Research.

Bartel, A. and Lichtenberg, F. (1987) 'The Comparative Advantage of Educated Workers in Implementing New Technology', *The Review of Economics and Statistics*, LXIX(1), 1–11.

Bennell, P. (1996) 'Rates of Return to Education: Does the Conventional Pattern Prevail in sub-Saharan Africa?', *World Development*, 24(1), 183–99.

Bennell, P. (1998) 'Rates of Return to Education in Asia: A Review of the Evidence', *Education Economics*, 6(2), 107–20.

Berman, E. and Machin, S. (2000) 'Skill-biased Technology Transfer: Evidence of Factor Biased Technological Change in Developing Countries', Boston University, available at www//econ.bu.edu/eli (mimeo).

Coe, D.T. and Helpman, E. (1995) 'International R&D Spillovers', *European Economic Review*, 39, 859–87.

Coe, D.T., Helpman, E., and Hoffmaister, A.W. (1997) 'North–South R&D Spillovers', *The Economic Journal*, 107(1), 134–49.

Coe, D.T. and Hoffmaister, A.W. (1999) 'Are There International R&D Spillovers among Randomly Matched Trade Partners? A Response to Keller', Working Paper No. 99/18, Washington, DC: IMF.

Keller, W. (1998) 'Are International R&D Spillovers Trade-Related? Analyzing Spillovers among Randomly Matched Trade Partners', *European Economic Review*, 42, 1469–91.

Mayer, J. (2000) 'Globalization, Technology Transfer, and Skill Accumulation in Low-Income Countries', Discussion Paper No. 150, Geneva: UNCTAD.

Nelson, R. and Phelps, E. (1966) 'Investment in Humans, Technological Diffusion, and Economic Growth', *American Economic Review*, 56, 69–75.

O'Connor, D. and Lunati, M. (1999) 'Economic Opening and the Demand for Skills in Developing Countries: A Review of Theory and Evidence', Technical Paper No. 149, June. Paris: OECD Development Centre.

OECD (1992) *Industrial Policy in OECD Countries, Annual Review*, Paris: OECD.

Parente, L.P. and Prescott, E.C. (1994) 'Barriers to Technology Adoption and Development', *Journal of Political Economy*, 102(2), 298–321.

Psacharopoulos, G. (1994) 'Returns to Education: A Global Update', *World Development*, 22(9), 1325–43.

Robbins, D. and Gindling, T.H. (1999) 'Trade Liberalization and the Relative Wages for More-skilled Workers in Costa Rica', *Review of Development Economics*, 3(2), 140–54.

UNCTAD (2000) *Handbook of Statistics 2000*, New York and Geneva: United Nations.

Wood, A. (1997) 'Openness and Wage Inequality in Developing Countries: The Latin American Challenge to East Asian Conventional Wisdom', *The World Bank Economic Review*, 11(1), 33–57.

Wood, A. and Mayer, J. (2001) 'Africa's Export Structure in a Comparative Perspective', *Cambridge Journal of Economics*, 25(3), 369–94.

World Bank (1995) *World Development Report*, Oxford and New York: Oxford University Press.

Appendix: coverage and sources

The group of low-income countries used in this chapter includes all developing countries that had a per capita level of GDP in 1995 of under US$800 and for which meaningful data are available. The group includes the following countries.

Low-income countries (forty-six countries). Afghanistan, Angola, Bangladesh, Benin, Burkina Faso, Burundi, Cameroon, Central African Republic, Chad, China, Comoros, Congo (Dem. Rep of), Côte d'Ivoire, Equatorial Guinea, Ethiopia, Gambia, Ghana, Guinea, Guinea-Bissau, Guyana, Haiti, Honduras, India, Kenya, Madagascar, Malawi, Mali, Mauritania, Mozambique, Nepal, Nicaragua, Niger, Nigeria, Pakistan, Rwanda, Sao Tomé & Principe, Senegal, Sierra Leone, Somalia, Sri Lanka, Sudan, Tanzania, Togo, Uganda, Zambia, Zimbabwe.

Developing countries with significant domestic R&D expenditures (fifteen countries). Argentina, Brazil, Chile, China, Hong Kong, India, Indonesia, Korea, Mexico, Pakistan, Singapore, Taiwan, Thailand, Turkey, Venezuela.

The breakdown of 'machinery and transport equipment' imports can be obtained upon application to the author of this chapter, or the editor of this volume. See also Mayer (2000). The term 'general-purpose technology' is used in this chapter to indicate technology that can be used in various industrial sectors. It thus differs from the meaning in some other publications where general-purpose technologies are characterized by an inherent potential for technical improvements and innovative complementarities in addition to pervasiveness.

6 Linkages between smaller and larger developing economies

The role of FDI

Linda Cotton and Vijaya Ramachandran

The importance of foreign direct investment

There are several reasons why foreign direct investment (FDI) has a significant impact on economic growth; this impact is magnified within a small economy. In particular, FDI impacts five variables – domestic investment, technology, employment generation and labour skills, the environment and export competitiveness.

Despite the substantial setbacks that are being experienced from the Asian financial crisis, the newly industrializing economies (NIEs) and Association of Southeast Asian Nations (ASEAN) have completely transformed their economies in a relatively short period of time. The extraordinary success witnessed in this part of the world have spurred other developing countries to follow in their footsteps in the hope of breaking out from the sidelines of the global economy and into the ranks of middle income countries. Emphasis in this chapter will be put on the fact that although the highly visible and exciting growth spurts of FDI and GDP growth rates in NIEs and ASEAN countries captured the world's attention they were nurtured by decades of political and economic stability.

The second section outlines some of the stylized facts of FDI flows. The third section is concerned with difficulties in investing in Africa, while the fourth section examines two case studies (Mozambique and Ghana). Finally, the fifth section concludes with some policy recommendations.

Global trends in FDI

Foreign direct investment has historically been concentrated in developed countries, particularly in the US, Japan and Western Europe. In 1998, FDI for the developed countries totalled US$460 billion in inflows and US$595 billion in outflows. During this year, North–North FDI was largely fuelled by high growth rates in developed economies and a flood of mergers and acquisitions among the world's largest transnational companies.

Until 1998, the developing country share of global FDI had been increasing annually during the 1990s, reaching 37 per cent in 1998. FDI flows jumped from 0.8 per cent of developing country GDP in 1991 to 2.7 per cent in 1997. Inflows of FDI to developing countries continue to be concentrated in only a few countries.

The top five host countries (China, Brazil, Mexico, Singapore and Indonesia) accounted for 55 per cent of FDI inflows to developing countries in 1998 (UNCTAD 1999).

The Asian financial crisis that began in 1997 was one of the main reasons for the decrease in FDI to developing countries the following year. In 1998, developing countries attracted US$166 billion in inflows of FDI, a 4 per cent decrease from 1997. In addition, economic growth and increased FDI in developed countries during these years pushed the developing country share down. Even though inflows to developing countries increased significantly to US$192 billion in 1999, this does not compare to the growth spurt that took place during the mid-1990s.

Finally, in 1998, less than 1.8 per cent of global FDI was directed at the least developed countries (LDCs) adding up to less than US$3 billion. The forty-eight countries designated as LDCs by the United Nations are mostly located in Africa. The LDCs hardly participated in the previous growth of the developing country share in overall investment, their percentage adding up to less than 1 per cent of global FDI inflows during most of the last two decades (UNCTAD 1999).

South–South FDI

A relatively new trend in global investment flows is evident in FDI originating in developing countries. These flows reached roughly 14 per cent of global FDI outflows in 1997, up from 5–7 per cent in the 1980s. Since the majority of these outflows originated in East Asia, the financial crisis in that area led to a reduction of 8 per cent in FDI originating in developing countries in 1998 (UNCTAD 1999).

Not surprisingly, about 80 per cent of this South–South investment originates in a few of the more successful developing economies; Hong Kong, Singapore, Taiwan, China, South Korea, Malaysia, Nigeria, Brazil, Argentina and Chile. By region, 90 per cent of FDI outflows from developing countries came from South, East and Southeast Asia in 1997. On a stock basis, 90 per cent of these Asian outflows were invested within the region. Intra-ASEAN flows fell sharply after 1997, severely affecting Laos, Cambodia, Vietnam, and Myanmar, which are very dependent on inflows from neighbouring countries.

Investment from South, East and Southeast Asia to Latin America and the Caribbean (LAC) has also been increasing during the 1990s (UNCTAD 1999). Of the FDI flowing out of the LAC region, a larger percentage is directed toward developed countries (about half, on a stock basis in the early 1990s). This figure may be skewed by Mexico, which directs more FDI to developed economies to the North than its regional partners. Unfortunately, sub-Saharan Africa (SSA) has been the least visible in the new South–South FDI trend. The developing countries that do invest in Africa are Asian rather than Latin American.

The majority of developing country FDI outflows are new sources of investment for other developing countries. Possible explanations behind this emerging pattern include the fact that the success of some developing countries has increased the differences within the rubric of 'developing countries'. Even though both investor and host are 'developing economies', they are usually heterogeneous in terms of size, level of development, efficiency and technology. Thus, significant comparative advantages can be found in these differences, provided they are not too large as to be prohibitive (UNCTAD 1999). Other analysts propose that the increase of South–South investment is partly because investors from Asian countries rely less on national trade promotion organizations or support institutions to pave the way into new markets than developed countries do (Bhinda *et al.* 1999). The quantity and success of investment with both origin and destination within ASEAN has been attributed to the fact that investors from neighbouring countries are more amenable to joint ventures with local partners and bring with them more compatible technologies, management styles and products (Chia 2000). Some analysts also contend that Asian investors may have more leeway than developed country investors because their environmental and labour rights practices are not as closely watched by non-governmental organizations (Chia 2000).

Asian FDI flows to sub-Saharan Africa

Of particular interest is the possibility of increasing investment from developing countries to LDCs, most of which are located in Africa, given the reluctance of developed countries to increase and change the nature of their investment on the continent.

Initial outflows from NIEs and ASEAN countries to Africa have indicated that this could be a new source of considerable growth (see Table 6.1). This chapter contends that the changes that need to be made in order to attract East and Southeast Asian investors to SSA, are the same basic changes that will attract developed country investors as well.

Countries such as China, Malaysia, Hong Kong, Taiwan and South Korea were increasing their activity in SSA until the financial crisis of 1997. Investors from these locations concentrated on the communications and construction industries. Flows rose from virtually nothing to an annual average of US$160 million in 1994–5 (Bhinda *et al.* 1999). Not surprisingly, most of this Asian investment was directed toward South Africa, but during the late 1990s, companies began to expand into Botswana, Ghana, the Seychelles, Tanzania, Uganda and Zimbabwe

Table 6.1 Outward FDI flows and stock from selected Asian countries to Africa (US$ million)

	China		*Malaysia*		*South Korea*		*Taiwan*	
	1991	*1995*	*1987*	*1997*	*1992*	*1997*	*1987*	*1997*
Flows	1.5	9.2	—	94.7	27.3	72.4	1	0
	1990	*1995*	*1987*	*1997*	*1987*	*1997*	*1987*	*1997*
Stocks	49.2	104.4	—	140.7	11.6	362.8	3.7	97.3

Source: UNCTAD (1999).

(Bhinda *et al.* 1999). Since 1993, South African companies have also increased investments in southern Africa, perhaps helping to bring about this expansion of Asian investment. Neighbouring countries are likewise investing in the new South Africa (Bhinda *et al.* 1999).

The greater part of the NIEs FDI to ASEAN was pushed by external factors and facilitated by favourable domestic characteristics. Asian investment within Asia will continue, but business associations and governments of Malaysia and Thailand are actively promoting the consideration of alternative African and Latin American destinations. Asian investment in Africa will most likely increase but will not provide enough investment to induce the high rates of growth needed to lift LDCs out of poverty. In addition, the Asian financial crises created significant corporate debt and the financial restructuring in those countries will be an arduous and lengthy process. Little is known about Africa in East and Southeast Asia.

A comparison of FDI flows into Asia and Africa

Many African countries today have similar economic situations to Southeast Asia in the 1960s (Lindauer and Roemer 1994). In general the similarities lie in the significant natural resources, colonial legacies inherent in political and economic structures and the great need for human capacity building. For this reason, it seems there is some basis for comparison and application of lessons learned (Court and Yanagihara 1998).

The surge of investment into ASEAN countries in the late 1980s was largely due to a convergence of specific external circumstances and desirable domestic characteristics such as stable political structures, good macroeconomic figures, relatively liberal investment policies and literate, productive workforces. FDI in Africa has largely been in the area of natural resources, namely oil and mineral extraction, in the countries that possess these resources: Nigeria, Angola, Botswana and South Africa. Significant reforms in macroeconomic policy and liberalization of trade and investment policies have taken place during the 1980s, but African countries have yet to reap the rewards. Clearly, more has to be done to reverse the decades of bad reputation in the minds of investors.

At the root of the matter is the question – how can African countries link to the global economy and reap some of the benefits of the extraordinary growth in international economic activity? The experience of the NIEs and ASEAN countries presents an alternative hybrid of market principles and some forms of protection. This creative adaptation coupled with the extraordinary growth of these economies from relatively the same level as many African countries has drawn attention to these countries as models.

Comparative advantage

At the moment, the general consensus of investors is that Africa's comparative advantage lies in natural resources, not just the extraction of such but in primary processing as well. Of course, domestic resources differ greatly from one country to another. However, to take an example from Asia, Indonesia grew for a decade based on foreign investments in oil and gas and slowly, with investments in infrastructure and human capital, FDI began to diversify into the manufacturing sector.

But what of the numerous small African economies without resources such as oil or diamonds? There are still many untapped opportunities in labour-intensive primary processing industries. A useful model for similar countries in Africa may be Singapore, a city-state lacking natural resources which skipped the resource-based manufacturing that took place in other ASEAN countries during the colonial period. Singapore pursued investments in export-oriented manufacturing from multinational corporations as early as the 1960s with very liberal investment and trade policies. The educational level of Singapore was higher at independence than it currently is in many African countries (Chia 2000).

In addition, instead of mandating that investors hire locally, Singapore invested in basic and advanced public education and professional training programmes. In this 'supply-side' approach, the increase in the supply of local skilled labour and managerial and executive staff meant that foreign companies voluntarily sought local employees to take advantage of assets such as language and cultural familiarity. Other created assets that attract FDI to Singapore are competent, non-corrupt government agencies, a transparent and well-established legal framework, sound macroeconomic management, excellent physical and financial infrastructure and liberal trade and investment policies.

The explosive growth in ASEAN has largely been in the electronics exporting sector. Industry analysts have not seen much interest in electronics export manufacturing in Africa. Experts contend that apparel and textile manufacturing seem much more promising for certain countries. The global electronics industry is extremely competitive. Success in this industry requires not just the technological know-how but also exceptional organizational expertise, supplier and customer networks and market knowledge and information (McMillan *et al.* 1999). Production and labour costs are on the rise in Asia, and a small number of firms are beginning to explore the cost potential of manufacturing in Africa (McMillan *et al.* 1999).

Policies for promoting investment

ASEAN countries have some of the same concerns as African countries regarding the impact of FDI on their economies. ASEAN trade and investment policies are a 'mixture of investment incentives on the one hand and restrictions, regulations and performance requirements on the other' (Chia 2000). ASEAN countries have found that they need to continuously decrease regulations and restrictions in order to attract FDI, especially since the Asian financial crisis. In addition, regional and global trade and investment agreements are moving in this direction. The World Trade Organization's Trade-Related Investment Measures (TRIMS) agreement phases out the use of local content requirements.

The lesson for Africa is that external conditions are unpredictable; countries can only take advantage of favourable situations that arise if fundamental investor concerns have been addressed ahead of time. Of course, no country will ever resolve all investor concerns; however, it seems that a minimum level of satisfaction is required in several areas. Unquestionably, the necessary but not sufficient conditions for investment in any part of the world are political stability and constant favourable macroeconomic indices.

If linkages to the domestic economy are valued, investment policies should not promote one type of FDI over another. In Southeast Asia, the partial openness of policies has led to fewer benefits from FDI such as technology transfer and industrial upgrading. Export promotion was super-imposed on the pre-established structure that promoted domestic import-substituting industries. The improvement of education levels in Africa, at both primary and advanced levels is extremely important. The ASEAN economies were able to shift into higher value added manufacturing due to the supply of skilled workers. As mentioned before, the cost of labour is only one factor in investor decision-making; productivity and education level are just as important. Long-term broad-based growth relies principally on the increase of existing indigenous capabilities.

The lack of domestic savings in Africa means that FDI will be the quickest way to stimulate significant growth in African countries. A key difference between Southeast Asia and Africa is the amount of domestic savings – Africa having generally half of Southeast Asian savings to GDP ratio. In addition, a large part of the fuel for growth in some of these countries has been domestic investment. In Thailand, for example, Thai corporate investment was twelve times that of foreign investment (Court and Yanagihara 1998).

During 1995–8, 15 per cent of FDI flows into the ASEAN region came from neighbouring countries. It seems very unlikely anything on the scale of the 'flying geese' pattern of manufacturing investment that cascaded from Japan to the NIEs to ASEAN could be replicated in Africa. Intra-ASEAN investment in Cambodia, Laos, Myanmar and Vietnam is the most important source of investment for these less developed countries.

South Africa could be a similar engine of growth and investment in Southern Africa. Namibia, Botswana and Mozambique are already some of the fastest growing economies on the continent, in great measure due to investment by South Africa. These investments are largely resource-based and while they do add greatly to GNP, there needs to be an increase in the type of investment that will create linkages with the domestic economy. If all of the above factors are successfully addressed within the twelve SADC countries this investment diversification is more likely to take place.

The Asian financial crisis has brought to the forefront the importance of good governance in public and financial sectors. As the ASEAN experience shows, there is no short cut to attracting FDI in high value-added manufacturing which brings about the impressive growth rates witnessed in the NIEs and ASEAN countries.

Additional constraints to investment in Africa

There are several reasons for low investment in the private sector. SSA continues to suffer from high trade barriers, both internal and to some extent, external.

It is estimated that domestic trade barriers cost the region as much as US$11 billion per year until recently (Madavo and Sarbib 1997). These barriers have had a significant impact on investment; during the first half of the 1990s, SSA received only about 1.6 per cent of total international private capital flows.

Macroeconomic reforms in many countries have often been implemented slowly and with difficulty. Governmental control over interest rates, over-regulation of markets and corrupt and burdensome tax regimes have taken their toll in Africa. Due to these problems, FDI flows to SSA for the late 1990s have lagged behind other developing regions. Only Nigeria has received more than a billion dollars of FDI in SSA. Total inflows of FDI in 1996 were over US$349 billion, of which Africa's share was just over US$5 billion or 1.4 per cent (Sachs and Sievers 1998). This share declined to 1.2 per cent for 1997 (UNCTAD 1999). Meanwhile, developing economies as a whole received 37.2 per cent of FDI, with Asia getting 21.7 per cent and the LAC getting 14 per cent in 1997. Table 6.2 describes the value of FDI flows to Africa in 1998.

In a very interesting analysis of investment flows into Africa, Bennell (1997) argues that a careful look at the numbers often reveals that actual investment flows are far lower than *approved* investment projects reported by government

Table 6.2 Foreign investment flows to sub-Saharan Africa, 1998

	FDI (*US$ million*)
Mauritius	21
Tunisia	370
Botswana	23
Namibia	52
Morocco	400
Egypt	740
South Africa	330
Swaziland	67
Ghana	255
Lesotho	17
Côte d'Ivoire	21
Zambia	58
Kenya	37
Uganda	135
Burkina Faso	3
Tanzania	190
Ethiopia	5
Mozambique	29
Cameroon	35
Zimbabwe	47
Malawi	17
Nigeria	1,720
Angola	290

Source: World Economic Forum (1998).

ministries. Often, only 20–30 per cent of these projects are actually implemented within 3–4 years of initial approval. Also, the three main components of FDI (direct investment, reinvestment and loans) are often not consistently reported over time, making FDI data from African countries hard to use.

In general, investor response to economic liberalization has been limited as well. UNCTAD's *World Investment Report 1999* argues that although macroeconomic reforms bode well for the region, they have not resulted in increased investment. It appears that investors are waiting to see if the reform process is sustainable. The key questions are – will the reforms hold through hard times? Can investors be confident that government policies and regulations surrounding investment will remain the same? What will happen to the reform process when governments change hands? Some researchers argue that investment flows will very much depend on the success in ending military conflict and the establishment of stable democracies (Bennell 1997). It is clear that on the whole, investors have adopted a 'wait and see' attitude with regard to Africa. Foreign investment in Africa thus far has been heavily concentrated in the agriculture and mining sectors. While these sectors have attracted significant amounts of FDI, they have largely failed to establish domestic production linkages and technological spillovers.

Incentive packages to attract foreign investment have also had limited success, largely due to the reasons described above. Macroeconomic reform to promote a stable environment, and to strengthen underlying institutional weaknesses including corruption are crucial to the success of these packages. Risk management strategies to reduce the perceived possibility of future policy reversals are also very important. African economics may have to do something to combat the 'neighbourhood effect' where investors confuse events in neighbouring African countries. Investors may also use a country's past performance to judge it, thereby ignoring recent reforms and making them difficult to sustain in the face of political opposition.

In a survey of foreign-owned firms in Africa, Sachs and Sievers (1998) found that the greatest concern of firm-owners is stability, both political and economic. Cumbersome tax regulations, inadequate supplies of infrastructure and corruption are also factors listed by foreign businesses. Tariff and non-tariff restrictions prevalent in Africa can substantially raise the cost of FDI to the host country. Table 6.3 describes tariff and non-tariff restrictions present in Africa in 1998.

Finally, there is the issue of domestic investment and the reacquisition of expatriated capital. Many of the preconditions that are necessary to attract foreign investment are necessary to increase African resources in the private sector. According to Crocker and Taylor (1999), SSA has the lowest *domestic* investment level of all developing areas. African investment is about 16–17 per cent of GDP and is not growing significantly. Capital flight remains a serious problem in Africa, perhaps more serious than anywhere else in the world. It is estimated that in 1990, about 39 per cent of African-owned wealth was being held outside the region versus just 10 per cent in Latin America and 6 per cent in Asia (Crocker and Taylor 1999). These numbers translate into capital flight per worker of

Table 6.3 Trade restrictions in Africa, 1998

	Un-weighted tariff rates		*Un-weighted non-tariff restrictions*	
	1984–7	*1991–3*	*1984–7*	*1991–3*
Côte d'Ivoire	23.3	n/a	6.6	n/a
Egypt	42.8	33.5	32.9	45.2
Ethiopia	29.0	29.6	n/a	22.5
Ghana	29.6	n/a	48.4	n/a
Kenya*	39.2	43.7	67.3	37.8
Malawi*	16.7	15.2	96.1	91.3
Mauritius*	34.9	27.6	n/a	35.2
Morocco	23.5	22.8	27.6	n/a
Nigeria	23.8	32.8	17.0	8.8
Tunisia	24.0	27.5	76.2	32.7
Tanzania*	32.1	29.8	62.2	79.7
Zimbabwe*	8.7	10.1	2.5	93.6
All Africa	26.3	25.7	43.7	42.9
Sub-Saharan	26.3	25.3	44.0	47.1
Latin America	26.6	12.3	30.2	8.6
South Asia	61.7	47.5	47.6	20.4
East Asia	17.9	16.7	21.2	3.6
All countries	27.0	22.1	37.7	23.7

Sources: World Economic Forum (1998) and UNCTAD (1999).

Note: * Denotes countries for which data are for 1984–7 and 1988–90.

US$683 per year and a total stock of US$150 billion being held outside Africa. Crocker and Taylor argue that a complete repatriation would increase capital stock in Africa by 64 per cent! Various measures such as tax reform, anti-corruption measures, new forms of financial instruments, amnesties and better exchange rate management need to be in place to address this problem.

There are some positive signs. During the latter half of the 1990s, the *magnitude* of investment flows has increased somewhat, from US$1 billion per year in the early 1990s to almost US$12 billion in 1996. African governments have embarked on ambitious plans of privatization and macroeconomic reform in order to attract foreign investment. There have also been important developments in African capital markets over the last few years. Financial markets have played a crucial role in increasing the efficiency with which capital is allocated. Fifteen African countries have stock markets and several other countries are in the process of building equity markets.

Some researchers argue that the industrialization strategy should be on the development of industrial firms owned and managed by Africans (Stewart *et al.* 1992). Analysis of available data shows that firms with foreign equity are more capital intensive than their local counterparts in SSA (Ramachandran and Kedia Shah 1999). There is a large literature on the role of foreign investment that describes a variety of benefits including new management skills, quality standards, new methods of worker training and new markets for export (UNCTAD 1999).

Also, technological development is driven by foreign investment; alternative means of technological upgrading are not as effective (Ramachandran 1993).

Recently, a great deal of attention has been focused on the promotion of joint ventures in Africa. Econometric evidence indicates that joint ventures may not be the best way to go. Using a World Bank data set of 200 firms from Kenya, Ghana and Zimbabwe, analysis shows that value added per worker increases with the share of foreign ownership in the firm (Ramachandran and Kedia Shah 1999). Firms with 100 per cent foreign equity have the highest value added in Zimbabwe and Ghana. Kenyan firms that are majority foreign-owned have significantly higher value added per worker than firms that are locally owned or minority foreign-owned. The World Bank data reveals that firms with foreign ownership are generally larger, which is not surprising. Foreign firms invest in worker-training programmes to a greater extent than locally owned firms and worker-training programmes are more prevalent in firms which have majority foreign ownership in Ghana and Zimbabwe. Firms with foreign ownership tend to have better trained managers, although this difference is particularly noticeable between wholly locally owned firms and firms with any degree of foreign ownership. Locally owned firms are concentrated in the textile and garment industry, whereas firms with a higher share of foreign equity are dispersed to a greater extent across food, metal-working and textiles.

The results indicate that majority foreign ownership of greater than 55 per cent raises the value added of the firm; a lesser degree of participation is not significant in terms of its effect on value added (Ramachandran and Kedia Shah 1999). Interestingly, a 50–50 split in equity between local and foreign firm does not raise value added significantly. What seems to matter is *clear* majority ownership by the foreign owner.

There may be several explanations for this result. Foreign ownership may bring with it many benefits that local ownership cannot provide; examples include the 'know-why' surrounding know-how, timely access to inputs, finance, maintenance personnel and sources of information about technology and markets. Another explanation is that amongst these benefits are often *intangible* benefits relating to differences in the *quality* of labour and capital between local and foreign firms, as well as differences in the type of training received within these firms. These differences are very difficult to measure but are often highly correlated with ownership and consequently with value added of the firm. A third possible explanation of our result is that foreign firms are able to exercise market power that results in a higher value of sales. It could be argued that multinational subsidiaries invest more in R&D, advertizing and other measures that raise barriers to entry. The results raise concerns about promoting joint ventures in Africa.

Country evidence from sub-Saharan Africa

Ghana and Mozambique are two interesting cases from SSA. Their recent experiences with regard to foreign direct investment are described here.

Mozambique

Mozambique's investment potential rests largely in the area known as The Maputo Corridor. This strip of land links the port at Maputo with Gauteng Province in South Africa. Prior to the start of Mozambique's civil war in 1975, about 40 per cent of exports from Johannesburg and Pretoria were routed through Maputo. The project to renew trade and investment in this area was launched in 1995, the year after both countries held their first democratic elections. A private consortium has begun work on the toll road that forms the spine of the corridor.

Privatization of the port and railways in Mozambique has been slow, causing delays in the launch of the Maputo Corridor (*Financial Times* Survey 18 October 1999). The World Bank agreed to lend US$100 million to upgrade the three major port-railway systems along the Maputo, Beira and Nacala corridors. The government will privatize operations and management as part of the deal (*AFX Europe* 15 October 1999).

The Deputy CEO of the Maputo Corridor Company (which groups government agencies from both sides), reports that investments worth as much as R45 billion, (around US$6.5 billion) mostly from the private sector have flowed into northern South Africa, Swaziland and southern Mozambique over the past few years, the bulk of which (R36 billion, or approximately US$5.5 billion) has flowed into the Maputo Corridor. He attributes the investment as being driven by two very large projects – Mozal and a project by Enron.

The lynchpin of the Maputo Corridor is Mozal's US$1.34 billion aluminum smelting plant, whose major investors are Billiton, a London-listed natural resources group (47 per cent of the equity), Japan's Mitsubishi (25 per cent), South Africa's Industrial Development Corporation (24 per cent) and the Mozambican government (4 per cent in preference shares). Export credit agencies and the International Finance Corporation are additional sources of finance. Incentives given to Mozal include 1 per cent of its turnover in tax, fixed in perpetuity. In addition to incentives, Mozal has benefited from cheap and plentiful supplies of electricity.

An analysis of Mozal by the Foreign Investment Advisory Service of the World Bank Group concludes that the project provides a model for future negotiations of large projects, solutions to various bureaucratic barriers and the identification of knowledgeable and influential government officials in Mozambique to whom future investors may turn (Wells *et al.* 2000). The premise underlying the government's extraordinary commitment to making this project take off was the belief that a small number of 'mega-projects' would demonstrate to other investors that Mozambique was a good place to do business.

Another project with significant potential is the Maputo Iron and Steel Project (MISP). The US-based Enron, South Africa's Industrial Development Corporation (a self-financing company acting on behalf of the government) and other partners are planning to build a new US$2.4 billion steel plant which will export 3.5 million tons of slab a year, bringing in an estimated US$700 million in revenues per year. Enron, in partnership with the state-owned ENH, plans to develop a natural gas field in Pande, Northeast of Maputo and build a pipeline to supply gas to the new plant. Iron ore and electricity will be imported from South Africa for this project. Negotiations on sites, contracts and financing are yet to be completed.

The pursuit of the MISP project also has a lot to do with the low cost of electricity in Mozambique. In 1998 talks were under way with the Electricidade de Mocambique (EdM) and the South African utility, Eskom, which supplies some of the world's cheapest electricity, to sign a 850 megawatt supply contract (*Financial Times* 28 June 1998). The economic impact of Mozal and MISP is enormous and could stimulate growth in the region. According to some estimates, MISP alone could increase Mozambique's GDP by up to 8 per cent. South Africa is also estimated to benefit from this investment. MISP says its project will provide five thousand jobs during construction and 1,000 during operations (*Financial Times* Survey 18 October 1999).

There is a serious skills shortage in Mozambique, with a low adult literacy rate of 45 per cent, compared to 59 per cent for SSA. The school enrolment rate of 25 per cent is one of the world's lowest. In general, there is consensus in the literature that foreign firms are more efficient than local ones, producing standardized goods on a larger scale. Large projects like Mozal have been useful in building worker skills. At the height of construction, Mozal had 9,000 workers, of whom 70 per cent were Mozambican. More than 5,000 workers will have been trained in basic building skills when construction is finished. When the plant opens later this year it will employ 800 workers, of whom 700 will be Mozambican. The Maputo Corridor's proponents claim the potential to create up to 35,000 jobs in the area once it takes off (*Independent* 10 November 1999).

South Africa and Mozambique have made job creation and training prerequisites for any contract to which they are a party. Also, all contracts relating to concessions involving state assets, or in which the state had a role, contained a defined minimum value of the contract to be given to 'emerging' contractors. Further strategies to support medium, small and micro-enterprises include the establishment of a regional fund to assist emerging small businesses. There is some evidence to suggest that these policies have paid off. By mid-1998, about US$3 billion had been committed and 12,000 jobs created in the Maputo Corridor (*Financial Times* 28 June 1998). Also, a World Bank study finds that investment in the Corridor has resulted in an increase in labour productivity by 30 per cent between 1992 and 1997, with clothing and textiles leading the way.

Mozambique's export competitiveness looks promising as well. Mozal will be contributing to exports in 2001 through the production and export of 250,000 tons of aluminium, or 1 per cent of worldwide production. It will be the second lowest-cost producer in the world according to its proponents, due to low cost of electricity, alumina and taxes. The Mozambique model is strikingly different from others in SSA. It is a case study of globalization and regionalization at work. Mozal's record on the environment is reportedly quite good as well. Development agencies in Maputo believe that the economy can quickly recover from the recent floods in the spring of 2000, especially if the transport infrastructure is repaired in a timely manner and farmers are provided with food until the next harvest. Flood stricken areas are among the least populated and fertile in the country (*Financial Times* 7 March 2000). Mozal and the Maputo Corridor have largely escaped the floods that recently damaged many other parts of the country.

Ghana

Ghana is another relatively attractive country for foreign investors in SSA. Efforts to attract FDI in Ghana were significantly increased when the government passed the 1994 Ghana Investment Promotion Act, creating incentives and reducing obstacles to FDI. The programme lifted foreign exchange controls, liberalized trade controls, established a stock exchange and began the privatization process of more than 200 state-owned companies. Since the establishment of the Ghana Investment Promotion Centre the same year, the office has registered 972 projects mainly in the service, manufacturing, tourism, building and construction and agriculture sectors (Ghana Investment Promotion Centre, *Statistics on Registered Projects, Fourth Quarter* 1999). Approximately one third of these projects are wholly-owned foreign investments, the rest being joint ventures. The leading foreign investors were the UK and China followed by India, the US, Germany, Lebanon, Korea, The Netherlands and others.

The government is aiming for Ghana to become a middle-income country by the year 2020, requiring a growth rate of at least 8 per cent per year. This growth rate depends to a great extent on investment in the private sector. An increase in private investment from 4 per cent of GDP to 20 per cent is necessary to achieve an 8 per cent growth rate; much of this investment will have to come from foreign countries (*Financial Times* 21 June 1998). In 1999, GDP grew at 4.6 per cent, one percentage point below forecast but higher than the 4.2 per cent growth rate of 1997 (*Financial Times* 4 November 1999).

Some companies outside the traditional mining sector have in fact done quite well. Unilever Ghana, despite the power crisis of 1998 and falling disposable incomes, saw its sales volumes increase. By mid-1998, the company had reached its profit target for the year. Other firms have struggled as the economy has shown slow or no growth in recent years. But in general, foreign firms continue to show interest in Ghana. Telekom Malaysia Bhd, Malaysian Shipyard and Business Focus Sdn Bhd have investments in Ghana (*Business Times Malaysia* 28 July 1998). Chevron's West Africa Pipeline Project supplies Nigerian natural gas to Togo, Benin and Ghana.

The advantages of exporting from Ghana include low-cost labour, improving financial markets, free export zones, quota free access to US and European markets and membership in the Multilateral Investment Guarantee Agency (*Institutional Investor Survey* August 1998). Also, Ghana has enjoyed relative fiscal and political stability. It is the belief of ECOWAS members that its regional trade liberalization scheme, if agreed-upon trade protocols are implemented, would create a large market of approximately 250 million people to attract foreign investors. Attached to this effort, Ghana is trying to be perceived as the gateway to the region with the creation of export processing zones and attractive foreign investment policies.

The US$56 million Gateway project, mostly funded by a soft loan from the World Bank, is focused on the Tema Export Processing Zone (EPZ) launched in July 1999. World Bank funds will be used to improve infrastructure within the zone. However, the Bank will not release funds for infrastructure improvement until movement is seen on the private sector front. The response from the private sector has been positive so far. Among other firms, Business Focus, a Malaysian company will invest US$300 million over the next six years, making the Tema EPZ the first privately developed EPZ. The company plans to bring in twenty subsidiaries eventually. EPZ incentives in Ghana include a 10-year tax holiday and a maximum corporate tax rate of 8 per cent thereafter. Wholly-owned foreign enterprises are permitted. The minimum wage is set at US$1 per day. In addition to the promotion of EPZs, the government plans to improve the efficiency of agencies like the Customs, Excise and Prevention Services, the Ports and Harbour Authority, the Ghana Civil Aviation Authority, the Immigration Services, the Free Zones Board and the Ghana Investment Promotion Centre.

Ghana does have some advantages that will work toward the gateway concept becoming a reality. The country is politically stable, English is the language of business, infrastructure has improved over recent years and it is located on the coast in the middle of West Africa. Yet the crises brought on by drought and a loss of hydroelectric power have proved to be devastating to many industries. Land tenure issues are also proving to be a barrier to the commercialization of agriculture and the diversification of agricultural exports. Cocoa has not been privatized and most likely will not be, as it is one of the last bastions of state control.

Conclusions

We can draw several conclusions from the African experience. The first is that many of the problems with regard to attracting FDI in small economies are not that different from those in larger economies in the developing world. In particular, lack of infrastructure, cumbersome government regulations and restrictions on equity holdings by foreigners are common to both large and small countries. These obstacles to FDI must be addressed early on in the development process in order for economic development to proceed at a good pace. FDI flows could be a lot higher in SSA if governments implemented a proper set of regulations that enabled investors to do business in a fair and consistent manner. If the government enforces regulations in an arbitrary manner or writes tax and business codes that are contradictory and unclear, investors will stay away and/or seek other countries where the investment climate is more favourable.

The second lesson is that in very small countries, a single large project can be very significant in terms of raising interest in FDI. Mozal in Mozambique has given the country greater visibility in the international arena. A single large project, backed by a multilateral agency, serves to raise a large amount of capital, attract the attention of the media and bring together a number of different players from around the world. Also, if a small country is able to successfully implement a large project, it establishes itself as a credible host for FDI, thereby attracting further investment and employment.

Third, attempts at regionalization are important, particularly for small countries. The Maputo Corridor links small economies to larger ones, thereby creating economic opportunities and increasing the size of the market. Cross-border projects are always useful in terms of increasing commerce and investment. They appear to be almost a requirement for very small countries with limited domestic markets.

References

AFX Europe (1999) 15 October.

Bennell, P. (1997) 'Foreign Direct Investment in Africa: Rhetoric and Reality', *SAIS Review*, Summer–Fall, 127–39.

Bhinda, N., Griffith-Jones, S., Leape, J., and Martin, M. (1999) *Private Capital Flows to Africa: Perception and Reality*, The Hague: Forum on Debt and Development, (FONDAD).

Business Times Malaysia (1998) 28 July.

Chia, S.Y. (2000) 'FDI Policy Regimes and Practices in ASEAN and Their Applicability to Africa', Geneva: UNCTAD, August, unpublished.

Court, J. and Yanagihara, T. (1998) 'Asia and Africa into the Global Economy, Background and Introduction', paper presented at the UNU-AERC Conference 'Asia and Africa in the Global Economy', Tokyo, Japan, August.

Crocker, C.A. and Taylor, M.P. (1999) 'Mobilizing African Resources for African Development', Unpublished manuscript.

Financial Times, various issues.

Ghana Investment Promotion Centre (1999) *Statistics on Registered Projects, Fourth Quarter*.

Independent, various issues.

Institutional Investor Survey (1998) August.

Lindauer, D.L. and Roemer, M. (eds) (1994) *Asia and Africa: Legacies and Opportunities in Development*, San Francisco: Institute for Contemporary Studies.

Madavo, C. and Sarbib, J.L. (1997) 'Africa on the Move: Attracting Private Capital to a Changing Continent', *SAIS Review*, Summer–Fall, 111–26.

McMillan, M., Pandolfi, S., and Salinger, B.L. (1999) 'Promoting Foreign Direct Investment in Labor-Intensive, Manufacturing Exports in Developing Countries', Consulting Assistance on Economic Reform II (CAER II) Discussion Paper No. 42, Harvard Institute for International Development, July.

Ramachandran, V. (1993) 'Technology Transfer, Firm Ownership and Investment in Human Capital', *Review of Economics and Statistics*, 75, 664–70.

Ramachandran, V. and Kedia Shah, M. (1999) 'Minority Entrepreneurship and Firm Performance in sub-Saharan Africa', *The Journal of Development Studies*, 36(2), 71–87.

Sachs, J. and Sievers, S. (1998) 'Foreign Direct Investment in Africa', in *The Africa Competitiveness Report 1998*, Geneva: World Economic Forum.

Stewart, F., Lall, S., and Wangwe, S. (1992) *Alternative Development Strategies in sub-Saharan Africa*, Basingstoke: Macmillan.

UNCTAD (1999) *World Investment Report 1999: Foreign Direct Investment and the Challenge of Development*, New York: United Nations Conference on Trade and Development.

Wells, L.T., Jr., Buehrer, T.S., Emery, J.J., and Spence, M.T. (2000) 'Cutting Red Tape: Lessons from a Case-base Approach to Improving the Investment Climate in Mozambique', in Administrative Barriers to Foreign Investment: Reducing Red Tape in Africa, Occasional Paper No. 14, FIAS.

World Economic Forum (1998) *Africa Competitiveness Report*.

7 The challenges posed by globalization for economic liberalization in two Asian transitional countries

Laos and Vietnam

Nick J. Freeman

Introduction

> Your country belongs to the Western seas, ours to the seas of the East. Just as the horse and the buffalo differ between themselves, so do we differ by our language, our writings and our customs. … Everywhere man has the same value, but his nature is not the same.[1]

It could be argued that few Asian countries are more aware of the potency of global forces, and the impact of external trends, than Laos and Vietnam. At first glance such an assertion may appear strange, particularly for two economies that were wholly closed to all foreign business before the late 1980s. Indeed, these two countries are regarded by many as insular, led as they are by avowedly communist parties that remain ambivalent towards the economic development orthodoxy held by most nations in East Asia.[2] But with the exception of highly externally-oriented economies like Singapore and Hong Kong, it is hard to identify other countries in Asia that have been more exposed to external economic and political forces this century than Laos and Vietnam. Both Laos and Vietnam were French colonies, and while the former was a 'colonial backwater', the latter was on the receiving end of substantial French capital inflows during the first three decades of the twentieth century.[3] Although neglected by French capital, the current Lao state was created by the French administration, at least in terms of its current borders and territorial extent, having previously constituted three petty kingdoms, outlying parts of which were subsequently absorbed by neighbouring countries.[4] The liberation struggle to eject the French from both Laos and Vietnam mutated and inflated into a conflict that became the primary cockpit of Cold War superpower rivalry throughout much of the 1960s and early 1970s. After the end of hostilities in 1975, both Laos and Vietnam had relatively brief flirtations with inward-oriented command economics, payrolled in large part by the Soviet Union. But since the late 1980s, both countries have sought – at least partially – to open their economies to foreign trade and capital inflows, propitiously timed to coincide with a global trend of rising investment and trading activity in emerging markets. And finally, as a result of substantial outflows of refugees during recent decades (particularly in the latter part of the 1970s), quite large Lao and Vietnamese communities now reside overseas, most notably in Australia, France and the US, remitting considerable sums to their respective home countries.

The above notwithstanding, the leaderships in Laos and Vietnam are clearly not comfortable with the current forces of globalization, perceiving them to be – at best – a rather mixed blessing. While foreign capital inflows and other economic inputs are undoubtedly welcome, much of the additional socio-political 'baggage' is less well received. Vietnam's leadership frequently warns its people to be on guard against 'peaceful evolution'; a process by which external forces will seek to covertly undermine the regime. Given Vietnam's long history of resisting external aggressors, it is perhaps not surprising that Hanoi continues to be vigilant against hegemonic intent. The Lao government too has intimated its desire not to see the country overwhelmed by foreign interests, although seems quite willing to have Vietnam as its principal mentor, Evans (1998).

The leaderships in Vientiane and Hanoi tend to depict their concerns about globalization as primarily pertaining to its impact on issues like local traditions, national culture and so on. However, the potential impact of globalization in diluting national sovereignty and contracting the authority of government are probably of even greater (and much more immediate) concern to Vientiane and Hanoi, although rarely expressed as such.[5] The leaderships are also not helped by adhering to an ideology – now largely abandoned in the economic sphere, but still espoused in the political realm – that does little to equip them with the tools needed to comprehend recent changes in international business patterns, let alone notions of the 'new economic paradigm'. Instead, it allies them with a diminishing community of socialist states that have yet to deliver a convincing strategy to deal with the forces of globalization. The leaderships in Vientiane and Hanoi are certainly not ignorant of globalization, but seem unsure how to respond, and – as discussed below – seem more focused on the perceived perils of globalization.

The second section presents a brief overview of the two economies. The third and fourth sections are concerned with the reform experience at the pre- and post-1997 Asian crisis. The fifth section looks at the way ahead, and the sixth section is by way of conclusion.

A brief economic profile of Laos and Vietnam

Sharing a common border, the Lao People's Democratic Republic and the Socialist Republic of Vietnam are states with some strong similarities, albeit with a few marked differences. Both are low-income developing countries.[6] Both regimes were established in 1975, after years of military conflict, and have since been led by communist parties (the Lao People's Revolutionary Party and Vietnam Communist Party). Although political pluralism is not entertained, both countries have been enacting economic liberalization programmes since the implosion of the socialist bloc in the late 1980s. Rather like China, they have sought to reform the economy, but not the political sphere. In Laos, this programme of economic reform is known as the 'new economic mechanism', and in

Vietnam it is referred to as 'doi moi'. Relations between Vientiane and Hanoi are fraternal, and the leaderships regard each other as close allies. Laos is a landlocked country, with a population of around 5 million, while Vietnam has a lengthy coastline, and has a populace of about 80 million. Laos's total land area is roughly 70 per cent that of Vietnam, resulting in a stark difference of population densities

Table 7.1 Laos and Vietnam's macro-economic profiles compared

	1994	*1995*	*1996*	*1997*	*1998E*
Real GDP growth (%)					
Laos	8.1	7.0	6.8	6.9	4.0
Vietnam	8.8	9.5	9.3	8.2	5.8
Agriculture sector as % of GDP					
Laos	57.5	55.6	53.3	53.3	52.6
Vietnam	27.4	27.2	27.8	25.8	26.0
Industry sector as % of GDP					
Laos	18.1	19.2	21.1	21.2	21.9
Vietnam	28.9	28.8	29.7	32.1	32.7
Services sector as % of GDP					
Laos	24.4	25.5	25.6	25.5	25.5
Vietnam	43.7	44.1	42.5	42.2	41.3
Consumer price index (%)					
Laos	6.8	22.6	13	19.3	90.1
Vietnam	14.4	12.7	4.5	3.6	9.2
Exports (% of GDP)					
Laos	19.5	17.5	17.4	18.3	26.7
Vietnam	26.2	26.2	31.6	38.4	40.3
Imports (% of GDP)					
Laos	36.6	32.9	37.3	37.3	43.8
Vietnam	33.9	37.1	45.2	47.7	50.9
Balance of payments on current account (% of GDP)					
Laos	−14.3	−13.2	−16.1	−16.1	−10.4
Vietnam	−8	−11	−10.3	−6.8	−4.1
Foreign investment approvals (number of projects)					
Laos	130	55	63	66	68
Vietnam	367	408	370	313	—
Foreign investment approvals (value US$ million)					
Laos	2,598	615	1,293	142	123
Vietnam	3,664	6,722	7,702	4,456	1,738
External debt outstanding (US$ million)					
Laos	1,971	2,068	2,175	2,323	—
Vietnam	6,670	7,756	9,657	11,612	14,861
Debt service ratio (% of exports)					
Laos	3.3	5.7	5.9	9.5	11.9
Vietnam	13.4	12.2	11	11.4	13.4
Exchange rate against US$1					
Laos (kip)	730	940	975	2,205	4,750
Vietnam (dong)	10,978	11,037	11,032	11,683	13,297

Sources: ADB (1999), various IMF Staff Country Reports and ING Barings.

between the two countries. The ethnic profile of Laos's population is extremely diverse, whereas Vietnam's citizenry is relatively uniform in this regard.

By global standards, the economies of Laos and Vietnam are relatively small. The GDP of Laos is a mere US$1.4 billion, while Vietnam's is around US$25 billion. In Laos, the agricultural sector employs the majority of people and accounts for about half of total GDP, with the service and industry sectors representing about a quarter of aggregate GDP each. In Vietnam, the agricultural sector also employs the majority of people (about 80 per cent of the labour force), but only accounts for about a quarter of total GDP, with the industry and service sectors representing 34 per cent and 42 per cent of total GDP respectively (Table 7.1). Prior to 1987, both countries operated centrally-planned economies, supported by not inconsiderable socialist bloc assistance, primarily sourced from the Soviet Union. Economic interaction with the West was minimal, with Laos in particular becoming relatively closed. Although some of the more extreme elements of central planning – such as obligatory collectivization of agriculture and a complete ban on private sector endeavour – were phased out at the end of the 1970s, the economic performance of both countries remained extremely lacklustre, until the advent of economic liberalization measures in the mid-1980s. These economic reforms succeeded in overcoming some of the deficiencies of the old system, thereby unleashing a commendable spurt of growth, as measured across a wide range of macro-economic indicators.

Economic liberalization prior to the 'Asian crisis'

If one plots growing globalization by rising levels of external trade (as a percentage of GDP) or foreign investment inflows (as a proportion of domestic investment), it is clear that both Laos and Vietnam have become much more 'globalized' since the commencement of economic reforms in the late 1980s. Key pillars in the economic liberalization programmes in both Laos and Vietnam were the opening up of the economy to foreign investment (to attract much-needed capital and business know-how) and the successful bid to increase external trade (to generate foreign exchange).[7] For example, Vietnam's export earnings grew from less than US$500 million in 1988 to slightly under US$9 billion in 1997; rising from less than 3 per cent of GDP to almost 38 per cent of GDP. Similarly, foreign investment pledges increased from less than US$400 million in 1988 to over US$8.6 billion in 1996; rising from roughly 10 per cent of domestic investment to roughly 30 per cent greater than total domestic investment.[8] Laos's performance in external trade and FDI inflows has not been as impressive as Vietnam's, but showed broadly the same underlying trend during the first half of the 1990s.

The timing of the 'opening up' of the Lao and Vietnamese economies to foreign capital inflows and external trade was propitious, coinciding with an unprecedented rally in investment and trade flows across global emerging markets in general, and Asia in particular (see figures in UNCTAD 1999 and Cotton and Ramachandran, Chapter 6, this volume). The forces of globalization were regarded as being relatively benign at this time, with integration into the global economy deemed necessary to revive their ailing domestic economies. While elements of the Lao and Vietnamese leaderships may have harboured reservations about this diversion in the socialist development path, these were subsumed by a more pressing need to reinvigorate their moribund and malfunctioning economies, at a time when the primary external sponsor (the Soviet Union) was unable to continue with its assistance.

The response of foreign venture capitalists to the 'opening up' of Laos and Vietnam was very favourable, discerning that some of East Asia's last frontiers were now being made accessible. The fact that Laos and Vietnam were located in a part of the world where so many other economic success stories were already apparent helped matters tremendously. For investors and traders seeking to penetrate new domestic consumer markets, Vietnam in particular offered the potential of over 70 million new customers. For investors seeking to find new low-cost labour platforms for producing manufactured goods, here were two countries where semi-skilled labour cost less than US$50 per month.

The role played by foreign investment – with its the value-added inputs of new technology, management know-how, access to foreign markets, and so on – in the economic liberalization programmes of Laos and Vietnam should not be underestimated. It is undoubtedly the case that Vietnam's 'doi moi' programme would have been far less successful without the inflow of substantial foreign investment between 1988 and 1996. Indeed, FDI was a critical motor of economic growth and development in both Laos and Vietnam, during their first decade of economic liberalization. To some extent at least, this trend mirrored a similar process – roughly sixty years before – with the inflow of French colonial capital in the 1920s playing a pivotal role in advancing the Vietnamese economy, Callis (1942). More than one author has noted that French capitalists were responsible for taking Vietnam on the 'next step along the road of economic change' during the early part of the twentieth century, Smith (1968). A similar role could be played by FDI in the 1990s, assisting Vietnam in taking its economy to a new level of production, by supporting the creation of an export-oriented manufacturing and processing base.

The 1990s wave of foreign investment did not seek to emulate the colonial notion of *mise en valuer* that was associated with French capitalist penetration of Laos and Vietnam in the early twentieth century. But another parallel between the foreign investment activity of the 1980–90s and the early twentieth century is perhaps worthy of note. More than any other colonial regime in Southeast Asia, France enacted various measures that virtually excluded all non-French foreign investors. As a result, one observer estimates that just 3 per cent of all investment in Indochina came from countries other than France.[9] Although no foreign power sought to dominate FDI activity in Laos or Vietnam in the 1990s, the former did encounter levels of Thai investment that far exceeded all others. But, more interestingly, in a sort of reversal of French colonial policy, the US maintained an investment embargo against Vietnam, until 1995, see Freeman (1993). This allowed European and several East Asian firms to steal a march on their US competitors in Vietnam, and added to the allure of this market. Once the embargo was lifted, numerous US firms made a concerted bid to enter Vietnam, in a drive that was probably the last major 'FDI push' into the country, prior to the onset of the Asian crisis.

Both Vietnam and Laos joined the Association of Southeast Asian Nations (ASEAN) in 1995 and 1997, respectively. There is little doubt that the primary reasons behind both countries joining were the perceived political and strategic benefits to be derived from being a member, particularly regarding relations with mighty China – with which both Laos and Vietnam have northern borders. (ASEAN's well-established principle of mutual non-interference in the domestic circumstances of fellow members will also have attracted Vientiane and Hanoi, see Funston 2000). However, the political benefits of ASEAN membership also come with economic obligations, including compliance with the ASEAN Free Trade Area (AFTA) and ASEAN Investment Area (AIA), both of which will place additional demands on the two countries' economies. For example, reducing import tariffs to comply with AFTA will reduce one important layer of protection currently used to defend state enterprises from much leaner overseas competition. Given a choice, both Vientiane and Hanoi would probably prefer an ASEAN that does not include AFTA and AIA commitments, but that choice does not exist, and the perceived political benefits of membership are deemed to outweigh the less economic obligations of membership. (The extended deadlines given to Laos and Vietnam for AFTA and AIA compliance – Laos must comply with AFTA by 2005 and the AIA by 2010; Vietnam must comply with AFTA by 2003 and the AIA by 2010 – has given the two countries some breathing space.)

The impact of the 'Asian crisis'

If the substantial increases of investment inflows to, and external trade with, Laos and Vietnam were regarded by Vientiane and Hanoi as being broadly benign during the early 1990s, this perception seemed to change around the mid-1990s, and particularly after the onset of the regional economic downturn – the 'Asian crisis' – in 1997. While it would be incorrect to assert that leadership perceptions of the forces of globalization were transformed from being completely benign to thoroughly malignant, it is true to say that the potential perils of becoming integrated into the global economy were brought to the fore, if only by those elements within the leaderships that had harboured misgivings about the speed (and depth) of economic liberalization measures all along. It almost became accepted wisdom that, had it not been for delays in liberalizing various elements of the economy (such as foreign exchange and the finance sector), the impact of the Asian crisis would have been much harder. Or put another way, if Laos and Vietnam had been more integrated with the global economy, the adverse effects of the regional downturn would have been much worse. This interpretation of events is spurious, but nonetheless has gained currency in Vientiane and Hanoi, and partially undermined the platform of pro-reform elements within the senior leaderships.

Laos

Despite having only the most rudimentary banking and financial system, the impact of the Asian economic crisis on Laos was marked, and most evident in the fortunes of its domestic currency, the kip. With an economy heavily oriented towards Thailand, both in terms of trade and investment, it did not take long for the Thai currency crisis to migrate across the Mekong River. Although officially illegal, the use of both the Thai baht and US dollars for domestic transactions (and savings) in Laos is widespread. At first, the Lao currency's value against the US dollar shadowed the decline of the Thai currency, but after the baht began to stabilize, the value of the kip continued to weaken against both the US dollar and the baht. This currency weakening persisted throughout 1998, resulting in a devaluation even greater than for Indonesia's rupiah. This in itself was quite peculiar, given that the fallout from the Asian economic crisis had an impact on Indonesia's economic, social and political spheres that was far greater than anything experienced in Laos. The sharp depreciation in the kip rapidly led to very high inflation, as imported goods (on which Laos is heavily reliant) became considerably more expensive in local currency terms. The spending power of urban Lao – including government officials – declined precipitously, forcing the government to enact a number of policies to mitigate the impact. These included reducing the hours of the working week, in order that civil servants could generate additional income from second jobs. While such measures may have helped a little, they did not wholly compensate for the woes felt by most urbanites. Displeasure at what had happened almost certainly played a part in the aborted demonstration that took place in Vientiane in October 1999, by students and teachers.

Having sourced the vast majority of its foreign investment from Thailand (72 per cent of aggregate inflows between 1994 and 1999), the sharp economic downturn in Laos's southern neighbour resulted in a sharp reduction in FDI inflows (Figure 7.1). The dire effect of the financial crisis on Thailand's corporates caused a number of Laos's largest foreign investors to cut back their plans for the country. To compound matters, a large proportion of total foreign investment pledges (and licence approvals) in Laos had been for an ambitious array of hydropower projects across the country (also see Table 7.2). Although far in excess of Laos's own power needs, the electricity generated was to have been exported to Thailand. However, Thailand's power demand projections have subsequently been sharply revised down, and a substantial proportion of the approved hydropower projects will not now proceed. And for those that do proceed,

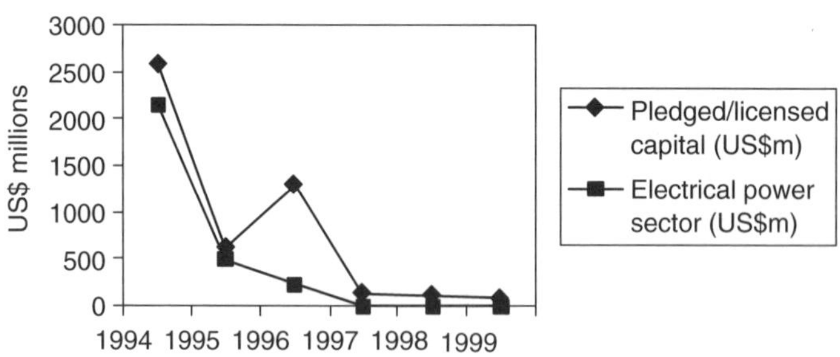

Figure 7.1 Foreign investment inflows in Laos, 1994–9.

Table 7.2 Major FDI patterns in Laos and Vietnam

Laos		*Vietnam*	
Top five foreign investors as % of total			
Thailand	46.9	Singapore	15.7
USA	26.6	Taiwan	13.0
Korea	5.7	Japan	9.5
Australia	5.1	Hong Kong	9.2
Malaysia	4.9	Korea	8.4
Top five foreign investment sectors as % of total			
Energy	66.1	Construction	18.4
Hotels/tourism	8.9	Heavy industry	16.5
Telecommunications	8.2	Hotels/tourism	13.5
Manufacturing	7.0	Light industry	10.8
Wood products	2.4	Telecommunications	8.6

Sources: OECF (1999) and *Vietnam Business Journal* (various issues).

Vientiane and Bangkok have been stuck in negotiations over the terms of the power purchasing deals. Laos's policy-makers had placed much emphasis on these power projects as a pillar of the country's economic development drive, which – with the benefit of hindsight – meant that they had placed 'too many eggs' in the hydropower 'basket'.

> When *imperialism* speeds up trade and services liberalization and globalization of investment, the rich countries become richer, and the gap between rich and poor countries widens.[10] [This author's italics.]

The above quotation is taken from a speech by the General Secretary of the Vietnam Communist Party, Le Kha Phieu, given in early 2000. These words provide a telling indication of the senior leadership's concerns about the forces of globalization, and the threat posed by 'hostile forces' seeking to 'wipe out the remaining socialist countries'.[11] While this concern was not wholly in abeyance prior to the Asian crisis, it was much less apparent. Perhaps the most tangible evidence of these concerns was the debacle that occurred at the APEC summit in Auckland, in September 1999, when Hanoi made an eleventh hour decision not to sign a 'normal trading rights' agreement with the US, having initialled a preliminary agreement a few months before (after nine rounds of negotiations). Such an agreement would have been the most significant development in Vietnam's process of rejoining the international business community since the lifting of the US embargo in 1995, and been the penultimate stop in a process that had begun in 1987, with the promulgation of its foreign investment law. Hanoi's decision not to sign in Auckland came as a body blow to already sombre sentiment towards Vietnam by most foreign investors, and took overseas business perceptions of the country to new lows, from which it will be hard to recover. On a more immediate note, the signing of a US–China trade agreement, just two months later, means that the latter will now have a distinct advantage over Vietnam in terms of its exports entering the US market. As a direct competitor to Vietnam in various exports, China now has the upper hand.

Unlike Laos, Vietnam did not witness a dramatic depreciation in its domestic currency (the 'dong'), during and immediately after the financial crisis in Thailand. Hanoi's currency strategy has resembled that of China, to maintain the fixed exchange rate, regardless of the impact this may have on export competitiveness, resulting from the currency depreciations by other countries in East Asia. (Although Vietnam's policy-makers may insist that the dong exchange rate has the ability to freely move within a permitted trading band, the incremental movements are so minute as to be inconsequential.)

Probably the greatest impact of the Asian crisis on Vietnam was felt in the foreign investment inflow figures, which have almost evaporated over the last 2–3 years. Although pledges of new FDI had probably peaked in 1996, both the pledges and disbursements of foreign investment began to trend down sharply after mid-1997. Unlike Laos, Vietnam's FDI inflows were not dominated by one country source and one sector: the industry sector (both light and heavy) comprises roughly one-third of all approved foreign investment, followed by hotels and tourism, construction, telecommunications and oil and gas exploration (see Table 7.2). Nonetheless, approximately 70 per cent of Vietnam's FDI inflows were being sourced from the Asia Pacific region, including those countries most affected by the financial crisis and subsequent regional economic downturn. Therefore, one would be right to attribute at least part of the FDI inflow decline to the impact of the Asian crisis. However, the regional economic downturn was not the only cause of the contraction in foreign investment, as indicated by the fact that FDI inflows peaked in 1996, ahead of the Asian crisis. Much of the initial euphoria towards Vietnam as a new investment destination began to wear off in 1996 (see Figure 7.2), and after the Eighth Party Congress of mid-1996 the economic reform process began to lose momentum, and it has yet to convincingly recover. As a result, foreign investors began to revise down their expectations for the country, as new economic liberalization measures were not forthcoming, and foreign firms began to hold back on proposing new projects.

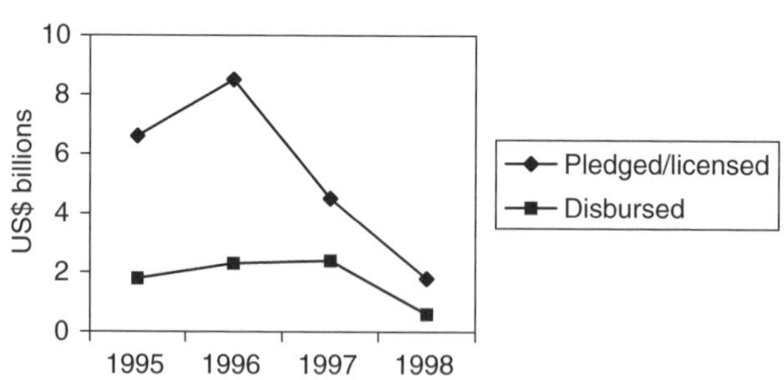

Figure 7.2 Foreign investment inflows in Vietnam, 1995–8.

Perhaps one area of Vietnam's economic policy-making that best displays the leadership's general anxiety over globalization, and a reluctance to enact business liberalization measures that go beyond what is deemed acceptable by the more conservative elements, has been in the field of capital markets. Since roughly 1991, Hanoi has been toying with opening a stock market. Yet despite establishing a securities regulatory commission in 1997, and issuing various pieces of regulatory paperwork, Vietnam has still to unveil a stock market.[12] While the reasons behind this delay are complex, and include genuine logistical problems, the fact that Hanoi has been so slow in overcoming various hurdles reflects in part a lack of leadership consensus on the issue. (And witnessing what happened to the stock markets of most East Asian countries during the Asian crisis has probably served to weaken leadership consensus even further.) A Chinese dissident remarked in 1997 that his country's stock market 'has that magic power that makes people concerned about the country's economic policy . . . once the will of the people is awakened, they will not sleep again'.[13] But a stock market also has the potential to act as a conduit for foreign portfolio investment into domestic enterprises listed on the market, which may also pose concerns for some in Vietnam's leadership, despite the fact that a shortage of capital (both credit and equity) has been the single largest problem facing the country's corporate sector for the last few years.

Until 1998, the slow pace of stock market development in Vietnam was mirrored by a similarly glacial approach to the divestment of non-essential state enterprises, with a host of practical hurdles cited as the reason for sloth. However, the pace of state sector divestment – known as 'equitization' in Vietnam – increased considerably in 1999, indicating that when sufficient political will is galvanized, economic liberalization measures can move forward quite rapidly.[14] Recent progress on 'equitization' was one of the very few bright spots on the economic liberalization 'front' for Vietnam in 1998–9.[15]

The way forward for economic reform

The extreme opacity of the decision-making process in Vientiane and Hanoi make it difficult for external observers to judge how the leaderships of Laos and Vietnam are debating issues relating to globalization. It is therefore hard to forecast whether they will come to terms with globalization, and whether they will choose to reinvigorate the economic reform process. While there is probably little prospect of Laos and Vietnam actually reversing the economic liberalization measures enacted since the late 1980s, it is conceivable that the recent 'non-policy' stance will persist in the coming years, until some sort of consensus within the senior leadership is arrived at, or events overtake the leadership. If so, we can expect to see the continuation of broadly pro-liberalization utterances, with incremental improvements made to the legislative and regulatory regimes that pertain to the business environment. In other words, a continuation of the modus operandi that has been in place since roughly 1996.

A more positive and convincing economic liberalization drive in the short-term would probably be only forthcoming if the distress to the economies of Laos and

Vietnam was of a level that prompted remedial action by the leadership, rather in the same way that the first tranche of economic reforms of 1986 was in response to dire economic plight. But such a situation in itself would not be a sufficient precondition, as it would also require a consensus within Vientiane and Hanoi that further economic liberalization measures provided the best chance of economic improvement, and that the potential rewards outweighed the perceived risks. And even then, it would remain to be seen whether the economic liberalization measures taken – regardless of their boldness – were the right ones for the job. At a time of increasing globalization, this not only requires competency, but also a degree of vision and imagination, in a field where the leaderships of Laos and Vietnam are relatively inexperienced.

One particular area of concern for this observer is that the sorts of 'micro' economic liberalization measures now being enacted in Laos and Vietnam – fine-tuning a business law here, adjusting an implementing regulation there – in a bid to regain economic momentum is of little utility, and indeed may even be counter-productive. The economic growth spurt of the late 1980s and early 1990s was attributable in large part to the activity of the private sector (both domestic and foreign firms alike), after having been restricted or wholly excluded in previous decades. Changes in the various laws, decrees and regulations opened up an avenue of economic endeavour that was seized by everyone, from local farming families to major foreign multinationals. And the sorts of laws and decrees that were drafted broadly complied with an established 'blueprint' for economic development that had been tried and tested by other Southeast Asian countries in the 1970s and 1980s. In the specific case of foreign investment, particular emphasis was placed on encouraging export-oriented production projects (everything from electricity generation in Laos for sale to Thailand, to garment manufacturing in Vietnam for sale to Europe), as exemplified by the export processing zones and industrial zones that sprouted up across Vietnam.

Foreign investors had an appetite for this sort of approach in the 1980s, and although this had begun to wane, they still had some lingering interest in establishing new plant in Laos and Vietnam during the 1990s. However, forces of globalization – particularly with regard to new efficiencies of production and the economies of scale to be derived from cross-border production networks – are helping to ensure that such appetite is now much-diminished. At a time of global overcapacity in many of the fields where Laos and Vietnam were seeking to develop capabilities, appetite for new power plants and car assembly plants has been almost wholly satiated. Yet, the micro liberalization measures being enacted by Vientiane and Hanoi are very much still within the mindset of the 'old economy blueprint'. While appropriate for that stage of transition in Laos and Vietnam, and appropriate for the business environment of the late 1980s and early 1990s, such policies may have less relevance in the next stage of transition, and in the new international business environment. In short, diminishing returns are beginning to set in for the reform agenda pursued by Laos and Vietnam since the late 1980s.

At worst, tinkering with existing laws and regulations – accompanied by poor performance in implementation – succeeds in only further complicating what has become a remarkably labyrinthine regulatory regime, for Vietnam in particular, thereby adding to the opacity of these host country business environments. At best, the benefits to be derived from 'micro' tinkering are wholly discounted by ongoing macro hurdles that confront both foreign and domestic business: non-convertibility of the currency; regulations that oblige firms to exchange any foreign exchange earnings into local currency; hassles incurred when dealing with a petulant customs service; scant recourse to law in areas such as intellectual property rights, etc. One observer recently commented that foreign 'investors will return [to Vietnam] only when the government demonstrates the necessary seriousness of purpose to convince prudent executives to put their money at risk' (Rushford 2000). The policy-makers in Laos and Vietnam know this, but are wrong to think that repeated redrafting of a few laws will be sufficient to display a seriousness of purpose. Above and beyond improving the legislative framework, the gestures have to be more convincing, more imaginative, and more oriented towards a rapidly changing international business environment. And they must not be undermined by references to 'imperialism' by the Secretary General of the Communist Party – the single most powerful man in Vietnam. A lot of foreign investors jumped into Laos and Vietnam with both feet during the early 1990s and promptly 'lost their shirts'; the next tranche are likely to be more cautious.

Laos and Vietnam's policy-makers do not seem to have developed a grasp of the sorts economic liberalization measures that are necessary for a developing country in the global economy of today, as opposed to a few decades ago. With most developing countries now offering liberal investment regimes and incentive packages as standard, the competition to attract foreign firms has moved on, to more macro-economic issues like: the quality – transparency and robustness – of the domestic financial sector (particularly post-crisis), the standard of infrastructure, the cost of communications, the level of human capital and so on. In these sorts of areas, Laos and Vietnam do not score highly. While some in Vientiane and Hanoi might be sorely tempted to dispense with foreign investment as part of their economic development process, such a notion would be self-deluding. Both countries need foreign capital, and arguably more importantly, they need foreign export markets, technology, and know-how. While Laos might be able to consider relying on external assistance (for example, bilateral aid and multilateral agency grants) alone, this sort of assistance also comes with strings attached, often in areas that are socio-politically contentious. Multilateral agencies are increasingly attaching conditionalities to assistance that relate to issues of economic and political governance, yet private investors rarely have conditionalities that go further than corporate governance. Hanoi and Vientiane profess that they remain keen to attract foreign firms, but the 'micro' policy prescriptions being used are not of the sort that will galvanize overseas investors nor salivate the creative juices of entrepreneurs.

Conclusion

Laos and Vietnam enacted economic liberalization measures in a bid to transform their economies into versions of the more vibrant economic models that surrounded them in Southeast Asia. Half way through doing so, Laos and Vietnam's leaders saw the Asian crisis partially discredit the economic models that they were seeking to emulate. And to make matters worse, forces of globalization now seem to point to a much more demanding liberalization agenda than was initially envisaged, with implications that may include various additional socio-political perils. Possibly having psyched themselves up for a relatively brief sprint to reach the 'transition line', the leaderships in Vientiane and Hanoi have discovered that globalization is more like a long-distance endurance race. Whether Laos and Vietnam possess the necessary stamina and volition to stay in the race remains to be seen.

Notes

1 Taken from an 1862 declaration, by the inhabitants of Go-Cong province in southern Vietnam, to the French, 'warning the invaders that they would fight to the death for the return of the territory ceded the previous year', see Smith (1968: 183).
2 This orthodoxy might be summed up as broadly entailing economic liberalization (including divestment of state firms, restructuring domestic corporates, encouraging the private sector to burgeon, allowing foreign corporates to enter, etc.), the fruits of which will subsequently be evidenced in improved economic growth.
3 France invested as much as 8 billion francs in colonial Indochina, prior to the Second World War, Callis (1942: 79–80).
4 Agreement by France and Siam to delineate much of the border along the Mekong River meant that a larger number of Lao found themselves living outside Laos than those left within its borders, Stuart-Fox (1997).
5 Even the World Bank recognizes that 'nation states are facing increasing limitations as territorial constructs', Rischard (2000: 3).
6 Laos has a nominal per capita GNP of US$258, and Vietnam has a nominal per capita GNP of US$310, according to Asiaweek (24 March 2000: 65). The UNDP's (1998) human development index, ranks Vietnam 122 and Laos 136 in its ranking of 174 countries.
7 To be precise, external trade volumes were not only increased, but also re-oriented, from trading with the socialist bloc countries to mostly Asian and European countries. Vietnam in particular did a remarkable job in re-orienting its external trade swiftly, and with little apparent dislocation.
8 The figures pertain to FDI inflow *pledges*, and not FDI *disbursements*.
9 Lindblad (1998: 14). This compares with 10 per cent non-British investment in Burma, 29 per cent non-Dutch investment in Indonesia, 30 per cent non-British investment in Malaysia, and 48 per cent non-US investment in the Philippines, as at 1937.
10 Le Kha Phieu, speaking at the seventieth anniversary celebrations of the VCP, January 2000. *Vietnam Business Journal*, February 2000, available at www.viam.com/02-2000/editorsnote.htm.
11 *Vietnam Business Journal*, February 2000 (editor's note), available at www.viam.com/02-2000/editorsnote.htm.
12 The State Securities Commission replaced a Capital Markets Development department, located within the State Bank of Vietnam.
13 Quote by Wu'er Kaixi, cited in Chancellor (1999: 330).
14 Between 1992 and 1997, just eighteen state enterprises were equitized. But in 1998 alone, 116 state firms were equitized, followed by another 260 in 1999, Nguyen (2000: 23–6).
15 Laos has a more impressive track record than Vietnam in the state sector divestment field, having been more willing to sell or lease state firms to both local and foreign private investors.

References

ADB (1999) *Asian Development Outlook 1999*, Washington, DC: ADB.

Callis, H.G. (1942) *Foreign Capital in Southeast Asia*, New York: Institute of Pacific Relations. (Re-printed in 1976 by Arno Press, New York.)

Chancellor, E. (1999) *Devil Take the Hindmost*, London: Macmillan.

Evans, G. (1998) *The Politics of Ritual and Remembrance: Laos Since 1975*, Honolulu: University of Hawaii's Press.

Freeman, N.J. (1993) 'United States' Economic Sanctions Against Vietnam', *Columbia Journal of World Business*, 28(2), 12–22.

Funston, J. (2000) *ASEAN and the Principle of Non-Intervention – Practice and Prospects*, Trends in Southeast Asia Paper No. 5, Singapore: ISEAS, March.

IMF (International Monetary Fund) (1999) *Vietnam: Selected Issues*, IMF Staff Country Report No. 99/55, Washington, DC: IMF, July.

IMF (International Monetary Fund) (1999) *Vietnam: Statistical Appendix*, IMF Staff Country Report No. 99/56, Washington, DC: IMF, July.

IMF (International Monetary Fund) (2000) *Lao People's Democratic Republic: Recent Economic Developments*, IMF Staff Country Report No. 3, Washington, DC: IMF, January.

Lindblad, J.T. (1998) *Foreign Investment in Southeast Asia in the Twentieth Century*, Basingstoke: Macmillan.

Nguyen, H.H. (2000) 'The Private Sector and the Process of Privatization in Vietnam', Draft paper.

Overseas Economic Cooperation Fund (1999) *The Lao Economy: Its Current Status and Future Challenges*, OECF Research Papers No. 30, Tokyo: OECF, February.

Rischard, J.-F. (2000) 'The New World Economy and Global Governance', paper presented at the Regional Outlook 2000–2001 Conference, Singapore, January.

Rushford, G. (2000) 'Vietnam at a Crossroads', *Asian Wall Street Journal*, 10 April.

Smith, R. (1968) *Viet-Nam and the West*, London: Heinemann.

Stuart-Fox, M. (1997) *A History of Laos*, Cambridge: Cambridge University Press.

UNCTAD (1999) *World Investment Report 1999: Foreign Direct Investment and the Challenge of Development*, New York: United Nations Conference on Trade and Development.

UNDP (1998) *Human Development Report 1998*, New York: United Nations Development Programme.

8 Protectionist tendencies in the North and vulnerable economies in the South

Matthew J. Slaughter

Introduction

This chapter examines whether protectionist tendencies, in terms of both policy preferences and policy actions, in 'northern' countries – looking in particular at the US – seem to be an obstacle to the integration into the world economy of vulnerable 'southern' countries. The chapter makes three related points. First, current trade barriers in the North appear to cost southern countries billions of dollars annually. Second, although some trade barriers in the North are declining under the guidance of the World Trade Organization (WTO), it appears that there is an increasing US resistance to further globalization via trade, investment and immigration liberalization. Third, the chapter speculates about what forces might be driving this rising northern resistance to further liberalization, and what this resistance may imply for the integration prospects of small, vulnerable economies.

How much do northern trade barriers cost southern countries?

Answering this question is rather difficult, both because general-equilibrium welfare estimates tend to require computable general-equilibrium (CGE) models, which are quite complicated, and because results from these CGE models tend to be sensitive to key modeling assumptions: for example, returns to scale of production technology, elasticities of substitution in production and consumption, etc. That said, there have been some carefully executed studies of the welfare impacts of some of the most-egregious northern trade barriers such as the Multi-fibre Arrangement (MFA) covering world trade in textiles and apparel.

This section reviews several of these studies. One important message of these studies is that southern countries in the aggregate are likely to gain from various northern liberalizations. Studies indicate this to be the case even for largely non-tariff barriers such as the MFA: even though southern countries lose quota-like rents from liberalization, these losses appear to be more than offset by pro-competitive gains from increased market access and output. A second important message is that even though southern countries may gain in the aggregate, it need not follow from this that every individual country gains – the distribution of gains may be quite disparate within this group.

Elimination of the MFA

First is an analysis of the MFA. Restraints on global trade in textiles and apparel date back to at least the US–Asian Short Term Agreements on Cotton Textiles in 1962. The first phase of the MFA came into existence in 1974, and evolved into an elaborate structure of tariffs and, especially, bilateral export quotas imposed mainly by northern importers on southern exporters. In the MFA importers granted exporting licenses to exporting-country governments, who in turn allocated the licenses among domestic producers. The 1994 Uruguay Round agreements called for a 10-year phasing out of the MFA under a new agreement called the Agreement on Textiles and Clothing (ATC). This phasing-out period consists both of raising quota levels and removing products from ATC coverage; by 1 January 2004, all ATC provisions are to be gone and this area will fall under normal WTO oversight.

What will MFA removal mean for the level and distribution of world welfare? Trela and Whalley (1990) offer a detailed estimates of the welfare effects, based on a CGE model of 'the world' simplified to three major importing regions (the US, Canada and the European Community), thirty-four exporting countries (mainly developing nations) and fourteen MFA product groups. The model is calibrated to actual 1986 data on MFA barriers, production, and trade flows; this baseline is then used for simulations of a complete elimination of all MFA barriers.

Their baseline estimate (table 3: 1199) is that worldwide welfare would be raised *annually* by about US$23.4 billion. This gain would be distributed both between the three importing regions (about US$15.3 billion) and among the thirty-four exporting countries (about US$8.1 billion). Among the thirty-four exporting countries twenty-nine are estimated to gain individually, with China the largest gainer at US$1.8 billion; four of the five losing countries lose less than US$30 million each, with Hong Kong the outlier at a loss of about US$0.5 billion. Sensitivity analyses which vary functional form or elasticity values find broadly similar results (table 5: 1202), as do Nguyen *et al.* (1993).

Trela and Whalley (1990) emphasize that the exporting countries gain in the aggregate despite their loss in quota rents enjoyed by quota-holding countries: quota-rent losses are more than offset by improved import-market access and thus higher production. This is true even for countries holding a relatively large share of the quotas, such as South Korea and Taiwan. It is also notable that the analysis finds that MFA removal does not merely reshuffle import-market shares among exporting nations with no net gain for this group in market share. Instead, these exporting countries each gain market share, with a net increase for this group being accommodated by reduced production in the importing countries themselves.

Kathuria *et al.* (1999) discuss how the distribution of southern gains from MFA removal can vary over time. Whalley (1999) discusses a couple of important recent changes in the pattern of worldwide production in textiles and apparel. First, regional trade agreements for the US and the European Union have shifted a lot of production into non-quota-constrained locations such as Mexico and

Central Europe. Second, within Asia production has shifted dramatically towards China, so that today it is estimated to account for over half of all Asian output in these sectors.

Kathuria *et al.* (1999) also emphasize the possibility of *dynamic* welfare gains from MFA removal, above and beyond the static resource-reallocation gains captured in CGE models like that of Trela and Whalley. Kathuria *et al.* highlight that 'a key feature of an outward-oriented development process seems to be the identification of industries where relatively high levels of productivity can be achieved… the presence, or continued threat, of export quotas (like the MFA) reduces the opportunity for developing countries to use the relative ease of adopting new technology in the clothing sector as a first step on the ladder of economic development' (1999, 5–6). They cite the example of Bangladesh, which for the past 25 years has realized annualized growth rates of clothing exports of nearly 100 per cent. Similarly, many commentators have pointed out that recent growth successes like South Korea and Taiwan started industrialization decades ago in textiles and apparel. Quantifying these dynamic welfare gains is very difficult, but they underscore that estimates of static gains might best be regarded as lower bounds.

Elimination of antidumping duties and countervailing duties

After the MFA, it seems that the northern trade restriction most troublesome to many southern nations is the class of non-tariff barriers known as antidumping duties and countervailing duties (AD/CVD). This is particularly so for the US, where AD/CVD use has increased dramatically in recent decades. But Prusa (1999) and Tharakan (Chapter 9, this volume) document that AD use has risen in recent years not just among 'traditional users' (US, the European Community, Australia, Canada and New Zealand) but among 'new users' as well, such as Mexico, Argentina, Brazil and South Africa – with many of these new users being involved in intra-South disagreements (Tharakan, Chapter 9, this volume). In fact, Martin and Winters (1996) report that many new users have patterned their new laws after their US counterparts. This all means that small, vulnerable countries face AD threats not just from many rich countries but increasingly from many middle-income countries as well.

How costly are AD and CVD barriers? I know of no study of their cost to the targeted countries. But Gallaway *et al.* (1999) report CGE estimates for the cost of these barriers imposed by the US to the US itself. Their framework is broadly similar to that of Trela and Whalley and others, but as many AD/CVD filings are made against narrow product categories in narrow industries, they use a CGE model with hundreds of product categories. They calibrate this model using data for ADCVD restrictions in place in 1993, and estimate that removing these barriers would increase US welfare by approximately US$4 billion. Given the ongoing MFA phase-out, these estimates indicate that post-MFA the costliest barriers to trade for the US will be this collection of AD/CVD restrictions.

What does Gallaway *et al.*'s (1999) estimate for US welfare suggest for the welfare of exporting nations targeted by these barriers? Gallaway *et al.* emphasize that the majority of the net US welfare loss stems from foreign suppliers raising their prices. Once an AD or CVD ruling is implemented in the US, it is subject to subsequent review and modification based on subsequent market developments. Thus, an initial ruling against foreign firms for charging 'too low' a price in the US can be partially or even entirely reversed if the ruled-against foreign suppliers subsequently raise their US prices. This peculiarity of US law which allows foreign firms to affect future margin determinations through their own pricing decisions *de facto* allows these firms to extract rents from the US economy, analogous to quota rents. Thus some of the estimated US$4 billion US welfare gain would come from the rent loss by foreign suppliers.

That said, Gallaway *et al.* (1999) find pro-competitive trade-expansion effects from their simulated liberalization, effects which presumably would benefit supplier nations. Prusa's (1999) estimates of the trade-reducing impact of AD rulings suggests these pro-competitive effects can be quite large. He finds that AD duties reduce imports from targeted countries by 30 to 50 per cent. Interestingly, he finds very similar trade reduction even in AD cases which are settled before duties go into effect – and he even finds trade reduction in AD cases which are rejected by the US government. AD/CVD cases severely restrict market access not just once duties are on the books but much more broadly through simple investigations which never lead to any duties being collected. Inferring from the MFA evidence of Trela and Whalley and others, the fact that AD/CVD barriers sharply restrict trade suggests that these barriers generate substantial welfare losses for the targeted countries.

Is there rising opposition to globalization in the North? US policy actions

Today in the US – and many other OECD countries as well – there appears to be rising opposition to policies aimed at further liberalization of international trade, foreign direct investment and immigration. A large number of political events of the past decade suggest a marked turn away from liberalization, and many prominent trade-policy specialists have raised alarms about this shift. For example, Hufbauer (1999) scores these events as being decisively won by opponents of further globalization:

> By my score, the global Backlash forces, in the US and elsewhere, have enjoyed seven victories since the WTO agreement was reached in Marrakesh in 1994 … Against this count, the Open Market forces have achieved three important victories since the WTO was established in 1994.

Here is a brief summary of several of these events, mainly in the US. Clearly, all these events may have involved issues beyond globalization – but opposition to globalization played a role in all of them. And it should be noted that many of these events have been concerned not just with liberalization in general, but liberalization with southern countries, including many small and vulnerable ones.

China–US Trade Agreement. The most volatile US trade issue at the time of writing this manuscript was the just-passed House of Representatives vote over whether to grant permanent, normal trade relations to China. This plan is expected to pass in the Senate, but the House vote was widely regarded as too close to call in the preceding months. The American labour movement waged a massive opposition campaign, 'its biggest lobbying campaign ever on trade matters' according to the front-page story of the 14 May *New York Times* (Greenhouse 2000). For example, on 12 April, thousands of AFL-CIO members rallied on Capitol Hill and lobbied dozens of House members against the bill. Eventually it passed the House on 24 May by a 237–197 margin, but with many free-trade supporters concerned over the intensity of opposition.

The African Growth and Opportunity Act. This bill will liberalize trade with dozens of small, vulnerable countries in Africa; in particular, it proposes eliminating a 17 per cent *ad valorem* tariff on US imports of African clothing. Although this bill finally passed through Congress in May, it had been stalled for about five years, in the face of sharp opposition widely regarded as originating from the major US textile union UNITE (Union of Needleworkers, Industrial and Textile Trades Employees) and from the textile-manufacturers lobby ATMI. Friedman (2000) conjectures that the opposition stems from 'Sheer knee-jerk protectionism – even though the bill has tough measures to protect against any surge in imports from Africa, and restricts free-trade status to African countries moving toward democracy, economic reform, and real worker protection'. And the actual liberalization is modest, with tariff reductions accompanied by strict quotas: African duty-free clothing imports cannot exceed 1.5 per cent of all US textile imports in the first year of the law, with the cap rising to only 3.5 per cent after eight years.

Public protests over the 1999 WTO Ministerial Meetings in Seattle and over the 2000 IMF/World Bank Annual Meetings in Washington. At both these meetings, tens of thousands of protestors representing labour unions, environmentalists and many other interest groups severely disrupted official proceedings (much more so in Seattle). Trade was the central issue in Seattle; at the Washington IMF/Bank meetings, trade was a major theme of the protests, but so too, were issues related to international finance such as external-debt relief for highly indebted southern countries and conditionality of IMF/Bank loans. Many commentators have credited the size and severity of the Seattle protests with contributing to the failure of the WTO delegates to initiate a new round of trade negotiations. At least 30,000 AFL-CIO members marched in various protest rallies aimed against freer trade.

The US delegation is reported to have generated strong animosity among developing-country negotiators on at least three fronts: insisting that labour standards somehow enter the WTO agenda; refusing to accelerate MFA phase-outs; and refusing to countenance restrictions on US AD/CVD filings. President Clinton was widely regarded as having contributed heavily to the animosity by stating in a mid-meetings radio interview that labour standards should be included in trade accords and that trade sanctions are a legitimate tool for addressing labour-standards violations.

All this discussion of labour standards and trade policy surrounded Seattle, despite a large body of empirical evidence indicating that developing countries do not generate any tangible edge in international markets from having labour standards different from those in the North. The OECD's (1996: 105) comprehensive labour-standards study concludes, 'core labor standards do not play a significant role in shaping trade performance. The view which argues that low-standards countries will enjoy gains in export market shares to the detriment of high-standards countries appears to lack solid empirical support'. Similarly, the OECD study reports no clear connection between labour standards and foreign direct investment (FDI) decisions by North-headquartered companies.

Death of the Multilateral Agreement on Investment. In December 1998 the OECD halted its efforts to ratify among its members a new FDI treaty aimed at ensuring that host governments treat equally domestic and foreign-owned firms. It is widely believed that a major force behind the collapse of this agreement was intense lobbying efforts of nongovernmental organizations, whose tactics included posting on the Internet a smuggled draft of the treaty.

Inability to renew fast-track negotiating authority. The Trade Act of 1974 granted the President the ability to negotiate trade agreements with Congressional oversight limited to a 'yes or no' vote, without the option of amending any particular element of any agreement, within 60 days of receiving any agreement from the President. Congress renewed this Act in 1979, 1988, 1991 and 1993. But in 1997 President Clinton asked House Speaker Newt Gingrich to kill House consideration of fast-track renewal; this request came after the White House realized it did not have enough votes to win renewal. In 1998 fast-track renewal was again considered in the House; this time it came to a vote, but it was defeated 243 to 180. After these two defeats the Clinton administration did not request renewal.

Debate surrounding the 1993 Congressional NAFTA vote. The summer and fall of 1993 brought an intense national debate over whether the US should extend the Canadian–US free-trade agreement to include Mexico. Destler (1995: 217) called these discussions 'the most prominent and contentious domestic debate on trade since the Smoot–Hawley Tariff Act of 1930'. NAFTA opposition was led by Ross Perot, who as an independent candidate received 19.1 per cent of the popular vote in the 1992 Presidential election.

Increased use of AD/CVD barriers. Despite the negotiation and ongoing implementation of the Uruguay Round trade liberalizations, a large number of countries are implementing AD/CVD barriers more frequently. As stated above, Prusa (1999) documents that AD use has risen in recent years among both traditional and new users. From 1987 through 1989 there were an average of 113 AD filings worldwide each year; from 1990 through 1997 this annual average more than doubled, to 232. And Tharakan (Chapter 9, this volume) reports that from 1987 to 1997, two-thirds of AD cases filed against small, vulnerable economies were filed by new users.

New immigration restrictions. As for immigration, border enforcement policies have toughened considerably in recent years. In 1994 California voters approved Proposition 187 which denied public services such as public education and health care to illegal immigrants. Since 1997 legislation has barred the use of federal money to cover Medicaid costs for poor legal immigrants during their first five years of residence.

Is there rising opposition to globalization in the North? US policy opinions

Some of the most recent and high-profile evidence comes from the *US News and World Report* (2000) cover story 'Backlash: Behind the Anxiety Over Globalization'. The new poll supporting this story finds that only 10 per cent of Americans characterize their preferences as being a 'free trader'. In contrast, 51 per cent of respondents characterize themselves as 'fair traders', and 37 per cent as 'protectionists'. So for every one American who supports free trade there are almost nine who support some form of interventionist trade policies.

The widespread opposition to freer trade is paralleled by widespread opposition to freer immigration, too. A December 1998 *Wall Street Journal* poll reported that 58 per cent of Americans think international trade is bad for the US economy because imports hurt wages and cut jobs, versus only 32 per cent who think trade is good because it stimulates demand for US products and thereby helps create jobs. Even more starkly, 72 per cent think current levels of legal immigration into the US should not be raised because immigrants cost US jobs and increase unemployment, versus only 20 per cent who think immigration levels should be raised because immigrants fill jobs that are otherwise troublesome to fill. Scheve and Slaughter (2001a,b) report similar anti-globalization majorities in recent National Election Studies (NES) surveys. In the 1992 NES survey, of respondents expressing a preference over US trade policy, 67 per cent favoured new restrictions on US imports to help protect American jobs, versus 33 per cent who oppose such restrictions because they raise US consumer prices and hurt US exports. In the NES surveys of 1992, 1994 and 1996, only about 10 per cent of respondents stated the US should increase legal-immigration levels by any amount. In contrast, each year large majorities wanted to reduce immigration levels.

So underpinning the rising policy actions in the US against globalization appear to be a persistent preference among the majority of Americans for less global integration – more trade restrictions, fewer immigrants. What accounts for this public sentiment against globalization? The following section offers a potential explanation.

Why are northern opinions so set against globalization? The skills-preferences hypothesis

In this section I offer a hypothesis about what drives this US sentiment set against globalization: US preferences about globalization cleave mainly across skills, and for about 25 years less-skilled US workers – who still constitute the majority of the overall labour force – have experienced poor relative and real-wage performance. Let me address each part of this hypothesis in turn.

The skills-preferences cleavage in the US: theory and evidence[1]

Standard economic models offer lots of rich predictions for what underlying economic forces should drive US preferences over trade and immigration liberalization. Start with the standard assumption that preferences depend on how policy affects income for factors of production, as current factor income is a major determinant of individual economic welfare.

For trade, it is well known from standard trade theory that trade's effect on current factor income depends crucially on the degree of intersectoral factor mobility, that is, on the degree of factor specificity. In a Ricardo–Viner (RV) framework where some or all factors cannot move to other sectors, factor incomes tend to vary by industry of employment. Here, trade-liberalization-induced changes in relative product prices redistribute income across sectors rather than factors. Sectors whose product prices fall – presumably comparative-disadvantage sectors – realize income losses for their specific factors while sectors whose product prices rise – presumably comparative-advantage sectors – realize income gains for their specific factors. As a result, trade-policy preferences are determined by sector of employment.

In contrast, in a Heckscher–Ohlin (HO) trade liberalization which changes relative product prices changes relative (and possibly real) factor prices according to the Stolper–Samuelson theorem: returns tend to rise (fall) for the factors employed relatively intensively in the sectors whose relative product price rises (falls). In this model it is usually assumed that protection is received by the sectors which employ relatively intensively the factors with which the country is poorly endowed relative to the rest of the world, because in opening from autarky to free trade these factors suffer income declines. Thus a country's abundant factors support freer trade while its scarce factors oppose it.

To summarize, in HO models factors evaluate trade policy based on their factor type while in RV models factors evaluate trade policy based on their industry of employment. What do these two models predict about trade-policy preferences in the US? Many studies (e.g. Leamer 1984) have documented that the US is well endowed with more-skilled labour relative to the rest of the world. According to the HO model, then, in the US more-skilled workers should support freer trade while less-skilled workers should oppose it. In contrast, the RV model predicts that US workers employed in comparative-advantage sectors should support freer trade while those in comparative-disadvantage sectors should oppose it. Note that both models may lead to the same policy outcome – US tariffs on unskill-intensive industries – but what is crucial is the different underlying preference cleavages.[2]

What about immigration-policy preferences? Well, these will depend on the skill-mix of immigrants relative to that of natives. It is reasonable to assume

Table 8.1 Estimated effect of increasing skill levels on the probability of supporting international trade restrictions

Variables	*Model 1*	*Model 2*	*Model 3*	*Model 4*	*Model 5*	*Model 6*	*Model 7*	*Model 8*
Occupational wage	−0.074 (0.012) [−0.095, −0.053]				−0.074 (0.012) [−0.094, −0.055]	−0.074 (0.013) [−0.097, −0.054]		
Education years		−0.132 (0.015) [−0.158, −0.107]					−0.132 (0.016) [−0.158, −0.106]	−0.133 (0.016) [−0.161, −0.106]
Sector tariff			0.012 (0.012) [−0.010, 0.032]		0.011 (0.013) [−0.011, 0.032]		−0.001 (0.012) [−0.021, 0.019]	
Sector net export share				−0.014 (0.013) [−0.035, 0.008]		−0.014 (0.013) [−0.035, 0.008]		0.000 (0.013) [−0.021, 0.021]

For each of the eight estimated models, we estimated using multiple imputation with a logit specification the effect of factor and industry exposure to international trade on individuals' trade policy opinions. Here we interpret those results by presenting the impact of a one standard deviation increase in each independent variable, holding other variables constant, on the probability that the respondent supports trade restrictions. For each of these changes, we report the mean effect, the standard error of that estimate, and a 90 per cent confidence interval.

Source: Scheve and Slaughter (2001a, table 2).

Note: Change in probability of supporting trade restrictions as a result of a one standard deviation increase in the independent variable for each model. Each triple of entries in the table begins with the mean effect from 1,000 simulations of the change in probability of supporting trade restrictions due to an increase of one standard deviation from the independent variable's mean, holding all other variables constant at their means. The standard error of this estimate is reported in parentheses. Finally, a 90 per cent confidence interval for the probability change is presented in brackets.

US citizens think that current immigrant inflows increase the relative supply of less-skilled workers. Borjas *et al.* (1997: 6) report that

> on average, immigrants have fewer years of schooling than natives – a difference that has grown over the past two decades, as the mean years of schooling of the immigration population increased less rapidly than the mean years of schooling of natives … immigrant contribution to the supply of skills has become increasingly concentrated in the lower educational categories.

Given this, a wide range of standard trade and labour models predict that less-skilled (more-skilled) Americans should oppose (favour) higher US immigration levels.

So standard economic models applied to the current US experience suggest that preferences over both trade and immigration policy may very well cleave across skill groups: more-skilled workers (less-skilled) workers will be more inclined to support (oppose) liberalizing policies.[3]

Do the data bear out this prediction? Yes. Scheve and Slaughter (2001a,b) find a strong skills-preferences correlation in their analysis of stated policy preferences from the 1992, 1994 and 1996 NES surveys. Tables 8.1 and 8.2 summarize their

Table 8.2 Estimated effect of increasing skill levels on the probability of supporting immigration restrictions

Increase skill measure from mean maximum	*Year*	*Change in probability of supporting immigration restrictions*
Occupation wage	1992	−0.086 (0.031) [−0.138, −0.036]
Education years		−0.126 (0.029) [−0.174, −0.081]
Occupation wage	1994	−0.337 (0.050) [−0.416, −0.252]
Education years		−0.112 (0.019) [−0.143, −0.081]
Occupation wage	1996	−0.201 (0.047) [−0.274, −0.120]
Education years		−0.085 (0.017) [−0.113, −0.057]

Source: Scheve and Slaughter (2001b: table 3).

Note: Using the estimates obtained from regressing stated policy preferences on a number of possible correlates including skill levels, this table simulates the consequences of changing each skill measure from its mean to its maximum on the probability of supporting immigration restrictions. The mean effect is reported first, with the standard error of this estimate in parentheses followed by a 90 per cent confidence interval.

findings on this issue. These tables show simulation results based on parameter estimates of individual policy preferences (either trade or immigration) on a number of potential explanatory forces, including individual skill levels measured either in terms of educational attainment (*Education Years*) or the national average wage in that individual's occupation (*Occupation Wage*).

Table 8.1 strongly support the hypothesis that individuals' skill levels determine trade-policy preferences, while little evidence is found consistent with the hypothesis that industry of employment influences policy preferences. Across all models in Table 8.1, higher skills measured either in terms of higher occupational wage or more education is strongly correlated with lower probabilities of supporting trade restrictions. The mean estimates of probability changes are much larger (in absolute value) than those for the industry measures, which show much more ambiguous effects. These mean estimates are virtually identical whether the specification includes just a skill measure or a skill measure and an industry measure. Moreover, they all are precisely estimated: all have 90 per cent confidence intervals strictly less than zero.

Table 8.2 shows similarly strong results for the hypothesis that individuals' skill levels also determine immigration-policy preferences. All simulations in Table 8.2 show more skills to be highly correlated with lower probabilities of supporting immigration restrictions. As before, all simulated effects are precisely estimated, with 90 per cent confidence intervals strictly less than zero.

Putting the skills-preferences cleavage in context: poor recent US wage performances

Tables 8.1 and 8.2 show that less-skilled workers are much more likely to oppose US liberalization. Figure 8.1 puts this fact into the context of the recent labour-market

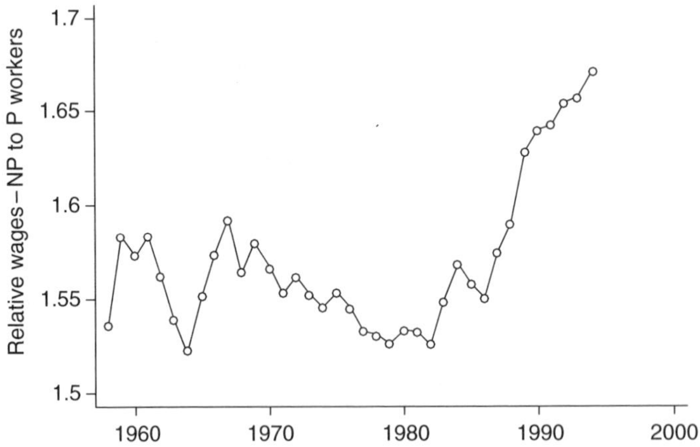

Figure 8.1 Wage inequality in US manufacturing, 1958–94.

Source: National Bureau of Economic Manufacturing Productivity Database.

Note: Skill premium is measured as the ratio of average annual wages of non-production workers to average annual wages of production workers in US manufacturing.

problems of these less-skilled US workers. This figure shows rising US wage inequality in terms of job classification. It shows for US manufacturing the average annual wage of a nonproduction worker relative to the average annual wage of a production worker. This 'skill premium' generally declined from 1958 until around 1979; since then it has risen almost continuously by about 10 per cent. This rise in the US skill premium has been going on since the late 1970s across all skill measures such as education, experience and job classification. Looking at the overall wage distribution reveals a similar picture of rising inequality. Between 1979 and 1994 the ratio of the earnings of a male worker at the ninth decile compared with one at the median rose from 1.73 to 2.04. At the same time the earnings differential between the median male worker and his counterpart in the first decile rose from 1.84 to 2.13.[4]

In addition to relative-wage changes, average real-wage growth in the US has been very sluggish since the early 1970s. Blanchflower and Slaughter (1999) report that from 1873 to 1973, US real average hourly earnings increased by about 1.9 per cent per year. But since 1973, CPI-deflated US real wages have *fallen* by about 0.4 per cent per year. Combined with the fact of rising wage inequality, this slow growth of average real wages has meant that less-skilled US workers have had close to zero or even negative real-wage growth for about 25 years. This real-wage stagnation differs sharply from earlier decades when real-wage growth was both faster and enjoyed across all groups.

And when we talk about less-skilled US workers, it is very important to remember that this category, as typically defined by labour economists, constitutes the majority of the US labour force. Table 8.3, from Johnson (1997), shows this quite clearly. Yes, the US labour force has been skill upgrading for decades. But that is a statement about the relative skill-mix of the US labour force. In absolute terms, even into the 1990s college graduates – the group typically defined as more-skilled workers – account for only about one in four US workers. The median US worker, even after 50 years of skill upgrading, is still relatively less-skilled – and this median worker has experienced poor wage performance in both real and relative terms for some 25 years.

Table 8.3 The skill-mix of the US labour force in recent decades

Year	*High-school dropouts*	*High-school graduates*	*Some college*	*College graduates*	*Relative supply*
1940	76	14	5	5	0.105
1950	66	21	7	6	0.137
1963	52	30	9	9	0.185
1970	45	34	10	11	0.217
1979	32	37	15	16	0.333
1989	23	39	17	21	0.435
1993	20	35	23	22	0.496

Source: Johnson (1997).

Notes: Each cell reports the share of the total US labour force accounted by that labour group in that year. The last column entitled 'relative supply' is a summary statistic of the US skill-mix across all labour types.

Taken together, the evidence presented in this suggestion offer a coherent picture for the strong US sentiment against globalization. Survey evidence in the US indicates that preferences over trade and immigration policies cleave strongly across skill groups. And the labour-market performance of the largest of these skill groups, relatively less-skilled workers who constitute the majority of the labour force, has been quite poor for at least two decades. Overall, it is not surprising that the median US voter wants more trade barriers and fewer immigrants.

Conclusions and implications for small, vulnerable economies

The chapter has made three related points. First, current trade barriers in the North appear to cost southern countries billions of dollars annually. Second, although some trade barriers in the North are declining under the guidance of the WTO, it appears that there is an increasing US resistance to further globalization via trade, investment and immigration liberalization. Third, this resistance may stem from the fact that less-skilled workers, who constitute the majority of the US labour force and who have been experiencing real and relative wage shortfalls for over 20 years, are much more likely to prefer less globalization.

What messages do these points carry for the integration prospects of small, vulnerable economies? If the conjecture about what drives US anti-globalization preferences is correct, one message would be that US resistance to liberalization with the South might diminish if the recent strong US economic performance continues. This resistance might also diminish if US policy discussions were to focus more on the wage problems of the less skilled.

A second, less hopeful message is that continued US liberalizations with small, vulnerable economies are likely to impart further wage pressures on the US economy. On the immigration side, Borjas (1999) examines how less-skilled US wages are likely to be pressured further if current US immigration policy is not altered to increase the skill-mix of arriving immigrants. On the trade side, Haskel and Slaughter (2000) have documented that the US tariffs remaining at the end of the Tokyo round were highest in the unskill-intensive sectors – in particular, textiles, apparel and footwear. This suggests there may be scope for future trade liberalizations – in particular, the MFA phase-outs – to pressure US unskilled wages.

A third message is that the world has been here before. The introductory chapter discusses research by economic historians highlighting that the world's protectionist outbreak from 1914 to 1945 was preceded by decades of shifting relative wages both in the US and Europe. After decades of shifting relative incomes, quite plausibly linked to globalization, many countries turned to trade and immigration restrictions. In principle, this kind of protectionist backlash could hit again.

Acknowledgements

This document draws on joint research done with Kenneth F. Scheve in Scheve and Slaughter (2001a,b). For helpful comments I thank Ki Fukasaku, Mansoob Murshed, and conference participants at the UNU/WIDER programme 'Globalization and the Obstacles to the Successful Integration of Small Vulnerable Economies'.

Notes

1 This section draws heavily from Scheve and Slaughter (2001a,b). See these studies for more complete discussions.

2 Of course, preferences may be consistent with both models, not just one. The RV model can be characterized as a short-run version of the more long-run HO model. For example, Mayer (1974) and Mussa (1974) compare wage changes in the two models, and Mussa (1978) formalizes how with intersectoral mobility costs an RV short-run gradually becomes an HO long-run. In reality, each model might be relevant over different time horizons.

3 In models without perfectly-competitive labour markets, equilibrium unemployment may give rise to policy cleavages across the employment/unemployment margin. For example, it may be the less-skilled unemployed workers demanding new trade barriers. This cleavage may be much more relevant in many European countries which have recently had much higher unemployment rates than the US.

4 Inequality has risen across education, experience and occupational groups as well as within these groups. The exact timing and magnitude of the changes vary somewhat with the measures used, but all standard measures show dramatic changes. For additional discussion, see Blanchflower and Slaughter (1999).

References

Blanchflower, D. and Slaughter, M.J. (1999) 'The Causes and Consequences of Changing Earnings Inequality', in A. Fishlow and K. Parker (eds) *Growing Apart: The Causes and Consequences of Global Wage Inequality*, New York: Council on Foreign Relations.

Borjas, G.J. (1999) *Heaven's Door: Immigration Policy and the American Economy*. Princeton, NJ: Princeton University Press.

Borjas, G.J., Freeman, R.B., and Katz, L.F. (1997) 'How Much Do Immigration and Trade Affect Labor Market Outcomes?' *Brookings Papers on Economic Activity*, 1, 1–90.

Destler, I.M. (1995) *American Trade Politics* (3rd edn). Washington, DC: Institute for International Economics.

Friedman, T.L. (2000) 'Don't Punish Africa', *New York Times*, 7 March, A31.

Gallaway, M.P., Blonigen, B.A., and Flynn, J.E. (1999) 'Welfare Costs of the US Antidumping and Countervailing Duty Laws', *Journal of International Economics*, 49, 211–44.

Greenhouse, S. (2000) 'US Labor Leaders Push Hard to Kill China Trade Bill', *New York Times*, 14 May, A1.

Haskel, J.E. and Slaughter, M.J. (2000) 'Have Falling Tariffs and Transportation Costs Raised US Wage Inequality?', National Bureau of Economic Research Working Paper No. 7539, February.

Hufbauer, G.C. (1999) 'World Trade after Seattle: Implications for the United States', *International Economics Policy Briefs*, No. 99–10. Institute for International Economics, December.

Johnson, G. (1997) 'Changes in Earnings Inequality: The Role of Demand Shifts', *Journal of Economic Perspectives*, 11(2), 41–54.

Kathuria, S., Martin, W., and Bhardwaj, A. (1999) 'Implications of MFA Abolition for South Asian Countries' (mimeo).

Leamer, E.E. (1984) *Sources of International Comparative Advantage*, Cambridge, MA: MIT Press.

Martin, W. and Winters, A. (1996) *The Uruguay Round and the Developing Countries*. Cambridge: Cambridge University Press.

Mayer, W. (1974) 'Short-Run and Long-Run Equilibrium for a Small Open Economy', *Journal of Political Economy*, 82(5), 955–67.

Mussa, M. (1974) 'Tariffs and the Distribution of Income: The Importance of Factor Specificity, Substitutability, and Intensity in the Short and Long Run', *Journal of Political Economy*, 82(6), 1191–203.

Mussa, M. (1978) 'Dynamic Adjustment in the Heckscher–Ohlin–Samuelson Model', *Journal of Political Economy*, 86, September.

National Bureau of Economic Research, Manufacturing Productivity Data Base (1997), available at www.nber.org.

Nguyen, T., Perroni, C., and Wigle, R. (1993) 'An Evaluation of the Draft Final Act of the Uruguay Round', *The Economic Journal*, 103 November, 1540–9.

Organization for Economic Cooperation and Development (1996) *Trade, Employment, and Labor Standards: A Study of Core Workers' Rights and International Trade*, Paris: OECD.

Prusa, T.J. (1999) 'On the Spread and Impact of Antidumping', National Bureau of Economic Research Working Paper No. 7404.

Scheve, K.F. and Slaughter, M.J. (2001a) 'What Determines Individual Trade-Policy Preferences?', *Journal of International Economics*, 54(2) August, 267–92.

Scheve, K.F. and Slaughter, M.J. (2001b) 'Labor Market Competition and Individual Preferences over Immigration Policy', *Review of Economics and Statistics*, 83(1), 133–45.

Trela, I. and Whalley, J. (1990) 'Global Effects of Developed Country Trade Restrictions on Textiles and Apparel', *The Economic Journal*, 100 December, 1190–205.

US News and World Report (2000) 'Backlash: Behind the Anxiety Over Globalization', 24 April.

Whalley, J. (1999) 'Note on Textiles and Apparel in the Next Trade Round' (mimeo).

9 The problem of contingent protection[1]

P.K.M. Tharakan

Introduction

The main instruments of contingent protection sanctioned by the World Trade Organization (WTO) are: anti-dumping (AD), countervailing duty (CVD) and safeguard (SG) measures. Figure 9.1 shows the share of each one of the three types of contingent protection investigations launched in 1999 by WTO members.

Among the aforesaid measures, AD requires closer scrutiny for various reasons. It accounted for more than 86 per cent of the contingent protection investigations launched in 1999. Other reasons include the ambiguity of the definition; fragility of economic rationale; the growing importance of the investigations undertaken; the recent spectacular proliferation of the mechanism among WTO members (hereafter 'members'); lack of transparency in implementation, and certain operational weaknesses. AD is now poised to become the most important trade-restricting device in the post-Uruguay Round world, see Gallaway *et al.* (1999). There is the danger that the increasing recourse to AD measures will erode the trade liberalization gains obtained through successive rounds of multilateral negotiations.

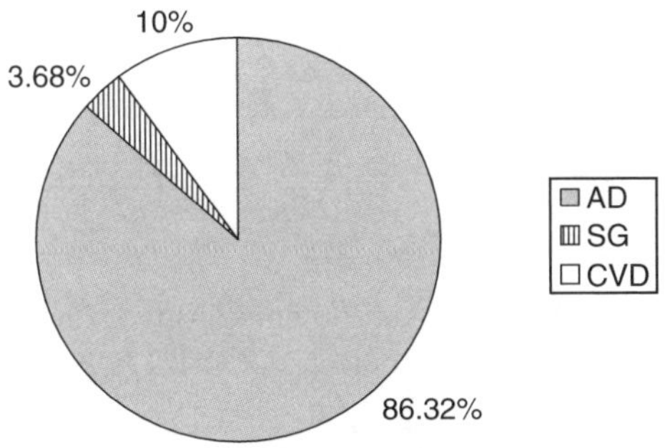

Figure 9.1 Contingent protection investigations initiated in 1999.

Source: Rowe and Maw (2000).

Notes: AD – Anti-dumping investigations; CVD – Countervailing duty investigations; SG – Safeguard investigations.

Countervailing duty investigations are less important in terms of the number of investigations undertaken. They accounted for only 10 per cent of the contingent protection measures initiated in 1999. An important distinction between the AD measures and CVD protection is that subsidies generally being the actions of governments themselves, the response such as CVDs often has a higher level of diplomatic visibility. Hence, the abuse of CVD provisions is more difficult than that of AD actions.

As far as the third instrument of contingent protection, that is, the SG provision, is concerned, its general nature and stringent preconditions make it more in conformity with the underlying principle of non-discrimination of the WTO. The Uruguay Round negotiations led to the 'Agreement on Safeguards' which introduced a certain amount of flexibility in the SG system. As I argue in this chapter, it is worthwhile considering whether the SG system could provide a building block in reforming the AD mechanism.

On the basis of the above-mentioned considerations, I shall concentrate on the AD system in this study. The plan of this chapter is as follows: the second section explains some of the conceptual and operational problems of the AD mechanism; the third section reviews the empirical results which have particular relevance for developing countries; and the fourth section proposes some policy measures to deal with the problem of contingent protection.

Some conceptual and operational problems of the anti-dumping mechanism

The conceptual and operational problems related to the AD mechanism are well known (see Deardorff 1990; Hindley 1991; Finger 1993; Tharakan 1995, 1999). According to WTO-consistent AD regulations, AD duties can be imposed only if it can be shown: (a) that dumping has taken place; and (b) that dumping has caused or is threatening to cause material injury to the like-product domestic industry. In certain jurisdictions (e.g. the EU) it must be further shown that the imposition of an AD duty is in the public interest.

Dumping

Some conceptual questions

Dumping, as defined in Article 2.1 of the WTO Anti-dumping Agreement (1994) has a narrow, technical meaning. According to Article 2.1 of WTO (1994),

> a product is considered as being dumped, i.e. introduced into the commerce of another country at less than its normal value, if the export price of the product exported from one country to another is less than the comparable price, in the ordinary course of trade, for the like product when destined for consumption in the exporting country.

The above definition contains two main notions of dumping: (i) international price discrimination (price dumping), and (ii) cost-dumping. Price dumping, or the charging of two or more different prices for a like product between two or more separated markets usually requires the following conditions: the segmentation of markets, dominant market position in the home market for the firm that dumps and a higher price elasticity of demand in the export market for the product concerned. If these conditions are satisfied, a firm might charge a lower price in the foreign market than at home in an attempt to maximize its profits. One cannot rule out the possibility of such conditions being satisfied even in cases of firms located in vulnerable, low- or middle-income economies.

While international price discrimination of the type mentioned above will fall within the scope of the definition of dumping given in Article 2 of the WTO (1994), it is difficult to provide a sound economic rationale for punitive action against such a practice. The imposition of duties generally leads to a loss in aggregate economic welfare because the diminution in the consumers' surplus will usually outweigh the domestic producers' gain from protection. The reason is that consumers will have to pay a higher price for the imported product and that the prices charged by the domestic producers of the importing country will remain high, compared to what they would have been, if there were no duties. But the reduction of the producers' surplus, and the job losses in the importing country are politically sensitive issues.

As textbooks in international economics point out (see e.g. Lindert 1991: 138–9), the optimal solution to the problems caused by the conflict between private and social costs and benefits is not trade protection. If the gains from the trade liberalization to the country exceeds the total losses incurred by some groups, it makes sense to spend part of the gains to strengthen the safety nets and adjustment tools rather than blocking the process which generates the gains. But such policies, particularly lump sum compensations to the 'losers' are not the optimal options for the political decision makers. Once paid off, the erstwhile losers will not necessarily vote for the politicians concerned in the next elections. This makes long-term protection attractive to policy makers.

During the Uruguay Round discussions on the AD question, some of the newly industrialized countries (Hong Kong, Korea and Singapore) raised the aggregate welfare problem of AD actions and insisted that the interests of the user industry as well as the cost of imposing dumping duties to the economy as a whole, must be taken into account (Kufuor 1998). But the Anti-dumping Agreement (WTO 1994) does not require the consideration of the economy-wide impact of AD actions or the state of competition in the domestic market. It only states that the users and representatives of consumer organizations should be given a hearing. The scope of the action of the consumers' organizations is limited in this context.

It is true that some of the relatively new developments in the international trade theory and industrial organization theory have provided interesting insights which question the conventional views on the welfare impact of dumping/AD. In the so-called 'strategic dumping' scenario, if the exporter's home market is foreclosed to foreign rivals, and if each independent exporters' share of their home market is of significant size relative to their scale economies, the exporters will have a cost advantage over foreign rivals, Willig (1997). Strategic dumping does not necessarily lead to the exit of rivals or the subsequent increase of prices. But it can lead to the distortion of competition and the creation of profitable market power. Nevertheless, its applicability is limited because if protection is to create significant economies of scale, home markets must be sufficiently large relative to the rest of the world's trading market. This, by definition, is unlikely in the case of firms located in 'small vulnerable economies'. However, under very special assumptions or conditions, examples in which action against price dumping is justifiable can be constructed.[2]

Cost dumping involves instances in which a seller chooses to sell below average total cost, or in some cases even below marginal costs for a certain period of time, see Trebilcock and Howse (1999) for an overview. Such sales will not be considered to be 'in the ordinary course of trade' stipulated by Article 2 of WTO (1994). Transactions which are not in the ordinary course of trade may be disregarded and the 'normal value' of the product may be constructed.

Cost dumping may or may not signal predatory price dumping, that is, low-priced exporting with the intention of driving rivals out of business in order to obtain a monopoly power in the importing market. If predatory pricing is involved, some form of corrective action would have an economic rationale because the consequent disappearance of competitive firms imply a clear welfare loss. But successful price predation requires very stringent conditions. First of all, the predator must have enough market power to recoup its price-cutting initial losses in the final stage of its predation. Further, as predation is impossible under complete information, it can occur only to the extent that the potential victim has doubts about the predatory nature of a price cut and that the predator manages to manipulate these doubts to its advantage, see Tharakan (2001). Again imperfections in the capital market have to be assumed in order to answer the question implied in the celebrated phrase of McGee (1980: 297): 'No one has yet demonstrated why predators could acquire the reserves they will need, while victims cannot'. Examples of successful international price predation by firms from small, vulnerable economies are not known. While confirmed cases of predation are rare, its occurrence cannot be ruled out. Competition authorities in certain countries have developed and deployed useful methods for detecting predation attempts. Recent empirical studies show that if such tests were applied, only a small proportion of AD complaints would have even reached the final stage of investigation.

Some operational problems

It is useful to state first in general terms, some of the problems which developing countries, particularly low-income vulnerable economies, would face at the operational level in coping with AD cases against them. New entrants into international trade in manufactures, such as low-income developing economies, may be easily perceived as carrying out dumping while the lower prices they offer might be simply due to their comparative advantage. Often, investigations can be initiated with relatively little evidence. Considerable time and expense are required by a company to defend itself against dumping allegations, Yano (1999). Firms from small, vulnerable economies are less well-equipped to cope with these difficulties and many may choose not to defend against the complaints. Lack of expertise, lack of manpower and lack of financial resources are some of the severe handicaps they face. Frequent investigations can constitute a harassment of the exporters, even if the complaints are finally rejected.

A direct comparison between the domestic price and the export price is often not possible. This could be because there may be no sales of the like product in the ordinary course of trade in the domestic market of the exporting country, or because of the particular market situation or the low volume of sales in the domestic market of the exporting country.[3] In such situations, the margin of dumping shall be determined either by comparison with the 'comparable price of the like product' exported to 'an appropriate third country' or with the cost of production in the country of origin plus a 'reasonable' amount for administrative, selling and general costs and for profits. Sales in the domestic market of the exporting country below unit costs of production plus administrative selling and general costs may be disregarded in determining normal value if made for an extended period of time in substantial quantities.[4]

A common underlying feature of the above-mentioned operational modalities is that they provide considerable discretionary power to the administrators who carry out the dumping determination. The decisions concerning questions such as those about 'comparable, like product', 'appropriate third country', 'reasonable amount for administrative, selling and general costs and profits' can all lead to finding 'dumping' where there is none, or inflate the margin of dumping. The use of 'best information available' in carrying out the calculations, and the 'strict confidentiality rule' used by some jurisdictions (e.g. the EU), leave little room for defence for defendants. As the political economy of contingent protection has amply illustrated, administrative discretion can lead to the abuse of the AD mechanism (Tharakan 1995). Developing countries risk AD findings against them because home market prices for domestically manufactured products might be higher than those in the export markets.

Injury

Some conceptual questions

Article 3 of WTO (1994) stipulates that it must be demonstrated that dumped imports, through the effects of dumping are causing injury. It cites a number of economic indicators which should be taken into account in evaluating the effect of dumping on the domestic industry. It further requires that the investigating authorities should examine many known factors other than dumped imports which at the same time could injure the domestic industry. Although injury is only one of the conditions required for imposing AD measures, most AD investigations are injury-driven, and the determination of injury is probably the weakest point in the AD system.

The like product industry in the complainants' country could manifest symptoms of injury due to a wide variety of reasons such as the nature of the market structure, lack of comparative, or competitive, advantage, mismanagement, competition from new sources of production, changes in consumer demand, rising costs of inputs, etc. It is, of course, not easy to disentangle the various causes of injury and ascribe to 'dumping' that part which it might have caused. In order to assess the effect of dumping on the like-product domestic industry, one has to ascertain how the condition of that industry would differ from its current state, had dumping not occurred, and then carry out a comparison with the factual world to determine the extent to which dumped imports change prices and/or quantities. Increased imports, allegedly dumped, could be easily seen as the cause of injury. But the effect of dumped goods on the like-product domestic industry may be insignificant. The 'strict confidentiality rule' followed in certain jurisdictions make it difficult for the respondents to verify the matter of causation. Developing countries did raise this issue at GATT (Kufuor 1998), but have not been able to obtain any concessions.

Some operational problems

I consider two specific operational aspects of injury determination which are of considerable importance to developing nations, particularly small, vulnerable countries.

Cumulation. The practice of cumulation leads to suppliers of small amounts of imports who would not otherwise have been found to be causing injury in isolation being punished. Equally important is the impulse which cumulation gives to the protectionist pressures. It encourages domestic industries not only to file more multiple country petitions, but also file more cases against countries with smaller import market shares. Research carried out by Hansen and Prusa (1996) concerning the US, and by Tharakan, Greenaway and Tharakan (1998) has shown that cumulation substantially increases the probability of an affirmative injury finding. In addition, both studies have independently confirmed that the protective effect of cumulation increases as the number of countries cumulated increases, holding import market share constant. This has come to be known as the 'super additive effect' of cumulation, and can be particularly detrimental to developing countries (see Tharakan, Vermulst and Tharakan 1998).

Absence of counterfactual estimates. The injury determination process in the AD proceedings consists of two important steps: (i) deciding whether there is evidence of material injury to the domestic like-product industry and, if so, whether it was caused by dumped imports; and (ii) measuring the margin of the said injury.

Ascertaining the existence of injury to domestic industry is done by taking into account a set of statutorily enumerated factors. They usually include: increase in the volume of 'dumped' imports; changes in the output of the domestic industry; utilization of production capacity; level of stocks; the impact on sales; changes in market share; actual or potential negative effects on cash flow; employment, wages, etc. But, as mentioned earlier, a causal relationship between the dumped imports and the injury to the domestic industry must be demonstrated. Nevertheless as Kaplan (1991) points out, the approach generally used is fundamentally flawed. The relationship between the condition of the domestic industry and the causation factors is unreliable and is never satisfactorily explained.

The measurement of injury margins raises further problems. Most jurisdictions use one or other variant of a method which measures the injury margin on the basis of comparison (after the usual adjustments) of the price of the domestic like-product and the imported product. In cases where the investigating authorities feel that the prices of the domestic producers have been depressed because of dumping, they will construct 'target prices' consisting of the full costs of the producers and a 'reasonable' or 'target' profit and compare the 'target price' with the 'dumped price'. As Tharakan *et al.* (1997) have pointed out, this will lead to an overestimation of the margin unless the entire price difference is due to dumping.

Review of the empirical evidence

General observations

Recent (April 2000) data on contingent protection compiled by Kempton and Stevenson at Rowe and Maw (2000) pertain to the year 1999, and show a massive increase in the AD activity. According to the above source, 328 AD actions were initiated by a total of twenty-two WTO members. This compares with the annual average of 232 cases per year during the preceding three years (Figure 9.2).

The composition of the countries initiating the AD cases has changed radically in recent years. Developing and newly industrialized countries are now active users of the AD mechanism. In 1998, South Africa initiated 41 cases, the USA 34 cases, India 30 cases, EU 22 cases and Brazil 16 cases. In 1999 the top 5 AD users were: EU (65 cases), India (60 cases), USA (45 cases), Australia (25 cases) and Argentina (21 cases).

The number of CVD (anti-subsidy) cases initiated by WTO members rose from 16 in 1997 to 38 in 1999. Traditionally, the US was the main user of the CVDs. The EU used to rarely make use of CVDs. But this may be changing. Out of the 38 cases opened in 1999, 18 were initiated by the EU and 10 by the US. The number of SG actions initiated have also increased in recent years, although the number involved remain small. Out of the 35 SG actions initiated during 1995–9, 10 were started by India and 7 by the US.

The most comprehensive set of empirical data on AD measures which are currently available are those compiled by the WTO Secretariat (Rules Division Anti-Dumping Measures Database). It has been subjected to extensive analysis by Miranda *et al.* (1998). Since the data-base used covers the period 1987–97, it avoids the problem of year to year fluctuations which often characterize AD measures.

As Tharakan (2001) notes, the most important fact that emerges from the WTO dataset is that the use of AD measures is no longer confined to a limited number of

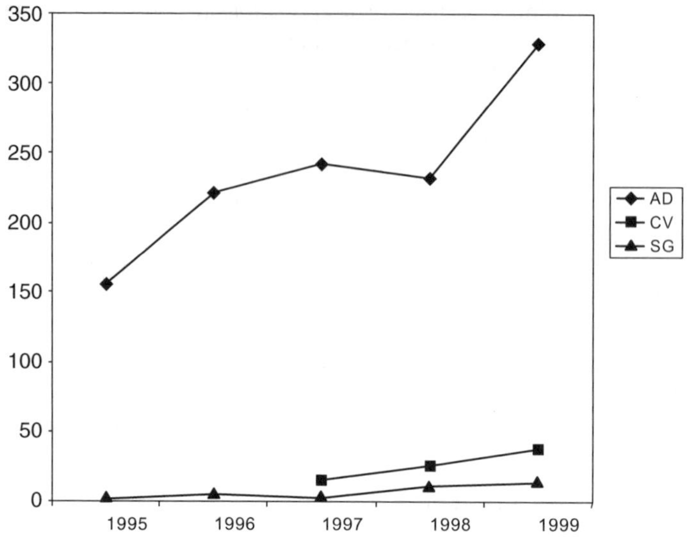

Figure 9.2 Contingent protection investigations initiated by WTO members.

Source: Rowe and Maw (2000).

Notes: AD – Anti-dumping; CVD – Countervailing duty investigations; SG – Safeguard investigations.

industrialized countries. At the beginning of the 1990s, a handful of industrialized countries (Australia, Austria, Canada, EU, Finland, Japan, New Zealand, Sweden and the US) accounted for more than 90 per cent of the total number of AD investigations initiated. But by 1997 their share of the investigations had declined to about 50 per cent. The year 1993 appears to have been a turning point, with the share of the new users (countries other than the ones mentioned above) rising sharply. This was mainly due to the large number of investigations launched by Mexico, Brazil and Argentina. The likely reason is that the firms which came under increased competition from abroad due to trade liberalization in the newly industrialized countries, like Mexico, stepped up their efforts for obtaining selective protection by filing more AD cases. The number of cases filed by the traditional users such as Australia, Canada, the EU and the US showed a decline at that time. There was some speculation that as more and more members started to use the AD system, traditional users realized the importance of reining in (Tharakan 1999). But this does not appear to be the case, as the latest available figures show that some of the traditional users like the EU have sharply increased the use of the AD mechanism.

Anti-dumping actions and the developing countries

During the 1987–97 period, out of the 807 AD investigations started against the developing countries, 26.8 per cent were initiated by other developing countries and the rest by the developed countries.

The AD investigations may lead to provisional, and subsequently definitive measures, being imposed. In some instances, the case may be terminated on the basis of an 'undertaking' provided by the respondent to limit the quantity or increase the price of the product concerned. In certain jurisdictions such as the EU, undertakings have played an important role in the past in the termination of AD cases. If no dumping or injury is found, the complaint will be rejected. But if an affirmative finding is made an AD duty may be imposed.

Out of a total of 1,034 definitive AD measures imposed by members during 1987–97, 73.6 per cent (769) were the result of decisions taken by the developed countries. In terms of numbers, these decisions affected developed and developing countries equally: 284 measures against developed countries and 283 decisions against developing countries. In addition, 194 definitive AD measures were taken against the economies in transition. Out of a total of 273 definitive AD measures imposed by the developing countries, eighty were against developed countries, eight-four against developing countries, and a clearly higher number (109) against the economies in transition.

In terms of the number of AD cases initiated and definitive measures imposed, developing countries have been targeting almost equally the developed countries and the developing world. Further, as the calculations of Miranda *et al.* (1998: 53–5) have shown, the proportion of investigations resulting in the imposition of definitive measures related to all completed investigations is higher against developing countries both in the case of the developed and developing countries.

Anti-dumping actions and small, vulnerable economies

The operational definition of small and vulnerable used here is a total GNP of US$50 billion or less, and a per capita GNP of US$800 in 1997. This includes a number of economies in transition. A total of thirty AD investigations were launched against small, vulnerable economies during 1987–97. This works out as 1.4 per cent of the total number of investigations during that period. These figures, while very small, should not be discounted, given the harassment effect of the investigations discussed above, and the scarce resources of the respondents.

Who were the plaintiffs in the AD investigations against the small, vulnerable economies? Out of the two investigations against Armenia, one was launched by Mexico, and the other by the US. The same two countries shared the two investigations against Azerbaijan. Brazil started two out of the three investigations against Bangladesh and the US started the third one. Again, Brazil was the plaintiff in the two complaints against Côte d'Ivoire. Brazil filed one case against Cuba, and Colombia filed the other. Out of the three investigations started against the Kyrgyz Republic, one was by the EU, another by Mexico, and the third was initiated by the US. Out of the three complaints against Moldova, one complaint was filed by Mexico, another one by Turkey and the third one by the US. South Africa filed the only case against Mozambique, and Costa Rica complained against Nicaragua. Sri Lanka faced two AD investigations during this period. Both of them were started by Brazil. Out of three investigations in which Tajikistan was the respondent, two were filed by Mexico and the third by the US. Mexico and the US started one investigation each against Turkmenistan, and a third complaint was filed by the EU. Vietnam faced one AD investigation by Colombia, and another by the EU. The only AD complaint against Zimbabwe was filed by South Africa.

The pattern that emerges from the above verification is sharp and clear. Two-thirds of the AD investigations against small, vulnerable economies during the period considered here were filed by developing countries defined broadly so as to include newly industrialized countries. Brazil and Mexico, together with the US lead as plaintiffs against small, vulnerable economies with each filing the same number (seven) of cases. The EU filed less than half the number of cases filed by the US against small, vulnerable economies. On the whole, one cannot escape the conclusion that the newly increased use of AD mechanism by the developing countries as well as the persistence of the US in starting investigations has worked against small, vulnerable economies.

A total of seven definitive AD measures were used against small, vulnerable economies during the period, 1987–97. Out of this, three were against Bangladesh. Kenya, the Kyrgyz Republic, Moldova and Zimbabwe all had one definitive AD measure imposed on them. Out of the three definitive measures against Bangladesh, two were imposed by Brazil, and the third by the US. The US also imposed one definitive AD measure each against Kenya and the Kyrgyz Republic. The definitive AD measure against Moldova was taken by Turkey, and the one against Zimbabwe by South Africa. So, as far as the use of definitive AD measures are concerned, the role played by the new 'developing' country users, and the traditional industrialized countries has practically the same weight, with a slight edge going to the former. But what is clear is that the proliferation of the use of the AD mechanism had adversely affected the situation of the small, vulnerable economies, although the numbers involved are small.

Anti-dumping actions and lower middle-income economies

Lower middle-income countries are those with less than US$3,150 per capita GNP. The bench-mark of vulnerability is defined here as a combination of the above-stated GNP per capita level with a GNP of US$100 billion or less in 1997. The total number of AD investigations directed against the lower income economies is about four times the number of those against the small vulnerable economies. Out of the 118 investigations, eighty-eight (72 per cent) were directed against the transition economies included in the group of lower middle-income countries (Belarus, Bulgaria, Georgia, Latvia, Lithuania, Romania, Ukraine and Uzbekistan).

The pattern in the case of the Philippines (nine cases) and Egypt (eight cases) is similar to that of the transition economies. The EU launched six out of the eight investigations against Egypt; the US and South Africa started one each. In the case of the Philippines, four of the traditional users – Australia, New Zealand, Canada and the US – together launched seven out of nine investigations. Brazil started two other investigations. But the case of Colombia is clearly different. The majority of the AD investigations against Colombia were started by the 'new' users: Argentina (two), Mexico (three) and Peru (one). In addition, Australia and the US also launched one investigation each. A total of fifty-eight definitive measures were applied against lower middle-income countries. Here two economies in transition suffered the most. Forty-four measures, representing 75.9 per cent of the actions taken against this particular category of countries were against transition economies. Romania and Ukraine together accounted for 62.1 per cent of them. The traditional users of AD measures imposed the largest number of definitive measures.

To sum up, the use of AD measures has sharply increased recently. It is no longer confined to a handful of industrialized countries. As for the definitive AD measures imposed against the small, vulnerable economies are concerned, developing and the newly industrialized countries took slightly greater number of measures than the industrialized countries. Lower middle-income countries have faced four times as many AD investigations as the small, vulnerable economies and have been subjected to a greater number of definitive measures. But in this case the traditional industrialized country users of the AD measures have been the main culprits.

Policy proposals

The AD mechanism which is increasingly being used by the WTO members is riddled with a number of conceptual and operational problems. The economic rationale of the system, except to combat 'monopolizing dumping' (particularly of the predatory kind), is open to question. At present, there is the danger that the AD practice will seriously erode the hard-won gains of multilateral trade liberalization.

There are authors who hold the view that the effect of the proliferation of AD is not altogether negative; that it might help countries – particularly developing countries – to move towards a more liberalized regime (Miranda *et al.* 1998: 64). Others argue that as long as the traditional users of the AD system continue to use it against developing countries, it is useful for developing countries 'to have the ability to hit back' (Vermulst 1997: 8).

The first best option for everyone concerned would be to dismantle the AD mechanism as a separate trade policy instrument and merge its defendable elements with the competition policy units of the members. Competition policy (anti-trust) units in some countries (like the US and the EU) have developed methods that should detect 'monopolizing dumping'. But there is likely to be no agreement on the 'best option' in the near future.[5]

The next best option, under the circumstances is to continue to question the rationale of the AD system in future multilateral negotiations, and attempt to limit its scope to predatory cases alone. At the operational level the so-called 'two-tier approach' used by the competition authorities in some countries, could be used with the necessary adjustments for detecting predatory dumping attempts. In the first stage of any investigation, the extent of the market power of the alleged predator is assessed. Only those cases in which the existence of market power is confirmed will pass on to the second stage where appropriate price–cost comparisons and other relevant factors could be taken into account.

It should be evident from what is said above, that the approach suggested is not one of pleading for special and preferential treatment for small, vulnerable economies in AD cases. Article 15 of WTO (1994) already contains the customary reference to 'the special situation of the developing country members' and need to explore 'constructive remedies' in their case. In the words of a leading specialist on AD, 'apart from any symbolic value it may have, in practical terms Article 15 is meaningless' (Palmeter 1996: 61). What is required is reform that would benefit all members; not 'special consideration' for some members in the continued functioning of a flawed system. And a reform along the lines suggested above would naturally benefit small, vulnerable economies

Given the political pressures that interest groups are likely to mount against such a reform, developing countries together with other like-minded members would be well advised to prepare 'fall-back positions'. One of the possible avenues to be explored is to replace the AD mechanism with a flexible SG system. There are those who fear that such a move could simply make AD type actions more respectable (Finger 1993: 59). Others have wondered whether in practice SG measures will always turn out to be less trade restrictive than AD measures (Miranda *et al.* 1998: 61). Nevertheless, as Messerlin and Tharakan (1999) argue, the SG system has certain merits. I shall very briefly refer to some of them here.

Article XIX of the GATT which furnishes the main international standards relating to SG,[6] allows the use of either import duties or quantitative restrictions. But it is aimed at providing 'temporary' relief from injury resulting from trade, recognizing that protection flows from the failure of the domestic industry – not from 'unfair' competition. This means that we can get away from the problem ridden procedure of 'finding dumping' and the enormous costs associated with it. The SG system is not a back-door to protection like the AD procedures. As long as an easy to use AD system remains available, even a revised SG system will remain much less used. The latter has a stronger non-discriminatory requirement. Injury has to be 'serious' as distinct from 'material' in AD cases. A certain number of concrete suggestions on this point have already been put forward in Messerlin and Tharakan (1999).

Let us now make the assumption that even the proposal for substituting a modified SG system for the AD mechanism proves to be unacceptable to the most influential WTO members. The next best option for all members – particularly small, vulnerable economies – would be to attempt to modify the current AD system. Here, the best strategy is to concentrate on those points on which common ground can be found with other members. These include the following.

If the AD instruments are to be used, give the competition authorities an official role in the investigation process, so that the contestability of the markets can be safeguarded. Hoekman and Mavroidis (1996) have elaborated this approach and have made some concrete proposals which are worth considering. Further, the injury determination process has to be seriously reformed. Priority should be given to doing away with the practice of cumulation of market shares in injury determination. This would be in the interest of all participants, particularly those with small market share. It is also important to make mandatory the use of some form of counterfactual analysis in determining the injury margins. The expertise built up by the US ITC in this field should be valuable for AD administrations in other countries that are willing to introduce such a system. A proper definition of the domestic like-product industry in accordance with economic considerations should be made mandatory and its use has to be transparent. Steps should be taken to make sure that a clearly defined public interest clause should be in place, considering not just the interests of producers.

It is evident that small, vulnerable economies do not have the necessary political clout to push through most of the proposals mentioned in this section. But by formulating proposals for reform which have a sound economic rationale and appeal to a broad spectrum of negotiating parties, the chances of safeguarding everybody's interests could be improved.

Notes

1 A fuller version of this paper is a UNU/WIDER Working Paper (see Tharakan 2000). Comments provided by Dr S. Mansoob Murshed and Dr Kiichiro Fukasaku were particularly useful in preparing this chapter.
2 For example, viewing AD legislation as the outcome of strategic interaction between governments, and using a variant of the reciprocal dumping model to characterize firm rivalry, Anderson *et al.* (1995), obtain unconventional welfare results under both Bertrand and Cournot competition for the strict enforcement of AD rules by both (implicitly all) countries.
3 A sufficient quantity must normally constitute 5 per cent or more of the sales of the product to the importing country (WTO 1994, Article 2.2, footnote 2).
4 Generally one year, but in no case less than six months. See WTO (1994 Article 2.2.1, footnote 4), and more than 20 per cent of the transactions (footnote 5).
5 One specialist guessed that it will take about forty years before AD measures are no longer actively employed (Yano 1999: 47).
6 Note also that Article XII and XVIII (B) of the GATT provided exceptions to deal with problems caused by balance of payments difficulties. Certain WTO texts and free trade area or customs union agreements provide similar instruments.

References

Anderson, S.P., Schmitt, N., and Thisse, J.-F. (1995) 'Who Benefits from Antidumping Legislation?', *Journal of International Economics*, 38(3–4), 321–37.

Deardorff, A. (1990) 'Economic Perspectives on Antidumping Law', in J.H. Jackson and E.A. Vermulst (eds), *Antidumping Law and Practice. A Comparative Study*, Henel Heupstead: Harvester Wheatsheaf, 23–9.

Finger, J.M. (1993) *Antidumping: How It Works and Who Gets Hurt*, Ann Arbor, MI: University of Michigan Press.

Gallaway, M.P., Blonigen, B.A., and Flynn, J.E. (1999) 'Welfare Costs of Antidumping and Countervailing Duty Laws', *Journal of International Economics*, 42(2), 211–44.

Hansen, W.L. and Prusa, T.J. (1996) 'Cumulation and ITC Decision-Making: The Sum of the Parts is Greater than the Whole', *Economic Inquiry*, 34(4), 746–69.

Hindley, B. (1991) 'The Economics of Dumping and Antidumping Action: Is there a Baby in the Bathwater?', in P.K.M. Tharakan (ed.), *Policy Implications of Antidumping Measures*, Amsterdam: North-Holland, 25–44.

Hoekman, B.M. and Mavroidis, P. (1996) 'Dumping, Antidumping and Antitrust', *Journal of World Trade*, 30(1), 27–52.

Kaplan, S. (1991) 'Injury and Causation in USITC Antidumping Determinations', in P.K.M. Tharakan (ed.), *Policy Implications of Antidumping Measures*, Amsterdam: North-Holland, 143–74.

Kufuor, K.O. (1998) 'The Developing Countries and the Shaping of GATT/WTO Antidumping Law', *Journal of World Trade*, 32(6), 167–96.

Lindert, P.H. (1991) *International Economics*, Homewood, IL: Irwin.

McGee, J. (1980) 'Predatory Pricing Revisited', *Journal of Law and Economics*, 23(2) 289–330.

Messerlin, P.A. and Tharakan, P.K.M. (1999) 'The Question of Contingent Protection', *The World Economy*, 22(9), 1251–70.

Miranda, J., Torres, R.A., and Ruiz, M. (1998) 'The International Use of Antidumping: 1987–1997', *Journal of World Trade*, 32(5), 5–71.

Palmeter, D.N. (1996) 'A Commentary on the WTO Anti-Dumping Code', *Journal of World Trade*, 30(4), 43–69.

Rowe and Maw (2000) 'Global Trade Protection Report 1999', compiled by Jeremy Kempton and Cliff Stevenson, London (mimeo).

Tharakan, P.K.M. (1995) 'Political Economy of Contingent Protection', *The Economic Journal*, 105(433), 1550–64.

Tharakan, P.K.M. (1999) 'Is Anti-Dumping Here to Stay?', *The World Economy*, 22(2), 179–206.

Tharakan, P.K.M. (2000) 'The Problem of Anti-Dumping Protection and Developing Country Exports', WIDER Working Paper No. 198, Helsinki, UNU/WIDER.

Tharakan, P.K.M. (2001) 'Predatory Pricing and Anti-Dumping' in G. Norman and J.-F. Thisse (eds), *Market Structure and Competition Policy: Game-Theoretic Approaches*, Cambridge: Cambridge University Press.

Tharakan, P.K.M., Greenaway, D., and Kerstens, B. (1997) 'Excess Anti-Dumping Margins in the European Union: A Matter of Questionable Injury?', University of Nottingham, CREDIT Research Paper 97/20.

Tharakan, P.K.M., Greenaway, D., and Tharakan, J. (1998) 'Cumulation and Injury Determination of the European Community in Antidumping Cases', *Weltwirtschafliches Archiv*, 134(2), 320–39.

Tharakan, P.K.M., Vermulst, E., and Tharakan, J. (1998) 'Interface Between Anti-dumping Policy and Competition Policy: A Case Study', *The World Economy*, 21(8), 1035–60.

Trebilcock, M.J. and Howse, R. (1999) *The Regulation of International Trade* (2nd edn), London and New York: Routledge.

Vermulst, E. (1997) 'Adopting and Implementing Anti-Dumping Laws: Some Suggestions for Developing Countries', *Journal of World Trade*, 31(2), 5–23.

Willig, R. (1997) 'Competition Policy and Antidumping: The Economic Effects of Antidumping Policy', Washington DC: Brookings Trade Policy Forum (mimeo).

WTO (1994) *WTO Anti-Dumping Agreement on Implementation of Article VI of the General Agreement on Tariffs and Trade 1994*, Geneva: WTO.

Yano, Katsuyuki (1999) 'Thirty Years of Being a Respondent in Antidumping Proceedings – Abuse of Economic Relief Can Have a Negative Impact on Competition Policy', *Journal of World Trade*, 33(5), 31–47.

10 WTO negotiation and accession issues

Rolf J. Langhammer and Matthias Lücke

Introduction

This chapter examines the challenge posed to vulnerable economies by the growing importance of the WTO as the main regulatory system for world trade in goods and services. In line with the focus of this volume, an economy is considered vulnerable if it is either least developed according to UNCTAD criteria or low-income[1] according to World Bank criteria. The accession of China (low-income but not least developed) to the WTO raises special problems and is therefore not discussed here (see Anderson 1997).

In an integrating world economy, sustainable economic growth in vulnerable economies (if and when it occurs) will be accompanied by growing exports of processed commodities or manufactures (see Ben-David *et al.* (2000) for the links between trade and poverty and growth). Secure market access for exports will, therefore, be more important than in the past, not least because contingent protection measures like countervailing duties and anti-dumping (AD) procedures are on the increase in major developed *and* developing countries (Tharakan, Chapter 9, this volume). At the same time, experience suggests that the preferential market access still enjoyed by many vulnerable economies is likely to be eroded if and when their exports become more competitive, and they are 'graduated' upwards by the donors. All this points to a need for greater reliance on the multilateral rules of the WTO system, including the Dispute Settlement Mechanism.

At the same time, the cost of acceding to the WTO as well as the cost of actively participating in the organization once countries have become members should not be underestimated. With the transition from GATT 1947 to the WTO Agreement, the range of issues covered by multilateral trade rules has expanded substantially (e.g. trade in services – GATS; and Trade-Related Intellectual Property Rights – TRIPS). Most of these new issues are of little relevance to improved export market access for vulnerable economies, while the implementation of the new rules involves a large administrative burden to them. This problem is particularly acute for those vulnerable economies that have been negotiating their accession to the WTO since 1995. Their trade-related policies are being scrutinized rather more closely than those of GATT 1947 members that became WTO members more or less automatically.

In this chapter the second section reviews the status of vulnerable economies *vis-à-vis* WTO membership. The third section examines the benefits and costs of WTO membership. The fourth section discusses the impact of post-Seattle developments in the WTO on vulnerable economies, particularly the future of preferential market access. The fifth section looks at ways of reducing the cost of WTO membership to vulnerable economies, especially through technical assistance and extended implementation periods. The sixth section concludes.

Country coverage: vulnerable economies and the WTO

Vulnerable economies constitute a large proportion of current non-members of the WTO. Among the thirty-two countries that had applied for WTO membership as of November 1999, five are both least developed and low-income (Cambodia, Lao People's Democratic Republic, Nepal, Sudan and Bhutan); three island states are least developed but not low-income (Western Samoa, Vanuatu and Cape Verde); and another five countries (Armenia, Azerbaijan, Moldova, China and Vietnam) are low-income economies though not least developed (Table 10.1). Of twenty-nine countries and territories that have not applied for WTO membership, nine are both least developed and low-income: Ethiopia, Yemen, Congo (Democratic Republic), Eritrea, Liberia, Somalia, Comoros, Sao Tomé & Principe, and Afghanistan. Kiribati and Tuvalu are least developed but not low-income, and Tajikistan, Turkmenistan and North Korea are low-income but not least developed.

At the same time, a total of forty-four current WTO members are either least developed or low-income economies (Table 10.2). This observation suggests that, whatever the obstacles, WTO membership is not necessarily out of the reach of vulnerable countries. However, of these WTO members, only Mongolia and the Kyrgyz Republic (both low-income but not least developed economies) have joined the WTO since 1995 and have thus gone through the lengthy process of accession negotiations under the new WTO rules.

An overview of the state of accession negotiations of vulnerable economies by November 1999 (Table 10.3) yields large differences within the group. Three countries (Armenia, Moldova and Vanuatu) had reached the most advanced stage, that is, the Draft Working Party Report, while half the candidates had not even gone through the substantive part of the process (questions and replies on the Memorandum and the documentation of all trade-related policies). In two cases, Cambodia and Sudan, the process was left pending for more than five years, obviously because of political reasons; whereas in the cases of Bhutan, Cape Verde, Lao PDR and West Samoa, applications for membership were launched only in 1998 and 1999 so that it is still too early to expect much progress in negotiations.

Table 10.1 Countries not currently members of the WTO (as of June 2000)[a]

Country	*Population (million) 1997*	*GNP per capita 1997*[b]	*Least developed (UNCTAD)*	*Low-income (1998 WDI)*	*ACP (LL: as least dev. country)*	*Diplomatic representative to international organizations in Geneva (April 1999)*
Current applicants						
CIS countries						
Armenia	3.8	560	No	Yes		Yes
Azerbaijan	7.6	510	No	Yes		Yes
Belarus	10.3	2,150				Yes
Kazakhstan	15.8	1,350				Yes
Moldova	4.3	460	No	Yes		Yes
Russian Federation	147.3	2,680				Yes
Ukraine	50.7	1,040				Yes
Uzbekistan	23.7	1,020				No
Other transition countries						
Albania	3.3	760				Yes
Bosnia and Herzegovina	2.3	c				Yes
Cambodia	10.5	300	Yes	Yes		No
China	1,227.2	860	No	Yes		Yes
Croatia	4.8	4,060				Yes
Estonia	1.5	3,360				Yes
Lao PDR	4.8	400	Yes	Yes		No
Lithuania	3.7	2,260				Yes
Macedonia, FYR	2.0	1,100				Yes
Vietnam	76.7	310	No	Yes		Yes
Other countries						
Algeria	29.3	1,500				Yes
Andorra	0.1	e				No
Bhutan	0.7	430	Yes	Yes		Yes
Cape Verde	0.4	1,090	Yes	No	Yes-LL	Yes
Lebanon	4.1	3,350				Yes
Nepal	22.3	220	Yes	Yes		Yes
Oman	2.3	d				Yes
(Western) Samoa	0.2	1,140	Yes	No	Yes-LL	No
Saudi Arabia	20.1	7,150				Yes
Seychelles	0.1	6,910			Yes	No
Sudan	27.7	290	Yes	Yes	Yes-LL	Yes
Taiwan	26.1	13,559				n/a
Tonga	0.1	1,810			Yes-LL	No
Vanuatu	0.2	1,340	Yes	No	Yes-LL	No
Observers, non-applicants						
Ethiopia	59.8	110	Yes	Yes	Yes-LL	Yes
Holy See (Vatican)	n/a	n/a				Yes
Non-observers, non-applicants						
Middle East						
Iran	60.9	1,780				Yes
Iraq	21.8	f				Yes

(Continued)

Table 10.1 (Continued)

Country	*Population (million) 1997*	*GNP per capita 1997*[b]	*Least developed (UNCTAD)*	*Low-income (1998 WDI)*	*ACP (LL: as least dev. country)*	*Diplomatic representative to international organizations in Geneva (April 1999)*
Libya	5.2	d				Yes
Syria	14.9	1,120				Yes
Yemen	16.1	270	Yes	Yes		Yes
Africa						
Congo (formerly Zaire)	46.7	110	Yes	Yes	Yes-LL	Yes
Equatorial Guinea	0.4	1,060	Yes	No	Yes-LL	No
Eritrea	3.8	230	Yes	Yes	Yes-LL	No
Liberia	2.9	c	Yes	Yes	Yes-LL	Yes
Somalia	8.8	c	Yes	Yes	Yes-LL	Yes
European and Asian transition economies						
FR Yugoslavia	10.6	f				Yes
Tajikistan	6.0	330	No	Yes		No
Turkmenistan	4.7	640	No	Yes		No
Island economies						
Bahamas	0.3	e			Yes	No
Bermuda	0.1	e				No
Cayman Islands		e				No
Comoros	0.5	400	Yes	Yes	Yes-LL	No
Federated States of Micronesia	0.1	1,920				No
Kiribati	0.1	910	Yes	No	Yes-LL	No
Marshall Islands	0.1	1,610				No
Sao Tomé & Principe	0.1	290	Yes	Yes	Yes-LL	No
Tuvalu			Yes	No	Yes-LL	No
Other countries and territories						
Afghanistan	25.0	c	Yes	Yes		Yes
North Korea	22.9	f	No	Yes		Yes
West Bank and Gaza	2.6	f				Yes

Sources: World Trade Organization for WTO membership (http://www.wto.org/wto/about/organsn6.htm); World Bank, World Development Indicators 1998 for low-income classification (http://www.worldbank. org/data/databytopic/class.htm); UNCTAD website for LDC classification (http://www.unctad.org/en/subsites/ldcs/country/sub1.htm); Geneva Networld for diplomatic representation (http://www.geneva.ch/missions.htm); Kennan and Stevens (1997) for list of ACP countries; Taiwan National Statistics (http://www.stat.gov.tw).

Notes

a In addition to the countries listed in this table, the status of many dependent territories is not entirely clear (for example, Greenland, Falkland Islands, the Channel Islands, French overseas departments). However, this is of little relevance to the present paper because these territories are not normally low-income areas.

b World Bank Atlas method except for Taiwan.

c Estimated to be low-income (US$785).

d Estimated to be upper middle-income (US$3,126 to US$9,655).

e Estimated to be high-income (US$9,656).

f Estimated to be lower middle-income (US$786 to US$3,125).

Table 10.2 Least developed or low-income WTO members (as of June 2000)

Country	*Population (million) 1997*	*GDP per capita 1997*[b]	*Least developed (UNCTAD)*	*Low-income (1998 WDI)*	*ACP (LL: as LLDS)*	*Diplomatic representative to international organizations in Geneva (April 1999)*
East and Southern Africa						
Angola	11.7	260	Yes	Yes	Yes-LL	Yes
Burundi	6.4	140	Yes	Yes	Yes-LL	Yes
Djibouti	0.6	g	Yes	No	Yes-LL	No
Kenya	28.6	340	No	Yes	Yes	Yes
Lesotho	2.0	680	Yes	Yes	Yes-LL	No
Madagascar	14.1	250	Yes	Yes	Yes-LL	Yes
Malawi	10.3	210	Yes	Yes	Yes-LL	No
Mozambique	16.6	140	Yes	Yes	Yes-LL	Yes
Rwanda	7.9	210	Yes	Yes	Yes-LL	Yes
Tanzania	31.3	210	Yes	Yes	Yes-LL	Yes
Uganda	20.3	330	Yes	Yes	Yes-LL	Yes
Zambia	9.4	370	Yes	Yes	Yes-LL	Yes
Zimbabwe	11.5	720	No	Yes	Yes	Yes
West Africa						
Benin	5.8	380	Yes	Yes	Yes-LL	No
Burkina Faso	10.5	250	Yes	Yes	Yes-LL	No
Cameroon	13.9	620	No	Yes	Yes	Yes
Central African Rep.	3.4	320	Yes	Yes	Yes-LL	No
Chad	7.2	230	Yes	Yes	Yes-LL	No
Congo	2.7	670	No	Yes	Yes	Yes
Côte d'Ivoire	14.2	710	No	Yes	Yes	No
Gambia	1.2	340	Yes	Yes	Yes-LL	Yes
Ghana	18	390	No	Yes	Yes	Yes
Guinea	6.9	550	Yes	Yes	Yes-LL	Yes
Guinea-Bissau	1.1	230	Yes	Yes	Yes-LL	No
Mali	10.3	260	Yes	Yes	Yes-LL	No
Mauritania	2.5	440	Yes	Yes	Yes-LL	No
Niger	9.8	200	Yes	Yes	Yes-LL	No
Nigeria	117.9	280	No	Yes	Yes	Yes
Senegal	8.8	540	No	Yes	Yes	Yes
Sierra Leone	4.7	160	Yes	Yes	Yes-LL	No
Togo	4.3	340	Yes	Yes	Yes-LL	No
East Asia and Pacific						
Indonesia	200.4	1,110	No	Yes		Yes
Mongolia	2.5	390	No	Yes		Yes
Myanmar	43.9	c	Yes	Yes		Yes
Solomon Islands	0.4	870	Yes	No	Yes-LL	No
South Asia						
Bangladesh	123.6	360	Yes	Yes		Yes
India	962.4	370	No	Yes		Yes

(Continued)

Table 10.2 (Continued)

Country	*Population (million) 1997*	*GDP per capita 1997*[b]	*Least developed (UNCTAD)*	*Low-income (1998 WDI)*	*ACP (LL: as LLDS)*	*Diplomatic representative to international organizations in Geneva (April 1999)*
Maldives	0.3	1,180	Yes	No		No
Pakistan	128.5	500	No	Yes		Yes
Sri Lanka	18.6	800	No	Yes		Yes
Europe and Central Asia						
Kyrgyz Republic	4.6	480	No	Yes		Yes
Americas						
Haiti	7.5	380	Yes	Yes	Yes-LL	Yes
Honduras	6.0	740	No	Yes		Yes
Nicaragua	4.7	410	No	Yes		Yes

Sources and notes as for Table 10.1.

Benefits and costs of WTO membership for vulnerable economies

Benefits

Among the candidates for WTO accession, all LDCs and LICs except Vietnam have small populations. Other common characteristics include remoteness from major markets (island and landlocked states), reliance on a small number of export goods, mostly raw materials, weak administrative capacities, great economic and ecological vulnerability, lack of market-oriented institutional infrastructure and political instability often compounded by civil disorder.

Given such characteristics, the gains from WTO membership seem to be small if they are assessed only in terms of improved market access for the traditional exports of LDCs and LICs. Raw materials mostly enjoy low or zero tariffs in OECD countries and supply bottlenecks on the LDC side (including inadequate transport facilities) seem to hamper export expansion more than policy-induced barriers on the demand side. Furthermore, although some raw material suppliers have been affected by AD procedures of major industrial countries, the LDCs are typically not price setters in the world markets of individual raw materials and, therefore, have not been targets of AD measures, quantitative restrictions or other NTBs.

Nevertheless, there are a number of good reasons for LDCs and LICs to join the WTO. First, WTO membership implies binding commitments to reforms in all trade-related policies. As the domestic reform momentum is often weak, external commitments can help reform-minded governments to contain anti-reform coalitions. This is especially important in LDCs and LICs where vested interest groups

Table 10.3 State of accession of vulnerable economies (as of November 1999)

Accession candidates	*Application received*	*Working party established*	*Memorandum*	*Questions and replies*	*Documentation (other)*	*Negotiations on goods and services*	*Draft working party report*
Armenia	November 1993	December 1993	April 1995	September 1995	1996–9	1999	August 1999
Azerbaijan	June 1997	July 1997	April 1999				
Bhutan	October 1999						
Cambodia	December 1994	December 1994	June 1999				
Cape Verde	November 1999						
Lao PDR	February 1998						
Moldova	November 1993	December 1993	September 1996	May 1997	1997–9	1998–9	October 1999
Nepal	May 1989	June 1989	February 1990; September 1998	June 1999	1998–9		
West Samoa	April 1998	July 1998					
Sudan	October 1994	October 1994	January 1999				
Vanuatu	July 1995	July 1995	November 1995	May 1996	1997–8	1997–9	November 1999
Vietnam	January 1995	January 1995	September 1996	March 1998	1998–9		

Source: WTO Document WT/ACC/7/Rev. 1.

often restrict access of private traders to so-called strategic resources, such as mineral commodities, fuels, maritime and touristic resources. Such groups collect monopoly rents from privileged access and often use resources inefficiently. By reducing the extent of state trading, these rents will be eroded.

Second, WTO membership, including the process of accession, leads to sizeable technical assistance in the form of training with respect to the legal framework of the multilateral trading system and its economic underpinnings. Such human capital is indispensable for building up institutional infrastructure, in particular, for anchoring private property rights. The WTO is institutionally prepared and financially endowed to help LDCs and LICs to form human capital in trade policy formulation and trade diplomacy that can also be used for other legal issues (for details, again, see Langhammer and Lücke 2001).

Third, the WTO is a shelter against unilateral pressure from powerful import markets. It can make conflicts transparent and offers 'good office' services embodied in the legalized dispute settlement procedure. Powerful members may be deterred from exerting unilateral pressure once the small country can publicize conflicts within the WTO. Powerful members include not only OECD countries. Countries like Bhutan and Nepal or Cambodia and Lao PDR strongly depend on economically powerful neighbours like India and Thailand, both as transit countries and trading partners.

Fourth, WTO membership encourages LDCs and LICs to open their domestic markets even if they can take a free ride under 'special and differential treatment' for a certain period. Apart from the medium-term allocative efficiency gains of import market opening in terms of lowering the implicit tax on exports and stimulating resource reallocation and export diversification, import market opening implies a concrete short-term gain: domestic prices of imports will often fall by more than the decline in import tariffs. It is well known from the experience of sub-Saharan Africa (SSA) (Yeats 1990) that countries with high tariff levels also pay higher cif-prices for imports because restrictive tariff regimes are inextricably intertwined with rent-seeking activities of traders and domestic producers.

Fifth, WTO membership will make domestic regulations more transparent to potential foreign direct investors and will enforce non-discrimination and national treatment. This may help to attract foreign direct investment.

To sum up, at first glance and given the existing export profile of LDCs and LICs, WTO membership does not seem overly urgent for them. Yet, this misses the point. Exactly because LDCs and LICs suffer from deep structural and natural barriers to international market integration, WTO membership (unlike GATT membership) can carry important positive indirect effects for human capital formation, institution building and structural reforms. By applying for membership and by actively participating in the various accession procedures, LDC and LIC governments can signal their willingness, in principle, to implement economic reforms.

Costs

Membership in the WTO is not costless. First, sovereignty is curtailed and short-term manoeuvring in trade-related policies is discouraged and also restricted, even for developing economies that invoke special and differential treatment. Politicians and interest groups who are used to acting selfishly will take the political cost involved in 'tying their hands' seriously.

Second, there are economic costs in terms of the opportunity costs of employing high-skilled personnel for the implementation of WTO commitments and active participation in WTO negotiations. Using this particularly scarce resource – provided it is available – in Geneva precludes its use at home and in other activities, perhaps including the private sector. During GATT times, the performance of skilled personnel playing in the 'theatre of trade diplomacy' was often belittled. Today, under the WTO with its multifaceted tasks to secure market access rather than only trade liberalization, there is every reason not to belittle active participation in WTO negotiations. Although training facilities are provided through external technical assistance especially for personnel from vulnerable economies (see below), the true opportunity costs arise in the aftermath of training when such personnel could likewise be employed productively in other activities. The proposal to economize on scarce human resources by bundling them regionally among several developing country partners encounters a lack of political will on the part of governments to surrender national sovereignty.

Third, a more liberal trade regime encouraged by WTO membership may expose companies in vulnerable economies to stronger competition from abroad, often from more advanced developing member states rather than from OECD countries. The result may be a short-term deterioration of the current account since higher imports due to market opening materialize faster than higher exports due to improved market access abroad. The external vulnerability of countries may thus be aggravated if the time lag between the two effects cannot be shortened. Yet, the positive experience of vulnerable economies in the WTO (for instance, recently with Mozambique until the February/March 2000 natural disaster) suggests that even these countries can benefit in the short run from market opening and rationalization of the trade regime. In any case, vulnerable economies can resort to long adjustment periods as they accede to the WTO.

Fourth, the fiscal costs of reducing import tariffs may be significant because taxes on international transactions are a major source of government revenue in many LDCs and LICs. This may be less of an issue in the early stages of trade liberalization when non-tariff barriers are tariffied and prohibitive tariffs are lowered and imports increase. In the medium- to long-run, however, substantial reductions in average tariff rates require a broadening of governments' tax bases. In the meantime, vulnerable economies may need to concentrate on reducing the dispersion of tariff protection across commodity groups in order to eliminate the resulting distortions, while reductions in the average level of protection remain limited by fiscal considerations.

Ultimately, it is the opportunity cost element of employing high-skilled personnel to deal with WTO matters which governments of vulnerable economies have to assess. Experience shows that during the GATT period, governments rated these costs as prohibitively high, and thus refrained from participation not least because the so-called principal supplier rule[2] practically excluded them from level playing field negotiations with the large trading partners. It was only during the Uruguay Round that vulnerable economies began to regard the advantages of participating in negotiations more positively.

Current trends in the multilateral trading system and vulnerable economies

Asymmetric benefits from future trade liberalization?

The fear has been expressed that the benefits from further trade liberalization will be skewed towards northern countries. For example, industrialized countries are dragging their feet over their commitment to liberalize their imports of textiles and clothing; some vulnerable economies are important suppliers of these goods. Some extensions of the GATT 1947 framework in the Uruguay Round, especially to trade in services (GATS) and TRIPS Agreement, are likely to benefit northern firms far more than southern firms. Demands for minimum standards for labour and environmental protection could burden southern countries in general and vulnerable economies in particular with short-term adjustment costs and perhaps even losses in net export revenues. The latter could arise not only because of declining exports but also because more expensive imported capital goods may be needed to meet environment standards.

However, a strong point in favour of vulnerable economies is that such changes in the WTO system cannot be implemented against their wishes because of the consensus principle for decisions in the WTO. For the time being, developing economies are united in opposing such changes, and the accession of vulnerable economies to the WTO can be expected to strengthen their position.

The future of preferential market access for vulnerable economies

For many years, LDCs and LICs have enjoyed non-reciprocal preferences under the multilateral trading system as well as under regional schemes and bilateral initiatives.

As concerns the *multilateral system*, GATT 1947, influenced by the theoretical underpinnings of the infant industry argument, allowed developing countries to deviate from GATT principles in their trade policies in order to promote their economic development (Article 18, Part IV of GATT 1947). Furthermore, under the Enabling Clause of 1979 agreed during the Tokyo Round, developing countries were granted special and differential treatment in almost all aspects of trade policies, including regional preferential arrangements that fell short of the requirements of Article 24 of GATT 1947 and also allowed longer implementation periods than for industrialized economies.

More recently, multilateral trade negotiations have sought to focus special and differential treatment on the poorest countries. In the Uruguay Round, developing countries were segmented into 'ordinary' developing countries and LDCs, with the intention to 'graduate' and eventually merge the former group with the industrialized countries and to confine special treatment to the LDCs only.

Consequently, different implementation periods for Uruguay Round commitments were agreed upon for industrialized, developing and least developed countries.

Unilateral generalized preference schemes of individual OECD countries (the so-called GSP), which were designed to facilitate developing countries' market access in processed goods, were integrated into the multilateral system through a long-term waiver. Again, LDCs were given special attention in that they were exempted from reforms that tightened GSP schemes in various OECD countries, for instance in the EU. Similar to the approach in the Uruguay Round Agreements, these reforms reduced the number of countries eligible for the GSP and restricted preferences to the poorest countries.

As regards regional preferences, the two most important schemes for many years have been the 1984 Caribbean Basin Initiative of the US operating under a waiver from GATT 1947 and the EU–ACP agreement (Lomé Convention). The latter provides extended preferences for the LDCs among the ACP members. The Fourth Lomé Convention expired in February 2000 and has been renegotiated. In the Uruguay Round, WTO members had agreed to monitor the mushrooming of preferential trading arrangements all over the world and submit existing and new arrangements to stricter WTO discipline and streamlining. Therefore, the EU proposed a long preparation (eight years) and implementation period (twelve years) toward so-called regional economic partnership zones which *de facto* would be free trade agreements between the EU and sub-regions of the ACP group. LDCs among the ACP group which are not prepared to join a partnership zone would be free to opt out.

Notwithstanding the agreement between the EU and the ACP members, reluctance to follow the EU proposals seems wide-spread among all ACP countries mainly for two reasons. First, ACP governments would lose import tariff revenues because preferences would be reciprocal (Wang and Winters 1998). Second, under reciprocal preferences ACP industries will be exposed to tougher competition from EU industries. Interestingly, the revision of the ACP Agreement has also created a conflict of interest between ACP LDCs and non-ACP LDCs since all LDC exports are eligible for duty-free entry into the EU from 2004 onward. To sustain their privileged position, ACP LDCs have requested compensation for the erosion of their preferences relative to non-ACP LDCs.

Bilateral preference schemes other than the GSP, such as those between the EU and individual Mediterranean countries, face the same fundamental challenges as multilateral and regional preferences: they are threatened by erosion due to the decline of MFN barriers and they are becoming subject to stricter screening with respect to their consistency with WTO rules.

Overall, the trend towards integrating regional and bilateral trade preferences into the multilateral system and thus making the former redundant is clear. Although LDCs will probably be the last group of WTO members to be graduated, the substitution of multilateral for regional and bilateral preferences could become a reality for them quite soon if WTO members agree on the proposed elimination of tariffs on all imports from LDCs. On the one hand, this could spur the WTO accession negotiations of those LDCs that are not yet WTO members in an effort to benefit from the tariff cuts. On the other hand, if such concessions were extended to all LDCs whether or not they are WTO members, efforts to complete the accession process could be discouraged.

Irrespective of the pace at which regional and bilateral preferences are replaced by multilateral preferences, the effectiveness of preference schemes, generally, in fostering economic growth appears doubtful. LDCs and LICs were granted the most generous and open-ended preferences in the sense that they stood at the peak of the 'pyramid of preferences' in EU and US non-reciprocal concessions (Stevens 1997). However, Harry Johnson's (1967) early critique, based on the 'protectionist (trade diverting) view on preferences', suggests that the generosity of donors went hand-in-hand either with trade diversion or with the inability of beneficiaries to transform preferences into export expansion. It is most likely that donors were fully aware of the low net trade effects and low adjustment pressure on domestic industries when they decided on the extent of their generosity. In fact, any preferences granted would probably have been curtailed if beneficiary countries had become significantly more competitive.

This sober assessment has empirical evidence on its side. Since the early 1970s, the share of LDCs and LICs in world trade of non-traditional products has remained negligible; the ACP countries' share in extra-EU imports even declined from about 7 per cent in the mid-1970s to less than 3 per cent in the mid-1990s. It is, of course, possible to argue that they did not benefit from preferences because of the low preference margins for commodities which still constitute their main exports (and traditionally face low MFN tariffs). However, this is only half of the story: even for identical primary commodities, suppliers in African LDCs and LICs performed worse than competing suppliers (Sharer 1998).

Furthermore, one needs to ask why preferential treatment did not contribute to export diversification. Many of the poorest countries, by relying on the infant industry argument, injected sizeable inefficiencies into their economies exactly by insisting on high border barriers. SSA countries, for instance, have been identified as being particularly reluctant to contribute actively to the multilateral negotiations in the Uruguay Round (Sorsa 1996; IMF 1998).

This is not to deny that external vulnerability coupled with ecological disadvantages and inadequate infrastructure has also contributed to the disappointing export performance of LDCs and LICs. However, the implicit taxation of exports through import substitution strategies would have impeded export expansion even if infrastructure bottlenecks had been removed through external assistance. Hence, supply-side inefficiencies prevented the countries from using their relatively easy access to industrialized markets.

In sum, while anchoring preferences in the WTO framework[3] has the advantage, compared with bilateral or regional schemes, of making them binding on all partners, such anchoring does not guarantee their effectiveness. This qualification is necessary because the infant industry argument as well as special and differential treatment still remain integral to the multilateral trading system (see Fukasaku, Chapter 11, this volume). It is obvious that many LDC and LIC governments do not yet appreciate how costly special treatment can be; hence, they believe that regional preferences (such as the clientelist EU–ACP Agreement) should be preserved and that stricter WTO discipline imposed upon regional preference schemes is detrimental to them. Such beliefs can only be overcome if domestic policy reforms enable LDCs to reap the gains from international integration. Without domestic reforms, LDCs and LICs will remain trapped in misleading perceptions of international integration as a zero-sum game.

Facilitating WTO accession for vulnerable economies

Technical assistance with negotiations

In recent years, various assistance programmes have been initiated by the multilateral organizations to help government officials in vulnerable economies understand and apply the rules of the game in multilateral trade negotiations. Programmes designed jointly by the UN organizations, Bretton Woods institutions, and the WTO have been funded by bilateral and multilateral donors. Such assistance is urgently needed in order to bridge the gap between the critical lack of manpower in trade diplomacy in vulnerable economies and the stock of expertise and knowledge which is required to defend country interests in increasingly sophisticated negotiations.

Two major support schemes are especially worth mentioning. First, selected vulnerable African economies who are already WTO members can benefit from a Joint Integrated Technical Assistance Programme to Selected Least Developed and Other African Countries operated by the ITC, UNCTAD and the WTO. This programme has been funded by the three institutions and thirteen donor countries which set up a Common Trust Fund. The main objectives are to establish national capacity to understand the WTO Agreements and their implications for the country, to bring policy and regulatory framework into conformity with the Agreements and to improve the country's capacity to take advantage of the Agreements through improved export readiness. By early 2000, four African LDCs (Benin, Burkina Faso, Tanzania and Uganda) and three LICs (Ghana, Ivory Coast and Kenya) together with Tunisia had participated in the programme.

Second, there is the 'Integrated Framework for Trade-Related Technical Assistance to Least Developed Countries' which is open to accession candidates. It is funded by the UN Organizations (UNCTAD, UNDP), the ITC, the two Bretton Woods Institutions and the WTO. The WTO module is targeted towards enabling officials from the accession candidates to attend WTO trade policy courses and to identify major stumbling blocks in physical and institutional infrastructure against export expansion and towards an allocatively efficient trade policy.

In the case of Bhutan, for instance, the WTO invited officials to attend trade policy courses and asked them to articulate the specific needs for support in training in a question-and-response-catalogue.[4] The result was a mixture of general adjustment issues (such as privatization), marketing, institution-building and links between the state and the private sector in the financing of physical infrastructure (to overcome the remoteness factor). These issues were mainly directed at the financing institutions rather than the WTO. Except for tariffs and import licensing, the Bhutan authorities provided little information on other trade-related policies such as those affected by the TRIMS, GATS and TRIPS Agreements. This may either demonstrate a lack of awareness or the non-existence of well-defined national policies in these areas.

Against the background of this country example, it is not surprising that an evaluation of the Integrated Framework by the donor organizations in mid-2000 finds that the programme has been largely ineffectual (BRIDGES Weekly Trade Digest, Vol. 4/2000, No. 25). While many beneficiary governments primarily looked upon the programme as a channel for obtaining additional aid for infrastructure development, donors emphasized technical assistance for policy formulation. The BRIDGES report recommends, nevertheless, that the programme be continued under the management of a single institution (the WTO) in order to achieve a better focus.

Clarifying developing or least developed country status

The availability of special and differential treatment under WTO rules raises the question of exactly which countries should benefit from it. Until 1990, eligibility for treatment as an LDC depended only on per capita income, the industry share in GDP and the literacy rate. In 1991, these were replaced by a more comprehensive set of criteria in order to account for long-term structural vulnerability and low levels of human resource development. Apart from GDP per capita and a maximum number of inhabitants, the new criteria include a so-called 'augmented physical quality of life index' APQLI, which is a composite index of life expectancy, calorie intake per capita, school enrolment ratios for primary and secondary schools, and the adult literacy rate. An 'economic diversification index' (EDI) is based on the industry–GDP ratio, industrial employment, export orientation and per capita electricity consumption. ODA–GDP ratios, vulnerability to natural disasters, access to open seas and population size of less than one million are additional criteria. Upper limits for each of the four criteria must not be exceeded, but there is flexibility concerning individual countries facing particularly difficult conditions. The essential criteria are EDI and APQLI; once both threshold levels are exceeded, a country may lose its LDC status even if its per capita GDP remains below the threshold level.

The new criteria are dynamic rather than static and point straight to the vulnerability aspect. Criteria directly addressing trade capacity such as export orientation (as part of the EDI) as well as indirect criteria such as a backward economic structure and low quality of human capital (deficiencies in literacy and nutrition) suggest, on the one hand, that these countries need special support in order to benefit from a rules-based world trading system.

On the other hand, countries with low scores on most of these criteria have failed to exploit their trade potential. Their exports are still dominated by primary commodities; they suffer from natural disadvantages and poor international market networking. For them, WTO membership is a necessary but not a sufficient condition for better participation in world trade. It is their trade potential rather than their current trade structure which makes WTO membership valuable to them. Without WTO membership and other international commitments, the momentum for economic policy reforms would be likely to remain weak.

Nevertheless, as conditions in many LICs are quite similar to LDCs, it is absolutely vital that institutional support is not confined to the LDCs in order not to drive an unreasonable wedge between the two groups. It is the advantage of the new, more flexible criteria that they focus on volatility and vulnerability rather than static measures of poverty. This should enable WTO members to define the borderline between the two groups less stringently.

Conclusion: to join or not to join the WTO?

Viewed from the current state of the integration of LDCs and LICs into the world economy, one might be inclined to view their accession to the WTO symbolic. This view would be based on the presumption that

- given their current export structure, market access for their exports cannot be significantly improved by WTO accession;
- they have only few interests in non-GATT related issues such as services, TRIPS or TRIMS and thus are GATT- rather than WTO-oriented;
- they will continue to rely on the MFN clause rather than actively participate in WTO negotiations, due to lack of personnel;
- they cannot influence WTO negotiations in a specific way due to their heterogeneity;
- the aspiration of the WTO to be taken seriously as the first universal rule-setting multilateral institution does not depend on whether some or all vulnerable economies become members.

This view relies both on past evidence about the limited role played by vulnerable economies in the multilateral trading system and on an extrapolation of a GATT-type setting into the WTO era. Both points of departure, however, must be questioned. First, many representatives of vulnerable economies see themselves either as victims of globalization or as outcasts that are bypassed by it. At the same time, they recognize that globalization calls for a wider set of global rules if cross-border externalities increase in importance and if they themselves are mainly affected by negative externalities. The only way to influence the setting of global trade rules is through membership and participation in the WTO.

Of course, the trend of being bypassed by foreign direct investment, for instance, cannot be corrected by WTO membership only. However, membership plus participation would send an important signal to capital markets that a country is serious about reforming its trade-related policies to the point of the government tying their hands by entering into internationally monitored obligations. This approach can reduce that part of economic vulnerability that is due to domestic policy volatility. At the same time, this approach will only be successful if a country 'owns' its reforms in the sense of assuming full responsibility for implementing them.

Second, the WTO, rightly or wrongly, is increasingly moving into territory not previously covered by GATT 1947. A recent example is the so-called precautionary principle: when future damages associated with the production or consumption of a good cannot be assessed today, such uncertainty (as distinct from risk) constitutes a legitimate reason to intervene in trade. Conservation of biosphere and biodiversity, protection of human and animal resources as well as good governance are already elements of multilateral treaties and impact upon trade and access conditions. Vulnerable economies are often threatened by depletion of their human, natural and physical capital stock. Hence, they are strongly affected by the new issues entering the WTO either directly or indirectly via the question of coherence between the WTO and other multilateral agreements.

WTO membership and participation should, therefore, be part of all efforts to create a greater momentum for economic development in vulnerable economies. When financial or personnel shortages are the main reason holding countries back from WTO accession or participation, public external assistance for this process will doubtless yield a high return.

Notes

1 In the following, the abbreviation LIC is used for low-income country and LDC for least developed country.
2 Under the principal supplier rule, only those partner countries negotiate with each other that can expect the largest counter concessions in exchange for their own concessions. Typically, these were the US, EU and Japan. Such a mercantilist view virtually excludes small countries from trade negotiations, whose outcomes are only extended to them indirectly through the MFN clause.
3 Interestingly, there is one type of preferential treatment for developing countries which was part of the multilateral system from the very beginning. This is the so-called Global System of Trade Preferences, a scheme among developing countries. However, it never gained importance and thus can be ignored.
4 See internet address http://www.ldcs.org/bhutan.

References

Anderson, K. (1997) 'On the Complexities of China's WTO Accession', *World Economy*, 20(6), 749–72.

Ben-David, D., Nordström, H., and Winters, L.A. (2000) *Trade, Income Disparity and Poverty*. WTO Special Studies No. 5, Geneva, available at www.wto.org.

BRIDGES (2000) *Weekly Trade Digest*, 4/2000, No. 25.

IMF (1998) 'Trade Liberalization in IMF-Supported Programs', prepared by a Staff Team led by Robert Sharer, IMF World Economic and Financial Surveys, February, Washington, DC.

Johnson, H.G. (1967) *Economic Policies towards Less Developed Countries*, London: Allen and Unwin, for Brookings Institute, Washington, DC.

Kennan, J. and Stevens C. (1997) 'From Lomé to the GSP: Implications for the ACP of Losing Lomé Trade Preferences', Institute of Development Studies, November, available at www.ids.ac.uk/ids/global/lomeox.pdf.

Langhammer, R.J. and Lücke M. (2001) 'Broadening WTO Membership: Key Accession Issues', in K. Deutsch and B. Speyer (eds), *World Trade Organization Millennium Round: Freer Trade in the Twenty First Century*, London: Routledge.

Sharer, R. (1998) 'Trade Liberalization: Building Export Competitiveness', paper presented at the Policy Dialogue 'Opening and Liberalization of Markets in Africa – A Response to Globalization?', Development Policy Forum of the German Foundation for International Development in cooperation with the German Ministry for Economic Cooperation and Development and the International Monetary Fund, 1–3 December, Berlin (mimeo).

Sorsa, P. (1996) 'The Burden of sub-Saharan African Own Commitments in the Uruguay Round. Myth or Reality?', *World Economy*, 19(3), 287–305.

Stevens, C. (1997) 'What Future for the EL's "Old" Regionalism?', Global Economic Institutions Working Paper Series 30, July, London.

Wang, Zhen-kun, L., and Winters, A. (1998) 'Africa's Role in Multilateral Trade Negotiations: Past and Future', *Journal of African Economies*, 7(1), 1–33.

World Bank (1999) *World Development Indicators 1998*, available at www.worldbank.org/data/databytopic/class.htm.

WTO (1999) 'Technical Note on the Accession Process', WT/ACC/7/Rev.1, 19 November.

Yeats, A. (1990) 'Do African Countries Pay More for Imports?: Yes', *World Bank Economic Review*, 4(1), 1–20.

11 Special and differential treatment for developing countries

Helping those who help themselves?

Kiichiro Fukasaku

Introduction

The General Agreement on Tariffs and Trade (GATT) and its successor the World Trade Organization (WTO) accord developing countries special rights and privileges that affect the ways they participate in the multilateral trading system. These special rights and privileges are collectively referred to as 'special and differential' (hereafter, S&D) treatment for developing countries. Since the early years of the GATT both developed and developing countries have long accepted the concept of S&D treatment for the latter,[1] but its orientation and emphasis have evolved over time. See, among others, Michalopoulos (2000), Whalley (1999) and WTO (1999a) for a detailed discussion of the origin and evolution of S&D treatment under the GATT–WTO trading system. Kessie (2000) also addresses the question of enforceability of the legal provisions relating to S&D treatment. Prior to the Uruguay Round of Multilateral Trade Negotiations (1986–94) it was primarily meant to accord developing countries special rights to nurture infant industries, preferential access to developed-country markets and non-reciprocity in trade negotiations. The principle of non-reciprocity allowed developing countries to opt out of MFN-based liberalization commitments. At the successful conclusion of the Uruguay Round, however, member governments adopted the 'single undertaking' approach that required both developed and developing countries to adhere to nearly the same set of agreements on trade rules. The concept of S&D treatment was then reoriented to address adjustment difficulties stemming from implementation of the WTO Agreements in many developing countries. Emphasis was also shifted to meeting the special needs of the least-developed countries (LDCs), the weakest partners in international economic relations. One of the main factors underlying this change was growing disenchantment with the development strategy based on import substitution.

Today more than 100 WTO members are developing countries, of which twenty-nine members are least-developed. Their development concerns thus must be adequately taken into account in the global trade rules. At the same time, these rules need to serve as an effective anchor for developing countries to enhance governance and implement necessary policy reforms to reap the full benefits of globalization. The traditional approach to S&D treatment has been stymied by the misconception that granting special privileges or exemptions is a 'benefit' to developing countries. This misconception has distracted the attention of policy makers from addressing the real issue: to improve effective market access for the products of primary interest to developing-country exporters and encourage good governance in economic policy making by subjecting domestic policies to multilateral discipline. Opinions differ considerably among policy makers and analysts about the future orientation of S&D treatment (see Amsden 2000; Krueger 1997; Langhammer 1999; Michalopoulos 2000; Oyejide 1998; Srinivasan 1999; Whalley 1999 and Wang and Winters 2000).

Given this background, the purpose of this chapter is to review main S&D provisions under the GATT–WTO trading system and discuss issues relating to the future of S&D treatment from the perspective of LDCs. The chapter argues that negotiations on S&D provisions in the next trade round must take the question of trade capacity building seriously. This would require WTO Members to make binding commitments to meeting the special needs of LDCs in terms of market access and technical assistance. Without such binding commitments, the effective participation of these economies in the WTO would not be guaranteed. The rest is organized as follows. The second and third sections review and highlight several key features of S&D treatment before and after the Uruguay Round, respectively. The fourth section discusses in more detail three issues – market access, trade capacity building and technical assistance – from the LDCs' point of view. Finally, the fifth section concludes.

Pre-Uruguay Round S&D treatment

A recent paper by the WTO Secretariat (WTO 1999a) presents a comprehensive list of S&D provisions that had been introduced into the GATT and then the WTO Agreements since the mid-1950s. These provisions fall into three broad categories: (a) those allowing fewer obligations or the easing of rules for developing countries; (b) those requiring positive actions in favour of developing countries; and (c) those meeting the special needs of the LDCs (Table 11.1).

From the 1950s to the 1970s the GATT embraced a variety of S&D provisions based on the traditional infant-industry argument. During this period a number of newly independent developing countries joined the GATT and wanted to nurture, through the flexible use of border measures, their domestic producers – national champions – that may have a potential competitive edge before facing up to full competition from foreign suppliers. This argument was invoked to ease the normal rules of the GATT for developing countries. The first major step in this direction was the redrafting of Article XVIII at the 1954–5 GATT Review Session. This Article allowed developing countries to withdraw tariff concessions and apply non-tariff measures under certain conditions, in order to promote a particular industry and deal with balance-of-payments difficulties. In a similar vein, the argument for infant-industry protection was further extended to the area of tariff negotiations (Article XXVIII bis) in which paragraph 3(b) recognized the needs of developing countries for a more flexible use of tariff protection for development and revenue purposes. Furthermore, the easing of normal GATT

Table 11.1 S&D treatment for developing countries under the GATT–WTO

Pre-Uruguay Round	*Post-Uruguay Round*
I. Allowing fewer obligations or the easing of rules for developing countries	
• The right to protect infant industries and to use trade measures to address BOP difficulties (Article XVIII of the 1947 GATT). • The principle of non-reciprocity (the Part IV Extension of 1965, Article XXXVI:8 and the 1979 Enabling Clause). • The right to establish, outside of Article XXIV, regional or global trade arrangements among developing countries (the 1979 Enabling Clause).	• A longer period of transition under the WTO agreements. • Greater flexibility in application of rules and disciplines under the WTO agreements.
II. Requiring positive actions in favour of developing countries	
• Preferential access to developed-country markets (the GSP, the Lomé Convention, etc.) under the legal cover of the 1979 Enabling Clause.	• Technical assistance to be made available in relevant provisions of the WTO agreements. • More favourable treatment for developing countries or their special groups in application of Safeguards, Subsidies/CV measures and Textiles and Clothing by developed countries under the WTO.
III. Meeting the special needs of LDCs	
• Special treatment of LDCs (the 1979 Enabling Clause).	• Requirement for conducting a periodic review of the special provisions in favour of LDCs and reporting to the General Council for appropriate actions (Article IV:7 of the Marrakesh Agreement Establishing the WTO). • Positive measures to be taken for LDCs in terms of market access, technical assistance and export promotion and diversification (the 1994 ministerial decision on 'Measures in Favour of Least-developed Countries').

Source: Fukasaku 2000.

rules on internal measures also began with regard to Article XVI:4 commitment (the ban of export subsidies on industrial products). When the contracting parties adopted in December 1961 the Declaration giving effect to the provisions of Article XVI:4 of GATT, this commitment was not made obligatory for developing countries.

Contracting parties took another major step in 1965 with the introduction of a special chapter on 'Trade and Development' (Part IV) into the GATT. Part IV contained provisions on the principle of non-reciprocity in trade negotiations between developed and developing countries. Article XXXVI:8 states that '[t]he developed contracting parties do not expect reciprocity for commitments made by them in trade negotiations to reduce or remove tariffs and other barriers to the trade of less-developed contracting parties'.

In the years following the introduction of Part IV, there was a growing demand for taking positive actions in favour of developing countries in terms of market access. Such demands led to the authorization of three waivers from Article I (the MFN obligation) of the GATT.

It should be noted in this conjunction that the most important area of positive action undertaken in favour of developing countries was, and has been, the GSP and other non-reciprocal trade preferences.[2] While the aggregate amount of imports covered by GSP appears to be substantial (see Table 11.3 later), the schemes suffer from a number of deficiencies and shortcomings, thereby making it difficult for LDCs to utilize such trade preferences.

Perhaps most significant as S&D treatment prior to the Uruguay Round was the 1979 Decision adopted by the contracting parties on 'Differential and More Favourable Treatment, Reciprocity and Fuller Participation of Developing Countries'. This Decision was widely known as the 'Enabling Clause' and provided a legal cover for S&D treatment in respect of the following four areas:

- preferential tariff treatment for developing countries in accordance with the GSP and other similar schemes, such as the European Commission's Lomé Convention with the ACP States;
- exemption from the Tokyo Round codes on the use of non-tariff measures (technical barriers to trade, government procurement, subsidies and countervailing duties, customs valuation, import licensing, and anti-dumping actions);
- regional or global arrangements among developing countries for the mutual reduction or elimination of tariffs and, subject to the approval of the contracting parties, non-tariff measures on products imported from each other; and
- special treatment of the LDCs as a distinct group defined by the United Nations in 'making concessions and contributions in view of their special economic situation and their development, financial and trade needs (paragraph 8)'.

As early as the 1980s, however, doubts were raised over the effectiveness of S&D treatment as a means of promoting trade and development of developing countries. The Leutwiler Report (GATT 1985), for example, commissioned in November 1983 by the then Director-General of the GATT, Arthur Dunkel recommended fifteen specific, immediate actions, one of which addressed the problem of trade and development. That recommendation reads:

> Developing countries receive special treatment in the GATT rules. But such special treatment is of limited value. Far greater emphasis should be placed on permitting and encouraging developing countries to take advantage of their competitive strengths and on integrating them more fully into the trading system, with all the appropriate rights and responsibilities that this entails.
>
> The Leutwiler Report (GATT 1985: 44)

Underlying this view was the growing recognition that developing countries may have missed the opportunity of gaining effective market access by having failed to participate actively in the Tokyo Round (1973–9) on a reciprocal basis. The tariff rates maintained by developed countries on products of export interest to developing countries, especially agricultural products, textiles and clothing and footwear, are much higher than average, and these products are either in whole or in part excluded from the GSP or subject to ceilings and other restrictions. Empirical evidence suggests that the benefits accruing from trade preferences granted to developing countries are very limited. This is why a number of developing countries decided to participate more actively in the Uruguay Round through the exchange of reciprocal tariff concessions, albeit not to the full extent.

Indeed, the Uruguay Round marked a clear departure from the traditional approach to S&D treatment, because all member governments accepted the concept of the 'single undertaking' that required both developed and developing countries to adhere to nearly the same sets of rules and obligations. Nonetheless, the WTO Agreements that resulted from the successful conclusion of the Uruguay Round do contain a variety of S&D provisions for both developing and LDCs. Put simply, the Uruguay Round constrained but did not eliminate S&D treatment.

Post-Uruguay Round S&D treatment

Now that the infant-industry argument for import substitution policy is widely disbelieved both on technical grounds (learning by doing) and because it is felt to encourage rent seeking, the justification of S&D treatment for developing countries rests primarily on the argument based on 'costs of adjustment' to market opening. As Table 11.1 indicates, much of S&D provisions are aimed at assisting developing countries in the implementation of the WTO Agreements by providing a longer period of transition, greater flexibility in application of trade rules and technical assistance. A synopsis of the main S&D provisions under the WTO Agreements is presented in Fukasaku (2000). In what follows, we highlight several salient features of these provisions.

First, developing country members are granted a longer time frame for implementation of the WTO Agreements than developed country members. The length of an initial period of transition, however, varies considerably from two years (SPS and Import Licensing), five years (TRIMS, Customs Valuation, and TRIPS), ten years (Agriculture) even up to an undetermined time (GATS). In the case of the Agreement on Subsidies and Countervailing Measures, there are specific conditions attached to the granting of a longer transition period, depending on both the specificity of countries and the nature of subsidies. On the other hand, in the case of the Agreement on Technical Barriers to Trade, there is no specific provision for a longer transition period for developing countries, perhaps due to 'generous' flexibility clauses contained in the Agreement.

Second, developing country members are accorded greater flexibility in application of most of the WTO rules and procedures. For example, both the Agreement on Agriculture and the Agreement on Subsidies and Countervailing Measures include flexibility provisions defined in a very specific manner in terms of scope and extent. On the other hand, the Agreement on TRIMS include S&D provisions of a blanket nature by providing for a further extension of an initial transition period under certain conditions. In between, developing country members may be granted 'specified, time-limited exceptions in whole or in part' from the obligations, provided that meeting these obligations is considered as inappropriate to their development, financial and trade needs (SPS and TBT) or to their administrative or financial capacities (Customs Valuation).

Third, the provision of technical assistance to developing countries has become part and parcel of S&D treatment under the WTO Agreements. It aims to assist developing country governments in their efforts to build institutional capacity needed to implement the Agreements and participate more fully in the multilateral trading system.

Fourth, the WTO Agreements include special provisions for the LDCs. The preamble to the 1994 Marrakesh Agreement Establishing the World Trade Organization recognizes that:

> [T]here is need for positive efforts designed to ensure that developing countries, and especially the least developed among them, secure a share in the growth in international trade commensurate with the needs of their economic development.

Moreover, Article IV:7 of this Agreement requests the Committee on Trade and Development to review periodically the special provisions for LDCs and report to the General Council for appropriate action. More specifically, the special provisions for LDCs include (a) complete or partial exemptions from commitments and obligations (Agriculture, Subsidies and Countervailing Measures, and TRIPS), (b) a further extension of transition periods (SPS and TRIMS), and (c) differential and more favourable treatment (Textiles and Clothing, TBT, Import Licensing, GATS, TRIPS and Dispute Settlement).

From the above review it would be safe to make two general observations. One is that the poor understanding of the adjustment process of the developing countries, especially that of the LDCs, has led to the *ad hoc* nature of S&D provisions that allow a longer period of transition and greater flexibility in application of rules. A priori, there is little reason to believe that these countries can manage to build institutional capacity sufficiently rapidly to comply fully with WTO obligations within the agreed time frame. In other words, there is a serious risk that, as was the case in the past, many poor countries would be kept outside the normal rules of the WTO, which would undermine their own initiatives to liberalize trade regimes and sustain domestic policy reforms.

Both the Committee on Trade and Development and the Sub-Committee on Least-Developed Countries have recently reviewed problems relating to implementation of the WTO Agreements and relevant S&D provisions (WTO 2000b,c). These reviews have uncovered a wide range of problems, many of which are closely linked to their own capacity to implement WTO obligations, and their concerns can be boiled down to three basic questions from the LDCs' point of view: (a) Has S&D treatment in terms of market access resulted in increasing trade opportunities for LDCs? (b) Has S&D treatment addressed squarely the LDCs' limited capacity for trade? and (c) Has technical assistance been effectively delivered to tackle the specific needs of LDCs? In the next section we will discuss these questions in more detail.

Issues relating to the future of S&D treatment

Market access

Four market access problems are of direct concern for the LDCs. First, even after the full implementation of Uruguay Round tariff concessions, tariff peaks (say, exceeding 12 per cent *ad valorem*) maintained by developed country members in such sectors as textiles and clothing and footwear continue to affect LDC exports, due to a high concentration of their manufactured exports in these sectors. In the case of agriculture, border measures such as quotas and variable levies have been converted to tariffs following the Uruguay Round Agreement on Agriculture. In most cases, such 'tariffication' process has resulted in the establishment of tariff rate quotas, involving very high rates (OECD 1999).

Second, the post-Uruguay Round bound tariff rates in major developing countries stay at high levels. OECD (1999) shows that the overall mean bound rate in the thirteen non-OECD countries remain as high as 43 per cent, compared with 5 per cent in Quad-4 countries and 19 per cent in other OECD countries (Table 11.2). The level of applied rates maintained by developing member countries against LDC exports is also generally high in all major product groups other than fuels and minerals (WTO 2000a).

Third, the practice of tariff escalation – sharply rising tariffs from low or zero duties on raw materials to higher duties on intermediate products and in some cases to peak tariffs on finished products – remains prevalent in such sectors as metals, textiles and clothing, and leather, rubber and wood products. And its impact varies considerably by both product and market (OECD 1997).

Table 11.2 Post-Uruguay Round simple mean bound tariff rates (%)

	All lines	*Agriculture*	*Industry*
Quad-4 OECD Countries[a]	5	10	4
Other OECD Countries[b]	19	40	18
13 non-OECD Countries[c]	43	63	39

Source: Dessus *et al.* (1999: table 1).

Notes

a Canada, EU-15, Japan and the United States.

b Australia, Czech Republic, Hungary, Iceland, Republic of Korea, Mexico, New Zealand, Norway, Poland, Switzerland, and Turkey.

c Argentina, Bangladesh, Brazil, Colombia, India, Indonesia, Malaysia, Romania, Sri Lanka, Thailand, the Philippines, Tunisia, and Venezuela.

Fourth, the benefit of trade preferences for LDCs under the GSPs and other non-reciprocal schemes has declined significantly as a result of continuing trade liberalization on an MFN basis. For instance, Amjadi *et al.* (1996) show that pre-Uruguay Round MFN tariff rates in three major OECD markets (the European Union, Japan and the US) on the imports of non-oil products from sub-Saharan African countries averaged 4.56 per cent and the margin of preferences was estimated at 4.25 percentage points. As a result of the Uruguay Round, these figures fell to 2.68 and 2.47, respectively. Therefore, the Uruguay Round resulted in a reduction of preference margins by 1.78 percentage points, some 40 per cent decline from the pre-Uruguay Round situation. Since multilateral tariff liberalization in industrial and agricultural products is most likely to continue in the next trade round, the margin of preferences will be further squeezed.

Table 11.3 presents a summary of GSP operations during the period of 1976–96 with regard to Quad-4 countries. It shows that the GSP schemes cover roughly half of dutiable imports into these markets and that the average utilization ratio of GSP remained at a low range of 50–5 per cent in the 1990s. It also highlights that the GSP imports from LDC beneficiaries accounted for less than 2 per cent of total GSP imports from all beneficiaries in 1996. It has been well documented, see OECD 1997; Onguglo 1999; UNCTAD 1998 and Wang and Winters 1998, that the operation of these preferential schemes suffers from a number of deficiencies.

1 The benefits of privileged market access have been concentrated in only a few countries and a few products.
2 These schemes suffer from many complex procedural requirements with respect to the rules of origin, quotas and ceilings.
3 There are mismatches between the exports of beneficiaries and the coverage of preferences, due to the exclusion of many sensitive products.

Table 11.3 Imports of Quad-4 OECD countries from beneficiaries of their GSP schemes, 1976–96 (US$ million and %)

	Total imports *[1]*	*MFN dutiable imports* *[2]*	*GSP imports (covered)* *[3]*	*GSP imports (received)* *[4]*	*Coverage ratio (%) [3]/[2]* *[5]*	*Utilization ratio (%) [4]/[3]* *[6]*
Quad-4[a]						
1976	126,152	47,266	21,364	9,277	45	43
1981	206,440	100,105	50,593	33,519	51	66
1991	376,278	255,421	120,528	58,637	47	49
1996	584,654	350,605	178,254	99,821	51	56
Memo item						
Imports from LDCs only						
1996	9,956	7,451	2,985	1,518	40	51
(% Share of total)	1.7	2.1	1.7	1.5	n/a	n/a

Sources: Compiled from OECD (1997: table 6) and UNCTAD (1998: Statistical Annexe, tables 1 and 2).

Notes

a Quad-4 OECD Countries: Canada, the European Union, Japan and the United States.

n/a not applicable.

Some efforts have been made to improve the current schemes of non-reciprocal preferences. For instance, recent revisions in the GSP schemes in the Quad-4 countries include duty-free access for a large number of industrial products and tariff reductions on agricultural products.[3] Thus, the non-reciprocal preference schemes may still play a role for some time in promoting exports from LDCs in those sectors in which import protection in developed-country markets remains high even after the implementation of Uruguay Round tariff concessions. These include, in particular, a number of politically sensitive sectors, such as certain agricultural products, processed food and textiles and clothing. However, the perceived benefits from trade preferences must be weighed against the potential costs arising from uncertainties in market access conditions inherent to the non-reciprocal nature of such schemes and disincentives for seeking MFN-based trade liberalization in the longer term.

In addition, the granting of non-reciprocal trade preferences to developing countries other than the LDCs has become less attractive as a policy option for the preference-giving countries. The recent experience of the European Union negotiating a successor agreement to the Lomé IV Convention *vis-à-vis* the ACP States is testimony to this point. More recently, the Quad-4 and several other member countries of the WTO have tabled a joint proposal for granting duty- and quota-free access to 'essentially all' goods from the LDCs as part of the preparatory steps to the next trade round (see *Financial Times*, 4 May 2000). If this proposal is genuinely to cover all sensitive products without any restrictions or conditions, then it will make existing non-reciprocal trade preferences redundant for the LDCs.

Trade capacity building

In order to reap the full benefits of further trade liberalization on a global scale, LDCs are increasingly aware of the importance of trade capacity building in their own economies. While the concept of trade capacity building is a very complex one, this can be thought of as comprising three dimensions:

1 capacity to negotiate with their trading and investment partners;
2 capacity to implement trade and investment rules; and
3 capacity to compete in the international market.

On the first point, Blackhurst *et al.* (1999) point to generally poor capacity of African members dealing with WTO issues in Geneva. What is more important is to have proper knowledge about what is at stake in WTO negotiations and give a priority to trade rather than political diplomacy in budget allocation. On the second point, Finger and Schuler (1999) highlight the high costs of implementing the reform programmes necessary to make domestic regulations in conformity with WTO rules.

From the analytical point of view, the third dimension of trade capacity building is probably the most problematic. In the context of sub-Saharan Africa's dismal economic performance over the past decade, there is a growing body of literature on why Africa has failed to export and grow as much as Asia or Latin America, despite more than a decade of macroeconomic and structural reforms (see Amjadi *et al.* 1996; Berthélemy and Söderling 2000; Bloom and Sachs 1998; Gugerty and Stern 1996; Oyejide 1998; OECD 1997; UNCTAD 1999; Rodrik 1998; Wang and Winters 1998; and Wood and Mayer 1998).

One of the main concerns for policy makers in this region has been a heavy dependence on exports of a few commodities (mostly, agricultural and mineral products) and services as the principal earner of hard currencies (see Annexe Table 11.A1). In a recent study of growth performance in six African countries,[4] Berthélemy and Söderling (2000) argue that the promotion of a greater degree of diversification is necessary to sustain long-term growth. This is because diversification can increase productivity by constantly introducing new, higher quality goods in an economy, on the one hand, and by spreading investment risks over a wider portfolio, on the other. In Africa, there are cases in which diversification based on dirigiste economic policies led to stagnation rather than growth (for example, Algeria, Côte d'Ivoire, and Senegal). On the other hand, one of the best known counter-examples is Mauritius, which has achieved a significant degree of diversification so as to withstand terms of trade shocks, encourage foreign investment, increase employment and accelerate the pace of growth. Another interesting example is Botswana, which has demonstrated that with a right set of policies the development of non-traditional exports can be compatible with the exploitation of a rich endowment in natural resources. There is thus a need for clarification regarding exactly what is meant by export diversification as a development strategy, since broadening the range of exportable goods and services would appear to contradict the notion of trade specialization based on comparative advantage (Mayer 1996).

In this conjunction it is important to stress that direct state intervention to promote exports has been increasingly restricted by the WTO Agreements. For instance, the use of subsidies for export promotion of industrial products has been brought under multilateral disciplines and surveillance under the Agreement on Subsidies and Countervailing Measures. Only the LDCs and certain developing countries whose per capita income is below US$1000 – the so-called Annexe VII countries – are exempted from the obligation to phase out export subsidies in eight years from 1995 (Article 27.2(a)). The case for export subsidies is empirically dubious (Panagariya 2000). S&D treatment of this sort provides little incentive for LDCs' policy makers to reform their own subsidy programmes and might help to lock them in the *status quo*. With respect to measures for export promotion and diversification, focus should be shifted away from sector-specific policies towards more generic policies, such as infrastructure development, human capital formation, customs and other administrative reforms.

Technical assistance

Technical assistance has come to play an important role as an instrument for meeting the special needs of the LDCs.[5] The first major effort to this end was undertaken in 1996 when the first WTO Ministerial Conference was held in Singapore. On this occasion, WTO Ministers adopted an Integrated Plan of Action for the Least-Developed Countries with the aim of improving the overall capacity of these economies to respond to the challenges and opportunities offered by the multilateral trading system. Pursuant to the Plan of Action, it was agreed by the WTO and five other international agencies (IMF, ITC, UNCTAD, UNDP and World Bank) to establish an Integrated Framework for providing trade-related technical assistance to LDCs, including human and institutional capacity-building. The inventory of existing trade-related projects suggests a wide rage of activities such as efforts to overcome supply constraints, trade promotion and trade support services, improving product quality standards and technical assistance towards the compliance with WTO Agreements.[6]

The Integrated Framework has been applied on a case-by-case basis to meet the development needs identified by individual LDCs through round-table meetings with donors and international agencies. This approach was endorsed by the High-Level Meeting on Integrated Initiatives for Least-Developed Countries' Trade Development, organized by the WTO in October 1997 and extended beyond the six original organizations to involve sixteen other multilateral and regional agencies and twenty-two bilateral donors.

At present, the mandated review of the Integrated Framework is being undertaken by the six core agencies. According to a recent review conducted by the WTO (2000d), concerns have been raised over the slow pace of implementation of the Integrated Framework. Another reason for concern is simply the lack of operational funds necessary to carry forward individual activities already identified. This has led some commentators to argue that 'as other negotiated commitments are binding, technical assistance commitments should be binding too' (Wang and Winters 2000: 16).

Conclusions

There is a fairly broad consensus that the past approach to S&D treatment based on the concept of non-reciprocity was disappointing, as it legitimized the 'free riding' on the part of developing countries and provided little incentive for them to participate more fully in the multilateral trading system. The 'single-undertaking' approach adopted at the Uruguay Round has rectified this problem to a certain extent but largely ignored the problem of domestic capacity constraints facing many developing countries in implementing the WTO Agreements. There is a serious risk that a large number of developing countries will be left out of the normal rules and procedures of the WTO.

Recently it has been argued that S&D treatment should be extended beyond the UN-sanctioned classification of LDCs to various groups of developing countries, such as small, island or land-locked developing countries. Given the *ad hoc* nature of some of the criteria for eligibility of S&D treatment, more discussions and negotiations would be required to identify what factors make a country a 'special case' for S&D treatment (see Read 2000).

Does S&D treatment help those who help themselves? The review and discussion of this chapter suggests that there is an urgent need for positive actions in the areas of both market access and technical assistance in the context of the next trade round. Without such actions, S&D treatment would hardly be relevant for the trade development of LDCs. More specifically, the following three points are worth noting:

- Granting duty- and quota-free access to all products from LDCs remains a top priority for international policy action, as the benefit of non-reciprocal trade preferences is very limited for them.
- The implementation of the WTO Agreements needs to be reassessed country by country, taking into account LDCs' development needs and the administrative and financial constraints.
- Binding technical assistance commitments are necessary to make S&D provisions more responsive to the specific needs of LDCs.

Acknowledgements

The author is grateful to Ulrich Hiemenz as well as Jörg Mayer, S. Mansoob Murshed, Robert Read, Matt Slaughter and other seminar participants for helpful comments and suggestions. A longer version of this chapter can be found in a UNU/WIDER working paper, Fukasaku (2000). The opinions expressed in this chapter are, however, those of the author alone, and do not reflect those of the organization to which the author belongs. All correspondence regarding this chapter should be addressed to kiichiro.fukasaku@oecd.org

Notes

1 The original GATT, however, strictly observed the non-discrimination principle despite the fact that eleven of the original twenty-three contracting parties were considered developing countries (Kessie 2000).

2 At present there are fifteen GSP schemes in operation offered by twenty-nine preference-giving countries, including the fifteen member countries of the European Union. Other non-reciprocal trade preferences are provided by the European Union to the ACP countries, by the US and Canada to Caribbean and Central American countries, by the US to Andean countries and by Australia and New Zealand to Pacific Island countries (UNCTAD 1998). See also Onguglo (1999).

3 Moreover, a number of developing countries, such as Egypt, Malaysia and Thailand, announced in October 1997 offers on non-reciprocal trade preferences to LDCs in the context of the Global System of Trade Preferences among Developing Countries (GSTP) – south–south preferences (Onguglo 1999).

4 Burkina Faso, Côte d'Ivoire, Ghana, Mali, Tanzania and Uganda.

5 Since 1955 the GATT Secretariat has been providing regular trade-policy courses for government officials from developing member countries.

6 See the Internet site of the Integrated Framework: http://www.ldcs.org.

References

Amjadi, A., Reincke, U., and Yeats, A.J. (1996) 'Did External Barriers Cause the Marginalization of sub-Saharan Africa in World Trade?', World Bank Discussion Paper No. 348, Washington, DC: World Bank.

Amsden, A.H. (2000) 'Industrialization under New WTO Law', Paper prepared for High-Level Round Table on Trade and Development: Directions for the Twenty-first Century, UNCTAD X, Bangkok, 12 February.

Berthélemy, J.-C. and Söderling, L. (2000) 'Emerging Africa: Is it Possible?', Paper presented at the 1st International Forum on African Perspectives, jointly organized by the African Development Bank and the OECD Development Centre, Paris, 3–4 February.

Blackhurst, R., Lyakurwa, B., and Oyejide, A. (1999) 'Improving African Participation in the WTO', Paper commissioned by the World Bank for a Conference at the WTO on 20–21 September.

Bloom, D. and Sachs, J.D. (1998) 'Geography, Demography, and Economic Growth in Africa', *Brookings Papers on Economic Activity*, 2, 207–95.

Dessus, S., Fukasaku, K., and Safadi, R. (1999) 'Multilateral Tariff Liberalization and the Developing Countries', Policy Brief No. 18, Paris: OECD Development Centre.

Finger, J.M. and Schuler, P. (1999) 'Implementation of Uruguay Round Commitments: The Development Challenge', Policy Research Working Paper No. 2215, Washington, DC: World Bank.

Fukasaku, K. (2000) 'Special and Differential Treatment for Developing Countries: Does it Help Those Who Help Themselves?', WIDER Working Paper No. 197, Helsinki: UNU/WIDER.

GATT (1985). 'Trade Policies for a Better Future' (The Leutwiler Report), March, Geneva.

Gugerty, M.K. and Stern, J. (1996) 'Structural Barriers to Trade in Africa', HIID Development Discussion Paper No. 561.

Kessie, E. (2000) 'Enforceability of the Legal Provisions Relating to Special and Differential Treatment under the WTO Agreements', Paper prepared for WTO seminar on Special and Differential Treatment for Developing Countries, 7 March, Geneva.

Krueger, A.O. (1997) 'Trade Policy and Economic Development: How We Learn', *American Economic Review*, 87(1), 1–22.

Langhammer, R.J. (1999) 'The WTO and the Millennium Round: Between Standstill and Leapfrog', Kiel Discussion Paper No. 352, Kiel: Kiel Institute for World Economy.

Mayer, J. (1996) 'Learning Sequences and Structural Diversification in Developing Countries', *The Journal of Development Studies*, 33, 210–29.

Michalopoulos, C. (2000) 'Trade and Development in the GATT and WTO: The Role of Special and Differential Treatment for Developing Countries', Paper prepared for WTO seminar on Special and Differential Treatment for Developing Countries, 7 March, Geneva.

OECD (1997) 'Market Access for the Least Developed Countries: Where are the Obstacles?', OCDE/GD (97)174, Paris: OECD.

OECD (1999) *Post-Uruguay Round Tariff Regimes: Achievements and Outlook*, Paris: OECD.

Onguglo, B.F. (1999) 'Developing Countries and Unilateral Trade Preferences in the New International Trading System', in M.R. Mendonza, P. Low and B. Kotchwar (eds), *Trade Rules in the Making: Challenges in Regional and Multilateral Negotiations*, Washington, DC: Brookings Institute and Organization of American States.

Oyejide, T.A. (1998) 'Costs and Benefits of "Special and Differential" Treatment for Developing Countries in GATT/WTO: An African Perspective', AERC Collaborative Research Project on Africa and the World Trading System, revised draft, February.

Panagariya, A. (2000) 'Evaluating the Case for Export Subsidies', Policy Research Working Paper No. 2276, Washington, DC: World Bank.

Read, R. (2000) 'The Case for Special and Differential Treatment of Small Island Developing Countries (SIDS) under the WTO' (mimeo).

Rodrik, D. (1998) 'Trade Policy and Economic Performance in sub-Saharan Africa', NBER Working Paper No. 6562, May, Cambridge, MA: National Bureau of Economic Research.

Srinivasan, T.N. (1999) 'Developing Countries in the World Trading System: From GATT 1947 to the Third Ministerial Meeting of WTO 1999', *The World Economy*, 22(8), 1047–64.

UNCTAD (1998) 'Ways and Means of Enhancing the Utilization of Trade Preferences by Developing Countries, in particular LDCs, as well as Further Ways of Expanding Preferences', TD/B/COM.1/20 and TD/B/COM.1/20/Add.1, New York and Geneva: UNCTAD.

UNCTAD (1999) *The Least Developed Countries: 1999 Report*, New York and Geneva: United Nations.

Wang Zhen K. and Winters, L.A. (1998) 'Africa's Role in Multilateral Trade Negotiations: Past and Future', *Journal of African Economies*, 7(Suppl. 1), 37–69.

Wang Zhen K. and Winters, L.A. (2000) 'Putting "Humpty" Together Again: Including Developing Countries in a Consensus for the WTO', CEPR Policy Paper No. 4, London: Centre for Economic Policy Research.

Whalley, J. (1999) 'Special and Differential Treatment in the Millennium Round', *The World Economy*, 22(8), 1065–93.

Wood, A. and Mayer, J. (1998) 'Africa's Export Structure in a Comparative Perspective', Study No. 4: African Development in a Comparative Perspective, Geneva: UNCTAD.

World Bank (1999) *World Development Indicators*, Washington, DC: World Bank.

World Bank (2000) *Global Economic Prospects and the Developing Countries*, Washington, DC: World Bank.

WTO (1999a) 'Developing Countries and the Multilateral Trading System: Past and Present', Background document prepared for High-Level Symposium on Trade and Development, 17–18 March, Geneva: WTO.

WTO (1999b) *Guide to the Uruguay Round Agreements*, The Hague: Kluwer Law International.

WTO (2000a) 'Market Access for Least-Developed Countries WTO Members', WT/COMTD/LDC/W/17, 25 January, Geneva: WTO.

WTO (2000b) 'Implementation of WTO Agreements: Possible Assistance to Least-Developed Countries', WT/COMTD/LDC/W/19, 26 January, Geneva: WTO.

WTO (2000c) 'Concerns Regarding Special and Differential Treatment Provisions in WTO Agreements and Decisions', WT/COMTD/W/66, 16 February, Geneva: WTO.

WTO (2000d) 'Integrated Framework for Trade-Related Assistance to Least-Developed Countries', WT/COMTD/LDC/7, 23 February, Geneva: WTO.

Annexe

Table 11.A1 Export profiles of LDCs in sub-Saharan Africa

Country	*1st export product (% of merchandise exports)*	*2nd export product*	*1st export service (% of service exports)*	*Export ratio of goods to services*
Type 1: Predominantly merchandise exporters (exports of goods are larger than exports of services)				
Type 1A: Highly dependent on agricultural exports				
Sao Tomé & Principe	Cocoa (96.4)	Copra (…)	Travel (56.7)	2.0
Guinea-Bissau	Cashew nuts (85.8)	Wood (6.3)	—	—
Burundi	Coffee (80.7)	Tea (7.8)	Transport (18.4)	9.7
Rwanda	Coffee (74.4)	Tea (10.0)	Travel (16.8)	1.6
Uganda	Coffee (69.0)	Cotton (2.2)	Travel (82.0)	3.5
Ethiopia	Coffee (63.5)	Hides (13.2)	Air transport (45.5)	1.4
Malawi	Tobacco (63.2)	Tea (6.7)	Transport (58.6)	16.5
Chad	Cotton (59.4)	Live cattle (10.9)	Travel (21.9)	2.5
Mauritania	Fish (56.3)	Iron ore (41.8)	Travel (40.1)	17.0
Mali	Cotton fibre (55.5)	Live animals (19.8)	Travel (32.2)	6.9
Benin	Cotton (49.6)	Petroleum (2.9)	Transport (56.8)	2.9
Burkina Faso	Cotton (42.2)	Live animals (18.9)	Travel (32.7)	3.9
Somalia	Live animals (40.0)	Bananas (6.9)	—	—
Togo	Cotton (29.8)	Phosphates (23.8)	Business services (32.5)	3.0
Sudan	Cotton (18.7)	Ovine (14.0)	Construction (66.3)	18.6
Madagascar	Coffee (18.0)	Vanilla (16.7)	Business services (33.4)	1.7
Tanzania	Coffee (17.7)	Cotton (16.3)	Travel (70.0)	1.5
Type 1B: Highly dependent on mineral exports				
Angola	Petroleum (74.6)	Diamonds (2.5)	Business services (39.0)	19.0
Guinea	Bauxite & alumina (59.9)	—	Transport (42.7)	5.7
Liberia	Iron ore (55.1)	Rubber (28.0)	—	7.1
Zambia	Copper (52.0)	Cobalt (11.3)	—	14.1
Niger	Uranium (51.9)	Livestock (…)	Travel (21.0)	8.7
Central African Republic	Diamonds (49.7)	Coffee (15.7)	Transport (18.1)	4.4
Equatorial Guinea	Petroleum (44.6)	Wood products (41.6)	—	35.0
Congo, Dem. Rep.	Diamonds (17.2)	Petroleum (11.4)	—	—
Type 1C: Highly dependent on manufactured exports				
Lesotho	Clothing (54.8)	—	Travel (45.9)	3.8
Type 2: Predominantly service exporters (exports of goods are smaller than exports of services)				
Gambia	Groundnuts (54.1)	—	Travel (68.8)	0.2
Sierra Leone	Diamonds (50.6)	Titanium (5.7)	Travel (65.9)	0.5
Mozambique	Shrimps (43.3)	Cotton (11.7)	Business services (76.7)	0.9
Comoros	Vanilla (42.5)	Ylang-ylang (26.5)	Travel (61.8)	0.3
Cape Verde	Fish products (62.6)	Bananas (11.7)	Air transport (38.5)	0.5

Source: Compiled from UNCTAD (1999: Table 18).

Notes

Countries in italics are not members of the WTO (as of April 2000).

Djibouti and Eritrea are not included here due to the lack of data.

12 Growth, economic development and structural transition in small vulnerable states

Robert Read

The process of decolonization and the recent fragmentation of some larger states have been responsible for the rapid increase in the number of sovereign small states in the global economy. Further, greater devolution of decision-making to increasingly smaller entities has occurred simultaneously with accelerating globalization and the emergence of supra-national regional trade blocs. Paradoxically, the increasing internationalization of economic activity has, therefore, been parallel to growing self-determination, including that of many sub-national regions. The growing number of small entities in the global economy has generated increased interest in explanations for their growth success, particularly given the additional challenges of small size and the globalization process.

This chapter reviews the theoretical and empirical literature relating to the economic growth of small states and the implications of globalization for their development. The rest of the chapter is organized as follows: the first section considers some conceptual issues and the second section discusses features of small states, the third section is concerned with growth, the fourth section critically reviews vulnerability indices, and, finally, the fifth section concludes.

Conceptual issues for the analysis of small states

The extensive analytical literature on small states covers a wide range of issues and while there is general consensus as to their inherent characteristics, there is little agreement concerning the concept of small size. Four principal indicators which can be used to measure small economic size are: population size, absolute economic size (GDP or GNP), geographic area and the ability to affect world prices. The last point is largely irrelevant, as only very few large economies (USA, Japan and the European Union (EU) as a whole) do not possess the characteristics of a small open economy. With regard to population, early studies of small economies utilized critical population thresholds of between ten and fifteen million (Kuznets 1960; Chenery and Taylor 1968; Chenery and Syrquin 1975), but the emergence of new and smaller states has resulted in the progressive lowering of this threshold to one million by many international institutions. The extensive empirical work by Armstrong and Read is based upon a natural break above Singapore at 2.9 million (Armstrong *et al.* 1996, 1998, Armstrong and Read 1998a, 2000). The problem with the imposition of specific thresholds is that population is a continuous variable such that the use of arbitrary structural breaks cannot be justified theoretically. The same problem applies to economic size (GDP or GNP). The difficulty with geographic size is that it only provides sufficient information for a crude proxy of potential resource endowments. It can therefore be used to complement demographic data to provide an indicator of population density and dispersion (Dommen 1980). Also, developments in the Law of the Sea have meant that some island states have acquired Economic Exclusion Zones (EEZs) which are far greater than their actual land areas.

There is a significant literature concentrating upon small island and archipelagic (multiple island) states as opposed to small states in general. Islandness is often treated as the critical determinant factor rather than small size *per se*, primarily because most small states are also island or archipelagic. Islands certainly face additional challenges, particularly relating to isolation, which may be compounded by small size, but many similar problems experienced by small land-locked states should not be overlooked. A consensus is now emerging that many of the issues encountered by small island states are similar to those of smallness in general (Dommen 1980; Armstrong and Read 1995, 2000; Armstrong *et al.* 1996, 1998; Briguglio 1995).

The economic analysis of small size raises critical issues with respect to the concept of sovereignty. Political sovereignty is defined according to four necessary criteria in the 1949 United Nations Charter: a permanent population; a defined territory; a representative government; and the capacity to engage in external relations. Political sovereignty however, is not a simple binary variable but is rather a discrete scale (Schaffer 1975) ranging from full independence to relative autonomy in regions of larger states and including autonomous self-governing territories, trust territories, colonies, dependencies, possessions and territories. The fundamental legal characteristic of a sovereign state is the absence of a recognized claim of ownership on its territory by another state.

The concept of economic sovereignty is primarily concerned with the effective level of economic policy formulation and implementation rather than ultimate territorial ownership. Economic sovereignty, therefore, relates specifically to autonomy over revenue-raising (via taxation), expenditure, the regulatory environment and monetary, fiscal, trade and exchange rate policies. Given the constraints on small states however, *de jure* economic sovereignty does not necessarily imply *de facto* economic policy autonomy (Read 1995).

The distinction between political and economic sovereignty is generally ignored in the literature on small states. The concern here is with the economic implications of small size so that the critical unit of analysis is territorial entities with economic sovereignty (Selwyn 1980; Jalan 1982a; Armstrong and Read 2000; Armstrong *et al.* 1996, 1998). The substantive economic difference between small politically sovereign states, territories and small regions of larger states, however, remains the potential of the latter two groups to receive fiscal transfers from the metropolitan state, see Armstrong and Read (2000).

Sub-optimality and size constraints on growth in small states

The economic analysis of small states has its origins in the insights of the papers in Robinson (1960) which have since been developed further into a robust analytical framework (notably by Jalan 1982b; Ashoff 1989; Srinivasan 1986; Streeten 1993; Armstrong and Read 1995, 2000; Armstrong *et al.* 1996, 1998). The analytical focus is based upon the impact of market imperfections upon the economies of small states and dispensing with the neoclassical economic assumptions of constant returns to scale, perfect competition and zero transport costs. This facilitates the conceptualization of the economies of small states as sub-optimal (Armstrong and Read 1995). This highlights the crucial impact of scale economies, indivisibilities, efficiency and competitiveness (Scitovsky 1960) as well as diseconomies of scope (Streeten 1996) on the potential to generate a 'critical mass' in domestic economic activity.

Unit costs of local production are increased by there being insufficient domestic demand to reach the minimum efficient scale (MES) necessary for the efficient output for many goods and services. This means that the range and extent of economic activity in a small state is a function of the shape of average cost curves below the MES (Knox 1967) and transport costs. Small states are therefore at a structural disadvantage relative to larger states with respect to nurturing large-scale industries as well as R&D. A small domestic market also inhibits competition in many domestic economic activities because of the small number of feasible incumbents (Kuznets 1960). The lack of competition further raises the prices of goods and services with knock-on effects on other activities, notably utilities and infrastructure. These effects are likely to be particularly severe for non-tradeables because of the potential cost of alternative imports but they will also affect those tradeables which are subject to diseconomies of scale and lack of competition in transportation and distribution as well as those prone to stock-outs. The cost of living in small states can, therefore, be expected to be relatively high, for reasons of scale and competition, together with a narrower range of consumer choice. These effects may be exacerbated in more geographically isolated small states because the extent to which many goods and services are traded is determined by transport costs.

The natural resource endowment of any state is partly a function of its geographic area as well as the result of serendipity. Although small size does not preclude an abundance of natural resources, states with small geographic areas are likely to have limited and relatively undiversified endowments. Many small states may lack the domestic capital to finance the exploitation of these natural resources. A small population imposes a severe constraint on the domestic supply of labour contrary to the standard model of structural transition in developing economies. Growth is more likely to arise from higher value-added activities intensive in human capital, skills and physical capital (Bhaduri *et al.* 1982). Investment in human capital is, therefore, critically important to the long-term economic health of small states.

Small states are, therefore, necessarily highly specialized and comparatively undiversified in the structure of their output and exports, possibly giving rise to an excessive dependence upon a few dominant activities, exports and export markets. This may be aggravated by the shallowness of local inter-industry linkages given the narrow domestic economic base (Selwyn 1975). Export concentration increases their exposure to exogenous shocks via unstable export prices and earnings, and possibly 'Dutch' disease. The potential for diversification in small states is highly constrained by the size of their domestic economy. Further, small states lack both the market power and the domestic resource base to fully ameliorate the impact of any external shocks since they cannot compensate for declining export earnings through increased export volumes.

The small domestic market is, therefore, unlikely to drive autonomous self-sustaining internal growth, thus limiting the potential for import-substituting growth strategies. Small states must, therefore, necessarily pursue highly open trade regimes and be well-integrated with the international economy (Kuznets 1960; Scitovsky 1960).

The structural openness of small states and the importance of trade to their economies mean that integration with the global trading system creates a critical risk asymmetry. Export price fluctuations are likely to be greater than for imports with serious implications for the balance of payments, foreign exchange for essential imports and the growth path (Erbo and Schiavo-Campo 1969; Thirlwall 1991). The high share of foreign currency transactions also means that small states have a high degree of international monetization. Many small states either use a hard currency or have a link to one (Read 1995; Armstrong and Read 1998a) so as to insulate against external volatility. This means the loss of monetary sovereignty, including the determination of interest rates and inflation, in the absence of capital controls (Helleiner 1982).

Openness means that low-cost trade links with the international economy are of paramount importance to small states. Land-locked states depend greatly upon neighbouring states for surface communications and port facilities and, therefore, for access to export markets and import sources. Many small archipelagic states are highly fragmented, so that internal communication may be as difficult and as costly as external links (Brookfield 1990; Selwyn 1978). Further, the impact of diseconomies of scale may be compounded by fragmentation in terms of providing essential economic and social infrastructure to outlying islands. The effect of remoteness and isolation on transport costs is similar to a tariff in terms of its impact on domestic production, consumption and welfare. The economic sub-optimality of small states implies that nearly all goods and services are tradeable at the margin. For remote and isolated small states, however, it may be less costly to produce certain tradeables and non-tradeables domestically rather than rely upon imports. Nevertheless, the supply of some goods and services may be infeasible.

These salient characteristics have critical implications to the extent that they are a significant constraint on the structure of activity and policy autonomy in small states. It is the general view in the literature that any potential advantages for small states conferred by their small size are greatly outweighed by the inherent disadvantages. This suggests that small states are likely to experience significant challenges in generating and sustaining economic growth relative to larger states.

The principal advantageous characteristic is size-induced openness to trade (Ashoff 1989) since their necessarily high degree of trade intensity requires small states to be internationally competitive. They are, therefore, more likely to favour export-led growth strategies than larger countries (Armstrong *et al.* 1996, 1998). Further, the potential gains from trade are also significant because of the magnitude of the trade multiplier (Ashoff 1989). International trade, however, cannot completely offset the adverse effects of small size because of the increased exposure to exogenous shocks. While small states are certainly potentially more responsive to change and more flexible in their policy-making, so promoting economic growth, the short distance and frequency of direct contact between decision-makers and constituents may also encourage harmful rent-seeking behaviour (Bräutigam and Woolcock, Chapter 13, this volume; Armstrong and Read 2000).

Explaining the growth of small states

Despite their small size, many small states, both developed and developing, have achieved sustained economic growth and relatively high levels of per capita incomes. Further, disproportionately fewer small states are to be found in the World Bank's lowest income categories (Armstrong *et al.* 1998). A small size does not, therefore, appear to be an insurmountable constraint on the growth of small states in spite of their inherent economic sub-optimality.

Country size is found to be insignificant in structural transformation (Chenery and Taylor 1968; Erbo and Schiavo-Campo 1969; Kuznets 1971; Chenery and Syrquin 1975; Chenery *et al.* 1986) and there is no evidence of any systematic adverse impact of small size on growth (Milner and Westaway 1993; Armstrong *et al.* 1996, 1998). Some evidence suggests that small states in Western Europe have actually out-performed comparable EU regions (Armstrong and Read 1995). These results do not preclude small size having an adverse effect on growth but rather suggest that any such effects are insignificant. Many small states have achieved sustained economic growth and increasing per capita incomes while many larger developing countries, have performed relatively poorly. This suggests that several other factors may play a critical role in this relative growth performance.

Trade is critically important to small states because of their need to finance essential imports. Further, it can alleviate many of the constraints associated with a sub-optimal domestic market size since increased specialization improves domestic efficiency and competitiveness. Openness therefore greatly increases the extent of their market. The magnitude of the trade multiplier means that these growth effects are particularly large. The gains from increased specialization through trade, however, must be offset against the greater risks of concentration and reduced diversification in the domestic economy.

Trade has a contestable impact upon domestic prices, efficiency and the competitiveness of small states because they are price-takers in imports and exports. These external cost and price pressures together with the need to assure market access means that the domestic output of tradeables must be internationally competitive. The high share of imports in consumption also means that the tradeable and non-tradeable sectors pay world prices for most intermediate inputs. Contestability, subject to transport costs, therefore, affects the entire tradeables sector and possibly some non-tradeables independent of the competitive structure of the domestic market (Armstrong and Read 1998b). The structural necessity to pursue highly open trade policies, therefore, requires the export sectors of small states to be founded upon their inherent comparative advantages. These lie in activities which are neither subject to increasing returns to scale nor reliant upon the intensive use of low-cost labour.

The sustained economic growth of many small states has led to increased theoretical and empirical interest in the critical determinants of this performance. There is increasing evidence to suggest that this growth success is associated with particular patterns of sectoral specialization and the effective use of endogenous policies.

Structural transition in developing economies is normally associated with Lewis-type industrialization with surplus agricultural labour shifting to more productive labour and technology intensive manufacturing (see Chenery and Syrquin 1975; Chenery *et al.* 1986). This development path is not open to most small states because of their relative lack of labour and the infeasibility of growth based upon large-scale, low-cost, labour-intensive manufacturing (Lewis 1955). Instead, small states can be expected to specialize in activities, such as natural resources and higher value-added niche manufacturing and service activities, which utilize human capital intensively and are less reliant upon scale economies (Bhaduri *et al.* 1982).

UNCTAD has developed a structural typology of small island developing states (SIDS), classifying them in four groups according to their principal economic activities (UNCTAD 1997). This is extended and modified by Armstrong and Read (1998a), shown in Table 12.1. Comparing average levels of per capita income and growth rates for each structural type, a strong economic performance is associated with specialization in services although there UNCTAD undertake no causal investigation of the relationship between sectoral specialization and growth performance. This relationship is investigated using conventional growth models and other techniques for an extensive global data set of small states (Armstrong and Read 1995, 2000; Armstrong *et al.* 1996, 1998). Growth success in terms of high per capita incomes is found to be associated with a rich natural resource base and a strong service sector, notably in financial services and tourism. A significant agricultural sector, however, is associated with a relatively poor growth performance. The positive impact of natural resources on growth runs counter to the argument of the 'resource curse' thesis (Auty 1993), possibly because their greater social cohesion makes small states more effective in sharing any such gains. The findings also suggest that advances in communication technology are of increasing benefit to remote small states in their provision of offshore services and long-haul tourism.

The high degree of structural openness to trade in small states has been identified as a critical growth factor because of its domestic multiplier effects although

Table 12.1 Classification of small economies: UNCTAD typology

Type I *external rental income, including aid > export and service income*		*Type II* *export income > service income*		*Type III* *service income > export income*		*Type IV* *significant manufacturing and service income*
Type Ia	*Type Ib*	*Type IIa*	*Type IIb*	*Type IIIa*	*Type IIIb*	
Falkland Islands	Cape Verde	American Samoa	Aruba	Andorra	Azores	Bahrain
Marshall Islands	Cook Islands	Brunei	Belize	Anguilla	Bahamas	Cyprus
Federated States of Micronesia	French Polynesia	Congo (Republic)	Bhutan	Antigua & Barbuda	Barbados	Estonia
Niue	Guam	Equatorial Guinea	Botswana	British Virgin Islands	Bermuda	Fiji
Northern Mariana Islands	New Caledonia	Faroe Islands	Comoros	Cayman Islands	Canary Islands	Latvia
Sao Tomé & Principe	Samoa	Gabon	French Guinea	Djibouti	Dominica	Lesotho
Tokelau	Tonga	Greenland	Gambia	Guam	Gibraltar	Macédonia FYR
Tuvalu		Guadeloupe	Guyana	Kiribati	Grenada	Malta
Wallis & Futuna		Guinea-Bissau	Iceland	Montserrat	Guernsey	Mauritius
		Kuwait	Jamaica	Turks & Caicos Islands	Isle of Man	Singapore
		Liberia	Martinique	US Virgin Islands	Jersey	Slovenia
		Mauritania	Mongolia		Liechtenstein	Trinidad & Tobago
		Mayotte	Namibia		Luxembourg	
		Nauru	Panama		Macao	
		Oman	Suriname		Madeira	
		Palau	Swaziland		Maldives	
		Qatar			The Netherlands Antilles	
		Reunion			St Kitts & Nevis	
		St Helena			St Lucia	
		St Pierre & Miquelon			St Vincent & Grenadines	
		Solomon Islands			San Marino	
		UAE			Seychelles	
					Vanuatu	

Source: Armstrong and Read (1998a).

there remains some scope for endogenous trade policy – functional openness. Structural openness, therefore, offers considerable potential growth benefits (Ashoff 1989) but some small states may choose a more protectionist trade policy stance. Investment in human capital can enhance the absorptive capacity for technology embodied in imports, particularly given the dearth of domestic R&D in small states (Briguglio 1995). The insights of endogenous growth theory suggest that small states are well placed to enjoy relatively high rates of growth because of their high degree of openness to trade and propensity for human capital formation, in spite of their economic sub-optimality.

International political economy is concerned with the strategic behaviour of countries according to rational self-interest but often giving rise to non-Pareto (second best) global welfare effects. This approach provides an appropriate context for analysing the interaction between endogenous policy choice and the growth performance of small states. Small states have the opportunity to exploit their relative unimportance in the global economy through international free-riding and rent-seeking which may generate considerable benefits at low cost.

Free-riding is probably most evident in defence given that most small states encounter significant diseconomies in its provision (Kuznets 1960). Instead, many of them eschew onerous domestic defence expenditure and gain significant positive externalities by relying upon the UN to uphold their territorial integrity. Small states are also likely to be major beneficiaries of a relatively liberal international trade regime through the positive externalities generated by the reciprocal multilateralism of the GATT and WTO. The adoption of a hard currency provides a means for small states to avoid the exchange rate and macroeconomic volatility associated with a high degree of openness and import dependence as well as free-ride on the currency's credibility. This strategy appears to have been particularly important for small states which have established successful offshore financial centres.

The rent-seeking strategy of most interest is probably the creation of a powerful lobby within the major international organizations. Since many decisions are based upon the principle of one country-one vote, small sovereign states have made use of their bloc vote to influence the shape of the international regulatory framework. Many small states have been surprisingly successful in securing critically important non-reciprocal asymmetric bilateral trade concessions with larger countries and regional trade blocs, notably the EU (Armstrong and Read 1995), to assure access to their key export markets. While such preferences incur few costs to the donor, they have the potential to generate significant rents for the beneficiaries. Perhaps surprisingly, however, very few small states participate in regional integration schemes although they are argued to be the greatest potential gainers (Balassa 1962). Many successful small states have also used their economic policy autonomy to establish appropriate regulatory frameworks and set strategic taxation rates so as to attract niche offshore financial activities through tax competition. Although there has been significant emigration of labour from some poorly developed small states, particularly in the Pacific, rent-seeking with respect to residency rights has been used to encourage immigration to alleviate specific skill-deficits.

Vulnerability and growth in small states

The vulnerability index

The growth and development of small states therefore incurs higher costs and risks because of their size (UNCTAD 1988) which can only be partially offset by appropriate endogenous strategies and limited domestic resources. The dominant methodology for the measurement and empirical analysis of vulnerability is based on the construction of an index, originally developed by Briguglio (1995). This approach has since been modified and extended, most recently, by the Commonwealth Secretariat (1998; summarized in Easter 1999) and the United Nations (2000). The index is a weighted composite measure of several critical variables which acts as an adjusted indicator of vulnerability intended to capture the special problems of small states.

The original Vulnerability Index is based upon three critical sources of vulnerability – small size, insularity/remoteness and susceptibility to natural disaster – measured by openness to trade, the share of transport costs in trade and the cost of natural disasters, respectively (Briguglio 1995). The data is normalized, weighted and converted into an index to create a vulnerability ranking for 114 states. The results suggest that the sample set of SIDS tend to be more vulnerable than both other developing countries and other countries, in general, and that a reliance upon GDP per capita data may therefore overstate the economic strength of small states (Briguglio 1995).

The most recent vulnerability indices are more comprehensive in their methodologies and tend to rely solely upon economic variables. The Commonwealth Vulnerability Index (CVI) uses three vulnerability impact variables significantly related to income volatility, export concentration, export dependence and the effect of natural disasters, together with absolute GDP to measure resilience (Commonwealth Secretariat 1998). Based upon data for 111 LDCs, the CVI assigns them to one of four broad vulnerability categories. The High Vulnerability category is dominated by states with populations below 2.2 million while the Higher Medium category has only ten states under 2.5 million but includes many larger but relatively poor sub-Saharan African LDCs. Only four small states feature in the lowest two categories. The UN Economic Vulnerability Index (EVI) is purely an economic index and uses a weighted average of five components; export concentration, export instability, agricultural output instability, share of manufacturing and services in GDP and population size (United Nations 2000). Of the 128 LDCs included in the index, some twenty-eight states with populations below 2.9 million are ranked in the fifty most vulnerable states while ten were ranked in the fifty least vulnerable.

There are a number of methodological issues relating to the construction of a robust index capable of capturing the impact of vulnerability effectively (see Read 2000). The most problematic of these is that the choice of impact vulnerability variables is determined in the first instance by the availability of quantifiable data for a sufficiently large array of countries. Even where data is available, vulnerability indices are likely to be sensitive to the use of alternative variables and differing weighting procedures. The variables in the CVI are determined endogenously according to their effects on income volatility while the EVI uses variables regarded as appropriate economic indicators of development. Islandness is included in the CVI and nearly all the SIDS lie in the High and Higher Medium categories. The EVI ignores islandness so that Fiji, The Maldives and Swaziland (High) and Barbados, Jamaica and Mauritius (High Medium) appear in the fifty least vulnerable states. The EVI, therefore, tends to rank larger and poorer states as the most vulnerable while the CVI is most concerned with SIDS. The apparently contradictory findings of these two quite sophisticated, but very different, vulnerability indices demonstrate the sensitivity of the results to the choice of impact variables.

All composite indices are likely to be extremely sensitive to the individual weights attached to components. Briguglio's original Vulnerability Index was dominated by the trade openness variable which comprised 50 per cent of the total weight. In the EVI, all five impact variables are assigned an equal weight. The CVI, however, avoids this problem by endogenizing the weights within the estimation procedure.

Any statistical analysis of LDCs and, in particular, small developing states is fraught with difficulty because of the lack of extensive and appropriately comprehensive data. This problem is particularly acute in the case of the smallest states, many of which lack sufficient resources to produce extensive economic and social data. These states, therefore, tend to be excluded from statistical analyses, resulting in sample selection bias favouring larger states (discussed in Armstrong *et al.* 1998) although this can be partly resolved by stratifying the data. All of the main vulnerability indices omit the smallest states, notably those in the Pacific.

A final issue relates to the explanatory power of vulnerability indices and whether they provide additional and relevant information in a manner that is easily comprehended and of use to policy-makers. To date, the principal methodological issues remain unresolved and the conflicting results of the main indices suggest that some degree of consensus concerning the critical impact variables is required. While it is clear that LDCs and other small developing economies are generally found to be the most vulnerable, the underlying principle of the Vulnerability Hypothesis still awaits statistical confirmation.

The impact of vulnerability on growth in small states

The exposure of any economy to external shocks has a dampening effect on its long-run growth path and increases instability around the underlying average trend rate of growth. The key premise of the Vulnerability Hypothesis is that the long-run growth of small states is adversely affected by their greater exposure to exogenous shocks, compounded by the lack of resources in many developing small states to fully assuage the impact of this volatility. Small states are, therefore, likely to experience lower long-run average rates growth characterized by greater amplitudes of fluctuation than larger states. While relatively wealthy small states can be expected to be better able to cope with such volatility, they may be exposed to much greater instability because of their greater dependence upon trade.

As a long-run phenomenon, the empirical veracity of the vulnerability hypothesis can be tested by including vulnerability as an additional conditioning variable in a neoclassical conditional convergence growth model. Using Briguglio's Vulnerability Index results for a limited number of small states, the vulnerability coefficient is found to be positive and significantly related to growth contrary to a priori expectations (Armstrong and Read 1998c). The most compelling explanation for this counter-intuitive result is the mis-specification of the external dependence variable which uses openness to trade as a proxy and its dominant weighting. The apparently paradoxical growth result, therefore, provides further support for the beneficial role of openness in growth. The impact of vulnerability itself, however, remains to be verified satisfactorily.

The Vulnerability Hypothesis represents an important extension to the theoretical literature on small states by incorporating the impact of exogenous shocks in a testable manner. In spite of a priori theorizing, however, the quantification of vulnerability has been fraught with methodological difficulties such that convincing empirical support for the hypothesis remains lacking. One particular conceptual difficulty with vulnerability is that, because it affects all small states, whether measured according to population and/or absolute GDP/GNP, the literature tends to adopt a fatalistic tone. The relative growth success of many states with small populations, however, suggests that the impact of vulnerability is uneven. Even normalizing for structural openness, location, isolation and predisposition to natural catastrophe, the impact of vulnerability may also be explained by the use of endogenous policies to at least partially offset the adverse effects of small size and, therefore, vulnerability. The critical determinants of growth success, therefore, appear to lie in effective endogenous policy-making in support of the pursuit of niche export strategies, openness to trade, and international free-riding and rent-seeking. A final, but nevertheless important, point relates to the a priori expectation that vulnerability is inversely correlated with per capita income levels. Growth success in small states increases the degree of exposure to and dependence upon the international economy such that their apparent vulnerability may in fact be greater. It is evident that a number of issues relating to vulnerability, therefore, still need to be resolved before its implications can be fully understood.

Summary and conclusions: small states and the impact of globalization

The primary concern of this chapter is growth, economic development and structural transition in small states. Low population size together with low absolute GDP/GNP is used throughout as a reference threshold. The importance of economic, as opposed to political, sovereignty highlights the potential insights to be derived from the additional inclusion of relatively autonomous territorial entities.

The discussion of the salient characteristics of small size applies to most, but not all, LDCs as well as those states with populations below three million and highlights the implications of economic sub-optimality and its adverse implications for growth. Bräutigam and Woolcock (Chapter 13, this volume) demonstrate that in a cross-sectional study of both large and small states the positive role played by high-quality institutions is similar in managing vulnerability.

Many states with small populations, however, have been relatively successful in achieving sustained economic growth and improved levels of per capita income. Explanations for this surprising growth performance focus on the critical role of several factors, namely openness to trade, sectoral specialization in accord with their narrow comparative advantage, location within particular global regions and the effective use of endogenous policies to promote growth, including free-riding and rent-seeking in the international economy. The concept of vulnerability captures the disproportionate long-run exposure of small states to a wide range of exogenous shocks. Methodological and data problems, however, mean that there is as yet little empirical confirmation of these effects.

It is evident that small states are likely to be extremely sensitive to the impact of globalization because of the interaction between their high degree of integration in the international economy and their inherent vulnerability. Although small states might be expected to be major beneficiaries of global trade liberalization, their narrow specialization and heavy export dependence makes them highly susceptible to adverse changes affecting specific categories of goods and services subject to protectionist pressures in both developed and developing countries (Armstrong and Read 1998a). Globalization has accelerated the move towards creating a level international playing field based upon comparative advantage and underlying competitiveness. This constitutes a severe threat to the continued prosperity of successful small states reliant upon niche market strategies aided by international free-riding and rent-seeking. Perhaps the most important current example of this trend is the action being taken by the OECD and EU against the offshore financial centres to be found in many successful small states. Further, this also suggests that it will be increasing difficult for small developing states to foster similar successful growth strategies in such an environment.

Acknowledgements

Robert Read, Lecturer in International Economics, can be contacted at the University of Lancaster, Lancaster LA1 4YX, e-mail : r.read@lancaster.ac.uk. This is a substantially revised version of a paper first presented at the UNU/WIDER Workshop on Globalization and the Obstacles to the Successful Integration of Small Vulnerable Economies held at UNU/WIDER, Helsinki, Finland 18–21 May 2000. The author is grateful to Mansoob Murshed for his guidance and comments, the comments of many participants at the Conference and those of an anonymous referee.

References

Armstrong, H.W., Jouan de Kervenoael, R., Li, R., and Read, R. (1996) *The Economic Performance of Micro-States*, Report to UK ODA.

Armstrong, H.W., Jouan de Kervenoael, R., Li, R., and Read, R. (1998) 'A Comparison of the Economic Performance of Different Micro-states and Between Micro-states and Larger Countries', *World Development*, 26, 539–56.

Armstrong, H.W. and Read, R. (1995) 'Western European Micro-states and EU Autonomous Regions: The Advantages of Size and Sovereignty', *World Development*, 23, 1229–45.

Armstrong, H.W. and Read, R. (1998a) 'Trade and Growth in Small States: The Impact of Global Trade Liberalization', *World Economy*, 21, 563–85.

Armstrong, H.W. and Read, R. (1998b) 'Trade, Competition and Market Structure in Small States: The Role of Contestability', *Bank of Valletta Review*, 18, 1–18.

Armstrong, H.W. and Read, R. (1998c) 'The Phantom of Liberty: Economic Growth and the Vulnerability of Micro-states' (mimeo).

Armstrong, H.W. and Read, R. (2000) 'Comparing the Economic Performance of Dependent Territories and Sovereign Micro-states', *Economic Development and Cultural Change*, 48, 285–306.

Ashoff, G. (1989) *Economic and Industrial Development Options for Small Third World Countries*, Occasional Paper No. 91, Berlin: German Development Institute.

Auty, R. (1993) *Sustaining Development in Mineral Economies: The Resource Curse Thesis*, London: Routledge.

Balassa, B. (1962) *Theory of Economic Integration*, Baltimore, MD: Johns Hopkins University Press.

Bhaduri, A., Mukherji, A., and Sengupta, R. (1982) 'Problems of Long-term Growth in Small Economies: A Theoretical Analysis', in B. Jalan (ed.), *Problems and Policies in Small Economies*, Beckenham: Croom Helm for the Commonwealth Secretariat, pp. 49–68.

Briguglio, L. (1995) 'Small Island Developing States and their Economic Vulnerabilities', *World Development*, 23, 1615–32.

Brookfield, H.C. (1990) 'An Approach to Islands', in W. Beller, P. d'Ayala and P. Hein (eds), *Sustainable Development and Environmental Management of Small Islands*, Paris: UNESCO, Man and the Biosphere Series, 5, pp. 23–33.

Chenery, H.B., Robinson, S., and Syrquin, M. (1986) *Industrialization and Growth: A Comparative Study*, Oxford: Oxford University Press.

Chenery, H.B. and Syrquin, M. (1975) *Patterns of Development: 1950–1970*, Oxford: Oxford University Press.

Chenery, H.B. and Taylor, L. (1968) 'Development Patterns: Among Countries and over Time', *Review of Economics and Statistics*, 50, 391–416.

Commonwealth Secretariat (1998) 'A Study on the Vulnerability of Developing and Island States: A Composite Index, Final Report', presented at the FCO Islands and Small States Conference, Wilton Park, 26–28 February (mimeo).

Dommen, E.C. (1980) 'Some Distinguishing Characteristics of Island States', *World Development*, 8, 931–43.

Easter, C. (1999) 'Small States Development: A Commonwealth Vulnerability Index', *The Round Table*, No. 351, 403–22.

Erbo, G.F. and Schiavo-Campo, S. (1969) 'Export Stability Level of Development', *Bulletin of Oxford Institute of Economics and Statistics*, 31, 263–83.

Helleiner, G.K. (1982) 'Balance of Payments Problems and Macro-economic Policy', in B. Jalan (ed.), *Problems and Policies in Small Economies*, Beckenham: Croom Helm for the Commonwealth Secretariat, pp. 165–84.

Jalan, B. (1982a) 'Classification of Economies by Size', in B. Jalan (ed.), *Problems and Policies in Small Economies*, Beckenham: Croom Helm for the Commonwealth Secretariat, pp. 39–47.

Jalan, B. (ed.) (1982b) *Problems and Policies in Small Economies*, Beckenham: Croom Helm for the Commonwealth Secretariat.

Knox, A.D. (1967) 'Some Economic Problems of Small Countries', in B. Benedict (ed.), *Problems of Smaller Territories*, London: Athlone Press, pp. 35–45.

Kuznets, S. (1960) 'The Economic Growth of Small Nations', in E.A.G. Robinson (ed.), *The Economic Consequences of the Size of Nations*, London: Macmillan, pp. 14–32.

Kuznets, S. (1971) *Economic Growth of Nations: Total Output and Production Structure*, Cambridge, MA: Belknap.

Lewis, W.A. (1955) *The Theory of Economic Growth*, London: George Allen and Unwin.

Milner, C.R. and Westaway, T. (1993) 'Country Size and the Medium-Term Growth Process: Some Cross-Country Evidence', *World Development*, 21, 203–12.

Read, R. (1995) 'Micro-States and Currency Systems: A Review of the Issues and Evidence', paper presented to the IESG Easter Mini-Conference, University of Manchester, 20–21 April (mimeo).

Read, R. (2000) 'The Characteristics, Vulnerability and Growth Performance of Small Economies', briefing paper for the WTO Seminar on Small Economies, Palais des Nations, Geneva, 21 October.

Robinson, E.A.G. (ed.) (1960) *The Economic Consequences of the Size of Nations*, London: Macmillan.

Schaffer, B. (1975) 'The Politics of Dependence', in P. Selwyn (ed.), *Development Policy in Small Countries*, Beckenham: Croom Helm, pp. 25–53.

Scitovsky, T. (1960) 'International Trade and Economic Integration as a Means of Overcoming the Disadvantages of a Small Nation', in E.A.G. Robinson (ed.), *The Economic Consequences of the Size of Nations*, London: Macmillan, pp. 282–90.

Selwyn, P. (1975) 'Industrial Development in Peripheral Small Countries', in P. Selwyn (ed.), *Development Policy in Small Countries*, Beckenham: Croom Helm, pp. 77–104.

Selwyn, P. (1978) 'Small, Poor and Remote: Islands at a Geographical Disadvantage', IDS Discussion Paper, No. 123, Sussex: University of Sussex.

Selwyn, P. (1980) 'Smallness and Islandness', *World Development*, 8, 945–51.

Srinivasan, T.N. (1986) 'The Costs and Benefits of Being a Small, Remote, Island, Land-Locked or Ministate Economy', *World Bank Research Observer*, 1, 205–18.

Streeten, P. (1993) 'The Special Problems of Small Developing Countries', *World Development*, 21, 197–202.

Streeten, P. (1996) 'Why Small Countries Succeed', paper presented at the Conference on The Effects of Economic Globalization and Regional Integration on Small Countries, Nicosia, 4–6 September (mimeo).

Thirlwall, A.P. (1991) *The Performance and Prospects of the Pacific Island Economies in the World Economy*, East-West Center, Pacific Islands Development Program, Research Report Series, No. 14.

UN (2000) 'Committee for Development Policy's Economic Vulnerability Index Explanatory Note', United Nations CDP2000/PLEN/21, New York: United Nations.

UNCTAD (1988) *Specific Problems of Island Developing Countries*, Geneva: UNCTAD.

UNCTAD (1997) 'The Vulnerability of Small Island Developing States in the Context of Globalization: Common Issues and Remedies', Geneva: UNCTAD, SIDS.

13 Micro-states in a global economy

The role of institutions and networks in managing vulnerability and opportunity

Deborah Bräutigam and Michael Woolcock

Introduction

Small states have always been more vulnerable in the global economy. This is not only because trade comprises a larger proportion of their economic activity than it does in large states (Table 13.1), but because they lack the power to set any of the terms or make any of the rules that govern globalization. Yet studies of small states tend to focus on the nature of their vulnerabilities, without considering that these countries have managed external pressures in different ways (Amstrup 1976). Moreover, smallness need not always be a liability. Globalization brings opportunities as well as risks, and a more integrated global economy may enable smaller, more 'nimble' states to adapt quickly to changing conditions, and more readily to identify and pursue strategic development policies.

Drawing on a unique data set on governance, growth, social development and inequality, we examine various hypotheses about the reasons for the development performance of small developing countries in the 1960–98 period. We define smallness as a population of five million or less in 1998, along the lines of Collier and Dollar (1999). We also examine, using case study evidence, a subgroup of countries that share the same medium-high rank in the Commonwealth Secretariat's 'Composite Vulnerability Index'. Our primary findings can be summarized as follows:

1 The differences between small and large countries are real, but concentrated in relatively few variables. Small countries experience more volatile growth rates and are more aid and trade dependent, when controlling for regional location, the initial level of economic development, the rate of growth and a number of other variables.
2 There are no significant differences between small and large countries in terms of the quality of their institutions. However, precisely because small countries are more vulnerable, the quality of their institutions matters even more than it does in large countries. We show that small countries with high quality institutions of conflict management and state capacity have less growth volatility, and those with stronger state capacity in particular are more likely to enjoy higher rates of economic growth.

Table 13.1 Summary of differences between large and small states

Variable	*N*	*Mean*	*SD*	*Variable*	*N*	*Mean*	*SD*
Size (<5M in 1998)				*Initial GDP/c (ppp)*			
Large	108			Large	98	2562.49	2655.70
Small	102			Small	72	3153.76	3793.73
Region (dummy)				*Annual growth rate*			
SSA	49			Large	99	1.46	2.73
E Asia/Pac	35			Small	76	1.38	2.49
Ethnic fractionalization				*Growth volatility*			
Large	84	42.56	30.94	Large	99	4.63	2.34
Small	29	38.31	26.41	Small	76	6.57**	4.18
Economic inequality				*Aid (% GDP)*			
Large	95	38.87	9.51	Large	84	5.97	8.39
Small	46	42.83**	9.85	Small	81	12.92**	17.69
Land inequality				*FDI (% GDP)*			
Large	72	63.56	16.24	Large	96	1.36	1.70
Small	38	66.91	15.69	Small	75	3.08**	3.76
Primary education				*Trade quantity (% GDP)*			
Large	90	82.95	21.79	Large	99	62.60	35.94
Small	54	83.72	18.41	Small	75	108.78***	46.80
Improving primary education				*Trade quality (dummy)*			
Large	88	5.44	16.47	Large	100	0.44	0.50
Small	50	0.38**	12.44	Small	79	0.28**	0.45
Secondary education				*Voice and accountability*			
Large	87	61.66	24.65	Large	107	−0.06	1.00
Small	52	66.21	20.15	Small	66	0.11	0.89
Improving secondary education				*Political instability*			
Large	86	10.83	20.28	Large	102	−0.12	0.96
Small	49	7.22	24.91	Small	53	0.17*	0.86
Mortality (<5 years)				*Government effectiveness*			
Large	105	82.13	74.63	Large	102	−0.08	0.96
Small	85	60.65**	64.38	Small	54	0.11	0.75
Mortality decline				*Regulatory burden*			
Large	96	−52.64	20.00	Large	106	−0.00	0.86
Small	54	−53.78	18.46	Small	60	0.01	0.79
Life expectancy				*Rule of law*			
Large	106	63.31	11.01	Large	106	−0.08	0.94
Small	91	66.08*	9.64	Small	60	0.15^{+}	0.88
Improving life expectancy				*Control of corruption*			
Large	103	13.65	8.69	Large	102	−0.09	0.94
Small	91	12.52	8.23	Small	53	0.16*	0.81

Notes
$^{+}p < 0.07$; $^{*}p < 0.05$; $^{**}p < 0.01$; $^{***}p < 0.001$

Small countries have traditionally been highly dependent on trade, but investors seem to be indifferent to the quality of their institutions, which are so important not only in their own right, but instrumentally for maintaining economic and political stability. Of greater concern is the fact that while aid donors are accurately targeting poor countries, their funds to small countries appear to go to those with institutions that are significantly *worse* than those who are less aid dependent. Closer attention to the institutional environment in small developing countries is likely to help both stabilize and increase growth rates, and thus make an important contribution to poverty reduction and social concerns, such as health and education.

The second and third sections review some of the literature that has explored the economic, social and political differences between small and large states, and then consider the possible reasons why some small states might be able to manage the risks and opportunities of globalization better than others. In the fourth section, we use regression analysis to test some of the arguments submitted in the second and third sections, focusing on institutions at the state level. The fifth section explores three case studies of small and vulnerable countries. The sixth section offers some conclusions.

Is small beautiful? Small states and large states

How do small states differ from large states in ways that might be relevant for understanding varying responses to globalization? Researchers have argued – often in contradiction to each other – that small states differ from larger states on economic, social and political factors. They may have higher per capita incomes and productivity levels, and better human development indicators, yet have higher poverty and inequality. They are also said to have greater economic openness, higher volatility in growth rates and higher levels of aid intensity per capita. A variety of studies on the political aspects of smallness argue that small states in general tend to have greater political centralization and possibly higher corruption levels. They also have larger public sectors, weaker state capacity, higher unit cost of public services and the handicap of a much higher level of perceived investment risk than objective indicators would suggest. Some researchers argue that small states are more flexible and can adjust more quickly to rapid changes.

Studies of small states often ask the question: is small beautiful? Streeten's 1993 review is one of many that have ranked the evidence for and against this question. Streeten argues that small states in general seem to depend more on the export of raw materials and to lag behind larger states in the development of a manufacturing base. Their greater openness and small size make an initial stage of import substitution industrialization very difficult. But small countries even more than large need to take advantage of the international economy. Streeten also suggests that collective action problems may be solved more easily in small countries where free-riding is more visible and people tend to know each other and meet face to face. Their small size should also make many transaction costs lower: information should flow more easily, and principal-agent problems should be fewer, with greater ease of supervision.

Controlling for OECD status, oil production and location by continent, Easterly and Kraay (2000) found that 'microstates' (those with populations under one million) are 'richer and have higher productivity levels' than large states. Small states also have better infant mortality statistics, educational attainment and life expectancy. The ratio of trade to GDP in these small states was 54 percentage points above average, showing their high degree of openness, yet microstates were 'not particularly open to financial flows'. Due to their relatively greater external exposure and an accompanying instability in their terms of trade, microstates (and possibly small states as well) tend to have growth rates that are much more volatile than other states. Yet at least in the group of microstates studied by Easterly and Kraay, this higher volatility does not lead to lower average growth rates for small states than for larger states with less volatility, suggesting that something is compensating for these swings in fortune.

In contrast, a study commissioned by the Commonwealth Secretariat found that small countries (those with populations of 1.5 million and below) seem to have larger problems, in particular, higher poverty and inequality, as well as greater vulnerability to shocks (Commonwealth Secretariat 2000). This may be a reflection of factors such as the fact that the widely dispersed populations of some small island states are spread over a number of islands, while the major economic activities are found mainly near the capital. In addition, they note that many small states are located in hurricane-prone regions, or are subject to the threat of volcanic eruptions.

Collier and Dollar (1999) examine the relationship among policies, growth and aid in small states. They find that when poverty levels and population are controlled, small states (with populations of five million and below) generally receive more aid, and that this aid does not seem to depend on the quality of their economic policies. However, this aid may be helping small countries compensate for another difference between small and large countries: an unwarranted perception of risk. Ratings done by risk agencies consistently rank small countries as more risky for investors than an objective review of their policy stance and history would support.

Most of the empirical research on the differences between small and large states has explored differences in economic and social variables. However, researchers have noted several possible differences in the way small and large states are governed, and the type of institutions they have. Katzenstein (1985) has argued that the small countries he examined all tended toward corporatist political arrangements, integrating major stakeholders in important government policy deliberations.

However, it is possible that these close-knit political arrangements and centralization can lead to higher levels of corruption in small countries, as their officials may be more accessible to clientelist and 'old boy network' pressures. Farrugia (1993) emphasizes the potential side effects of small scale in his exploration of the 'special' environment faced by high level bureaucrats in very small states. He suggests that relationships are more 'closely knit' and 'highly personalized'. In a similar vein, Armstrong and Read (1998) point out that in small states, these close ties may also promote clientelism and rent-seeking.

In general, small states tend to have proportionately larger governments. Public sector wage bills in the Commonwealth Secretariat group of small countries were considerably higher at 31 per cent of GDP than in larger states, which averaged

21 per cent of GDP (Commonwealth Secretariat 2000: 17). As the study points out, part of the explanation is likely to lie in the fact that small countries have few economies of scale, which raises the cost of providing public services. However, the economies of scale argument regarding the public sector is challenged by studies that do not find a productivity disadvantage due to increasing returns to scale in the economy in general (Easterly and Kraay 2000). The larger public sectors found in small states could also be related to the fact that small countries have more open economies. In general, countries that have more openness to trade historically have larger, rather than smaller, public sectors, with the extra spending required by efforts to cushion their citizens from the impact of greater volatility and the risks associated with greater flexibility (Cameron 1978; Rodrik 1998b).

Addressing the impact of volatility and risk requires a capable state, but research suggests that in general, small countries may have weaker state capacity. Small countries may have smaller pools of qualified people to select from in staffing their bureaucracies (Streeten 1993). As noted above, small countries receive disproportionately more aid, but high levels of aid intensity have been correlated with poor quality of state institutions, an effect that holds even when economic decline is controlled (Bräutigam 2000a). This might disproportionately affect the quality of governance in small countries that receive high levels of aid.

Why might some small states succeed at globalization?

As with large countries, small countries with macroeconomic stability, open to the skills and innovation benefits possible from joint ventures, and some kinds of foreign direct investment (FDI), are likely to do better than others at integrating with the global economy. Yet compared with the variety of studies that try to determine how small and large states differ, there is much less empirical research on the reasons why some small states do better than others. Armstrong and Read (1998) report that regional location constitutes the principal explanation of growth performance among small states. Having abundant natural resources, and strong financial and tourism sectors, also were important for growth, while having a large agricultural sector tended to work against economic growth. In general, the quality of state institutions can go far in explaining the variety of growth and human development performance found in developing countries. Two kinds of political institutions seem particularly important: those that reflect higher levels of state capacity, and those that manage social conflicts.

State capacity

The East Asian 'miracle' focused attention on the *quality* of state intervention, not merely whether the state intervened or not (Wade 1990; Evans 1995). Recently, this theme has been revisited with the much longer time series data now available on developing countries, and the compilation of several new indicator sets that give measures of bureaucratic quality, rule of law and corruption. Research by Knack and Keefer (1995), and more recently by Campos and Nugent (1999), suggests that bureaucratic quality and other governance indicators are important in explaining growth. In a related study, Fedderke and Klitgaard found that 'higher [bureaucratic] efficiency is associated with higher educational levels, lower levels of land and income inequality, and lower ethnolinguistic fractionation' (1998: 472). Easterly's (2000) work has shown that good institutions can help mediate the latent social conflicts associated with ethnic and economic inequality.

Reducing social conflict and instability

A second strong theme in the literature on successful globalizers is the importance of institutions that ameliorate the social impact of instability and mediate conflicts. Among the institutions that might have this effect are democratic rules that enable countries to 'institutionalize' their conflicts through the democratic system, while affording various important social groups a voice in the decisions about adjustment. Other important institutions are likely to be those that protect human rights, the rule of law, greater equality (through land access, or redistributive taxation) and social insurance.

Early examples of these kinds of institutions can be found in the small social democracies of Europe. Forced to be highly open to trade and capital flows by their small size, Europe's small countries concentrated on enhancing their ability to adjust flexibly to external conditions, while protecting their populations from the insecurity generated by continual adjustment. A number of studies have found that states that are more open to trade also have larger governments, presumably to manage and compensate for the costs of continual adjustment (Rodrik 1998b). In a recent article, Goldsmith (1999) argues that the African states with the largest public sectors, Botswana and Mauritius, are also two of the continent's most consistently good performers.

In a series of recent publications, Rodrik (1998a, 1999, 2000) demonstrates the importance of the institutions that states use to manage conflict, and links this to their ability to successfully navigate economic shocks. Rodrik uses indicators for 'the quality of governmental institutions, rule of law, democratic rights, and social safety nets' to represent institutions of conflict management. These institutions establish the rules and practices that can soften the distributional impact of the adjustment required by external shocks, and seem to have allowed countries with rules already in place to adjust more rapidly (and presumably equitably). A related factor might be that stronger social protections engender more trust in the government and its ability to protect their people's basic needs. This could reinforce 'social capital' (Woolcock 2000) and help to underpin adjustment with stability (and a human face).

Empirical analysis

There is little agreement over what actually constitutes a 'small' country. Recent research by Easterly and Kraay (2000: 2014) on 'microstates' includes those 'having an average population over the period 1960–95 of less than one million'.

Others have used population figures of one and a half million (Commonwealth Secretariat 2000); three million (Armstrong and Read 1998); five million (Collier and Dollar 1999), and ten million (Kuznets 1960; Streeten 1993). We use the figure of five million (1998 population) as our cut-off, since this is approximately the median population of all countries in the world. Globalization we define as integration with the global economy, as measured by trade as a proportion of GDP, trade openness and direct foreign investment. We also consider the 'quality' (as opposed to the 'quantity') of globalization, as measured by the degree to which exports are based on manufacturing (rather than resource extraction).

We consider the quality of governance using a comprehensive aggregated data set recently compiled by Kaufmann, Kraay and Zoido-Lobaton (KKZ) (1999). These authors have compiled six measures of governance: 'voice and accountability'; 'political instability'; 'rule of law'; 'government effectiveness'; 'controlling corruption'; and 'regulatory burden'. We examine each of these dimensions to discern whether there are differences in governance between small and large states.

We then further develop two broad categories of governance – conflict management and state capacity – that we propose are vital for countries seeking to negotiate the challenges and opportunities of globalization. Various plausible measures can be proposed for each of the two aspects of governance. *Conflict management* refers to institutions such as democracy, human rights, free press, collective bargaining arrangements, social programmes and the rule of law, which collectively entail clear procedures, mechanisms for information dissemination, support for weaker groups and independent forums in and through which differences can be resolved. On the basis of their comprehensiveness, we have selected 'voice and accountability' and 'rule of law' from the KKZ list of variables to best measure *conflict management*. Proxies for *state capacity* could include size of government, absence of corruption, quality of bureaucracy and nature and size of national tax base. We have selected two aggregated variables from KKZ – 'government effectiveness' and 'controlling corruption' (again, for reasons of comprehensiveness) – to best capture *state capacity*.

Our dependent variable is development performance in small states in a context of increased globalization. By 'development performance' we mean the trajectory and stability of economic growth rates attained over the 1960–98 period. We also examine various measures of education (primary and secondary enrolment) and health (life expectancy and under-five mortality).[1]

We begin by examining twenty-four different social, economic and governance variables, gathered from a sample of 102 small and 105 large countries (a population of 5 million in 1998 being the cut-off point). These variables are presented in Table 13.1, and show that, on the face of it, small countries have:

- higher economic inequality
- slower improvement in primary education
- lower child mortality rates
- longer life expectancy

- higher levels of foreign aid
- stronger rule of law
- higher levels of foreign investment
- higher trade quantity
- lower trade quality
- higher growth volatility
- more political stability
- less corruption than large countries.

Of course, these differences in means may not be a function of size *per se*, but rather some other factors. Table 13.2(a) presents results from regression analysis on the socioeconomic variables, controlling for initial level of development, rate of economic growth and regional dummies; Table 13.2(b) does the same for the governance variables, but also controlling for land inequality and ethnic fractionalization (joint proxies for social divisions). This analysis whittles down the number of variables on which small countries actually differ from large countries to:

- growth volatility
- trade quantity
- FDI
- trade quality
- foreign aid.

This suggests that while governance *per se* is not significantly better or worse in small countries, it nevertheless still matters a lot, given that small countries have a demonstrably more volatile relationship with the global economy than large countries. In the next stage of the analysis – Table 13.3 – we investigate whether growth volatility, FDI and foreign aid remain high in small countries, even after controlling for initial wealth, economic inequality, economic growth, globalization (trade quality and quantity), regional dummies and two sets of governance variables – conflict management, measured by the 'voice and accountability' and 'rule of law' variables, and state capacity, measured by the 'government effectiveness' and 'control of corruption' variables.

The results show that, controlling for quality of institutions in addition to standard socioeconomic variables, small states remain significantly different from large countries on just two dimensions: growth volatility and aid share. In these regressions, growth volatility is shown to be negatively related to country size and positively related to the absence of democratic decision-making institutions. Levels of direct foreign investment are positively related to levels of trade and government effectiveness (the sub-Saharan Africa dummy is strongly negatively significant, suggesting a conspicuous anti-Africa bias on the part of foreign investors). Foreign aid flows are allocated as one might initially expect – primarily to small, poor, slow-growing, high-trade economies – but, despite their rhetoric regarding the importance of human rights and anti-corruption, donors seem largely indifferent to the quality of government in the countries to which

Table 13.2(a) Socioeconomic development variables and country size

Dependent variables[a]	*Economic inequality* (log *Gini*)	*Primary education* (*% increase*)	*Under 5 mortality rate* (log)	*Life expectancy* (log)	*Growth volatility* (log)	*FDI* (log)	*Trade quantity* (log)	*Trade quality* (*dummy*)	*Aid share* (log)
Independent variables									
Small state	0.11	−3.37	0.02	0.009	0.36	0.82	0.59	−0.23	1.48
(dummy)	(2.60)*	(1.26)	(0.28)	(0.67)	(4.49)***	(4.05)***	(8.22)***	(3.60)***	(6.77)***
Initial GDP/c	−0.05	−2.34	−0.73	0.09	−0.08	0.001	0.09	0.12	−1.53
(PPP) (log)	(2.16)*	(1.53)	(14.59)***	(10.91)***	(1.77)	(0.01)	(2.00)*	(3.14)**	(10.92)***
Median growth rate	0.005	0.46	−0.10	0.01	−0.06	0.04	−0.002	0.07	−0.16
	(0.58)	(0.64)	(6.13)***	(5.09)***	(3.89)***	(0.92)	(0.17)	(4.80)***	(3.78)***
Sub-Saharan Africa	0.13	2.63	0.54	−0.19	−0.06	−0.87	−0.04	−0.28	0.37
(dummy)	(2.18)*	(0.70)	(5.46)***	(10.35)***	(0.58)	(3.09)**	(0.39)	(3.05)**	(1.31)
East Asia/Pacific	0.008	−3.16	0.001	−0.02	−0.09	0.24	0.12	−0.14	−0.09
(dummy)	(0.13)	(1.44)	(0.01)	(1.03)	(0.73)	(0.77)	(1.08)	(1.43)	(0.27)
N	130	128	164	170	170	152	164	157	148
R^2	0.201	0.080	0.778	0.779	0.182	0.207	0.343	0.360	0.603

Notes

* $p < 0.05$; ** $p < 0.01$; *** $p < 0.001$. Absolute value of t-statistic in parentheses.

a These nine variables are those that show statistically significant differences ($p < 0.05$) between the means of large and small countries (see Table 13.1).

Table 13.2(b) Governance variables and country size

Dependent variables[a]	*Political instability*	*Rule of law*	*Control of corruption*
Independent variables			
Small state	0.202	0.096	0.239
(dummy)	(1.11)	(0.60)	(1.38)
Log of initial	0.574	0.617	0.735
GDP/c (PPP)	(6.28)***	(7.57)***	(8.44)***
Land inequality	−0.925	−1.256	−1.22
(log)	(3.07)**	(4.61)***	(4.36)***
Ethno-linguistic	−0.002	−0.002	−0.001
fractionalization	(0.55)	(0.78)	(0.27)
Sub-Saharan Africa	−0.364	−0.307	0.061
(dummy)	(1.38)	(1.34)	(0.24)
East Asia/Pacific	0.224	0.350	0.156
(dummy)	(0.86)	(1.47)	(0.63)
N	77	80	77
R^2	0.575	0.649	0.650

Notes

*$p < 0.05$; **$p < 0.01$; ***$p < 0.001$. Absolute value of *t*-statistic in parentheses.

a These three variables are those that otherwise show statistically significant differences ($p < 0.05$) between the means of large and small countries (see Table 13.1).

Table 13.3 Development variables regressions

Dependent variable	*Growth volatility* (log)	*Foreign direct investment* (log)	*Aid share* (log)
Socioeconomic variables			
Small state (dummy)	0.451 (4.93)***	−0.060 (0.21)	0.952 (3.00)**
Initial GDP/c, PPP (log)	0.094 (1.61)	−0.194 (1.14)	−1.502 (7.67)***
Economic inequality (log)	−0.269 (1.56)	−0.024 (0.05)	−0.369 (0.65)
Median growth rate	−0.010 (0.42)	−0.027 (0.39)	−0.213 (2.67)**
Sub-Saharan Africa (dummy)	0.214 (1.92)+	−1.238 (3.87)***	0.409 (1.13)
East Asia/Pacific (dummy)	0.043 (0.37)	−0.113 (0.33)	−1.011 (2.21)*
Globalization variables			
Trade quantity (log)	0.019 (0.25)	1.055 (4.48)***	0.942 (3.13)**
Trade quality	0.157 (1.57)	−0.499 (1.72)	−0.227 (0.65)
Governance variables			
Conflict management			
Voice and accountability	−0.173 (2.51)*	0.078 (0.37)	0.425 (1.91)+
Rule of law	0.065 (0.68)	−0.062 (0.23)	−0.060 (0.19)
State capacity			
Controlling corruption	−0.185 (1.43)	−0.466 (1.22)	−0.569 (1.20)
Government effectiveness	−0.157 (1.15)	0.926 (2.32)*	0.277 (0.58)
N	110	105	89
R^2	0.539	0.404	0.694

Notes

+$p < 0.07$; *$p < 0.05$; **$p < 0.01$; ***$p < 0.001$. Absolute value of *t*-statistic in parentheses.

they lend: if anything, they assist more democratic countries, but not to those with strong rule of law, who are less corrupt, or have high-quality public institutions.

In the final series of regressions, we restrict our sample just to small countries. Because the number of countries with full data is rather small at this level, the four institutional variables are entered separately into the various regressions (since they are naturally somewhat correlated with one another). Again, however, we see that institutions of conflict management and state capacity matter. Small countries with superior state capacity (controlling for initial wealth, inequality, region and levels of globalization) have higher growth rates (Table 13.4(a)), while all four conflict management and state capacity variables are positively related to growth stability (Table 13.4(b)). Importantly, foreign investors seem indifferent to the quality of institutions in small countries (none of the institutional quality variables is significant for FDI; results not shown), whereas aid donors appear to seek *bad* institutional environments (Table 13.4(c)). It is clear that investors and donors alike would better serve both their own interests and those of their clients in poor small countries if they took more serious consideration of the institutional quality prevailing in the countries in which they are operating (or would like to operate).

Table 13.4(a) Economic growth and governance in small countries

Dependent variables	*Economic growth (median 1960–98)*			
	(1)	*(2)*	*(3)*	*(4)*
Socioeconomic variables				
Initial GDP/c, PPP (log)	0.226 (0.41)	0.091 (0.16)	0.461 (0.91)	0.564 (1.20)
Economic inequality (log)	−0.761 (0.48)	0.104 (0.06)	0.972 (0.56)	1.002 (0.61)
Trade quantity (log)	0.604 (0.76)	0.120 (0.14)	1.074 (1.26)	1.143 (1.47)
Trade quality	0.745 (0.85)	0.865 (0.98)	0.432 (0.49)	0.350 (0.42)
Sub-Saharan Africa	1.344 (1.33)	0.814 (0.86)	1.126 (1.21)	1.294 (1.49)
East Asia/Pacific	1.730 (1.95)$^+$	1.353 (1.51)	0.366 (0.39)	0.339 (0.39)
Governance variables				
Conflict management				
Voice and accountability	0.651 (1.20)			
Rule of law		0.682 (1.39)		
State capacity				
Controlling corruption			0.879 (1.98)$^+$	
Government effectiveness				1.079 (2.43)*
N	33	32	29	30
R^2	0.304	0.297	0.394	0.454

Notes
$^+p < 0.07$; $^*p < 0.05$; $^{**}p < 0.01$; $^{***}p < 0.001$. Absolute value of *t*-statistic in parentheses.

Table 13.4(b) Growth volatility and governance in small countries

Dependent variables	*Growth volatility* (log)			
	(1)	*(2)*	*(3)*	*(4)*
Socioeconomic variables				
Initial GDP/c, PPP (log)	0.175 (1.25)	0.257 (1.82)	0.144 (1.33)	0.067 (0.60)
Economic inequality (log)	0.474 (1.18)	0.122 (0.32)	−0.051 (0.14)	−0.088 (0.22)
Trade quantity (log)	0.096 (0.48)	0.213 (1.04)	−0.044 (0.24)	0.069 (0.37)
Trade quality	0.260 (1.18)	0.282 (1.35)	0.382 (2.05)$^{+}$	0.337 (1.71)
Sub-Saharan Africa	−0.270 (1.06)	0.173 (0.77)	0.136 (0.69)	−0.057 (0.28)
East Asia/Pacific	−0.447 (2.00)$^{+}$	−0.181 (0.85)	0.105 (0.53)	0.010 (0.05)
Governance variables				
Conflict management				
Voice and accountability	−0.403 (2.95)**			
Rule of law		−0.416 (3.58)**		
State capacity				
Controlling corruption			−0.501 (5.31)***	
Government effectiveness				−0.504 (4.75)***
N	33	32	29	30
R^2	0.388	0.471	0.643	0.578

Notes
$^{+}p < 0.07$; $^{*}p < 0.05$; $^{**}p < 0.01$; $^{***}p < 0.001$. Absolute value of t-statistic in parentheses.

Case studies

Quantitative cross-country comparisons are useful in many respects, but they are less helpful in designing specific policy proposals. In this section we briefly compare three small countries, Mauritius, Jamaica and Sierra Leone. All three fall into the same 'higher medium vulnerability' category, according to the Commonwealth Secretariat. Yet all three have dealt differently with the risks and opportunities presented by their openness and geography.

We need to begin with a brief discussion of the decisions each country made regarding the economic policies that promote efficient globalization. These vary sharply. Mauritius had far less government ownership of the economy, compared with Jamaica. Both had intervention, but in Mauritius it was generally targeted toward improving the country's position in its global interactions, or toward improving the equitable distribution of the fruits of globalization. In contrast, Jamaica's stance toward globalization has been characterized as 'unfocused … merely following to a limited extent world economic fashion' (King 2000). Sierra Leone in contrast did little either to intervene effectively, or to promote private investment. In

Table 13.4(c) Foreign aid and governance in small countries

Dependent variables	*Aid dependence* (log *of aid as share of GDP*)			
	(1)	*(2)*	*(3)*	*(4)*
Socioeconomic variables				
Initial GDP/c, PPP (log)	−1.300 (2.94)**	−1.071 (2.56)*	−1.310 (3.56)**	−1.489 (4.21)***
Economic inequality (log)	0.108 (0.08)	−0.355 (0.30)	0.046 (0.04)	0.044 (0.04)
Trade quantity (log)	0.051 (0.08)	0.692 (1.02)	0.458 (0.71)	0.482 (0.81)
Trade quality	−0.256 (0.37)	−0.026 (0.04)	0.243 (0.39)	0.262 (0.44)
Sub-Saharan Africa	−0.472 (0.57)	−0.098 (0.15)	−0.204 (0.32)	−0.574 (0.94)
East Asia/ Pacific	−0.651 (0.85)	−0.365 (0.53)	0.004 (0.01)	−0.009 (0.01)
Governance variables				
Conflict management				
Voice and accountability	−0.380 (0.84)			
Rule of law		−1.003 (2.39)*		
State capacity				
Controlling corruption			−1.340 (3.54)**	
Government effectiveness				−1.444 (3.78)***
N	30	29	26	27
R^2	0.539	0.617	0.687	0.705

Notes

$^{+}p < 0.07$; $^{*}p < 0.05$; $^{**}p < 0.01$; $^{***}p < 0.001$. Absolute value of *t*-statistic in parentheses.

particular, the three countries also made different decisions regarding strategies of manufacturing for export, one of the possible pathways out of the extreme vulnerabilities suffered by countries that are inherently small, and dependent on commodity exports. The decision the government in Mauritius made was to use its abundant unemployed labour in labour-intensive manufacturing for export, while underwriting social security for the population in general, has been key to the island's success, as was its early and successful stabilization after the economic turmoil of the late 1970s and early 1980s. Jamaica, on the other hand, has been a 'reluctant reformer' (King 2000) with sluggish growth rates and far less structural change. Governments in Sierra Leone have done almost nothing to improve the quality of the country's global economic links and the country is currently embroiled in a civil war.

As for development performance, as Table 13.5 shows, all three countries have experienced improvements in life expectancy and infant mortality since 1970, with Jamaicans gaining double the number of years gained by Sierra Leoneans, and Mauritians tripling the latter's gains. Mauritius also had far greater improvement

Table 13.5 Case study country comparisons

Factor	*Jamaica*	*Mauritius*	*Sierra Leone*
Years added to life expectancy at birth, 1970–97	6.5	9.2	3.2
Reduction in deaths, infant mortality rate, 1970–97	37	44	24
Infant mortality rate, 1997	10	20	182
Change in GDP per capita (1987 US$), 1975–97	−152	1654	−97
Average annual ranking, political and civil liberties, Freedom House, 1972–99	2, 3	1, 2	5, 5
Average spending on social services, % total, 1980–98	31	40	n/a
Adult literacy rate, 1998	86	84	31

Sources: UNDP (1999), World Bank (1997b), King (2000), Bräutigam (2000b).

in infant mortality, although by 1997, Jamaica had the lower rate. On income per capita measures expressed in 1987 US dollars, both Jamaica and Sierra Leone have declined since 1975, while Mauritius has more than doubled its real GDP per capita.

State capacity

One aspect of state capacity is the ability of the state to assure domestic and foreign investors that it will carry out its financial obligations. One way to explore this is through credit ratings given by firms like Institutional Investor, which rates countries from 0 (low) to 100 (World Bank 1997a). A glance at the credit ratings for 1981–3 suggests that Mauritius (at 19.0 compared with Switzerland's 95.2) was only marginally above Jamaica (at 15.9), while Sierra Leone stood at 8.2. Over the next ten years, however, Mauritius improved its rating by an average of 2.34 points per year, the most dramatic improvement of all the rated countries. Jamaica also improved, but only by 0.77 points per year, while Sierra Leone declined at an average of −0.09 points per year. While this is a narrow view of state capacity, it does suggest that Mauritius's ability to manage its economic affairs, and therefore its vulnerability, is likely to be superior to the other two.

State capacity is also affected by the broad quality of the educational system that feeds graduates into the bureaucracy. In 1980, fifteen years or so after independence, Mauritius had a 93 per cent primary enrolment, and 50 per cent secondary. Jamaica was even better. But Sierra Leone was enrolling only 54 per cent in primary school, and only 14 per cent in secondary (World Bank 1997a). Both Jamaica and Mauritius had a sufficient base from which to draw their civil servants, while the base in Sierra Leone was much thinner.

Conflict management

These should help countries manage the conflicts engendered by globalization. Here we look primarily at democratic decision making, but also at instruments of social policy, as reflected in levels of household inequality and social insurance.

All three countries were once British colonies, and all three have experienced substantial and gradual enlargement of suffrage and inclusion of local people in governance. Jamaica had a long history of representative government, dating from the eighteenth century. Legislative council elections were held in Mauritius in 1886, although the franchise was severely limited. Sierra Leone held its first legislative council elections in 1924, electing Africans to the council (Collier 1982: 39). At independence, all three adopted democratic constitutions. Mauritius (independent in 1968) and Jamaica (independent in 1962) maintained their democracies over time, despite some rough spots. Sierra Leone had lively multiparty competition until 1978, when an authoritarian leadership adopted a new constitution, making Sierra Leone a single party state. Now it is in a state of civil war.

Since 1972–3, Mauritius has averaged '1' on the Freedom House measure of political liberties, and '2' on the Freedom House measure of civil liberties, the same score held by the UK, making it among the most 'democratic' of small developing countries (Freedom House 2000). Over the same period, Jamaica averaged a more modest but still low '2' on political liberties and '3' on civil liberties, while Sierra Leone has averaged '5' on political liberties and '5' on civil liberties. If democratic institutions help ameliorate the impact of trade liberalization and engagement with the global economy, Mauritius should benefit the most, while Sierra Leone should find little help.

An effective social safety net is a final component of a system of conflict management. Unfortunately, we lack quantitative data to compare each country's history of social insurance. Studies suggest, however, that Mauritius and Jamaica have had a relatively long history of social protections, while the safety net in Sierra Leone depended on subsidies and controls on the price of rice sold in the urban areas, a feature that served to keep the price low for rural producers. In Mauritius, social expenditures (education, health, universal old age pensions, housing and social assistance and food subsidies) absorb about 40 per cent of government spending, and this pattern has lasted for four decades or more (Bräutigam 2000b). Mauritius has a compulsory contributory pension system, and in 1983, the country passed an unemployment relief act that provided minimum, means-tested payments to unemployed heads of households. Social services in Jamaica make up a smaller percentage of public expenditure, averaging 31 per cent between 1980 and 1998 (King 2000: 31).

It is clear that Mauritius, as the most successful 'globalizer' of the group, also had the strongest institutions, particularly those reflecting levels of state capacity, and the ability to manage social conflicts.

Conclusion

Small countries will remain vulnerable to an unpredictable global economy. But while they cannot control the winds of economic fortune that blow at their borders, they do have some control over the shape of their own domestic rules and institutions. Our results suggest that high quality institutions can make a difference in the ability of small countries to manage globalization. If we are certain of one thing about institutions, it is that they change slowly. Still, the trend over the past twenty years has been one of reducing the role of government. Our results suggest that attention needs to be paid to the reasons why so many states have poor capacity, and ways in which state capacity can be strengthened.

We also need much more creative thinking about the ways in which states can manage their societal conflicts, create trust in their institutions and maintain their ability to protect their vulnerable populations from the instability that accompanies openness. The European experience is one that should be studied for its possible lessons for today's small countries. Small countries in Europe combined economic flexibility and openness with democracy and social insurance. Yet these successful strategies may be difficult to replicate today in many developing countries. There is always a trade-off, and in this instance, the trade-off came from higher taxes to finance social protections for flexible workers. Under relentless pressure to remain competitive and to trim their spending, even Europe's social democracies are finding that the demands of integration are putting pressure on their social safety nets. Institutional quality matters in large and small countries alike. It matters even more in small countries, however, given their high degree of exposure to – and weakened power to influence – the turbulence of the global economy.

Note

1 Many of the variables used come from the data set on social cohesion, institutions and growth compiled for Ritzen, Easterly and Woolcock (2000), hereafter REW. Also socioeconomic data from the World Bank's *World Development Indicators* (World Bank 2000) database, Deininger (1999) and KKZ (1999) were used. The exact description and source of each variable used in this chapter can be obtained by application to the authors.

References

Amstrup, N. (1976) 'The Perennial Problem of Small States: A Survey of Research Efforts', *Cooperation and Conflict*, 3.

Armstrong, H.W. and Read, R. (1998) 'Trade and Growth in Small States: The Impact of Global Trade Liberalization', *World Economy*, 21(7), 563–85.

Bräutigam, D. (2000a) *Aid Dependence and Governance*, Stockholm: Almqvist and Wiksell International for the Swedish Ministry of Foreign Affairs.

Bräutigam, D. (2000b) 'Social Security and Globalization in Mauritius', Paper prepared for the XVIIIth World Congress of Political Science, International Political Science Association, Québec City, 1–5 August.

Cameron, D.R. (1978) 'The Expansion of the Public Economy: A Comparative Analysis', *The American Political Science Review*, 72(4), 1243–61.

Campos, N.F. and Nugent, J. (1999) 'Development Performance and the Institutions of Governance: Evidence from East Asia and Latin America', *World Development*, 27(3), 439–54.

Collier, R. (1982) *Regimes in Tropical Africa: Changing Forms of Supremacy, 1945–1975*, Berkeley: University of California Press.

Collier, P. and Dollar, D. (1999) 'Aid, Risk, and the Special Concerns of Small States', Development Research Group, Washington, DC: World Bank (processed).

Commonwealth Secretariat (2000) 'Small States: Meeting Challenges in the Global Economy', Report prepared for the Commonwealth Secretariat/World Bank Joint Task Force on Small States, Washington, DC, April.

Deininger, K. (1999) 'Measures of Land Inequality', Washington, DC: World Bank (mimeo).

Easterly, W. (2000) 'Can Institutions Resolve Ethnic Conflict?', Policy Research Working Paper No. 2482, Washington, DC: World Bank.

Easterly, W. and Kraay, A. (2000) 'Small States, Small Problems? Income, Growth, and Volatility in Small States?', *World Development*, 28(11), 2013–27.

Evans, P. (1995) *Embedded Autonomy: States and Industrial Transformation*, Princeton, NJ: Princeton University Press.

Farrugia, C. (1993) 'The Special Working Environment of Senior Administrators in Small States', *World Development*, 21(2), 221–6.

Fedderke, J. and Klitgaard, R. (1998) 'Economic Growth and Social Indicators: An Exploratory Analysis', *Economic Development and Cultural Change*, 46(3), 455–89.

Freedom House (2000) 'Annual Survey of Freedom Country Ratings, 1972/73 to 1999/00', available at www.freedomhouse.org/ratings/ratings.pdf.

Goldsmith, A.A. (1999) 'Africa's Overgrown State Revisited: Bureaucracy and Economic Growth', *World Politics*, 51(4), 520–46.

Katzenstein, P.J. (1985) *Small States in World Markets: Industrial Policy in Europe*, Ithaca: Cornell University Press.

Kaufmann, D., Kraay, A., and Zoido-Lobaton, P. (1999) 'Aggregating Governance Indicators', Policy Research Working Paper No. 2195, Washington, DC: World Bank.

King, D. (2000) 'The Evolution of Structural Adjustment and Stabilization Policy in Jamaica', Centro de Prensa, Comisión Económica para América Latina y el Caribe (ECLAC) Paper No. 65 LS/L.1361, Santiago, Chile, May.

Knack, S. and Keefer, P. (1995) 'Institutions and Economic Performance: Cross-Country Tests Using Alternative Institutional Measures', *Economics and Politics*, 7(3), 207–28.

Kuznets, S. (1960) 'Economic Growth of Small Nations', in E.A.G. Robinson (ed.), *Economic Consequences of the Size of Nations*, London: Macmillan.

Ritzen, J. Easterly, W., and Woolcock, M. (2000) 'On "Good" Politicians and "Bad" Policies: Social Cohesion, Institutions, and Growth', Policy Research Working Paper No. 2448, Washington, DC: World Bank.

Rodrik, D. (1998a) *The New Global Economy and Developing Countries: Making Openness Work*, Baltimore, MA: Johns Hopkins University Press for the Overseas Development Council.

Rodrik, D. (1998b) 'Why Do More Open Economies Have Bigger Governments?', *Journal of Political Economy*, 106(5), 997–1032.

Rodrik, D. (1999) 'Where Did All the Growth Go? External Shocks, Social Conflict, and Growth Collapses', *Journal of Economic Growth*, 4(4), 385–412.

Rodrik, D. (2000) 'Participatory Politics, Social Cooperation, and Economic Stability', Paper presented at the annual meeting of the American Economic Association, Boston.

Streeten, P. (1993) 'The Special Problems of Small Countries', *World Development*, 21(2), 197–202.

United Nations Development Program (UNDP) (1999) *Human Development Report*, New York: Oxford University Press for the UNDP.

Wade, R. (1990) *Governing the Market: Economic Theory and the Role of Government in East Asian Industrialization*, Princeton, NJ: Princeton University Press.

Woolcock, M. (2000) 'Managing Risk, Shocks, and Opportunity in Developing Economies: The Role of Social Capital', in G. Ranis (ed.), *Dimensions of Development*, New Haven, CT: Yale Center for International and Area Studies, 197–212.

World Bank (1997a) *World Development Report*, New York: Oxford University Press.

World Bank (1997b) *World Development Indicators*, Washington, DC: World Bank.

World Bank (2000) *World Development Indicators*, Washington, DC: World Bank.

14 Globalization and the island economies of the South Pacific

Rukmani Gounder and Vilaphonh Xayavong

Introduction

The South Pacific island economies have become part of the globalization process of the last two decades. The concern of many less developed countries (LDCs), and in particular small island states, is that they will be disadvantaged in the emerging global economic order and some will be further marginalized in world trade, investment, commodities and capital markets. Size and vulnerability are important factors for small states in terms of economic and environmental threats (see, Read, Chapter 12, Bräutigam and Woolcock, Chapter 13, this volume). This chapter examines the impact of globalization on the economies of Fiji and the Solomon Islands. The first section presents an overview of the economic characteristics of these two small island states. Financial and trade flows over the past two decades are examined along with the effects of globalization on the growth performance of two South Pacific island countries in the second section. In the third section we evaluate whether capital flows: foreign direct investment (FDI) and foreign aid, and trade affect growth. Other conditioning factors, such as inflation, real effective exchange rate, savings, growth in main trading partners, are included to analyse the dynamic link to economic growth. The final section presents the policy implications of the study.

Economic characteristics of island states

The South Pacific Islands have shown slow economic growth and development in the past two decades compared to similar island economies in other regions. For the period 1983–93, the average growth rate of real gross domestic product (GDP) for the Pacific Islands was 2.1 per cent per annum, lower than real GDP growth rates for the Caribbean, and the African and Indian Ocean regions for the same period at 3.2 per cent and 5.4 per cent per annum, respectively (World Bank 1996). On average Fiji achieved an annual GDP growth rate of 1.6 per cent and the Solomon Islands achieved 3.7 per cent for the period 1981–97 according to the Asian Development Bank (ADB 1998). Within the Pacific economies, GNP per capita in 1998 varied considerably, ranging from US$2,110 in Fiji, a lower middle-income economy, to US$750 in the Solomon Islands, a low-income country (World Bank 2000).

There are considerable differences in average per capita GNP of Fiji and the Solomon Islands as well as their economic structure as shown in Table 14.1. Agriculture forms a major component of GDP for the Solomon Islands, while for Fiji as per capita income rises, industry and service sectors account for a growing share of GDP compared to agriculture. The service sector tends to be the most important, with tourism and the provision of offshore financial services particularly contributing to growth in this area. Industry as a source of income is underdeveloped for the Solomon Islands, and Fiji's agriculture sector in the 1990s face the problem of unclear land rights (see Economic Intelligence Unit (EIU) 1999;

Table 14.1 South Pacific Islands: macroeconomic indicators and resource flows

Year	*1980*	*1985*	*1987*	*1990*	*1995*	*1997*
GDP growth (annual %)						
Fiji	−1.6	−4.0	−6.6	2.6	1.4	−1.8
Solomon Islands	−6.0	0.8	2.4	1.8	7.7	−0.5
GNP per capita (constant 1995 US$)						
Fiji	2,267	2,017	1,962	2,322	2,365	2,340
Solomon Islands	538	633	749	763	846	797
Economic activity[a]						
Agriculture, value added (% of GDP)						
Fiji	22.1	18.3	22.9	19.1	22.8	17.6
Solomon Islands	34.7	36.3	32.1	—	—	—
Industry, value added (% of GDP)						
Fiji	22.0	19.5	21.1	20.6	27.4	26.3
Solomon Islands	4.3	2.7	3.2	—	—	—
Services, etc., value added (% of GDP)						
Fiji	55.8	62.2	56.1	60.3	49.8	56.1
Solomon Islands	43.2	16.7	16.2	—	—	—
Merchandise export (% of GDP)						
Fiji	47.7	44.5	44.7	60.3	55.5	57.2
Solomon Island	73.2	50.2	51.3	45.2	64.2	63.9
Merchandise import (% of GDP)						
Fiji	54.6	48.9	46.2	70.6	64.3	63.5
Solomon Island	100.8	77.3	79.3	77.5	72.9	81.5
Inflation, consumer prices (annual %)						
Fiji	14.5	4.4	5.7	8.2	2.2	3.4
Solomon Islands	13.1	9.6	11.0	8.7	9.6	8.1
Foreign direct investment, net inflows (% of GDP)						
Fiji	3.0	1.9	1.0	6.7	3.6	0.6
Solomon Islands	2.1	0.4	6.4	4.7	5.5	5.9
Aid (% of GNP)						
Fiji	3.0	2.9	3.5	3.8	2.4	2.2
Solomon Islands	41.3	13.6	35.1	22.1	14.9	11.4

Sources: World Bank (1999) and AIDAB (1991).

Note

a Economic activity data for Solomon Islands do not add to 100% as the subsistence sector (food) is not included in any of the three sectors shown for GDP sectoral composition.

Gounder 1999a). The Pacific Islands also experienced their worst growth performance in 1998 with a steep decline in output estimated at 4.6 per cent: The Solomon Islands recorded negative growth rates estimated at 10 per cent, UNCTAD (1999). Political developments, and ethnic strife, adversely affected economic performance in Fiji and the Solomon Islands. The 1987 military coups in Fiji led to a temporary suspension of aid. Fiji also experienced a decline in tourism earnings and a drop in private sector investment.

Globalization and resource flows

Globalization and its effects on island economies

It is unclear whether the Pacific Island economies have in fact benefited from the globalization of international markets. Experiences of the last two decades show that these states increasingly have negative growth rates (ADB 1998, World Bank 1996). Fiji and the Solomon Islands have implemented reforms that include trade liberalization, exchange rate adjustments with the goal of improving competitiveness and the attainment of external and internal balance. Tax reforms have focused on greater competitiveness, the elimination of disincentives to investment and the enhancement of entrepreneurial activities. The achievement of a more market oriented regime, as well as sound macroeconomic management, are both crucial.

Net flow of resources to island nations

Investment

The need for FDI is necessitated by the scarcity of domestic capital. This specially applies in the natural resource, tourism, transport and financial service sectors. This reflects a shift from the traditional investment area of plantations, which has now declined in relative importance compared to other sectors.

In recent years there has been a large inflow of FDI to the Asian and Pacific region. Most of this investment has been directed to Southeast Asia and China. The Pacific economies have generally been bypassed, receiving only about one per cent of total FDI to developing countries in the Asia and Western Pacific region between 1985 and 1990 (UNESCAP 1997). See Table 14.1 and Figure 14.1 for FDI flows to Fiji, and the Solomon Islands. The ADB (1998) also points out that Government deficits have crowded out investment and caused serious problems for financial systems. In the Solomon Islands there is an attempt to strengthen the economy, gold deposits are being developed along with heavy government investment in agriculture, livestock, agro-industries, export assembly industries and tourism (Keith-Reid 1998: 206). Fiji has encouraged diversification in its agri-business, fishing, tourism and manufacturing sectors (FTIB 1994, AusAID 1995).

Fiji and the Solomon Islands have introduced various policies to attract foreign investment, see UNESCAP (1997: 134). These countries' emphasis on private

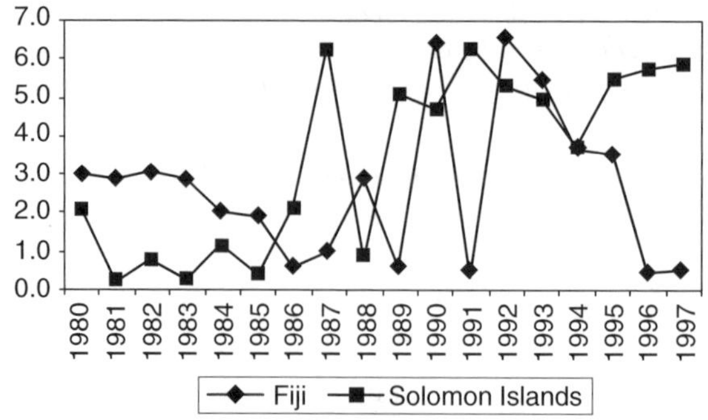

Figure 14.1 FDI/GDP (%).
Source: World Bank (1999).

sector development will require the government to ensure a stable macroeconomic regime, international competitiveness, clear and enforced property rights, a non-discriminatory regulatory environment, skilled labour and the provision of physical infrastructure. The main constraints that hinder investment opportunities for these island economies are political uncertainties, unclear property rights, macroeconomic instability, lack of skilled manpower and an inefficient administrative process.

Foreign aid

Foreign Aid or Official Development Assistance (ODA) has been a dominant feature in the Pacific Islands for over the past two decades. Developing countries in Oceania have an ODA/GNP ratio among the highest in the world, equal to 16 per cent on average (OECD 1987: 103). Where competition for aid between and within countries is growing, there is an increasing pressure for countries to use their existing aid flows more effectively, as well as the need to attract more private flows to finance development. Burnside and Dollar (1997) and the World Bank (1998) indicate that aid has a positive effect in a well-managed environment. Foreign aid flows to selected islands have remained high, but from 1990 there has been a declining trend. Japan, Australia, New Zealand and France are the major donors to the Pacific Island economies. Between 1980 and 1992, ODA to Pacific Islands amounted to almost 27 per cent of GDP. This average, however, conceals the variation of aid flows to individual islands. Aid hovered below 5 per cent of GDP for Fiji, while at the higher end, the Solomon Islands aid ratio amounted to 40 per cent in 1980, declining to 12 per cent of GDP in 1997 (Figure 14.2).

In the Solomon Islands, the development budget is mainly aid driven; thus aid may be a major determinant of growth. However, the ability of aid to influence growth depends on its form and utilization. For Fiji, Gounder (1999a) shows that total foreign aid, and aid in a decomposed form (bilateral aid, grant aid, technical cooperation grants), contributes positively to growth.

Trade

The South Pacific region accounts for a minuscule share of world production and trade, realizing less than 2 per cent of total world trade. The reliance is mainly on the export of a few primary products. Table 14.1 and Figures 14.3 and 14.4 demonstrate import dependence; the import share is much higher than the export to GDP ratio. Usually, net receipts from international services and transfers, particularly from foreign aid, offset trade deficits and the other net receipts come from tourism, financial services and remittances.

South Pacific Islands have trade arrangements with Australia, New Zealand, Japan, the US and countries in Asia and Europe under the South Pacific Regional Trade and Economic Cooperation Agreement, the Lomé Convention and the Generalized System of Preferences. Export destinations for Fiji and the Solomon Islands altered in the 1980s indicating a shift from traditional ties to more market-based arrangements. Also, the benefits arising from preferential access to protected markets (sugar to the US and Europe, copra to Europe, textiles to the Pacific), will diminish over time as these preferences are to be phased out.

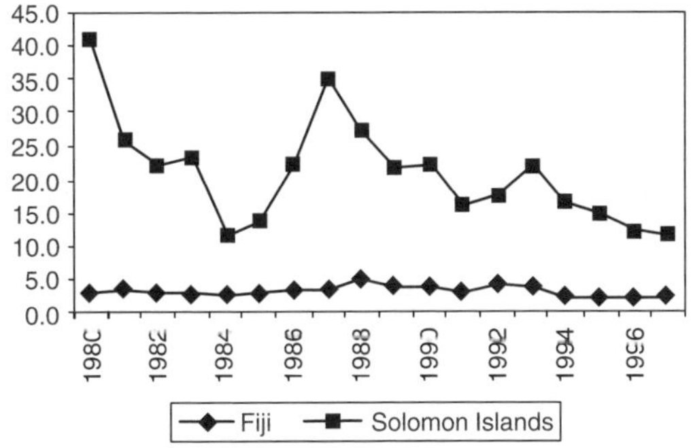

Figure 14.2 Aid/GDP (%).
Source: World Bank (1999).

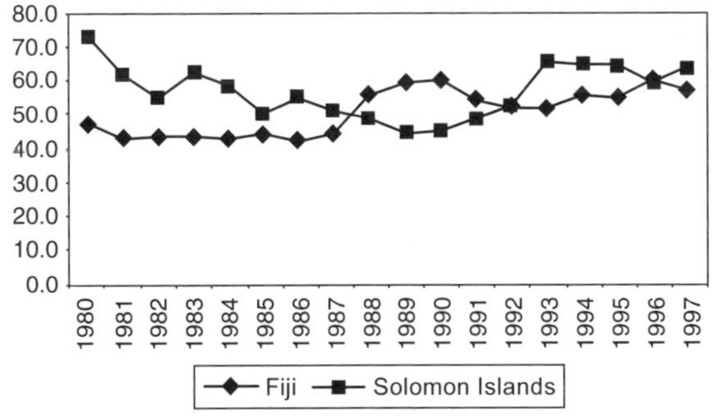

Figure 14.3 Exports/GDP (%).
Source: World Bank (1999).

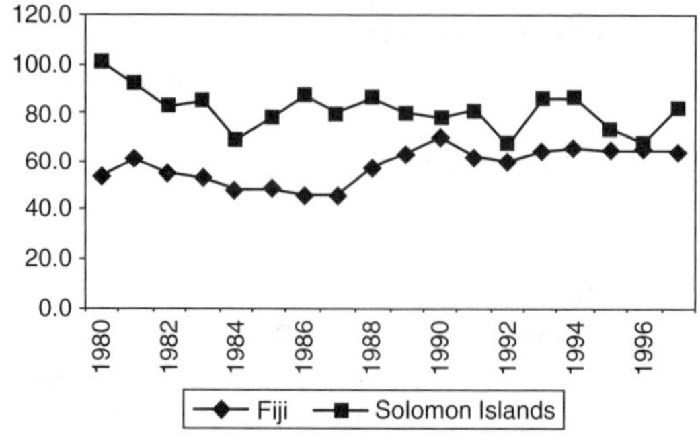

Figure 14.4 Imports/GDP (%).
Source: World Bank (1999).

Models, data and methodology, estimated results

Models, data and methodology

This section analyses the link between economic growth and globalization. To study the impact of capital flows and trade on the development of the island nations, the standard neoclassical measure of growth is modified to integrate several aspects of the impact of capital flows on the economy, as explained in the two-gap model. The simulation model tracks the impact of capital flows through its direct and indirect effects on investment, international trade and growth. The model consists of four behavioural equations: domestic investment, exports, imports, national savings and a resource gap identity equation.

Behavioural equations

$$I/Y_i = f_1(\dot{Y}_i, S/Y_i, FDI/Y_i, Aid/Y_i, Inf_{i(-1)}) \quad (1)$$

$$X/Y_i = f_2(\dot{Y}^*_i, I/Y_i, REX_i) \quad (2)$$

$$M/Y_i = f_3(\dot{Y}_i, I/Y, REX_i) \quad (3)$$

$$\dot{Y}_i = f_4(I/Y_i, \dot{L}_{\text{eff}_i}, Z_i) \quad (4)$$

Identity equation

$$\frac{(S_i - I_i)}{Y_i} = \frac{(X_i - M_i)}{Y_i} \quad (5)$$

where I/Y is domestic investment to GDP ratio, $\dot{Y}$ is growth rate of income, Aid/Y is foreign aid to GDP ratio, S/Y is the savings to GDP ratio, Inf is inflation rate, $\dot{L}_{\text{eff}}$ is the growth rate of effective labour force, measured as secondary, tertiary, vocational educational attainment to total labour force, X/Y is exports to GDP ratio, M/Y is imports to GDP ratio, $\dot{Y}^*$ is the weighted average by trade share of growth in per capita income of the trading partners, REX is real exchange rate, Z represents all other factors that may affect growth, that is, political instability, oil shocks and/or externalities, i is country i, that is, Fiji or the Solomon Islands, and S, I, X, M, Y is total savings, investment, exports, imports and GDP, respectively.

Equation (1) presents the macro impact of investment through FDI flows, aid, savings and inflation. Inflation is included as it affects the economy through higher price levels, which has an impact on investment decision-making. Equation (2) is the export function and equation (3) is the import function.

Equation (4) presents the growth function. The common variables that enter the growth model include the annual growth rate in the labour force and the investment share in GDP. Human capital is included in the growth process by creating an index that comprises secondary, tertiary and vocational educational enrolment to the total labour force as a proportion of population, called the effective labour force in this study. The Z vector in (4) includes all other factors that may affect growth: political instability, oil shocks and externalities. Equation (5) presents a balance of payments equation relating to a two-gap (saving-investment) model. FDI and aid can affect investment, imports and exports explicitly, and the balance of payments implicitly.

The model involves time series techniques as outlined in Harvey (1990) and Hendry (1995), using procedures that minimize the possibility of estimating spurious relations, while retaining the long-run information. Based on the results for each behavioural equations (1)–(4), with equation (5) as the identity equation, we undertake the ex-post simulation for each country. Overall the equations have a high explanatory power and the model diagnostics suggest no concern. Dynamic simulation techniques are employed to study the validity of the model, as well as generate multipliers to measure the impact of foreign capital flows and trade on growth. We utilize ordinary least squares (OLS) estimates. The estimation period for Fiji is 1968–97, for the Solomon Islands is 1970–97. The data source for the variables employed is World Bank (1999).

Empirical results for Fiji

The simulated values capture the fluctuations and trend over the period for most actual data quite well except for some years in the post-coup period due to political instability and also uncertainty caused by the implementation of the 1990 Constitution. The effect of globalization is measured by a dynamic multiplier analysis to understand the impact of foreign capital inflows and other factors on various macroeconomic variables that determine growth. The dynamic multiplier analysis shows how the endogenous variables may change over time in response to a change in a particular exogenous variable. In this study, the impact and long-run multipliers for five endogenous variables ($\dot{Y}$, *IY*, *XY*, *MY*, *SY*) are computed with respect to eight exogenous variables, namely, the growth rate of effective labour force ($\dot{L}_{eff}$), foreign direct investment (*FDI*), foreign aid (*A*), real exchange rate (*REX*), inflation (*Inf*), external shocks causing negative growth (*D1*), uncertainty affecting FDI in the post-coup period (*CFDI*) and growth rate in income of trading partners (*LGYTRP*). The coefficients estimated for the dynamic multiplier effects are presented in Table 14.2. The estimated value of the coefficient in each column represent the multiplier effect on the endogenous variables for every US$1 million increase in the exogenous variables. The short-run or impact multiplier measures the first period impact of the change in the endogenous variables due to the change in the exogenous variables.

Foreign direct investment as an important component of growth shows positive short-run and long-run multiplier values for the effect on $\dot{Y}$, *IY* and *MY*. This result suggests that FDI flows that are channelled through the private sector positively affects growth. FDI also has a positive relationship with domestic investment (*I/Y*), which has backward and forward linkages. The impact of FDI in the long-run increases substantially, and supports the view that domestic investment benefits from exposure to foreign technology. The FDI multiplier value is negative on savings; thus it does not stimulate domestic savings and therefore indirectly may not

Table 14.2 Short-run and long-run multipliers for the Fiji model

DEPVAR	*FDIY*	*Aid*	*CFDI*	$\dot{L}_{eff}$	*D1*	*Linf*	*REX*	*LGYTRP*
Short-run (impact multiplier)								
$\dot{Y}$	0.42	0.09	−0.33	−0.002	0.11	0.03	−0.001	0.003
IY	0.57	0.12	−0.44	−0.02	0.70	0.03	0.02	0.33
XY	−0.29	−0.06	0.23	0.004	−0.16	−0.02	−0.05	0.79
MY	0.02	0.12	−0.45	0.58	0.12	0.04	−0.08	0.36
SY	−0.03	−0.06	0.24	−0.03	1.22	−0.02	0.06	0.76
Long-run multiplier								
$\dot{Y}$	0.21	0.04	−0.16	0.17	−6.67	0.01	0.02	0.16
IY	1.87	0.38	−1.45	−0.09	3.59	0.11	0.15	1.49
XY	−1.66	−0.34	1.28	0.08	−3.18	−0.10	−0.36	2.67
MY	1.65	0.34	−1.28	0.13	−5.04	0.10	−0.49	1.31
SY	−1.44	−0.29	1.11	−0.14	5.45	−0.09	0.28	2.84

Notes

DEPVAR – dependent variable, $\dot{Y}$, *IY*, *XY*, *MY*, *SY* are growth rate of GDP, investment, exports, imports and savings to GDP ratio, respectively.

FDIY and *Aid* – foreign direct investment and aid to GDP ratio.

CFDI – interactive coup dummy for FDI.

$\dot{L}_{eff}$ – growth in effective labour force.

D1 – dummy for external shocks.

Linf – lagged inflation.

REX – real exchange rate.

LGYTRP – lagged growth of the income of the trading partners.

increase gross national investment. Nor does FDI fill the gap caused by low export earnings.

Aid inflows directly raises economic growth, investment and imports and lowers savings in Fiji. This implies that foreign aid is used to finance increased public investment and pay for imports. Essentially, aid is tied to imports of the donor country, and this effect is explained by the positive coefficient on the import multiplier both in the short- and long-run. However, the impact of aid on growth declined from 0.09 to 0.04 in the long-run.

It is not surprising that the extent of the impact of FDI on the components of aggregate supply is larger than the impact of foreign aid. This supports the view that FDI flows into productive sectors while foreign aid is usually used to finance social and physical infrastructure projects. Therefore, FDI directly contributes to economic growth, while aid contributes only indirectly to economic growth. The actual impact of military coups on foreign capital flows and its effect on other endogenous variables is measured by an interactive dummy variable (*CFDI*). The negative *CFDI* multiplier values in the short- and long-run indicate that economic growth, investment and imports have been adversely affected by coups. Gounder's (1999b) study of the impact of political instability on Fiji's economic growth shows a negative impact on capital and labour inputs of coups, leading to lower growth. The majority of the emigrants after the 1987 coups were Indo-Fijian professional and technical workers. In the case of Fiji, various actions immediately after the military coups in 1987 led to changes in government structures, abrogation of the 1970 Constitution and the coup leader, (then) Colonel Sitiveni Rabuka, becoming the Prime Minister of Fiji. Moreover, the 1990 Constitution (protecting the rights of the indigenous people in terms of political supremacy and land) was seen as racially prescriptive in nature, causing an international outcry (EIU 1998). The impact effect of growth in the effective labour force ($\dot{L}_{\mathrm{eff}}$) on GDP is negative in the short-run, due to political instability. In the long-run, however, increases in the effective labour force have a positive impact on growth. The negative effect of the lack of skilled manpower on investment increased in the long-run from -0.02 to -0.09. The emigration of skilled labour also contributes to lack of savings; the $\dot{L}_{\mathrm{eff}}$ impact multiplier value on savings (*SY*) increases from -0.03 to -0.14 in the long-run.

The results obtained for the impact of inflation (*LINF*) is consistent with the theory that an increase in inflation reduces exports and savings through real exchange rate appreciation and a decline in real interest rate, respectively. Overall, as Fiji has a low inflation rate, there are no adverse effects on growth, imports and investment. The *LGYTRP* coefficients (income of the trading partners) indicate a positive impact on all endogenous variables. The *XY* multiplier increases from 0.79 to 2.67 in the long-run, this reflects an increase in demand for goods from Fiji as its trading partners' income grow.

The steady-state concept assumes that all growth variables grow at a constant rate, however, the results in Table 14.2 show that in the short-run most of the factors that contribute to growth do not follow a similar trend.

Empirical results for the Solomon Islands

The dynamic simulation for the Solomon Islands covers the period 1976–97. The dynamic impact for five endogenous variables ($\dot{Y}$, *IY*, *XY*, *MY*, *SY*) are computed with respect to six exogenous variables (i.e. foreign direct investment (*FDI*), foreign aid (*A*), growth rate of effective labour force ($\dot{L}_{\text{eff}}$), real exchange rate (*REX*), inflation (*Inf*), and growth rate in income of the trading partners (*LGYTRP*). The coefficients estimated for the impact and long-run multiplier are presented in Table 14.3.

The FDI impact multiplier reveals a positive impact in the short-run on growth, exports and savings, however, the long-run multiplier values obtained are negative for all the endogenous variables except for exports. Therefore, factors such as technology, foreign capital and skills associated with FDI do not contribute to Solomon Islands growth. This may be due to lack of domestic skilled manpower and the associated physical infrastructure required by foreign investors, which in turn has an impact on Solomon Islands long-term development. Note also that the long-run coefficient for the effective labour force is negative (−0.07) in relation to the endogenous investment variable, providing support for the view that the Solomon Islands lacks human capital. Removing restrictions on capital should attract more FDI, creating jobs and integrating labour in international systems of production. While liberalization makes it easier to import goods, rising productivity increases the demand for skilled labour. Moreover, the unrest experienced in June–July 2000 caused the country's largest company, Solomon Taiyo, to repatriate all its foreign workers, following suspension of its operations. Such effects also lead to other negative effects via backward and forward links to other sectors.

The negative sign of FDI on the *MY* variable implies that FDI flows have not been a major force of rapid globalization through increased imports. The positive

Table 14.3 Short-run and long-run multipliers for the Solomon Islands model

DEPVAR	*FDIY*	*Aid*	$\dot{L}_{\text{eff}}$	*LINF*	*REX*	*LGYTRP*
Short-run (impact multiplier)						
$\dot{Y}$	0.09	−0.09	0.01	0.005	−0.001	−0.001
IY	−0.05	0.05	−0.005	−0.003	−0.001	−0.003
XY	0.14	−0.14	0.01	0.008	0.06	0.04
MY	−0.14	0.14	0.01	−0.008	−0.017	−0.002
SY	0.23	−0.22	−0.002	0.014	0.07	0.04
Long-run multiplier						
$\dot{Y}$	−0.29	0.28	−0.28	−0.017	−0.008	−0.004
IY	−0.72	0.69	−0.07	−0.043	−0.002	−0.001
XY	0.22	−0.21	0.02	0.013	0.24	0.16
MY	−0.49	0.46	0.07	−0.029	−0.08	−0.001
SY	−0.02	0.02	−0.13	−0.001	0.32	0.16

Notes as for Table 14.2.

coefficient on the *XY* variable suggests that foreign-owned enterprises generate a net positive flow of export earnings in the Solomon Islands. This may be due to tax incentives given to promote the export sector. FDI has a negative effect on savings in the long-run. Thus, the role of FDI as a supplement to domestic savings is unclear.

Aid inflows directly raise economic growth, investment, imports and savings in the Solomon Islands in the long-run. Thus, foreign aid may be used to finance increased public investment and imports. The impact of aid on growth increased from −0.09 to 0.28 in the long-run; it suggests that the Solomon Islands is heavily dependent on foreign aid to provide for its needs. The relationship between aid and investment is positive, which increases substantially from 0.05 to 0.69 in the long-run, thus aid supplements government resources to finance public investment that contributes to growth. Therefore, aid directly raises total investment (*IY*) through the increase in public expenditure and indirectly via private investment through an increase in income. Aid fills the savings gap in the long-run. The extent of the impact of aid on the components of aggregate supply is larger than the impact of FDI for the Solomon Islands. This may be because aid is used to finance social, physical infrastructure and other investment projects that contribute to growth. Whereas FDI flows are not large enough, it does not greatly affect the productive sectors, so the impact on growth is not established.

The impact of growth in effective labour force ($\dot{L}_{\text{eff}}$) on growth is negative in the long-run, this result supports the view that Solomon Islands has a low growth of skilled labour. According to the study by Ram (1996), the labour coefficient is generally negative, he points out that 'the labor parameter is not statistically significant in any model, which is a fairly typical scenario in the estimates of such growth equations for the LDCs' (Ram 1996: 1374). The negative impact of effective labour force is also seen in the investment sector where shortage of skilled manpower affects investment opportunities. Another problem the Solomon Islands faces is school dropouts. The lack of skilled labour causes the negative investment multiplier to increase from −0.005 to −0.07 in the long-run.

The results obtained for the impact of inflation are consistent with the theory that an increase in inflation causes negative effects on growth, investment, imports and savings. The Solomon Islands Government's chronic fiscal imbalance has created inflationary pressures, and is a major factor in retarding economic growth. Growth in trading partners' incomes has a positive impact only on exports. Thus, demand for goods increases as Solomon Islands trading partners' income grows. However, as the Solomon Islands is an exporter of a few primary commodities the earnings from the export sectors do not substantially contribute to increases in GDP.

The steady-state growth feature also does not fit the Solomon Islands due to the varying impact of the growth variables. The characteristics of smallness, lack of infrastructure and skilled labour has contributed to declining economic growth. Therefore, in the long run we observe a negative performance of various exogenous variables in relation to the endogenous variables, Table 14.3.

Furthermore, the backward and forward linkages necessary for growth are not sufficient.

Policy implications

The points raised here focus on the structural issues and constraints that island economies face in their effort to attract investment and develop the export sector. They are as follows:

- Due to openness on both trade and capital accounts, island states are vulnerable to external economic shocks and find it difficult to offset them through macroeconomic management. Reductions in official finance will adversely affect the development budget of small islands and reduce current spending which in turn depresses economic activity. Improvements in the conduct of monetary and fiscal policies are essential to offset these trends and shocks.
- As small island countries are more constrained in their access to external sources of private finance, smaller states like the Solomon Islands will still depend heavily on official aid to meet their resource needs. However, with a declining trend in foreign aid, these countries will have to compete for aid, and also strengthen their capacity to mobilize other resources, both domestic and foreign.
- Export diversification is required to secure earnings. Also if resources are excessively committed to slow growing segments in world trade, price and quantity movements may be offset, giving rise to earning instability. While Fiji has experienced considerable diversification of its export earnings in recent years, the Solomon Islands has lagged behind. Invisible earnings from tourism, offshore banking and other financial services have been extended, however diversification via the growth of manufactured exports as well as non-traditional primary products has not taken place. Money laundering is also becoming a growing problem.
- Countries in the South Pacific face the problem of unclear delineation of land titles. While Fiji has developed land legislation, the recent expiry of agricultural land leases, and the blockades of hotels by traditional landowners have shaken the confidence of investors. Where land disputes have been delayed, the lack of faith in previous land contracts has impaired investment and ultimately export-led growth in most Melanesian countries.
- Deterioration of law and order is a serious constraint to development in most Pacific islands, particularly, Fiji and Papua New Guinea, where it is reflected in rising operating costs, and a decrease in relative competitiveness.
- Poor skill development and relatively low levels of educational attainment are major constraints to the development of small island economies. Fiji, to some extent, possesses skilled labour and management capable of dealing with sectoral shifts. However, political instability in that country has led to an outflow of skilled manpower.

The concern of many small island economies is that they will be further marginalized in the emerging global economic order. These island nations have a narrow resource base; their exports are confined to a few primary products and they are heavily reliant on imports. A major challenge for Fiji and the Solomon Islands is the improvement of their competitiveness through domestic policy reforms that will enhance their prospects for growth through greater integration into the global economy. Political stability and good governance are of paramount importance.

References

Asian Development Bank (1998) *Asian Economic Outlook*, New York: Oxford University Press.

AusAID (1995) *The Economy of Fiji: Supporting Private Investment*, International Development Issue No. 40, Canberra: AusAID.

Australian International Development Assistance Bureau (1991) *The Solomon Islands Economy Prospects for Stabilization and Sustainable Growth*, International Development Issue No. 21, Canberra: PDP Australia Ltd.

Burnside, C. and Dollar, D. (1997) 'Aid, Policies, and Growth', Policy Research Working Paper 1777, World Bank Development Research Group, Washington, DC: World Bank.

Economic Intelligence Unit (1998) *EIU Country Profile: 1st Quarter*, Kent: Redhouse Press.

Economic Intelligence Unit (1999) *EIU Country Profile: 1st Quarter*, Kent: Redhouse Press.

Fiji Trade and Investment Board (1994) *Fiji Trade and Investment Board 1994 Annual Report*, Suva.

Gounder, R. (1999a) 'The Role of Development Assistance and Economic Growth: Empirical Results for Fiji', Department of Applied and International Economics Discussion Paper 99.14, New Zealand: Massey University.

Gounder, R. (1999b) 'The Political Economy of Development: Empirical Evidence From Fiji', *Economic Analysis and Policy*, 29(2), 133–50.

Harvey, A. (1990) *The Econometric Analysis of Time Series* (2nd edn), London: Phillip Allan.

Hendry, D.F. (1995). *Dynamic Econometrics*, Oxford: Oxford University Press.

Keith-Reid, R. (1998) 'Cook Islands, Kiribati, Samoa and Solomon Islands', in *The World of Information: The Asia and Pacific Review 1998* (17th edn), Essex: Walden Publishing.

Organization for Economic Cooperation and Development (1987) 1987 Report, *Development Cooperation in the 1990s: Effort and Policies of the Development Assistance Committee*, OECD. Paris.

Ram, R. (1996) 'Productivity of Public and Private Investment in Developing Countries: A Broad International Perspective', *World Development*, 24(8), 1373–8.

United Nations Conference of Trade and Development (1999) *Least Developed Countries Report*, New York: United Nations.

United Nations Economic and Social Commission for Asia and the Pacific (1997) *Enhancing Cooperation in Trade and Investment between Pacific Island Countries and Economies of East and South-East Asia*, Vol. 1 – Issues, Bangkok: UNESCAP.

World Bank (1996) *Pacific Island Economies: Building a Resilient Economic Base for the Twenty-First Century*, Washington, DC: World Bank.

World Bank (1998) *Assessing Aid*, New York: Oxford University Press.
World Bank (1999) *World Development Indicators*, Data on CD ROM, Washington, DC: World Bank.
World Bank (2000) *World Development Report 1999/2000*, New York: Oxford University Press.

15 Global integration and growth in Honduras and Nicaragua

Manuel R. Agosin

Introduction

Honduras and Nicaragua are two small neighbouring Central American countries with a common history and similar economies. Together with other countries in the region, both countries are emerging from decades of civil war and unrest; they are in the process of consolidating democratic governments, and have embraced a market-oriented growth strategy. This strategy stresses privatization of state enterprises and trade liberalization. It attaches special importance to export growth and diversification as the main pillar of development. Both countries have been members of the Central American Common Market (CACM) since its creation in the early 1960s and recognize the importance of regional integration for their development strategies.

These two economies are very poor, small and dependent on foreign trade (Table 15.1) After Haiti and Bolivia, they are the poorest countries in the Western Hemisphere. They are also examples of countries that are diverging from the world leader (the US). For the last twenty-five years, their per capita GDPs in purchasing power parity terms have been falling relative to the US' per capita GDP. At the same time, we are dealing with very open economies, where the importance of

Table 15.1 Basic economic indicators for Honduras and Nicaragua

	Honduras	*Nicaragua*
Per capita GDP, 1997 (US$, PPP)	2,220	1,950
Per capita GDP relative to the United States		
1975	10.1	20.3
1985	9.4	9.3
1997	7.7	6.9[a]
Population, 1997 (millions)	5.99	4.69
Export-GDP ratio (%)		
1990–2	32.4	22.6
1996–7	46.9	41.9

Source: Author's calculations, based on World Bank (1999).

Note

a 1995.

trade has been growing sharply over the last decade. So, in a sense, these countries provide a counterfactual to the Sachs–Warner hypothesis that open economies tend to converge on the output level of the world leader (Sachs and Warner 1995).[1]

This chapter discusses why, in site of considerable progress in the 1990s toward opening up to the world economy and in achieving macroeconomic equilibrium, these two economies have so far failed to achieve sustained growth and a visible improvement in living standards. The second section discusses the new political environment in Central America. The third section describes the opening up of the Honduran and Nicaraguan economies in the 1990s. The fourth section reviews the modest growth record of both countries during the past decade. In the fifth section we attempt to attribute causes for the failure of both countries to generate export-oriented growth, in spite of the policy progress achieved. The sixth section offers some conclusions and policy recommendations.

The importance of peace as a precondition for growth

All countries in the region except Costa Rica had faced left wing armed insurgency of a regional character during the 1980s. Democratic institutions were rebuilt, and the rule of law was re-established in the 1990s. Although Honduras was not at the centre of the conflict, it suffered its consequences. These took the form of intermittent threats to its government's authority and the use of its territory as sanctuary by combatants from other countries in the region, especially from bordering Nicaragua.

As armed opposition to the Somoza dictatorship grew in strength, Nicaragua suffered very severe civil upheavals since the early 1970s. The Sandinista forces that overthrew the Somoza Government in 1979 faced permanent armed threats from their opponents. In addition to civil strife, the economic and social fabric was subjected to severe strains, as the main orientation of policy swung first toward an attempt to implant a socialist, state-led model of development and, later, even before the Sandinistas left office, toward a more market-oriented approach. Since the assumption of an elected government in 1990, the strengthening of the market economy has been a major policy objective. As part and parcel of this approach, foreign trade has been freed from controls, macroeconomic policy has emphasized adjustment and disinflation and state enterprises have been or are in the process of being privatized.

Today, all Central American countries have democratically elected governments committed to market-oriented reforms, the armed forces are increasingly subordinated to civil authorities, and human rights violations are no longer state policy. Economically, pacification has yielded a large peace dividend. Specially in Honduras and Nicaragua, military spending as a share of GDP has declined remarkably: from 8.4 per cent of GDP in 1989 to 1.3 per cent in 1996 in Honduras, and from 28.3 per cent of GDP to 1.5 per cent in Nicaragua during the same period (ERDHS 1999).

However, there are still several important problems to be resolved in relation to human rights and personal security. Crime rates are high, and people continue to have a sense of insecurity about life and property. In Nicaragua, protection of property rights is still inadequate. Consequently, both countries have serious problems of governance.

Policies to achieve greater global integration

As already suggested, both countries have shifted their growth strategies toward greater market orientation and integration into the global economy. We examine three aspects of the new policy package: macroeconomic adjustment, opening up to trade in the context of 'open regionalism' and policies toward foreign direct investment (FDI).

Progress in macroeconomic adjustment

The conventional wisdom is that prudent fiscal and monetary policies are key to structural adjustment, which in itself is a precondition for success in the global economy. Perhaps the single most important reform in this regard is the reduction of the public deficit. If the objective of achieving a new, growth-promoting insertion into the world economy is to be preserved, expenditure cuts must fall on items other than investment in education and health. Indeed, in most countries, such expenditures will have to increase. Where the tax burden is low, an important contribution to the needed reductions in the deficit will have to come from tax reform aimed at raising revenues.

Nicaragua's adjustment programme, implemented with the return to democracy in 1990, consisted in first using the exchange rate as an anchor for domestic prices while bringing down drastically the budget deficit, which was due to the inefficiency of nationalized enterprises and, above all, to a swollen military budget. Inflation fell from over 13,000 per cent per annum in 1990 (January–December) to between 10 and 20 per cent in the second half of the 1990s (see Agosin 2001 for more details on inflation, fiscal balances and the real exchange rate in the two countries). The price was currency appreciation in real terms, supported by official capital inflows. The reductions in government spending and employment were draconian. Public employment fell from 208,000 workers in 1990 to 100,000 in 1994. Most of the cuts took the form of reductions in the armed forces, from more than 100,000 soldiers to barely 24,000 over the same period (Agudelo 2000).

Nicaragua has also implemented tax reform and has succeeded in raising its tax burden from 15 per cent of GDP in 1990 to over 30 per cent in 1998. As part of the effort to put its fiscal house in order, the Nicaraguan government has made efforts to charge users for public services. The conjunction of spending cuts and revenue increases resulted in the reduction of the deficit from over 20 per cent of GDP in 1990 to 2.2 per cent in 1998 (Solórzano 2000). However, the public sector continues to rely heavily on foreign aid (about 8 per cent of GDP).

Honduras did not suffer from the serious macroeconomic disequilibria that afflicted Nicaragua until 1989. However, the authorities have not been successful in bringing inflation down to a single digit level (see Agosin 2001). In spite of some progress, the fiscal deficit remains problematic, and there is still considerable room for raising the tax burden. It is not possible to accurately estimate the share of aid in government receipts, presumably it is close to the difference between total government receipts and tax revenues, which amounts to about 3–4 per cent of GDP. Accounting for debt refinancing, an extra 3 percentage points of GDP ought to be added.

The challenges of 'open regionalism'

After a long period of protection, in the 1990s all Central American countries adopted an export-oriented model of development. At the beginning of this decade, the bulk of tariffs in members of the CACM ranged from 5 to 95 per cent, with occasional tariff peaks well over 100 per cent. Countries also resorted to a variety of non-tariff measures to restrict imports. As a result of negotiations to revive the CACM, at the end of 2000 all CACM members (Costa Rica, El Salvador, Guatemala, Honduras and Nicaragua) will have tariffs in the range of 0–15 per cent on about 90 per cent of their tariff lines. Most non-tariff barriers have been eliminated.

Buffeted by the disintegrating effects of civil strife and the external debt crisis, the CACM unravelled in the 1980s. With the reestablishment of peace, signatories have been in the process of bringing the CACM back to life. A new CET was agreed, and the share of regional trade in the total foreign trade of member countries has staged a comeback (see Table 15.2).

The CET contains only four tariff rates. A zero rate applies to raw materials, intermediate goods and capital goods not produced in Central America. Raw material produced in the region carry a duty of 5 per cent. Capital goods produced in the region are subject to a tariff of 10 per cent, and a tariff of 15 per cent is applied to finished goods. Some examples of goods excluded from the CET are certain agricultural goods, meat, poultry, tobacco, non-alcoholic and alcoholic beverages, petroleum and automobiles. Tariffs on these goods can be much higher than the maximum of 15 per cent agreed to for the CET. However, these higher rates are often justifiable on government revenue or equity grounds.

Efforts to establish a CET have been undermined by other unilateral actions as well. In the first place, individual countries are able to negotiate exceptions to the

Table 15.2 Intra-regional trade in Central America, as a share of total trade (%)

	1960	*1968*	*1980*	*1985*	*1990*	*1998*
Exports	6.8	23.5	25.4	13.9	17.0	20.2
Imports	—	21.3	18.5	9.9	9.7	13.3

Source: Author's calculations, based on data of SIECA and on World Bank (1989).

Note: Central America covers Costa Rica, El Salvador, Guatemala, Honduras and Nicaragua.

CET. Nicaragua has obtained agreement from its partners to reduce its top two tariff rates to 5 and 10 per cent, respectively. In some cases, tariff surcharges that affect other member countries are imposed without consultation. Second, each country has bound its tariffs in WTO at different rates. Honduras' entire tariff is bound at 35 per cent, and Nicaragua's is bound at 40 per cent. This means that, faced with balance of payments difficulties, the CET could once again unravel. Third, countries are pursuing free trade agreements with third parties in an individual manner. For example, Nicaragua has signed a comprehensive free trade agreement with Mexico; Honduras, El Salvador and Guatemala are negotiating their own joint agreement with that country. Fourth, groups of countries within CACM are pursuing the formation of more exclusive 'clubs'. Before their dispute over maritime jurisdiction in early 2000, Nicaragua had started negotiations with Honduras toward the formation of a complete customs union by 2002. In May 2000 Honduras announced that it was joining El Salvador and Guatemala in a customs union.

There are other challenges ahead for the CACM. One of them is agreement on a uniform drawback and export-subsidy scheme for exports outside the region. The distortive effects of excluding these policies from regional harmonization efforts are bound to grow as integration deepens. A second concern is failure to arrive at a common regional approach toward FDI in general and toward Export Processing Zones (EPZs) in particular. Third, effective integration will require a concerted effort to improve regional infrastructure. Finally, greater exchange rate and macroeconomic coordination will have to be pursued.

In spite of these difficulties and while much remains to be done, the efforts to strengthen regional integration can be judged as very successful. Moreover, regional integration is being pursued in the context of a very significant reduction of tariffs on a Most Favoured Nation (MFN) basis, which, for small economies, undoubtedly has greater development potential than the protectionist policies of the past.

Opening up to FDI

The liberalization of FDI regimes is part and parcel of global integration, and the Central American countries have understood this well. Accordingly, Honduras and Nicaragua (together with other CACM members) have considerably liberalized their FDI regimes. National treatment is guaranteed to foreign investors. In addition, they have complete freedom to invest in any sector of the economy (except related to defence) and to remit earnings or repatriate their capital abroad. No performance requirements are imposed on investors. Both countries have signed the Multilateral Investment Guarantee Agreement (MIGA).

In Nicaragua, foreign investors who register with the Foreign Investment Committee enjoy additional assurances from the Government and can benefit from specific sectoral incentives that are available to national investors. However, such registration is not a legal requirement, and most investors do not register. Foreign investment legislation is in the process of being simplified.

Table 15.3 FDI, as a share of GDP (%)

	1990–2	*1993–5*	*1996*	*1997*	*1998*
Honduras	1.5	1.5	2.2	2.7	1.9
Nicaragua	0.3	2.8	4.9	8.6	10.2

Sources: World Bank (1999) and Central American Monetary Council.

Up to now, Nicaragua has been more successful than Honduras in attracting FDI. In recent years, FDI in Nicaragua has represented a significant share of GDP (see Table 15.3). Beginning in 1996, there have been important new investments in the energy and mining sectors. Other sectors that have received significant foreign investment are hotels, shrimp farming and cellular telecommunications. The low figures for Honduras could be somewhat deceptive, since multinational enterprises (MNEs) in EPZs operate mostly through domestic subcontractors.

Both countries have attempted to attract foreign investors to EPZs set up for foreign firms or for domestic subcontractors of MNEs assembling products with imported parts for the international market. Firms in EPZs enjoy complete tariff exemptions over imported inputs and income tax holidays. The latter are permanent in Honduras, and have a duration of 15 years in Nicaragua (Gitli 1997: 202–10, see also Jenkins *et al.* 1998). Owing to greater political stability and more clearly defined property rights, Honduras has been more successful in this activity.

The growth record

The growth performance of these two countries was quite different in the 1990s. Despite considerable structural change, GDP in Honduras did not grow in per capita terms. By contrast, despite less structural change, in Nicaragua there was positive per capita growth in the 1990s, after two decades of economic contraction (see Table 15.4). In fact, in Honduras, the growth rate decelerated somewhat in the second half of the decade. In Nicaragua, once the disinflation and adjustment of the first half of the decade had been completed, there was a visible improvement in growth performance in the second half.

There is evidence that, in Honduras, investment is overestimated, and that GDP is probably underestimated (Ramos Lobo 2000), so that recorded rates of investment in recent years in excess of 30 per cent of GDP are hardly credible, especially in view of stagnation in per capita output. In Nicaragua, the gross investment to GDP ratio declined from an annual median of 25 per cent in the 1980s to an annual median of slightly under 20 per cent in the 1991–7 period.

Since global integration is one of the key objectives of the new development strategies adopted by both Honduras and Nicaragua, particular importance attaches to the evolution of exports in the 1990s. A good sign that change has begun is, indeed, the performance of the export sector. Exports have led economic growth in both countries in the 1990s, and there is evidence that export growth is

Table 15.4 Rates of growth of GDP and GDP per capita, 1970–99 (%)

	Honduras	*Nicaragua*
GDP		
1971–80	5.4	0.0
1981–90	2.4	−1.5
1991–9	3.1	3.2
1991–5	3.4	1.7
1996–9	2.6	5.2
Per capita GDP		
1971–80	2.1	−3.2
1981–90	−0.8	−4.1
1991–9	0.2	0.3
1991–5	0.4	−1.2
1996–9	—	2.3

Sources: World Bank (1999) and CEPAL (1999).

accelerating at an annual average of 3.3 per cent and 5.0 per cent respectively in Honduras and Nicaragua during the 1991–9 period. In Honduras there was a strong pick up in the growth of exports beginning around 1995. Up until 1998, export growth had been very strong. The 1999 figures were affected by the adverse impact of Hurricane Mitch. In Nicaragua, high export growth was sustained through 1997. In 1998–9, poor export performance can be attributed to the elimination in 1998 of export incentives benefiting non-traditional exports and to the effects of Hurricane Mitch.[2]

The transformation of the structure of exports since the early 1990s has been remarkable, particularly in Honduras. The share of traditional commodity exports (bananas, coffee, sugar, cotton and meat) fell significantly in the 1990s in both countries; in the case of Honduras, the decline was dramatic (Table 15.5). Since the arrival of peace, new export crops have been developed, especially fruits and vegetables (so-called 'dessert products'), ornamental plants, new agricultural staples, cultivated shrimp, tobacco products, prepared fruit products and some light manufactures such as soaps and detergents. Exports to Central America have grown very rapidly, but so have non-traditional exports to destinations outside the region.

In addition, Central America has emerged as a big assembler of garments (and, marginally, of other manufactured goods, such as plastic goods, metal products and consumer electronics) for the US market (Gitli 1997; Jenkins *et al.* 1998). Honduras has taken the lead in this regard, with over 100,000 jobs generated in EPZs by foreign firms and their domestic subcontractors. These *maquiladoras* are concentrated in a corridor outside San Pedro Sula, which has become the main industrial centre in the country.

The heavily globalized garment industry is built around a dozen or so layers of subcontractors. The entrepreneurial structure can be viewed as a pyramid of

Table 15.5 Traditional and non-traditional exports: shares in total exports and average annual rate of growth, 1990–8 (%)

	Share in total		*Growth 1990–8*
	1990	*1998*	
Honduras			
Traditional[a]	82.7	37.0	1.0
Non-traditional	17.3	41.3	24.5
Central America	(4.2)	(11.3)	(26.2)
Rest of the world	(13.0)	(30.0)	(23.9)
Maquila value added	—	21.7	45.2[c]
Total	100.0	100.0	9.8
Total (US$ million)	831.5	2,011.0	
Nicaragua			
Traditional[b]	79.2	56.5	4.2
Non-traditional	20.8	32.7	15.0
Central America	(13.2)	(19.2)	(13.8)
Rest of the world	(7.6)	(13.5)	(16.8)
Maquila value added	—	10.7	96.2[d]
Total	100.0	100.0	8.7
Total (US$ million)	330.5	642.2	

Sources: Author's calculations, based on data from Banco Central de Nicaragua, Secretaría de Integración Económica de Centro América (SIECA), Banco Central de Honduras, Consejo Monetario Centroamericano and Gitli (1997).

Notes

a Basically coffee and bananas. It includes modest values of other unprocessed primary products.

b Coffee, bananas, marine shrimp, gold, silver, cattle molasses, and cotton.

c 1991–8.

d 1992–8.

subcontractors, which has at its apex a big production or marketing MNE. When one reaches the Central American layers, one finds a few US, Korean, and Taiwanese MNEs with their own facilities, as well as domestic enterprises working on a subcontracting basis for a MNE. From the point of view of the development of domestic entrepreneurship this is a favourable development.

The growth of the *maquiladora* industry has been phenomenal (Table 15.6). In 1990, in Honduras national value added by *maquiladoras* constituted barely 4 per cent of total export earnings from goods, and they employed 17.5 thousand workers. In Nicaragua, there was no *maquiladora* industry at all in 1990. In 1998, national value added represented 21.7 per cent of the value of goods exports in Honduras. In Nicaragua, where this activity is still in its infancy in 1998, the share of national value added by *maquiladoras* in export revenues was 10.7 per cent. In Honduras, employment in *maquiladoras* accounts for nearly 50 per cent of total manufacturing sector employment.

Table 15.6 Importance of the *maquiladora* industry

	1990	*1998*
Honduras		
National value added (US$ million)	31.6	436.4
Percentage of exports	3.9	21.7
Employment (thousands)	17.5	100.0[a]
Percentage of industrial employment	22.3	50.0[a]
Nicaragua		
National value added (US$ million)	—	68.7
Percentage of exports	—	10.7
Employment (thousands)	—	11.0[b]
Percentage of industrial employment	—	30.0[a]

Source: Gitli (1997: 32–4, 38).

Notes
a Estimate.
b 1996.

Some explanations for weak growth performance

In spite of very significant policy reform, both of these two countries have yet to generate a process of sustained economic growth. Market-oriented reform is a necessary but not sufficient precondition for growth. More is clearly needed. What this 'more' entails is a complex matter. Some of the explanations for weak growth are outlined below.

Weak linkages between export activities and the domestic economy

Since the early 1990s, the fastest-growing sector of the Honduran economy has been the *maquiladoras*. They have been responsible for the dynamism of the region around San Pedro Sula and have transformed that city into the most prosperous in the country. Unfortunately, the dynamism of the *maquiladoras* has not translated into faster growth for the country as a whole. Besides labour, electricity, rents and a few other services, firms operating in the sector purchase practically nothing in Honduras. Thus export processing generates few backward linkages to other sectors of the economy.

In Nicaragua, export activity has been considerably less dynamic. Although new export sectors did emerge in the course of the 1990s, they are far from becoming consolidated. In fact, non-traditional exports suffered a severe setback in 1998–9. The main source of growth has been the recovery of domestic demand from the shocks associated with macroeconomic adjustment. Unless the economy can generate an export-oriented growth momentum, the relatively satisfactory performance of recent years could be short-lived.

Weak signals encouraging export production

Signals arising from the opening up of the economy have favoured non-tradables rather than the export sector. This is mainly because national currencies in both countries, especially in Nicaragua, have tended to become overvalued. There have been two major causes for currency overvaluation, a 'double Dutch disease in the tropics', see Agosin (2001, figure 1). In the first place, both countries have come to count on wage remittances to meet their foreign exchange needs. This boosts imports, and helps to prevent real exchange rates from depreciating. Official balance of payments figures consistently underestimate the value of remittances. In Nicaragua, wage remittances are estimated to be in the range of US$400–600 million, compared with total export earnings from goods of about US$700 million. The second cause is heavy reliance on foreign aid. Both countries, and particularly Nicaragua, are heavy recipients of official development assistance, mostly soft loans.

Table 15.7 presents estimates of foreign aid and wage remittances. Nicaragua has had to continuously refinance heavy debt service requirements that it is unable to meet, accounting for between 30 and 40 per cent of GDP. Even excluding such refinancing, estimated net aid receipts plus wage remittances are above 10 per cent of GDP. The situation is somewhat less dramatic in Honduras, although net foreign exchange receipts from these two sources also account for between 5 and 10 per cent of GDP. Even so, it is likely that our calculations continue to underestimate wage remittances, since keeping track of them can be notoriously difficult. Both countries are likely to be accepted to the HIPC Initiative in 2000.[3] This would wipe out 80 per cent of the net present value of outstanding debt.

Export subsidies, used quite successfully during the 1980s and early 1990s in neighbouring Costa Rica, have proven difficult to implement in Honduras and Nicaragua. True enough, outward-bound assembly for the US market enjoys generous income tax exemptions. However, neither country has a genuine drawback system on imported inputs used in export production located outside EPZs. Moreover, they do not avail themselves of the leeway they have as low-income members of the World Trade Organization (WTO) to use subsidies to encourage the emergence of new exports.

Table 15.7 Estimates of foreign aid plus wage remittances, 1996–8 (as % of GDP)

	1996	*1997*	*1998*
Honduras			
With debt refinancing	15.5	11.5	8.8
Without debt refinancing	12.9	8.6	5.5
Nicaragua			
With debt refinancing	46.2	53.8	34.7
Without debt refinancing	3.1	11.7	10.8

Source: Author's estimates, based on IMF (2000) data.

Until early 1998, Nicaragua used to grant exporters of non-traditional goods exemptions on income taxes on their profits earned in export production, as well as Tax Benefit Certificates (*Certificados de Beneficio Tributario*) equivalent to a certain proportion of export earnings. These Certificates could be used to pay income tax or could be sold to third parties. This incentive was patterned after Costa Rica's very successful *Certificados de Abono Tributario* (CATs), which operated until the 1990s, and were instrumental in diversifying exports away from primary commodities towards manufactures. Nicaragua wrongly eliminated both of these incentives in 1998 and replaced them by subsidy of 1.5 per cent of the value of exports (applicable to all exporters) in lieu of a drawback on duties paid on imported inputs. The use of export subsidies to stimulate the emergence of new exports is particularly appropriate in the light of the structural problems that affect these countries' real exchange rate and which are very difficult to deal with successfully.

Inadequate investment in human capital and health

Since the pioneering paper by Barro (1991), levels of human capital have been considered essential initial conditions explaining subsequent economic growth. Both of these countries had very inadequate levels of educational achievement at the beginning of the past decade. In countries where education and health indicators are at very low levels, it is certain that access to such services is very heavily concentrated in a few well-off segments of society. This means that most of the population will be unable to participate in the modern economy, especially as it integrates into the global economy. Honduras and Nicaragua also have severe problems of gender equality, which lower the participation rates of women in the labour force and reduce the quantity and quality of educational and health services available to women. Thus, women contribute less than their potential to economic growth.[4]

We look at four major dimensions of human development: the demographic transition,[5] basic health indicators, child malnutrition indicators and education indicators.

Honduras and Nicaragua still have very high rates of population growth, more than double Costa Rica's (see Agosin 2001: table 12). Their high fertility rates imply that the share of dependent young people in the total population will remain high for a long time, making it difficult to provide education for all who need it and reducing the saving rate of households. Fertility rates are kept high partly because of inadequate investment in the quantity and quality of education. An improvement in education, particularly at post-primary levels, would probably result in a fall in fertility rates, which would then yield an important one-off demographic dividend.

One particular problem in these two countries is the abnormally large size of the informal sector, evidence of the inability of the formal sector of the economy to provide productive employment for all those who are able and willing to work. Part of the problem arises from urban–rural migration. Average living conditions for workers in the informal urban sector may be no better than in the countryside. However, migration occurs because there is a non-zero probability of having access to higher wages in the formal urban sector, in the spirit of the Harris–Todaro model (1970).

In Nicaragua, in addition, the rate of open unemployment is high, mainly as a consequence of the dramatic shrinkage of the state sector during the adjustment of the early 1990s. While measured unemployment receded gradually from its high of 17.8 per cent in 1993, it still was 12.5 per cent of the labour force in mid-1999 (Solórzano 2000). In Honduras, measured unemployment is much lower, but much that passes for 'employment' is at such low levels of productivity that it is really disguised unemployment.

Micro enterprises represent a problem and an opportunity. If ways could be found to help them improve their technological level, and if credit were more readily available to them, it might be possible to raise living standards, wages and employment. Some micro enterprises may eventually be in a position to produce import-competing goods or inputs for export production.

Conclusions and policy recommendations

It is evident that Honduras and Nicaragua are beginning to shift away from a reliance on primary commodities for export and production of import substitutes for the home market towards a mix of simple manufactures and processed primary products for international markets. Honduras is more advanced in this direction than Nicaragua. On the other hand, Nicaragua appears to be a few steps ahead of Honduras in macroeconomic stability and in having raised its tax burden to levels that are compatible with the investments in human resources that will be needed for successful global integration.

In spite of considerable progress toward greater openness and stability since the early 1990s, these economies have not taken off. The main problems they face are:

- poor governance;
- inadequate protection of property rights, particularly in Nicaragua;
- weak growth impulses emanating from new exports;
- absence of strong backward linkages from exports to the rest of the economy;
- weak supply responses to the price signals emanating from the economic reforms;
- low levels of investment in human capital and in health.

The experience of these two countries shows that passive liberalization policies are insufficient to spur export-oriented growth. In low-income countries there are two basic requirements for successful integration into the global economy. In the first place, market signals emanating from policy change must be strong and unequivocal. Second, supply responses must be encouraged through deliberate policies to stimulate investment and develop appropriate human resources, see Agosin (1999b) and Agosin *et al.* (2000a).

Both countries need to align the structure of incentives more closely with the goal of encouraging export diversification. This will involve correcting currency overvaluation or counteracting its effects. The first option – attempting to fight currency appreciation – is not easy under any circumstance, much less when the sources of overvaluation are in some sense desirable. Wage remittances raise the living standards of those who receive them, who are among the poorest segments of society.

In the first place, Honduras and Nicaragua must become accustomed to decreasing amounts of foreign aid, not only because such resources appreciate their currencies. The degree of support that these countries can expect from the international community in the future will undoubtedly diminish, especially if they are both admitted to the HIPC Initiative. For this to happen, public saving must rise. Nicaragua has done much to raise tax revenues and cut current expenditure. It still has space to cut non-essential expenditure to make room for investment in education and health. As it succeeds in replacing foreign aid with domestically generated resources, the córdoba should depreciate. As regards Honduras, it is essential that it raise its tax burden to levels that will allow it to finance needed investment in human resources. There is also a need to cut expenditures unrelated to investment in human capital and health.

Some positive results could be obtained from encouraging recipients of wage remittances to save a larger proportion of their receipts. This could be done through special housing programmes or educational schemes tied to prior saving.

A clear picture of what awaits Nicaragua and Honduras is provided by the experience of El Salvador, where wage remittances, about two-thirds of goods exports, are the main factor behind the severe currency appreciation that has taken place since the early 1990s. Since it maintains a fixed nominal exchange rate, El Salvador has had to face a continuous accumulation of reserves. Policies of sterilizing the monetary impact of reserve accumulation have kept domestic interest rates very high and have inhibited private investment. So, El Salvador is stuck with the worst of all possible worlds: an appreciated real exchange rate that renders exportables uncompetitive and a high real interest rate, which discourages investment generally.

One way to dampen real exchange rate appreciation in Honduras and Nicaragua would be for the Central Bank to accumulate reserves and to sterilize their monetary impact by issuing dollar-denominated paper backed by Central Bank reserves (rather than paper denominated in domestic currency). This would prevent domestic interest rates from rising, but would certainly have a cost. In order to make the dollar-denominated paper attractive to private investors, the Central Bank would have to wind up paying interest rates in excess of what it receives on its own reserves. This loss would, in effect, represent a subsidy to the production of tradables.

An alternative to fighting this form of Dutch disease would be to subsidize the production of new export products, something that the Nicaraguan government seems to be ideologically opposed to at the present time. The Honduran government has less clear positions in this respect. As developing countries with a GDP below US$1000, Honduras and Nicaragua are exempted from WTO injunctions against export subsidies. These countries must use this space to design a temporary and moderate mechanism to support non-traditional exports to non-Central American markets.

A mechanism such as the 'simplified drawback' used by Chile with great success since the mid-1980s ought to be considered (see Agosin 1999a, for a description).[6] The simplified drawback consists of a subsidy of up to 10 per cent of the 'fob' value of exports which benefits all firms that export goods belonging to tariff lines whose total value of exports does not exceed US$20 million. The subsidy is granted in lieu of the regular drawback of duties paid on imported inputs used in the production of exports. When exports of a particular tariff line exceed the US$20 million threshold, all exporters of the good lose the right to the subsidy and must apply for a regular drawback.

As a minimum, Honduras and Nicaragua should implement a drawback on duties paid on imported inputs used by direct and indirect exporters.[7] By not having such benefits, exporters are being penalized artificially in favour of competitors from other countries.

In order to transform the *maquiladora* industry into a true 'development pole', greater attention must be devoted to encouraging the growth of stronger linkages with the rest of the domestic economy. In addition, governments are not making efforts to target specific sectors and firms to attract to their EPZs. Products other than textiles, such as, assembly of electronic and plastic goods, have greater potential for developing stronger linkages with the domestic economy, and their producers are less footloose than garment assemblers. This is exactly what Costa Rica has done in the field of electronics. If countries are serious about the Common Market, this ought to be done at the regional level. For starters, EPZ legislation ought to be harmonized across countries. A uniform length for tax holidays of 5–10 years ought to be adopted by all countries.

Another element of a growth-oriented strategy toward the *maquiladora* industry would be an effort to encourage the development of strong regional industries supplying inputs to the *maquiladoras*. One way of doing this is to institute a region-wide programme of tariff drawbacks for suppliers of inputs to the *maquiladoras*. Other useful policies in this regard could include setting up special training and capacity building programmes, attractive to aid donors. This approach also highlights the link that exists between successful global integration and investment in human capital and health.

Countries ought to sign double taxation treaties with the US, the main home country of foreign investors in EPZs. As regards foreign investors, double taxation treaties with the US (and other countries of origin) are probably just as useful as tax exemptions. Once such a treaty is in place, taxes paid in Central America would simply be credited to their (presumably lower) income tax liabilities back home.

Finally, the problems of micro and small enterprises also need to be tackled vigorously. As already noted, a key problem is the lack of finance for these firms. In both Honduras and Nicaragua, financing for this segment of the enterprise sector is available only from NGOs and other not-for-profit organizations. It is time to convert these institutions into real banks, as has been done in neighbouring El Salvador (see Trigueros 2000). Micro finance institutions can only be successful when they operate as banks offering a wide variety of financial services. See, for example, Morduch (1999) and Agosin (1999a). When borrowers come to understand that they will be cut off from future access to finance if they do not service their loans in a timely fashion, non-performing loans tend to fall dramatically. Therefore, simple reforms enabling the creation of banks specializing in servicing the financial needs of micro and small enterprises would be a move in the direction of easing these firms' financial constraints.

Acknowledgements

I am thankful to Dr Mansoob Murshed for useful comments on a previous draft.

Notes

1 To be fair to Sachs and Warner, it is conceivable that trade liberalization, which dates back to the early 1990s in both countries, has been too recent to yield growth dividends.
2 Based on interviews with exporters, analysts and government officials in July 1999 and May 2000.
3 HIPC stands for 'highly indebted poor countries'. The HIPC Initiative is a programme of the multilateral financial institutions to provide debt relief to poor countries that have made progress toward macroeconomic adjustment. For a discussion of the HIPC Initiative in the context of Honduras' and Nicaragua's debt problems, see Esquivel *et al.* (1998).
4 For a fuller examination of human development issues in Central America, see Agosin *et al.* (2000b).
5 A decline in fertility rates lead to higher saving and investment and to more investment in the quality of children and, hence, in labour productivity over the long run. Of course, the impact of demographic variables is not permanent.
6 This instrument will be dismantled at the end of 2002 because it is inconsistent with WTO rules. As less developed countries, Honduras and Nicaragua would not have legal impediments to utilize an instrument of this nature.
7 Indirect exporters are producers who sell inputs to exporters.

References

Agosin, M.R. (1999a) 'Private Finance for Development: Analytical Underpinnings and Policy Issues', New York: Office of Development Studies, United Nations Development Programme. Processed.

Agosin, M.R. (1999b) 'Trade and Growth in Chile', *CEPAL Review*, 68, 79–100.

Agosin, M.R. (2001) 'Global Integration and Growth in Honduras and Nicaragua', WIDER Discussion Paper 2001/31, Helsinki: UNU/WIDER available at www.wider.unu.edu.

Agosin, M.R., Bloom, D.E., and Gitli, E. (2000a) 'Globalization, Liberalization, and Sustainable Human Development: Analytical Perspectives', UNCTAD/UNDP Global Programme, Geneva, March. Processed.

Agosin, M.R., Bloom, D.E., and Gitli, E. (2000b) 'Globalization, Liberalization, and Sustainable Human Development in Central America', UNCTAD/UNDP Global Programme, Geneva, March. Processed.

Agudelo, I. (2000) 'Implicaciones de la Reforma Económica para el Desarrollo Humano Sostenible en Nicaragua', UNCTAD/UNDP Global Programme, Managua, March. Processed.

Barro, R. (1991) 'Economic Growth in a Cross Section of Countries', *The Quarterly Journal of Economics*, 106, 407–43.

CEPAL (1999) *Balance Preliminar de las Economías de América Latina y el Caribe*, Santiago: CEPAL.

Esquivel, G., Larraín, F., and Sachs, J.D. (1998) 'The External Debt Problem in Central America: Honduras, Nicaragua, and the HIPC Initiative', Development Discussion Paper No. 645, Cambridge, MA: Harvard Institute for International Development, Harvard University.

Estado de la Región en Desarrollo Humano Sostenible (ERDHS) (1999) Proyecto Estado de la Nación, San José, Costa Rica.

Gitli, E. (1997) *La Industria de la Maquila en Centroamérica*, San José: International Labour Office.

Harris, J.R. and M.P. Todaro (1970) 'Migration, Unemployment, and Development: A Two-Sector Analysis', *The American Economic Review*, 60, 126–42.

IMF (International Monetary Fund) (2000) *International Financial Statistics*, May, Washington, DC: IMF.

Jenkins, M., Esquivel, G., and Larraín, F. (1998) 'Export Processing Zones in Central America', Development Discussion Paper No. 646, Cambridge, MA: Harvard Institute for International Development, Harvard University.

Morduch, J. (1999) 'The Microfinance Promise', *Journal of Economic Literature*, 37, 1569–614.

Ramos Lobo, M. (2000) 'Implicaciones de la Reforma Económica para el Desarrollo Humano Sostenible en Honduras', UNCTAD/UNDP Global Programme, Tegucigalpa, March. Processed.

Sachs, J.D. and Warner, A. (1995) 'Economic Reform and the Process of Global Integration', *Brookings Papers on Economic Activity*, 1, 1–117.

Solórzano, O. (2000) 'Implementación de Reformas de Política Económica en Nicaragua: Temas Principales y Estrategia', UNCTAD/UNDP Global Programme, Managua, March, Processed.

Trigueros, A. (2000) 'Promoviendo el Desarrollo Humano Sostenible por Medio de las Microfinanzas y la Microempresa en El Salvador', UNCTAD-UNDP Global Programme, San Salvador, May. Processed.

World Bank (1989) *Trade Liberalization and Economic Integration in Central America*, March 1989, Report No. 7625-CAM, Washington, DC: World Bank.

World Bank (1999) *World Development Indicators, 1999*, Washington, DC: World Bank.

16 Botswana and Zimbabwe

Relative success and comparative failure?

Guy Mhone and Patrick Bond[1]

Introduction

Neighbours in Southern Africa, Botswana and Zimbabwe represent two cases of differential access to the world economy. Notwithstanding its lack of diversification and its reliance on a primary mineral export, Botswana has prospered; despite its once strongly-diversified, manufacturing-led economy Zimbabwe has fallen into a deep crisis. In both cases, size and vulnerability are key factors, but in very different ways. Historical and comparative evidence allows us to transcend the superficial presumption common to much policy discourse, namely, that the basis for success depends upon simple-minded adherence to the 'Washington Consensus'. We argue instead that there are much deeper problems and possibilities that Botswana and Zimbabwe unveil, which relate largely to developmental linkages and in economic management and planning (Fine and Rustomjee 1997).

To begin with Botswana, increasing integration into the global economy since political independence from Britain in 1966 poses a number of questions about the nature of presumed opportunities and threats. At one level, Botswana's experiences appear to confirm the presumed benefits of globalization based on conventional macroeconomic management (Williamson 1990). Concern is growing over the terribly uneven experiences of many developing countries in the world economy over the past quarter-century or so, because in many instances countries that loyally following the Washington Consensus still continue to be marginalized. Yet upon closer examination, Botswana's development trajectory calls into question fundamental assumptions about the accommodating nature of the global environment, for the economic restructuring and export diversification required to transform Botswana's growth into balanced development has not happened.

In Zimbabwe, meanwhile, the most recent international integration process has been more obviously unsatisfactory. International trade, investment and financial flows have disappointed Zimbabwean proponents of neo-liberal macroeconomics. During the 1980s, the first decade of independence, advocates of liberalization persistently argued that in the context of an exhausted import-substitution industrialization strategy, growth and job creation would occur only if the economy became more export-oriented, catalyzed by foreign investors in a deregulated financial and trade environment. The regulatory context changed dramatically from around 1990 when structural adjustment policies were introduced, but poor conceptualization and phasing of the reforms generated dramatic declines in living standards and rapid deindustrialization. The most recent three-year period is especially instructive, for President Robert Mugabe has made international headlines with controversial policies (ranging from land reform promises to patronage expenditure to involvement in regional warfare) which are understood to have upset macroeconomic balances.

Both economies' experiences are addressed in turn, in the second and third sections, and the fourth section concludes. What appears, superficially, as two cases which correspond to orthodox argumentation about international integration, are not actually so clear cut.

Botswana: economic success, development failure

Botswana's success story

Botswana has won international recognition for consistently high rates of economic growth, the prudence with which the country's macroeconomic balances have been managed, and the political stability (including relatively deep-rooted democratic traditions) achieved in the process. Botswana's large expanse of underdeveloped, semi-arid land generated very little of a marketable character, aside from cheap migrant labour for export to South African mines, and livestock as a basis for beef exports to Europe. The Botswana economy had evolved – as did those of Swaziland, Lesotho and Namibia – through peripheral dependency upon South Africa, from which it imported manufactured and industrial goods as part of the Southern African Customs Union. Monetary policy was also set in Pretoria, through the Common Monetary Area. Thus at independence the economy of Botswana was one of the poorest in Africa and the country's prospects appeared bleak.

Botswana has a small population (about 2 million) but occupies an enormous geographical area. Thanks to three decades of rapid growth, its per capita income, at over US$3000 is higher than that of South Africa, and more than five times greater than Zimbabwe. Botswana ranks seventh amongst fifty African countries on the UNDP's Human Development Index (97th overall), behind the Seychelles (52), Mauritius (61), Libya (64), Tunisia (81), Algeria (82) and South Africa (90).

But Botswana's economy remains vulnerable in a number of ways. Its geographical location in a semi-arid part of the African continent makes the country prone to drought. The large expanse of the country, coupled with the dispersed nature of the population, also drives up costs (of transport, service provision and infrastructure construction) and militates against economies of agglomeration. Botswana's economic vulnerability is underscored by its dependence on mining, particularly diamonds, which account for about one-third of gross domestic product (GDP), about three-quarters of export earnings, and nearly half of government revenue. The economy thus remains far less diversified than Zimbabwe's, notwithstanding the latter's relative poverty.

As a consequence of the discovery of diamonds and judicious economic and political management based on a calculated predisposition to the market and adherence to democratic forms of governance, Botswana elevated itself to one of the fastest growing countries in the world. Between 1966 and 1980, Botswana's GDP grew at an annual rate of 14.5 per cent, while industrial production grew at 18 per cent per year and manufacturing at 23 per cent per year. Per capita GDP quintupled over the first 20 years of independence. Throughout this period Botswana managed to escape the fate of most African countries.

Botswana fortuitously benefited from the discovery of diamonds, which have enjoyed a relatively sustained demand in the international market, and whose supply was for decades adroitly managed by an international selling monopoly (DeBeers' Central Selling Organization). But many developing countries also enjoy similar mineral bonanzas, and yet have not been able to manage windfalls judiciously. For many such countries, income flows have, sooner or later, been interrupted by secular declines in export prices of their valued commodity. Alternatively, the benefits of primary products have been offset by weak domestic policies, endemic corruption and the manifest symptoms of 'Dutch disease'.

The IMF (1999: 4) observes that the Botswana authorities 'struck a balance in the use of mineral revenues by investing part of them abroad and investing in domestic infrastructure and social services, such as education and health'. The scale of Botswana's success is particularly impressive in view of the fact that it is surrounded by neighbours whose economies have been afflicted by both economic and political mismanagement, as well as conflict. Commentators have attributed Botswana's success to a number of other factors (IMF 1999; Salkin *et al.* 1997):

- good macroeconomic management reflected in stable and neutral fundamentals;
- commitment to market forces, liberalization and an outward-looking policy framework;
- commitment to democracy and good governance;
- judicious government spending and intervention in spite of a relatively large and growing public sector;
- the strong influence of rural exporters on economic policy;
- the presence of an open trade environment in the form of the Southern African Customs Union, hence the absence of an administered trade regime;
- low levels of corruption;
- an early demographic transition that has reduced the dependency ratio; and
- well developed human resources.

Assessing Botswana's success

Yet Botswana's success also raises troubling questions about international economic integration (Tsie 1993; Mhone 1993; Salkin *et al.* 1997). First, with respect to unemployment, the IMF (1999: 45) concedes that 'Despite the strong growth, Botswana has experienced persistent and rising unemployment, owing not only to the weakness in the agricultural sector but also to the lack of adequate employment creation in the non-agricultural sectors'. According to the IMF (1999: 8), unemployment stood at 10 per cent of the labour force in 1981, increased to 17 per cent in 1984, and reached 22 per cent by the late 1990s. Employment increased markedly between 1983 and 1992, averaging about 8 per cent per year, and began to stagnate thereafter to a low of about 0 per cent per year since 1992, a trend that has continued to the present.

Notwithstanding rising unemployment, some scholars argue that income inequality of Botswana citizens is declining to some degree. According to Hudson and Wright (1997), Botswana's income gains have been distributed widely, once the incomes of expatriates are excluded, income inequalities have declined in Botswana relative to those in other African countries and many other developing countries. Trends in poverty studied by Jefferis (1997) are hopeful, including a decline in households falling below the poverty datum line from 49 per cent in 1985/6 to 37 per cent in 1993/4. Yet 23 per cent of households remain 'very poor'. The poverty data suggest that growth elasticities with respect to the proportion of the poor that can be lifted above the poverty line as a consequence of a given percentage increase in GDP have historically been very low.

Second, Botswana remains locked in an extractive economic mode. Relying on ogive and entropy indices to measure the degree of diversification, the IMF concludes that the Botswana economy has made little headway, and instead suffers from 'concentration of economic activity in the mining sector and the over-reliance on diamond exports' (Table 16.1). The economy achieved its highest degree of diversification between 1979 and 1984 when mining accounted for about 30 per cent of GDP and was least diversified between 1984 and 1989 when mining accounted for about 45 per cent of GDP (IMF 1999). There have been slight improvements in diversification in recent years, due to active promotional measures being undertaken by government.

Botswana has not witnessed particularly spectacular foreign direct investment (FDI), in spite of sound macroeconomic fundamentals, political stability and the proximity of larger markets in South Africa and Zimbabwe. Net FDI was negative in 1993 (−US$296 million) and 1994 (−US$24 million), before turning positive from 1995 onwards (rising to US$167 million in 1998). Moreover, FDI has tended to be lumpy and associated with one-off megaprojects (such as the

Table 16.1 Aggregate sectoral diversification indices, Botswana, 1979/80–1997/8

	1979/80–1983/4	*1984/5–1988/9*	*1989/90–1993/4*	*1994/5*	*1995/6*	*1996/7*	*1997/8*
In units indicated							
Ogive index	0.7	1.5	1.1	0.8	0.9	1.0	1.1
Entropy index	2.0	1.8	0.4	2.0	2.0	1.9	1.9
Average annual % change							
Ogive index	6.4	19.5	−12.5	−11.6	6.4	17.1	4.5
Entropy index	0.1	−2.5	2.5	1.4	−1.0	2.3	−0.8

Source: Fund staff estimates (IMF Country Report 1999).

Hyundai motor assembly plant) whose sustainability has been questionable, especially when incentives expire.

Meanwhile, domestic entrepreneurship has primarily been restricted to cattle farming and entry into small-scale service industries taking advantage of the fast-growing service sector. Livestock farming has been the mainstay of the local bourgeoisie, and ownership of cattle and farms has historically been skewed, even if there is evidence that income from such activities is shared through intra-kinship transfers. The sixth National Development Plan noted that between 45 per cent and 54 per cent of rural households did not own any cattle, and about 15 per cent of the households accounted for about 75 per cent of the national herd (Mhone 1993). Not only are the majority of rural households excluded from market-related cattle farming, but the government's main pro-entrepreneurial policy interventions have favoured livestock.

Diamonds may have generated a Dutch disease (see Bevan *et al.* 1990). The problem arises from temporary or permanent booms induced by increases in prices of a major export commodity, which in turn induce major shifts in resource allocation. In underdeveloped economies, such resource flows sometimes prevent balanced, equitable forms of growth and development. They also heighten the vulnerability of the economy to external shocks if commodity prices decline substantially. Botswana has been fortunate that despite cycles in the diamond market, prices have followed an upward trend. Yet this may not continue, especially given the recent surrender of DeBeers' monopolistic position in diamond distribution in favour of entry into diverse luxury-goods markets. Diamond dependence has resulted in a shift of resources away from other sectors, such as agriculture. Although mining output increased by 10 per cent in 1995/6, 6 per cent in 1996/7 and 10 per cent in 1997/8, growth in agricultural output was negative. The non-tradable construction sector increased output dramatically. The boom also permitted strong growth in the public sector. In the absence of countervailing state interventions, the boom increased savings rates, consumption and public sector revenues, but in ways that reinforced the monocultural heritage of the economy.

Government policy challenges

Decades of rapid GDP growth and export success were insufficient to diversify and develop Botswana's economy. Typically, blame for such an outcome can be traced to the inadequacy of domestic policies, to structural failures in the economy for which orthodox policies may not be sufficient, or to constraints arising from the global economy. These factors have not been adequately considered in the literature on the Botswana economy, in part due to overenthusiasm of analysts intent upon proving Botswana's role as a success story, and in part due to the general dominance of conventional views of economic management and globalization among policy analysts specializing in Africa.

In Botswana, the government has not been oblivious to the concerns raised above. Indeed every development plan has clearly articulated the need to diversify the economy and generate adequate income-generating and employment opportunities. The main policies aimed diversifying the economy and promoting employment are (IMF 1999):

- Financial Assistance Policy: This scheme provides employers with grants based on the size and location of new investment, the number of unskilled workers employed and the cost of training programmes. The grant is limited to five years and covers entrepreneurs in manufacturing, small-scale mining, mineral processing, agriculture other than beef production and tourism.
- Local Preference Scheme: This scheme is aimed at encouraging non-mining investment in the Selibe-Phikwe area and allows for 15 per cent reduction in corporate tax over 20 years. This programme has been integrated into a general promotional programme for manufacturing under the Investment Promotion Agency also entailing a 15 per cent reduction in corporate tax for all manufacturing activities.
- Arable Lands Development Programme: This programme assists farmers with on-farm investment packages related to cattle farming aimed at increasing livestock production, management and husbandry, as well as land conservation and improved land tenure.

These policies suggest a desire by the government to influence the structure of the economy through proactive measures. Unlike the similarly proactive approach adopted in Mauritius, however, the outcome of these interventions for economic diversification and employment generation has been lacklustre. While deemed necessary by the government, these policies are not normally what would be recommended by the Washington Consensus, given that they retard or redirect market processes. This, in turn, reflects a realization by Botswana's policymakers that under certain conditions, market forces exacerbate distortions in the economy, thereby leading to perverse outcomes even in the face of economic growth.

There appear to be three major structural constraints confronting the Botswana economy which require state intervention. First, increased growth arising from mining has resulted in mining wages distorting economy-wide wages. Wages in other sectors tend to increase faster than productivity increases would warrant, thereby discouraging investment. Prospects for diversification have been further undermined by the smallness of the economy and the lack of minimum thresholds of demand that would warrant lumpy investments to meet local (or export) demand. Second, Botswana has failed to transform its high saving rates into investment. During the 1990s, the savings rate was around 40 per cent, while gross investment was between 25 per cent and 30 per cent, suggesting a low capacity to absorb savings in site of the backlog in unemployment. It should be noted, nonetheless, that both the savings and investment rates are quite high by any standards. Third, Botswana's rural economy is characterized by extremely unequal access to land and livestock, both of which militate against the broadening of the economic base and the development of industry based on domestic demand.

Zimbabwe: from dirigism to structural adjustment and back

Zimbabwe's post-independence financial, trade and investment record is, essentially, one of residual social injustice and economic stagnation under conditions of inherited state regulation. Initially this legacy was addressed through a gradualist, ineffectual export-oriented strategy (1980s), and later by a failed structural adjustment and liberalization package (1990s). The extreme disarticulation of economy and society characteristic of 'Rhodesian' settler-colonialism was exacerbated by the structural adjustment policies, and look set to continue at least through the 2002 presidential elections.

By way of historical background, the economy experienced uneven relations with the world economy, depending upon both global conditions and local policy impulses. The initial macroeconomic regulatory techniques were established by the nascent Rhodesian state during the 1920s, enhanced during the 1950s and cemented during the 1965–79 period of Unilateral Declaration of Independence (UDI) by approximately 200,000 white settlers. Table 16.2 summarizes the experience of oscillating inward and outward economic policy orientations, with corresponding economic and development conditions (Bond 1998; Phimister 1988; Seidman 1986; Sowelem 1967; Stoneman 1981).

Table 16.2 Phases of inward/outward macroeconomic policy in Zimbabwe, 1920s–present

Period	*Relevant policy*	*Economic conditions*
1920s	Protection for local manufacturers	Beginning of industrial development
1930s–40s	Relative isolation	High growth and inward maturation of secondary industry
1950s	Increasing financial and trade regulation	Large inflows of foreign investment, but overproduction problems and unsustainable financial and trade relations
1960s–70s	Heightened financial/trade regulation coincident with sanctions	Initial dramatic recovery, followed by a crisis of overproduction and civil war
1980s	Gradual loosening of financial/trade restrictions and strong export drive	Enhancement of developmental state's human capital functions, yet uneven economic record
1990s	Rapid liberalization of finance and trade	Dramatic volatility and vulnerability in many markets, de-industrialization, underdevelopment
1997–present	Uneven return to a few dirigist policies (exchange controls accompanied by capital flight, currency peg, luxury import tariffs followed by regional free trade agreement, foreign debt defaults, uncontrolled budgetary growth) under conditions of desperation	Deepening crisis across all sectors of the economy

The Zimbabwe government's failure to deal more conclusively with the inherited distribution of economic resources during the 1980s contributed to the problems of the lack of effective domestic demand and outdated production processes. When, by late 1997, this became evident, the government's response was, tragically, a self-destructive return to dirigism plus corruption/malgovernance, without the structural transformation required to correct earlier problems.

Post-independence stagnation and debt crisis, 1980–90

Upon taking power, the new Zimbabwe African National Union (ZANU) government of Robert Mugabe maintained the bulk of Rhodesian-era regulatory controls initially, and good rains plus a business cycle upturn led to a very rapid growth rate in 1980–1. Economic managers – especially Finance Minister Bernard Chidzero – were soon committed to both financial and trade liberalization. The World Bank (1983: 13) soon initiated 'important policy directions – including an outward-looking, export-oriented industrial strategy'. By 1987 the World Bank suggested that 'it is highly difficult to predict which manufacturing subsectors will enjoy rapid growth, but there is sufficient evidence on the responsiveness of Zimbabwe's manufacturing sector to be optimistic on its export prospects'.

Yet the majority of Zimbabwe's domestic manufacturers preferred protection from international competition (Riddell 1983). In spite of continual complaints about foreign exchange shortages, manufacturers had access to a World Bank Manufacturing Rehabilitation Loan (1981), a Bank Manufacturing Export Loan (1983) and the Export Incentive Scheme, as well as enjoying generous depreciation allowances introduced during the Rhodesian era (thus keeping fixed capital costs extremely low). Their hesitancy to expand into global markets was not for lack of opportunity or investment financing.

As a result of stagnant fixed investment, the government's main strategy to increase export revenues was periodic currency devaluation. In 1984 devaluation reached nearly 40 per cent within eighteen months, for example, and was accompanied by massive cuts in development spending and an unpopular reduction of the maize subsidy. The main beneficiaries were agricultural and minerals exporters, but the devaluations simply cheapened goods temporarily, rather than structurally improving Zimbabwe's export capacity.

Relations with international financial markets during the 1980s were also disappointing. Mugabe initially resisted – but then under pressure agreed upon – the repayment of foreign debt inherited from the illegal Rhodesian UDI regime at independence. But servicing the debt became increasingly difficult as real interest rates soared from negative 1970s levels to very high early 1980s levels. The World Bank (1982: 3) issued a report which stated that: 'The debt service ratios should begin to decline after 1984 even with large amounts of additional external borrowing'. Zimbabwe accepted large new foreign loans, as a result. But even as the world economy began to rapidly improve, Zimbabwe's debt servicing ratio spiralled upwards to an untenable 35 per cent of export earnings by 1987. Of US$420 million per annum in new loans during the 1980s, an average of

US$110 million came from commercial banks. Reflecting its capacity to apply leverage, the IMF terminated a US$315 million line of credit due to a larger than expected fiscal deficit in 1984 (*Herald* 23 August 1984).

The *quid pro quo* for access to commercial loans and the Bank's seal of approval included not only fiscal constraints, high interest repayments and Zimbabwe's hesitancy to ask for rescheduling of payments. There were also specific conditions on US$700 million in new loans by the World Bank (Zimbabwe's single largest foreign lender), culminating in the 1991–5 Economic Structural Adjustment Programme (ESAP).

Structural adjustment and economic crisis, 1991–2000

ESAP projected that by the end of 1995 there would be a 25 per cent cut in the civil service, and the demise of all labour restrictions, price controls, exchange controls, interest rate controls, investment regulations, import restrictions and government subsidies. Parastatal privatization was practically the only major ingredient in the typical structural adjustment recipe that Zimbabwe was allowed to delay (World Bank 1995: 35). ESAP made the following ambitious claims:

- Reaching 5 per cent growth annually, the economy would have grown in excess of 4.3 per cent for eight consecutive years (1988–95) – the longest stretch of positive growth since 1973 had been just three years.
- The overall budget deficit would shrink to 5 per cent of GDP. Although Zimbabwe's foreign debt would initially increase from US$2.4 billion in early 1991 to a projected US$4 billion in 1995, repaying the debt would become easier. The debt service ratio (repayments as a percentage of export earnings) – which peaked at 35 per cent in 1987 and fell to 24 per cent in 1990 – would drop further, to 18.5 per cent by 1995, in spite of the addition of US$3.5 billion in new loans in the intervening years (US$1.9 billion of which would meanwhile be repaid).
- Private sector investment would rapidly overtake government investment, doubling from levels of the late 1980s, and total investment, which averaged less than 20 per cent of GDP from 1985–90, would reach 25 per cent by 1993 and remain there.
- Inflation, running at 20 per cent in early 1991, would be down to 10 per cent by 1994.
- Exports would grow by about one-third from late 1980s levels; specifically, mining exports would increase from less than US$400 million in 1990 to more than US$500 million in 1994, manufacturing exports would double from US$400 million in 1988 to US$800 million in 1995, and agricultural exports, which were in decline since 1988, would grow steadily through 1995.
- Except for 1991, Zimbabwe would have better terms of trade in its dealings with the world economy over the subsequent five years.
- New FDI would come in (US$30 million a year from 1992–5) notwithstanding the fact that such investment flooded out during the 1980s.

In reality, growth only reached 5 per cent during one year (1994), and averaged just 1.2 per cent from 1991 to 1995. Inflation averaged more than 30 per cent during the period, and never dropped anywhere near the 10 per cent goal. The budget deficit was more than 10 per cent of GDP during the ESAP era, with no prospect of getting down to the targeted 5 per cent from a drought-related high of 13 per cent in 1994/5.

It is true that forces external to the logic of reforms – the 1992 and 1995 droughts, durable fiscal deficits and severe losses by parastatals – all threw the plan off track. Conceptually, it is extremely difficult to control for the drought factor, although historically, the previous period of sustained economic crisis, from 1974/8, was a time of extremely good rains, while the late 1960s and early 1970s period of booming growth witnessed years of severe drought.

The trade deficit, following liberalization, rose rapidly during the early 1990s. Exports dropped by 17 per cent in US dollar terms between 1990 (US$1.753 billion) and 1992 (US$1.531 billion) (World Bank 1995: 163). This was not purely due to agricultural failure or the temporary rise in demand for formerly-exported food products in 1992. Manufactured exports fell 19 per cent in US dollar terms in 1991 (from US$537 million to US$434 million) (ZCTU 1996: 52). The demise of some export incentives was often blamed, and government succumbed to pressure to revive incentives in subsequent years.

The capacity to export was weak partly because the favourable 1964 trade agreement with South Africa expired in 1992. Also, Zimbabwe failed to qualify as a 'least-developed country' except for the purposes of gaining additional World Bank loans (at a lower interest rate); and because, as the ZCTU (1996: 49) concluded, trade liberalization 'has tended to turn manufacturers into traders … (as) firms have tended to stop manufacturing products locally, preferring to import them directly and then sell them to local consumers'.

The manufacturing sector's real (factor cost) contribution to GDP during the 1990s fell 18 per cent from a peak of Z$4.530 billion in 1991 (in constant 1990 terms) to Z$3.724 billion in 1995, and did not subsequently recover much ground. Total manufacturing output fell from an indexed peak of 143 (with 1980 = 100) in 1991 by 24 per cent to 109 in 1999, as deindustrialization ravaged the textiles (−64 per cent), metals (−35 per cent), transport equipment (−31 per cent) and clothing (−28 per cent) subsectors. One of the only positive aspects of manufacturing performance, according to the World Bank (1995), was that 'Labor intensive sectors, such as wood products and textiles, have benefitted from the sharp reduction in real wages, reinforcing the expansion of exports'. But the drop in wages was disastrous for local effective demand (ZCTU 1996). Unemployment remained rampant, with a tiny fraction of the 200,000 annual school-leavers able to find formal sector employment.

Adding this to the falling 'social wage' – thanks largely to new cost recovery policies for health, education and many other social services, as well as the unprecedented interest rates on consumer credit – workers and poor people faced an unprecedented financial crisis during the early 1990s. The trends generated by Zimbabwe's exemplary social policy during the first decade of independence – reducing infant mortality from 86 to 49 per 1000 live births, raising the immunization rate from 25 to 80 per cent and life expectancy from 56 to 62 years, doubling primary school enrolment, etc. – witnessed ominous reversals (to which HIV/AIDS also contributed). For example, primary school dropout rates soared during the 1990s, with girls particularly prone to suffer when school fee increases were imposed; and likewise, just as the HIV/AIDS pandemic hit Zimbabwe, from 1990 to 1995, per capita spending on care fell by 20 per cent in real terms (UNDP 2000: 33, 36).

Foreign debt also ballooned. ESAP was to require US$3.5 billion in new foreign loans over five years (as against existing external debt of US$2.5 billion). But during the 1992–3 fiscal year, interest payments on both foreign and domestic debt soared 15 per cent more than projected, due to exorbitant interest rates and dramatic exchange rate depreciation (World Bank 1995: 35). Still, Zimbabwe avoided rescheduling and default. One of the main causes of untenable foreign debt was that with financial liberalization, large domestic corporate borrowers (including banks) began seeking funding overseas, discovering in the process that the nominal cost of overseas funds was as low as 7 per cent, compared to in excess of 35 per cent for domestic loans.

The IMF and World Bank insisted on tighter monetary policy in mid-1991, and as a result, short-term interest rates rose from 27.5 to 44 per cent in a single day, shattering the stock market and leading merchant banks to 'sharply curtail lending to clients pending the stabilization of the money market' (*Financial Gazette* 31 October 1991). The interest rate increases did not increase savings rates (which remained below 20 per cent of GDP), given the desperate state in which most Zimbabweans found themselves at that stage (Muzulu 1993). One way in which high interest rates did affect savings, however, was in attracting a flood of 'hot money' to Zimbabwe, which played havoc with the stock market. Hot money inflows also required 'sterilization' through yet higher interest rates, so as not to contribute further to inflation (*Financial Gazette* 28 June 1995).

The 1991–7 period during which ESAP was implemented can thus be considered a failure in many crucial respects. Popular opinion was reflected in 'IMF Riots', including the 1993 bread riots which broke out in high-density suburbs of Harare, and in the city centre in 1995. Public workers went on strike in 1996, and other private employees (including plantation workers) followed at an unprecedented rate in 1997. By the time that political opposition consolidated in 1998–9, leading to a new, labour-led political party that nearly won the 2000 parliamentary elections, leading ZANU ministers had come to the conclusion that ESAP was their most important policy error.

Still, the government was able to claim the following accomplishments during the period, in line with ESAP's 1991 commitments (World Bank 1995: 20):

- 18,000 government jobs were abolished (with 7000 retrenchments) and the civil service wage bill was reduced from 15.3 per cent of GDP in 1990 to 11.3 per cent in 1994;
- the foreign exchange control system was dismantled;

- tariffs were lowered (except for some 'import-competing activities') to the 15–25 per cent range below the WTO requirement of 30 per cent, which was only meant to take effect by the year 2005);
- there was extensive liberalization of foreign investment regulations;
- price controls were eliminated;
- many local zoning and trading restrictions were abolished; and
- labour markets were largely deregulated.

If ESAP was largely implemented, and if the implementation was unsatisfactory, the subsequent period suggests that the political costs and social instability generated by ineffectual international economic integration are substantial. One sign of impending economic collapse was the crash of the massively overvalued Zimbabwe Stock Exchange beginning in September 1997. This was soon followed by three controversial political calculations by Mugabe – first, to raise rhetorical (and later actual) conflicts surrounding land maldistribution; second, to grant large pension fund payouts to veterans of the 1963–79 Liberation War; and third, to involve Zimbabwean troops in the Democratic Republic of Congo war. As punishment, investors simply ran from Zimbabwe. On the late morning of 14 November 1997, the Zimbabwe dollar lost 74 per cent of its value over a four-hour period. As a result, unprecedented inflation was imported, leading in January and October 1998 to urban riots over price increases for maize and fuel, respectively. Mugabe and the ZANU government reacted to the threat – essentially from the political left – by itself moving back into dirigist policy territory: imposing a mid-1998 price freeze on staple goods, a late 1998 tariff on luxury imports, and several minor technical interventions to raise revenues, slow capital flight and deter share speculation.

Government policy challenges

Liberalization and increased economic integration has evidently had a devastating impact on Zimbabwe. The country's current *Human Development Report*, sponsored by the United Nations Development Programme but involving both officials and leading civil-society intellectuals, came to similar conclusions. The report (UNDP 2000: 82) makes six recommendations for government economic development policy, that are antithetical to earlier ESAP policies. They are:

1. Overall objective: restore confidence by creating conditions of fulfillment of basic human material and social needs, and by opening up democratic space for dialogue in all sectors of life …
2. The hitherto neglected responsibility of ensuring conditions for the reproduction of labour and ensuring a life of dignity must form the core of the new strategy …
3. Better integration of gender concerns …
4. A well-focused land reform and agricultural regulation policy framework …
5. Restore production and safeguard the domestic market from external competition in respect of essential commodities and services, as a basic complement

to fiscal and monetary tools. Probably considered subsidies and tariff protection might be necessary.

6 Carry out an audit of imports and introduce measures to cut down all inessential imports and luxury products. Carry out a similar audit of debt, retire illegitimate debts and negotiate with the creditors for the payment of the legitimately incurred debts on the *principle of joint responsibility*. Put in place capital controls, regulate the banking sector and review financial liberalization measures to develop an indigenously led banking sector.

Conclusion

Murshed (2000) identifies both endogenous and exogenous obstacles to successful integration of small economies into the global economy. For Botswana, asymmetrical benefits from global integration raise the problem of translating growth into sustainable, long-term development for all the country's citizenry, based on economic diversification and resolution of unemployment and under-employment which still afflict the majority of the labour force.

On the one hand, the Botswana economy has relied on relative openness and a market orientation to achieve high rates of economic growth over a number of decades. While the presence of diamonds may have been fortuitous, the country's growth was reinforced and sustained by judicious management of the economy, along lines similar to the Washington Consensus. Yet on the other hand, beyond its primary product exports, the benefits of globalization for Botswana are not evident. This not only demonstrates the ambivalent implications of international economic integration for a small and vulnerable developing country that remains a price taker, and cannot significantly influence the pattern of FDI in its favour. It also shows the limits of the anticipated trickle-down effects of growth on the domestic economy.

In terms of policy conclusions, there is a need for more effective ways of channelling foreign investment to small developing economies and to open up the markets of developed economies so as to facilitate the diversification of small economies away from traditional primary-product exports.

Zimbabwe's story is unequivocally gloomy. Two decade-long periods of inward-oriented accumulation (1932–41 and 1965–74) were the eras of greatest GDP growth and generation of economic linkages, albeit under circumstances which entailed the adoption of brutally racist policies. From the 1980s, the overall structure of Zimbabwe's economy and society left it ill-suited for rapid liberalization and international economic integration, given that these were accompanied by extremely high real interest rates, a dramatic upsurge in inflation and devastating cuts in social welfare spending. Although Mugabe often confused matters by using rhetoric that was extremely hostile to the Washington financial institutions, finance ministers and Reserve Bank governors followed a fiscally-conservative, deregulatory agenda until late 1997.

The results of orthodox policies, especially the trade/financial liberalization and conditionality associated with ESAP, included an amplification of existing high levels of inequality. As a direct result of funding cuts and cost-recovery policies, exacerbated by the AIDS pandemic, Zimbabwe's brief 1980s rise in literacy and health indicators was dramatically reversed. In contrast, the stock market reached extraordinary peaks in mid-1991 and mid-1997, but these were followed by crashes of more than 50 per cent within a few months along with massive hikes in interest rates. The standard of living of the average Zimbabwean citizen fell even further. The damage done to a once strong industrial base must be repaired. This will probably entail, as the UNDP (2000) recommends, a substantial reversal of international economic integration.

Both small countries have relatively high profiles in international markets. While issues of size appear in the difficulty Botswana has experienced in broadening its industrial base, the same was true in Zimbabwe only insofar as luxury-goods import substitution industrialization generated problems of subsequent stagnation. In both countries, had basic needs commodities been the subject of investment, a far better balance would have been achieved. Remedial measures, we have argued, are based on the fundamental premise that for Botswana and Zimbabwe, several broad economic development objectives – better internal linkages, economic diversification, and socio-economic equality (with attendant environmental effects) – are all, now, excessively threatened by globalization.

Note

1 The authors are, respectively, Professor and Director of the School, and Associate Professor. A longer version of this chapter is available as a WIDER Discussion Paper at www.wider.unu.edu.

References

Bevan, D., Collier, P., Gunning, J.W., Bigsten, A., and Horsnell, P. (1990) *Controlled Open Economies: A Neoclassical Approach to Structuralism*, Oxford: Clarendon Press.

Bond, P. (1998) *Uneven Zimbabwe: A Study of Finance, Development and Underdevelopment*, Trenton: Africa World Press.

Fine, B. and Rustomjee, Z. (1997) *The Political Economy of South Africa: From Minerals-Energy Complex to Industrialization*, London: Hurst and Johannesburg: Wits University Press.

Hudson, D. and Wright, M. (1997) 'Income Inequality in Botswana', in J.S. Salkin, D. Mabanga, D. Cowan, J. Selwe, and M. Wright (eds), *Aspects of the Botswana Economy: Selected Papers*, Gaborone: Lentswe la Lesedi Publishers and Oxford: James Currey Publishers.

IMF (International Monetary Fund) (1999) *Botswana: Selected Issues and Statistical Appendix*, IMF Country Report No. 99/132, Washington, DC: IMF.

Jefferis, K. (1997) 'Poverty in Botswana', in J.S. Salkin, D. Mabanga, D., Cowan, J. Selwe, and M. Wright (eds), *Aspects of the Botswana Economy: Selected Papers*, Gaborone: Lentswe la Lesedi Publishers and Oxford: James Currey Publishers.

Mhone, G. (1993) 'Botswana: Debunking the Myth of Africa's Economic Cinderella', *Southern Africa Political and Economic Monthly*, 6 (12).

Murshed, S.M. (2000) 'Globalization, Marginalization and Development', WIDER Working Paper No. 175, Helsinki: UNU/WIDER.

Muzulu, J. (1993) 'Exchange Rate Depreciation and Structural Adjustment: The Case of the Manufacturing Sector in Zimbabwe, 1980–91', Doctoral dissertation, University of Sussex.

Phimister, I. (1988) *An Economic and Social History of Zimbabwe, 1890–1948: Class Struggle and Capital Accumulation*, London: Longman.

Riddell, R. (1983) 'A Critique of Zimbabwe: Government Policy and the Manufacturing Sector: A Study Prepared for the Ministry of Industry and Energy Development, April 1983, Submitted by Dr Doris J. Jansen', Unpublished paper, Confederation of Zimbabwe Industries, Harare, July.

Salkin, J.S., Mabanga, D., Cowan, D., Selwe, J., and Wright, M. (eds) (1997) *Aspects of the Botswana Economy: Selected Papers*, Gaborone: Lentswe la Lesedi Publishers and Oxford: James Currey Publishers.

Seidman, A. (1986) *Money, Banking and Public Finance in Africa*, London: Zed Press.

Sowelem, R.A. (1967) *Towards Financial Independence in a Developing Economy*, London: George Allen and Unwin.

Stoneman, C. (1981) 'The Economy', in C. Stoneman (ed.), *Zimbabwe's Prospects*, London: Macmillan.

Tsie, B. (1993) 'The Political Context of Botswana's Development', *Southern Africa Political and Economic Monthly*, 6 (12).

United Nations Development Programme (2000) Poverty Reduction Forum and Institute for Development Studies, *Zimbabwe: Human Development Report 1999*, Harare.

Williamson, J. (1990) 'The Progress of Policy Reform in Latin America', in *Policy Analyses in International Economics*, Washington, DC: Institute for International Economics.

World Bank (1982) 'Report and Recommendation of the President of the IDA to the Executive Directors on a Proposed Credit in an amount equivalent to US$1.2 million to the Government of Zimbabwe for a Petroleum Fuels Supply Technical Assistance Project', Energy Division, Eastern Africa Regional Office.

World Bank (1983) 'Report and Recommendation of the President of the International Bank for Reconstruction and Development to the Executive Directors on a Proposed Loan in an Amount Equivalent to US$70.6 million to the Republic of Zimbabwe for a Proposed Manufacturing Export Promotion Project', Eastern Africa Projects Department.

World Bank (1987) 'Zimbabwe: A Strategy for Sustained Growth', Southern Africa Department, Africa Region.

World Bank (1995) 'Performance Audit Report: Zimbabwe: Structural Adjustment Program', Operations Evaluation Department, Washington, DC: World Bank.

Zimbabwe Congress of Trade Unions (1996) *Beyond ESAP*, Harare.

Index